Iraq from Monarchy to Tyranny

Florida A&M University, Tallahassee
Florida Atlantic University, Boca Raton
Florida Gulf Coast University, Ft. Myers
Florida International University, Miami
Florida State University, Tallahassee
University of Central Florida, Orlando
University of Florida, Gainesville
University of North Florida, Jacksonville
University of South Florida, Tampa
University of West Florida, Pensacola

Iraq from Monarchy to Tyranny

From the Hashemites to the Rise of Saddam

Michael Eppel

University Press of Florida

Gainesville · Tallahassee · Tampa · Boca Raton

Pensacola · Orlando · Miami · Jacksonville · Ft. Myers

09 08 07 06 05 04   6 5 4 3 2 1

Library of Congress Cataloging-in-Publication Data
Eppel, Michael, 1947–
Iraq from monarchy to tyranny: from the Hashemites to the rise
of Saddam / Michael Eppel.
p. cm.
Includes bibliographical references and index.
ISBN 0-8130-2736-5 (cloth: alk. paper)
1. Iraq—History—Hashemite Kingdom, 1921–1958.
2. Iraq—History—1958–1979. I. Title.
DS79.E67 2004
956.704—dc22   2004049333

The University Press of Florida is the scholarly publishing agency
for the State University System of Florida, comprising Florida A&M
University, Florida Atlantic University, Florida Gulf Coast University,
Florida International University, Florida State University, University
of Central Florida, University of Florida, University of North Florida,
University of South Florida, and University of West Florida.

University Press of Florida
15 Northwest 15th Street
Gainesville, FL 32611-2079
http://www.upf.com

Contents

Preface

When Saddam Husayn took total control of the government in Iraq in 1979, that country became a venue for international crises and an important focus of world attention. Iraq was involved in three wars with regional and global ramifications: the Iraq-Iran war, 1980–88, the Kuwait war, 1990–91, and the war against the United States and Great Britain in 2003. In the wars against Iran and Kuwait, Iraq was the aggressor, initiating the war. The third, when the United States and Britain initiated the action, was the culmination of a long-term crisis in the relationship with the United Nations and the United States.

The wars that Iraq initiated against Iran and Kuwait, and the suspicion that Saddam Husayn tried to develop unconventional weapons, leading to international sanctions and the war with the United States and Britain, incurred tragedy for the population of Iraq, led to the collapse of Iraqi society, and sowed destruction and blight on the Iraqi economy. Saddam Husayn's regime was one of the most despotic, cruel, and sophisticated totalitarian regimes of the modern era. It flourished under conditions unique to Iraq and the regional and global political climates and ideologies of the second half of the twentieth century.

From the time of its establishment after World War I, Iraq suffered from internal weakness, due to its many and varied population groups and external threats from its larger and stronger neighbors. The weakness of the resultant national cohesiveness combined with external threats created conditions whereby Iraq's foreign policies were aggressive and expansionist under the flag of Arab unity. Iraq's assumption of a leadership role in the Arab world and its status as a regional power in the Middle East were fueled by the innate internal weaknesses in Iraq's societal and national structure and the threats from its neighbors.

Iraq was the first Arab state, beginning in the 1930s, to foster the ideology of pan-Arabism as a means of achieving its goals in the international and regional arena and as a means for gaining legitimacy and support in its domestic political arena. Iraq was the first Arab country in which, starting in 1936, military coups occurred. Furthermore, Iraq was the only Arab country in which anti-British fervor led to a military clash with Great Britain during World War II, in 1941. Even though, for most of its existence (1921–58), Iraq was governed by a relatively mild conservative government and enjoyed a lively political life, violent disturbances broke out in 1936, 1941, 1948, 1952, and 1956.

Between 1958 and 1968, Iraq was governed by the radical revolutionary regimes of ʿAbd al-Karim Qasim and the brothers ʿAbd al-Salam and ʿAbd al-Rahman ʿArif. Despite the fact that they were military dictatorships, they allowed some social and political expression; they worked to develop and modernize the country—without governmental terror and without the murders that characterized the later regime of Saddam Husayn.

The political developments, based in turn on social and economic developments, that created the conditions enabling the Baʿth Party to seize control of the government are examined in this book. Understanding the conditions under which Saddam Husayn rose and built his regime requires a detailed examination of the politico-social forces and conditions in Iraq. Especially critical is an examination of the fall of the constitutional monarchy that ruled after World War II and that of the radical revolutionaries who ruled from 1958 until the rise of the Baʿth Party. Difficulties in developing a coherent civilian political force in Iraq, due to its multiethnic population, fraught with multiple antagonisms and conflicts, created the conditions whereby Saddam became the totalitarian ruler.

Based on extensive research, this book primarily deals with the history of Iraq between World War II and the Baʿth Party's takeover of the government in 1968 and the beginning of the Saddam tyranny. The period since 1968 requires additional historical research. At the same time, in order for the reader to be able to relate to the dramatic events around and in Iraq since 1968, a general outline of Iraq's history until Saddam Husayn's fall was added in chapter 11.

A broad historical discussion entails a temptation to concentrate on historical issues that are important in and of themselves. But in this case, that would draw the book away from its central focus. Therefore, despite the tremendous temptation to pause and go into depth on the history of the Jews in Iraq and their emigration, on the developments among the Shiʿites, or on the status of women, I chose to avoid doing so. I devoted only paragraphs, isolated comments, and one subchapter to these subjects. Many studies have been written on these and other subjects, and much room remains for many more studies, but including them in this book would disrupt its flow. The reader would be drawn away from the book's central theme, a description and analysis of Iraq's political development, based on domestic social and economic circumstances and its relationship to developments in the international, regional, and global arenas. In-depth history of Iraq from the time the

Ba'th Party took the reins of government, and especially the period of Saddam Husayn's rule, is a subject for future research.

Years of research have gone into this book, which is based on many primary and secondary sources. My primary sources were Iraqi newspapers, memoirs of Iraqi politicians, the archives in the British Public Records Office and the U.S. National Archives, official Iraqi publications, and economic and statistical data published by the United Nations and the Iraqi government. Primary material of immense importance for studying the period of the Hashemite monarchy and that of the Qasim regime can be found in the minutes of the Mahadawi trials—the revolutionary court that was established after the Qasim revolution. The rulers of the Hashemite monarchy were tried there first; later, the court tried those who opposed the revolutionary regime. The minutes are encompassed in twenty-three volumes filled with important evidence and documents from the Iraqi archives. Furthermore, I attempted to get to most secondary sources: studies, books, and articles written in Hebrew, English, Arabic, and Russian. Understandably, I was able to cover only some of the literature on the subject. Most of the chapters in the book rely on a combination of primary sources and independent research that has been done and published in the past. However, the wide range of subjects and historical issues encountered required that certain chapters rely on secondary resources and on others who have conducted research relying principally on primary resources available.

I want to thank a long list of people who helped me. Of course, all of the opinions and errors are my sole responsibility.

First, I want to thank Haggai Erlich of Tel Aviv University for his tremendous encouragement, his valuable advice, and his assistance.

A special thanks to Amatzia Baram of Haifa University, whose advice and extensive knowledge of Iraq and especially of Saddam Husayn's regime were of great help.

My gratitude goes to Ofra Bengio of Tel Aviv University, an expert on Iraq, from whose advice and comments I learned a lot. Similarly, I want to thank my colleagues in the Iraqi Studies Department of the University of Haifa, Noga Efrati and Ronen Zeidel, with whom I shared many discussions on important issues in the history of Iraq.

During the course of the research that led to writing this book, I consulted with experts in various fields, who assisted me in researching various aspects of Middle East history. My heartfelt thanks to Israel Gershoni of Tel Aviv University; Yehoshua Porath of Hebrew University in Jerusalem; Itamar Rabinovich and Ehud Toledano of Tel Aviv University; Menahem Rosner of Haifa University, Gad Gilbar, Kais Firro, Gabriel Warburg, Reuben Snir, Uri

Kupferschmidt, Onn Winckler, and Mahmud Yazbak, all from Haifa University.

For preparing the maps, I want to thank Shai Shpiller for his assistance.

I have the pleasant duty of thanking Sharon Neeman and Marsha Brown for their devoted work in preparing and editing the English version of this book, enabling its publication.

Similarly, my gratitude to the Research Authority of Haifa University, especially to Shantal Asher, the Jewish-Arab Center in University of Haifa, and Oranim College of Education in Kiryat Tivon.

A very special thanks to my sons, Amir, Sagi, and Shai, and my wife, Tali, for their unwavering encouragement and patience throughout the process of writing this book.

This book was written with hope for all the people of the Middle East: for peace, tolerance, equality, prosperity, regional cooperation, and meaningful and good lives.

1. Iraq.

IRAQ

BASRA

ZUBAIR

Rumailah Oil Field ▲

IRAN

KHORRAMSHAHR

ABADAN

Shatt al-'Arab River

UMM QASR

WARBA ISLAND

FAW

KUWAIT

BUBYAN
ISLAND

PERSIAN
GULF

(ARAB GULF)

KUWAIT CITY

2. Shatt al-ʿArab River, Iraq's outlet to the sea.

3. Iraq and the Kurds in the Middle East. The area marked in gray is populated by the Kurds. The composition of the Iraqi population is complex: Most of the Shi'ites living in southern and central Iraq are Arabs; the Sunnis in central and southern Iraq are also Arabs; the Kurds are mostly Sunnis, and some 300,000 Turkmen are mostly Sunnis, speak a dialect of Turkish, and live around Kirkuk.

I

Historical Perspective of Iraq before 1941

Mesopotamia up to the Twentieth Century

In the plains of the Euphrates and Tigris Rivers, in the eastern part of the Fertile Crescent, between the expanses of desert to the south and west and the lofty mountain ranges to the north and east, humankind made several of its great strides forward at the beginning of its technological and organizational political development and the advancement of written communication. Like the Nile Valley, Mesopotamia—the name given to it by the ancient Greeks— was one of the cradles of human culture. The area was known to the ancient Jews as Aram-Naharayim; the Arab and Muslim tribes of the Middle Ages called it al-'Iraq; during the nineteenth century, it was sometimes referred to as Wadi al-Rafidain (the Valley of the Two Rivers). It was the center of the ancient kingdoms of Sumer, Akkad, Babylon, Assyria, and New Babylon. Its conquest by Alexander the Great (334–33 B.C.) linked the area with the Mediterranean basin, which became the greatest cultural center since the rise of Greece and Rome.

In the seventh century, the valley of the Euphrates and the Tigris, which had been fought over by the Byzantine Empire and the Sassanian Persian Empire, was conquered by the Arab tribes under the banner of Islam. The names of the commanders of the Arab-Muslim forces—Muthanna bin al-Kharitha, Khalid bin al-Walid, and Sa'd bin Abi Waqqas—who conquered the area of the Euphrates and the Tigris, and the names of the battles in which the Arab Muslims vanquished the Persians (such as al-Qadisiyya) have become, in the modern era, milestones in Arab nationalist discourse in Iraq and symbols of the building of the Arab-Iraqi nation.

Admittedly, the center of the Arab Islamic Empire established under the Umayyads (661–750) was in the western part of the Fertile Crescent, and its capital was Damascus. Nonetheless, the territory now known as Iraq was of great importance to that empire. The establishment of the 'Abbasid Empire in 750 transferred the focus of the Muslim state to central Mesopotamia. The 'Abbasid Empire (750–1258) was basically universal Islamic in nature; although it was dominated by Sunnites, other influences also prevailed within it—Shi'ite, Persian, and (starting in the ninth century) Turkish as well. Its capital, the city of Baghdad, founded by Caliph al-Mansur (754–775), was not only the administrative and political center of the strongest and most sophisticated empire in the world at that time, but also the most important cultural, scientific, and intellectual center on Earth. The gradual deterioration and decay of the 'Abbasid Empire, starting in the mid-ninth century, led to the neglect of the complex irrigation system and the economic decline of the area. Following the Mongol conquest in 1258, which put an end to the remnants of the 'Abbasid Empire and razed the city of Baghdad to the ground, the area fell into a deep depression. The population between the Euphrates and the Tigris, which had numbered (according to various sources) between 8 and 16 million residents in antiquity and during the 'Abbasid period, was reduced to less than 1 million in the thirteenth, fourteenth, and fifteenth centuries. Only at the end of the twentieth century did the population of Iraq again exceed 15 million. The Mongol conquest reduced the number of residents in Baghdad, estimated at about 800,000 during the 'Abbasid period, to less than 60,000. It took Baghdad 600 years, to the mid-nineteenth century, to again reach even 100,000 residents. The urban culture and the centralist state, which had the ability to impose their sovereignty on the entire area, enabling the development of economic and cultural activity and the development and maintenance of a network of irrigation systems, were utterly destroyed. Following the decline of the 'Abbasid Empire and the destructive Mongol Conquest, the various types of tribal social organization and the tribal production system became dominant. Under those conditions, it was no longer possible to establish a strong central administration that would be capable of ruling the entire area. The tribal forces that were dominant in the area between the Euphrates and the Tigris had neither the capacity nor the motive for maintaining and rehabilitating the complex irrigation systems or even preventing their decay. At the same time, following the lack of a central strong rule and the consequent decline of the security situation in the area, and as a result of political and economic developments in Europe and the Mediterranean basin, the importance of the trade routes from the Far East, India, and Persia through Mesopotamia to Europe declined. From the standpoint of the various states and empires that conquered the area by turns, starting in the thirteenth century—the short-lived Mongolian Empire, the Shi'ite Persian Empire, and the Ottoman Empire—the area between the Euphrates and the Tigris was a miserable, impoverished outland, far from the political and cultural centers of the respective empires and with only marginal economic importance. Thus, for hundreds of years, the powers that nominally ruled the area had no interest in its rehabilitation.

Starting in the early sixteenth century, when the area was conquered by the Ottomans and the Shi'ite Safavite Empire flourished in Persia, Iraq became the front line of a series of wars which ranged at intervals between the two empires for 250 years. The territories of Iraq were conquered gradually by the Ottoman Empire between 1514 and 1534, under the rule of sultans Salim I and Sulayman the Great. The Safavite Persians reconquered Baghdad in 1623; only eleven years later, in 1634, it was reconquered by Sultan Murad IV and again became part of the Ottoman Empire. These wars wrought havoc and destruction in Baghdad and throughout the area. The wars between the Ottomans and the Persians ended only in 1823, and the relative stability of this border was achieved following the Erezrum Treaty of 1847 between the Ottomans and the Persian Qajar Dynasty.

The decentralist trends apparent at intervals in the Ottoman Empire, along with the inability of the Ottoman administration, which had become entangled in wars in Europe, to allocate sufficient forces to defend the territories of Iraq, created conditions for the growth of local forces—tribal federations and urban local-Ottoman elites dominated by the Mamluks (military elites of slaves who recruited their manpower from the Caucasus Mountains). The Mamluks mingled with urban notable families and became dominant local forces centered in Baghdad and Mosul; in practice, these forces established autonomous rule in Baghdad (at first intermittent and later continuous) in 1702. Among scholars, a difference of opinion exists between the widespread approach which emphasizes the "Mamluk" military nature of the ruling elites in Egypt and Baghdad, who drew their manpower from the Caucasus Mountains, and the approach which emphasizes the local-Ottoman nature of the ruling households.[1] Starting in 1749, the power of the local-Ottoman-Mamluk households who ruled autonomously in Baghdad increased and continued to do so until 1831. The strong local rulers of Baghdad—the Mamluks, Sulayman the Great (1780–1802), and Dawud Pasha (1816–31)—established connections with agents of the British East India Company, which expanded its activity in the Gulf, Basra, and Baghdad during the eighteenth century. The local-Ottoman-Mamluk forces of Baghdad were forced to compete against many powerful rivals: Shi'ite Safavite Persia (and the Qajar dynasties of Persia, starting at the end of the eighteenth century), the strong tribal federations, the Kurdish Baban dynasty, which also maintained autonomous rule in the mountains of Kurdistan to the north, and the threat of Wahhabite invasion from the south (Bedouin raids under the banner of the Wahhabite doctrine—purist-extremist Sunnite Islam—against the Shi'ite areas of the south). The Wahabite raids from the Arabian Peninsula inflicted grievous damage on the Shi'ite holy cities. Karbala was conquered for a brief period of time and looted in 1801; Najaf was under siege twice.

The autonomy of the local-Mamluk forces in Baghdad and Mosul came to an end when the Ottoman Empire entered a phase of centralization in the nineteenth century. The autonomy and power of the local forces ran counter to the centralist effort which was immanent to the attempt to bring about reforms in the Ottoman Empire under Sultan Mahmud II (1808–1839). The moves made by Sultan Mahmud II toward reform and toward increasing the effectiveness of centralized government in the Ottoman Empire led him into conflict with local autonomous forces in Baghdad and Mosul and to clashes with the governor of Egypt, Muhammad 'Ali.

In 1831, following a siege imposed by the Ottoman Army on Baghdad, the local-Mamluk rule of the city was wiped out. The city itself was severely damaged, and great numbers of its population perished due to the siege, the plague, and the flood which swept through the city. In 1834, the autonomous local-Mamluk rule of Mosul was eliminated. The area between and surrounding the Euphrates and the Tigris was subordinated to the centralized but lax and inefficient Ottoman rule. Quite possibly, the elimination of autonomous rule by local-Ottoman-Mamluk forces put an end to the abortive beginnings of nineteenth-century Iraqi statehood. Following the conquest of Baghdad and Mosul, the local-Ottoman elites who were to develop in those cities were closely related to the Ottoman administration. The modernization of the territories of Iraq, like that of Syria, now continued within the framework of the centralist Ottoman state.

Notwithstanding the establishment of direct Ottoman rule, the *vilayets* of Iraq remained marginal, impoverished, and neglected, and the implementation of reform was slow, partial, and intermittent. Only after the appointment of Midhat Pasha, the most effective and determined of the Ottoman reformers, as *wali* of Baghdad and Basra, which were unified into a single vilayet, did the reforms accelerate. During his brief administration (1869–1872), Midhat Pasha succeeded in establishing centralized, effective Ottoman control of the entire area and in promoting reforms in administration, economics, transportation, and education. Admittedly, the brevity of his term in office prevented him from achieving in-depth reforms; still, the measures adopted by Midhat Pasha accelerated the processes of change which retained social, economic, and political significance over the long term.[2]

Midhat Pasha took measures to implement the Ottoman Land Law, enacted in 1858. By implementing the law, Midhat Pasha sought to break the strength of the tribal federations, to weaken the tribal leaders, and thereby to reinforce the sovereignty of Ottoman rule. Implementation of the law, together with the changes in economic conditions which resulted from the expansion of trade and the growth of the market economy, contributed to the weakening and eventual crumbling of the tribal federations and gave the Ottoman rule and the city a position of supremacy over the tribes. However, notwithstanding the expectations of the Ottoman rulers, they did not succeed in establishing a strong, independent peasantry. The implementation of the law and the changeover to a market economy were exploited by traditional urban notables, who had found their place in the new Ottoman bureaucracy and had developed trade relations with the West, as well as by tribal notables, who sought to take over the lands of their tribes. This process, which continued into the first half of the twentieth century, gradually transformed the tribesmen into *fellahin*—landless or nearly landless serfs, while the tribal notables became major landowners with a guaranteed source of income: production for markets.[3]

During the centuries of Ottoman rule, the relations between the tribes and the urban local-Ottoman-Mamluk administration were complex. They embodied a system of rivalries and struggles for dominance, on one hand, and interactions involving economic connections and mutual influence, on the other. Among the tribal population, differences and rivalries prevailed among the tribes, at times reflecting the conflicts and struggles for control of the most basic resources between the nomadic shepherds and the fellahin, and between the tribes which controlled the water sources and irrigation systems and the tribal groups which yearned to control them.

The unstable relationship between the local-Ottoman-Mamluk administration, centered in the cities, and the tribes and tribal federations persisted until the late nineteenth century. The tribal federations and the tribal social frameworks began to disintegrate, due to the centralizing elements of the Ottoman reforms, the strengthening of the state and its organizational and military capacity, and initial changes in the economic, production, and transportation conditions. In a complicated process, which developed at different rates in different sections of the vilayets of Iraq during the second half of the nineteenth century, the tribes gradually became weaker and the central administration and the cities became stronger. The tribal frameworks and loyalties continued to constitute a factor in the social relations and political arena of Iraq in the twentieth century, following the contribution made by the British occupation in World War I and the policy of the Iraqi state to strengthen the tribal notables. (The conservation, albeit with changes, of tribalism in the Iraqi state was a direct consequence of the new kinds of interaction which had arisen between the tribal notables, now major landowners, and the central administration and political system.)

The political, social, and ideological developments among the Shi'ite population of southern and central Iraq admittedly were affected by interaction with the remaining sections of the vilayets of Baghdad and Basra; nonetheless, due to factors exclusive to the Shi'ites, they took place (to a great degree) within a separate channel. The Ottoman administration, albeit suspicious of the Shi'ites, intervened only minimally in the Shi'ite holy cities, which in practice constituted more or less autonomous salients. The Shi'ite cities of Najaf and Karbala had flourished, from the economic viewpoint, since the late eighteenth century and had become Shi'ite intellectual centers. The developments among the Shi'ites in India and Persia, as well as the subsidence and eventual conclusion of the Persian-Ottoman wars, following the rise of the Qajar dynasty to power in Persia in the mid-eighteenth century and the Persian-Ottoman peace since 1823, led to an increase in the number of pilgrims to Najaf and Karbala, with the concomitant financial contribution to the prosperity of those cities. A similar increase took place in the number of caravans, which brought the bodies of deceased orthodox Shi'ites who had been wealthy in their lifetimes, from India and Persia, for burial near the graves of the Shi'ite holy men. The donations arriving from Persia and India paid for the digging of canals, which were to improve the conditions for agriculture around the Shi'ite cities. The development of the schools turned both cities into the most important centers for Shi'ite study and thought in the world. The connections between Najaf and Karbala and the Shi'ite communities in the East played an important part in this development, while direct Western influence played only a limited role. Simultaneously with the urban Shi'ite development, a process of conversion to Shi'ism took place among many tribes in the vicinity of Najaf and Karbala. The economy of many tribes was related to the guiding and guarding of the caravans on their way to the holy cities and supplying agricultural produce to the expanding urban markets. They were able to fulfill the needs of the expanding urban markets and supply this produce due to the improvement of agricultural conditions around those cities, following the investments in the irrigation system. The trauma of the brief but destructive Wahabite conquest of Karbala in 1801 and the desire to secure the roads which led the caravans to the holy cities impelled the leadership of those cities to extend their influence over the Sunnite tribes by disseminating Shi'ite Islam. The centrality and status of Najaf and Karbala as holy cities, centers for Shi'ite study and thought, and economic foci, in the absence of any parallel Sunnite religious centers and in view of the weakness of the Ottoman administration, assisted in the propagation of Shi'ite influence. The provinciality of Baghdad and the weakness of the Ottoman rule promoted the process whereby many Sunnite tribes or parts of tribes became Shi'ite in the course of the nineteenth century.[4]

By contrast to most of the Ottoman Empire, Western influences began to reach the territory of Iraq from the East, from India, through the Persian-Arab Gulf and the port of Basra.[5] The first foreign merchants to reach Basra were Portuguese and Dutch seamen who arrived via the Indian Ocean. Beginning in the eighteenth century, however, Britain became the principal Western power active in the Gulf and the city of Basra. British commercial activity developed slowly, and its influence was limited up to the mid-nineteenth century, despite the fact that the strong local-Ottoman-Mamluk rulers, especially Dawud Pasha (1816–1831), attempted to avail themselves of the British to reinforce their military strength and their autonomy. (It should be remembered that the dominant British interest, starting in the 1830s and up to shortly before World War I, favored strengthening and preserving the Ottoman Empire, rather than that of autonomous forces which could hasten its demise. Accordingly, with regard to the vilayets of Iraq, the conflict of interest and the differences in world outlook among the British—specifically between the East India Company and its rivals in London—became evident.) During the nineteenth century, Britain took active measures to ensure its hegemony in the Persian Gulf, in accordance with a concept which viewed this area as the frontline for the defense of British India.

Starting in the 1830s, several British delegations examined the possibility and feasibility of operating a transport system from the Syrian ports on the Mediterranean to the Euphrates River, down the river to the Persian Gulf, and on to India. British consideration of the valley between the Euphrates and the Tigris as a transportation route to India stemmed from Britain's strategic and economic imperialist interests. Britain lost interest in the Euphrates Route once it had taken over the Suez Canal Company and opened the Suez Canal. However, British activities regarding sailing on the Euphrates led to the operation of steamboats on both that river and the Tigris. The operation of a regular line of steamboats on the two rivers reinforced the connections between Basra and Baghdad, at least at the administrative and commercial levels. (The development of transport, combined with the strengthening of the market economy, were among the major factors which led to change in the social and agrarian conditions prevailing in the vilayets of Iraq.)

Throughout the nineteenth century, Britain was chiefly concerned by the spread of French influence; at midcentury, it also feared the infiltration of Russian influence into Persia and the Persian Gulf area, as a bridgehead to India. Toward the end of the nineteenth century, following its unification by

Bismarck, Germany began to show an interest in the Ottoman Empire in general and the vilayets of Iraq in particular—both as a strategic route to the British colony in India and to central Asia, and as a possible future source of cotton for German industry. The German interest in the valley of the Euphrates and the Tigris in particular, and the reinforcement of competition between the colonialist-capitalist powers in general, increased Britain's interest in preventing any other Great Power from penetrating into the Persian Gulf. In accordance with Britain's interest in securing its own dominance in the Gulf, an agreement was signed in 1899 between Britain and the ruler of Kuwait, Shaykh Sabah. (The Ottomans considered Kuwait as part of the vilayet of Basra; however, Shaykh Sabah—who claimed that his dynasty had ruled Kuwait since the eighteenth century—was an autonomous ruler who maintained an independent foreign policy. The British exploited the weakness of the Ottoman Empire, which officially ruled Kuwait, and reached an agreement with Shaykh Sabah without Ottoman consent. The circumstances under which Kuwait achieved its status as a political entity separate from the vilayet of Basra, which belonged to the Ottoman Empire, enabled Iraq to claim, in the twentieth century, that Kuwait constituted an integral part of Iraqi territory and that its separation resulted from exploitation of the impotence of the Ottoman Empire by Britain.)

Germany made efforts to obtain a concession for the construction of a railway from Istanbul to Baghdad. Such a railway would have created a direct overland connection between the vilayets of Iraq and Vienna and Berlin. The strategic threat to the status of Britain in the area led to intensive British activity aimed at blocking that possibility. However, following the intervention of German financiers, Germany obtained the concession to build a railway to Baghdad in 1903. In 1913, when the Germans succeeded in reaching an understanding with the other parties who had expressed objection to the railway, France and Russia, Britain withdrew its opposition, provided that the railway would end at Baghdad and would not reach Basra. (In practice, the railway took many long years to complete, and the Istanbul-Baghdad line began operations only in 1940.)

The strategic and economic importance of Iraq increased along with the rising importance of petroleum in the world economy following the discovery of petroleum in Persia in 1908 and the start of its production in 1912. Control of the vilayets of Baghdad and Basra became vital to the protection of the refining facilities constructed in the Persian city of Abadan on the Shatt al-'Arab River, which was the border between Persia and those vilayets. At the same time, the almost certain possibility that petroleum would be found in Iraq increased German, British, and French efforts to obtain the concession for oil prospecting and production.

Early in the twentieth century, competition for the concession for oil prospecting and production in the vilayets of Iraq developed between British-Dutch, German, and American companies and groups.[6] In 1914, a British-Dutch-German-Ottoman partnership obtained the long-awaited concession. According to the agreement signed in March 1914 between the governments of Britain and Germany and the National Ottoman Bank, the Turkish Oil Company was granted the concession. This company constituted a partnership between the British- and Dutch-owned Royal Dutch Oil Company, the Anglo-Persian Oil Company, the Deutsche Bank, and an Armenian businessman named Gulbenkian. As a result of this move, Britain obtained the majority of the shares in the company which held the concession in the vilayets of Iraq. (Production of petroleum began only in 1927, at which point the company was renamed the Iraq Petroleum Company, or IPC.)

The founding of modern schools in Baghdad, Basra and Mosul, the establishment of the modern Ottoman administration and bureaucracy during the Tanzimat period (1839–1876) and especially during Midhat Pasha's term in office, and the strengthening of ties with the West led to the growth and development of a thin stratum of Iraqis with modern Western educations. The development of this stratum—which initially included members of the rich, notable families, and subsequently also more and more members of the traditional middle stratum—created conditions favorable to the beginning of political activity. (This stratum, which expanded with each graduating class of the schools which offered some kind of modern education, adopted Western dress and modern political language, and deviated from traditional social frameworks, was sometimes known in Arabic-speaking society as the effendiyya.)

Significant political organization began in Baghdad following the "Young Turks" revolution in Istanbul in 1908.[7] The first step involved the establishment in Baghdad of a branch of the Committee of Union and Progress, or CUP, the political organization of the "Young Turks," who had seized power in the Ottoman Empire. Shortly thereafter, an additional organization of Baghdadi notables arose, under the leadership of the Naqib al-Ashraf of Baghdad, the head of the aristocratic families said to have been descended from the prophet Muhammad. In 1912, branches of Hizb al-Hurriyya wa-al-Itilaf (the Liberty and Accord Party), which had been established in 1911 in Istanbul as an opposition party to the ruling Committee of Union and Progress, were opened in Baghdad and Basra. These and other organizations represented a duality of local Baghdadi, Mosuli, or Basran identity, with a feeling of common destiny among the three cities and local self-image as part of the Ottoman Empire. Most of the activists in these organizations belonged to the old notable families; a minority were members of the traditional middle stratum who had acquired modern educations and wealth. In 1913, a secret society known as al-ʿAhd was established in Istanbul; its members were officers in the Ottoman Army, and most of them came from the cities of Iraq. This society, Arab nationalist by nature, aimed to achieve autonomy for the Arab nation within the framework of the Ottoman Empire. In light of the deterioration of the Empire, so pronounced that its very existence was called into question, more extreme currents aimed at Arab independence began to appear within the society. In Basra, a connection was formed between Sayyid Talib, a traditional "strong man" and landowner in the area, and the new political forces. Sayyid Talib was a Sunni notable who sought to bolster his own autonomous status, or even to obtain the status of independent ruler of the Basra area and perhaps of areas populated by Arab tribes in southwestern Persia (ʿArabistan-Khuzistan) as well. He was involved in the political organization (Jamiyat al-Basra al-Islahiyya—the Reformist Society of Basra) which was founded in 1911 in that southern city. Starting in 1912, Sayyid Talib formed contacts with British officials, with a view to obtaining their support for his ambitions. Before any of these organizations could form a coherent ideological and organizational platform, however, the outbreak of World War I totally changed the global and regional political reality.

Immediately prior to World War I, the vilayets of Iraq were impoverished and abandoned, and most of the population suffered from hardship. However, the beginning of oil production in neighboring Persia, the certainty that great amounts of petroleum were also to be found in the vilayets of Basra and Baghdad, and the Russian and German ambitions to reach the Indian Ocean increased the strategic importance of the area in the eyes of the Western powers. The modern political organization of residents of the area, still in its initial stages, reflected the transformation of the urban notable families and their adaptation to the new conditions. The awareness of modern national consciousness was a very new development among the few members of the modern Westernized stratum, the effendiyya. The various leanings toward identities—Ottoman, Arab, Iraqi—had not had time to mature when World War I broke out. In the historical reality dictated by global developments following the outbreak of World War I, the elimination of the Ottoman Empire and the British conquest, a new political configuration arose—the Iraqi state—which included all of the heterogeneous population groups of the vilayets of Baghdad, Basra, and Mosul, the valley known to the West as Mesopotamia.

The Establishment of the Hashemite Monarchy, the Construction of the Iraqi State, and the Development of Its Relations with Britain

The Conquest of Mesopotamia by the British in World War I and the Establishment of the Iraqi State

In November 1914, shortly after the outbreak of World War I, British forces sent in from India conquered the city of Basra and its environs. This move was intended to ensure their control of the important strategic area at the head of the Persian-Arab Gulf surrounding the oilfields of southern Persia. In the autumn of 1915, the Ottoman forces halted the British advance up the Tigris toward Baghdad. A large British force was encircled by the Ottomans at Kut al-ʿAmara on the banks of the Tigris and surrendered to them, following a siege, in April 1916. Renewing their offensive in December 1916, the British took Baghdad on March 11, 1917. The British takeover of the Mosul area and southern Kurdistan took place only in 1918; parts of that area were conquered by the British even after the cease-fire with the Ottoman Empire on October 20, 1918.[8]

Because the British forces which conquered Mesopotamia had come from India, their commanders and administrative officers supported the long-standing colonialist attitudes among the leaders in the British government and bureaucracy. Sir Percy Cox, the former foreign minister of the British government in India, who was appointed civil commissioner of Mesopotamia, ignored the organizations of educated urban activists and their nationalist-political demands, and instead formed connections with the tribal notables and the strong tribal leaders. In accordance with this trend, in 1918, the British authorities promulgated the Tribal Criminal and Civil Disputes Regulations, which awarded extensive juridical and administrative powers to tribal leaders and notables (an initial version of these regulations had been published as early as 1916). This British policy ran counter to the Ottoman efforts to weaken the tribes and tribal leaders and reinforce the central administration. The legitimacy given by the British conquerors to tribal customs and tribal law (the ʿurf), which had become decreasingly valid since the second half of the nineteenth century, helped the tribal notables to reinforce their status and to exploit it by taking over the lands of their tribes and turning them into their own private property. These regulations constituted the legal basis for the conservative land regime; moreover, in actual practice, they conferred state-backed legitimization upon the inferior status of women. The Tribal Disputes Regulations, which became an Ordinary Law in December 1924 and were confirmed by the Constitution of Iraq in 1925 (see paragraphs 88/2 and 113, 114 of the Constitution),[9] reinforced the juridical basis for the power of the tribal landowners and became an important factor in shaping the social and political conditions of twentieth-century Iraq. British tribal policy and the policies of the Iraqi state hampered the growth of a strong, independent peasantry.

Since the British occupation in 1918, political opposition to British rule had been steadily growing in the holy Shi'ite cities of Najaf and Karbala. In both of those cities, political societies were founded. These societies, Jamiyat al-Nahda al-Islamiyya (the Islamic Renaissance Society) in Najaf and al-Jamiyya al-Wataniyya al-Islamiyya (the Islamic Patriotic Society) in Karbala, tried to organize the population against the British rule. In 1919, Shi'ite activists in Baghdad founded a nationalist political party, Haras al-Istiqlal (the Guardian of Independence), which demanded independence for Iraq.

In June 1920, an anti-British insurrection erupted in the northern Euphrates area. In July, the insurrection spread to the south as well. It was put down relatively easily in the north; in the south, however, the British encountered stubborn resistance, which persisted until November. The insurrection, which was anarchic and chaotic in nature, was devoid of any political leadership and continued until the end of that year.[10] The principal players in the insurrection of the Shi'ite tribes were primarily from the Euphrates area and the Shi'ite cities. The Shi'ite religious leadership—which played an important role in the outbreak of the revolt—attempted to lead it as well. An additional group which attempted to take charge of the insurrection were members of the Arab nationalist al-'Ahd. The members of al-'Ahd were former Ottoman Army officers who had established a secret Arab nationalist society as early as 1914. During World War I, members of al-'Ahd joined the rebellion against the Ottomans under the leadership of the Hashemite family, the traditional rulers of Hijaz and Mecca. During the reign of the Hashemite King Faysal in Damascus (1918–1920), members of al-'Ahd held key positions in his regime. Several of the officers of al-'Ahd, with the encouragement of King Faysal in Damascus, were involved in increasing the unrest in Iraq between 1919 and 1920, and they tried unsuccessfully to assume the role of leaders of the insurrection. The Shi'ites and tribesmen, however, were not prepared to accept the sovereignty of Sunnite urban officers. (Not all members of al-'Ahd identified with the insurrection; some of its members considered cooperation with Britain to be the best way to achieve Arab nationalist ambitions, and viewed the revolt in Iraq as a tribal and Shi'ite ethnic phenomenon.)

Scholars of Iraq differ in their opinions concerning the nature and significance of the insurrection. From the standpoint of Iraqi and pan-Arab nationalist historiography, this was a national insurrection in which Shi'ites and Sunnites joined forces in a common struggle against British colonialism. Elie Kedourie viewed it as primarily Shi'ite in nature. The Iraqi-Shi'ite historian

Fariq Muzhir al-Farʿun stressed its tribal nature. Amal Vinogradov emphasized the socioeconomic transformations that took place in the population of
Iraq as an important factor in this rebellion and viewed it as both a nationalist Iraqi and a "genuine national" Arab insurrection.[11] While it is true that the
insurrection also gave evidence of unprecedented Shiʿite-Sunnite cooperation, the active force in the insurrection was definitely the tribal Shiʿite population of the Euphrates area and some of the Shiʿite population of the holy
cities. The Shiʿite religious leadership, which had adopted a militant anti-
British line ever since 1918–19, played an important part in encouraging the
unrest which led to the outbreak of the insurrection. Social changes and
unrest among the fellahin and junior tribal notables against the landowners—urban and tribal alike—were also factors of some importance in the
outbreak of violence in several areas along the Euphrates. Later, from the
1920s on, the myth of the 1921 insurrection was nourished and propagated
by Iraqi historians and Iraqi schools in the process of nation-building, becoming a national Iraqi-Arab symbol.

After the suppression of the insurrection, Supreme Commissioner Cox
established a sort of local government, the Council of State. Appointed to
head the Council was ʿAbd al-Rahman al-Kaylani, the Naqib al-Ashraf (the
head of the aristocratic families said to have been descended from Muhammad the Prophet) of Baghdad. Sayyid Talib, the "strong man" of Basra,
was appointed as foreign minister; Haskail Sassoon, an important leader of
the Jewish community of Baghdad, became minister of finance; Jaʿfar al-
ʿAskari, a former Ottoman officer who had joined forces with Faysal and had
been governor of Aleppo during the latter's reign in Syria, was named as
minister of defense.

At the same time, members of the British "Cairo Office" began to exert
pressure on Faysal, who had been expelled from Syria by the French in June
1920, to agree to be crowned as king of Iraq. Other British officials wanted
to offer the throne of Iraq to Sayyid Talib or ʿAbd al-Rahman al-Kaylani, or
even to a strong tribal leader in southern Iraq and southern Persia, Shaykh
Khazaʿil of Muhammara. The British decision in this matter was reached at
a conference of senior British officials held in Cairo in March 1921 under the
leadership of the colonial secretary, Sir Winston Churchill.[12] In accordance
with the British decision at the Cairo Conference, the Hashemite Faysal ibn
Husayn was chosen to lead Iraq. Pursuant to this decision, and after making
suitable preparations among the notables of Iraq, the British crowned Faysal
on August 23, 1921.

The borders of Iraq were established in agreements between Britain and
the countries adjacent to Iraq. The border with Najd was set forth in the
Muhammara Agreement of 1922, the Uqair Protocol of 1923, and the Bahra

Agreement of 1925. The border of Kuwait was defined in 1923—although Iraq itself claimed that Kuwait was part of the vilayet of Basra and should not be separated from Iraq.

The issue of the future of the Mosul area raised a large number of complex questions.[13] The Kurdish population of the area objected to its inclusion within the Arab-Iraqi state, and the Kurdish leaders sought to obtain independence, as they had been promised by the Sevres Treaty. The Kurdish objection to British rule and to the inclusion of Kurdistan within the Arab-Iraqi state gave rise to a series of rebellions, starting in 1919, under the leadership of Shaykh Mahmud Barazanji, who sought to establish a Kurdish state under his own rule. Turkey, which had waived its claims to Arab-speaking areas during the rule of Kemal Ataturk, was not willing to renounce its claims to the Mosul area, because of its wealth of petroleum and because it viewed the Kurds as part of the Turkish nation.

Two opposite orientations existed within the British administration. One of these, whose principal proponent was the secretary of state for the colonies, Sir Winston Churchill, held that the establishment of a Kurdish state under the protection of Britain, which would separate Iraq from Turkey, would assist Britain in maintaining its control of an area of strategic importance to the defense of the Middle East and Iraq from the north and would help it maintain dominance over the wealth of petroleum in the area. The other orientation, supported by Cox and British officials in the Middle East, preferred to annex the Mosul area to Iraq. This orientation sought to give the Iraqi state a sound economic basis, so as to ensure that it would not depend upon British economic support. The proponents of this policy also believed that the integration of the Mosul area into Iraq would make it easier for Britain to ensure its control of the oil in that area. Annexing the mountainous area around Mosul would give Iraq and Britain control of the strategic heights vital to the defense of the Euphrates and Tigris plains. An additional consideration in favor of the annexation of the Mosul area to Iraq was the desire to increase the Sunnite component in the population of Iraq, given the overwhelming Shi'ite majority in the areas of Basra and Baghdad. At the end of the day, the policy supported by the local British officials—the annexation of Mosul to Iraq—prevailed. Under heavy British pressure, which succeeded in isolating Turkey in the international arena on this issue, in 1926 Turkey agreed to renounce its claim to that area, which was finally and officially annexed to Iraq.

The British moves in Iraq following its conquest had far-ranging consequences on the formation and development of the Iraqi state. The establishment of a single political entity in what had been the separate vilayets of

Baghdad and Basra resulted in the assemblage of a heterogeneous population, mostly Shi'ite with a Sunnite minority, within a single political structure. The addition of the Mosul area to Iraq in 1926 added a significant
Kurdish and Turkoman population group to the already complex mosaic of
Iraq. Indeed, this transformed the heterogeneous nature of Iraq's population
into one of the central factors in forming the social and political conditions
within the new state. Granting control of the new political entity to the
Sunnite Arab urban notables created a situation whereby the Sunnite Arabs—who constituted a minority throughout the twentieth century—became
the dominant element in the Iraqi state. The Shi'ites, notwithstanding their
majority within the population, became a political minority. This gave rise to
a political and social reality in which the politicians, the elites, and the regimes (the Hashemite monarchy until 1958 and the radical regimes thereafter), all headed by Sunnite Arabs, adopted a mixture of suppression and
controlled integration into the state with regard to the Shi'ite majority and
the Kurds. The elites and regimes dominated by Arab-Sunnites, while clev-
erly integrating certain Shi'ite and Kurdish politicians and bureaucrats into
the state apparatus and fostering Iraqi integrative nationalism and pan-Arab
ideology, strove for preservation of their status and class interests. In practice, this perpetuated Sunnite Arab dominance under the banner of Arab and
Iraqi nationalism. The national identity fostered by the various regimes ran
the gamut from Iraqi-Arab identity, in which precedence was given to Arab-
speaking Sunnites, Shi'ites, and Christians, to Iraqi-territorialist identity, in
which the Kurds and Turkmen, Christian Assyrians and other Aramaic-
speaking minorities were also included as equals.

By crowning Faysal, head of the Hashemite family of Hijaz, the British
had set up as head of the Iraqi state a member of a dynasty who was foreign
to most of the country's population. This situation reinforced Faysal—who
had been identified, from the time of the Arab revolt against the Ottomans
and his own brief rule in Syria, as the leader of the Arab nation—in his
reinforcement of Arabism and his vision of Arab unity. In the eyes of the
educated stratum, the effendiyya within Iraq, this policy became the means of
legitimizing his rule, as well as a tenet of the foreign policy intended to bring
Syria under Iraqi-Hashemite control.

The British moves and regulations which were intended to reinforce the
status of the tribal notables, and thereby to create a counterbalance to the
urban Sunnite dominance of Iraq, set up a dynamic which assisted the Shi'ite
tribal landowners in gaining strength and power within the Iraqi state and
the Hashemite regime. This gave rise to conditions which fostered the conservative nature of that regime.

The Building of the Iraqi State and Its Institutions in the 1920s

During the 1920s, the foundations of the Iraqi state were laid and the patterns of its regime were formulated.[14] The building of the Iraqi state and its institutions took place within a reality characterized by a heterogeneous society fraught with tension, suspicion, and contradictions. Large portions of Iraq's heterogeneous population felt alienation and mistrust toward any central administration, especially for the Iraqi state and the ruling urban Sunnite elite. King Faysal and the ruling elite (which was itself internally divided) sought to build a state, to formulate a collective identity for its residents, and to achieve complete independence from Britain, while ensuring Britain's continued support of Iraq against its neighbors and against the centrifugal tribal and ethnic forces within it. The British sought to build the Iraqi institutions according to British patterns and worldviews in line with British interests. The British decisions and moves—forming a single political entity in what had been three separate Ottoman vilayets, determining its borders, establishing a constitutional monarchy, and crowning Faysal, thus reinforcing the status of the tribal leaders—laid the foundation and created a framework for the development of the Iraqi state.

In 1922–23, elections were held for the Constituent Assembly, which ratified the Iraqi Constitution in 1925. The Hashemite monarchy, the Iraqi Constitution, and Parliament constituted the basis for a regime which depended upon the urban Sunnite Arab elite, the Sunnite and Shi'ite major tribal landowners, and the enlistment of support among the modern middle stratum, the effendiyya. The fostering of Arab identity and pan-Arab ideology was intended not only to provide a common denominator for the Arab-speaking majority of Iraq's population but also to enlist the support of the middle class. The British, by means of advisors, retained supervision over most of Iraq's government ministries, which were established and took shape throughout the 1920s. An exception was the Ministry of Education, where British supervision had come to an end in the early 1920s—meaning that the British waived their influence precisely in the area which was subsequently revealed, in the 1920s and 1930s, to be of decisive importance in the formation of the collective consciousness and national identity of the modern middle class and of the entire population of Iraq.

The Iraqi Army (which had been founded in January 1920, even before the establishment of the Iraqi monarchy) was under scrupulous British supervision and remained limited in scope—about 7,500 troops—until 1932.[15] In addition to supervision of the Iraqi Army, the British established a unit of Iraq Levies (conscripts), which remained under direct and complete British command. This unit consisted principally of minorities (Assyrians, Kurds, and tribesmen) and constituted a counterbalance to the Iraqi Army. It was disbanded only after Iraq received its independence.

The question of conscription remained a source of contention within the Iraqi political arena and in Iraqi-British relations throughout the 1920s. Conscription into the national army is a basic and vital component in the construction of any state in the modern era. The nationalists in Baghdad, who sought to reinforce the power of the Iraqi state, considered conscription as essential for building the state and the Iraqi-Arab nation. Vehement objection to conscription was voiced by Shi'ite and Kurdish tribes and tribal notables. They considered the Iraqi Army and the Iraqi state as basically Sunnite-Arab organisms. They had no interest whatsoever in strengthening the Iraqi Army, where the officers were Sunnites and the enlisted men were Shi'ites. Reinforcement of the Iraqi Army would mean the relative weakening of the tribes vis-à-vis the Iraqi state. (This objection on the part of Shi'ite tribal notables diminished during the 1930s, as they became landowners with an interest in reinforcing the state against the unrest of the tribesmen, who became fellahin.) The British, although they had established the Iraqi state and given it an inherent possibility of control, were not interested in its developing what they viewed as too much power. The issue of conscription embodied the tension between the building of a centralist national state with the ability to force military service on its citizens, and the ethnic and tribal interests which sought to preserve their autonomy within a decentralized state. One of the first moves by the Iraqi state, following the end of the British Mandate and the receipt of independence in 1932, was the enactment of the Conscription Law, which led to the rapid expansion of the Iraqi Army and its increased political and social importance during the 1930s.

King Faysal's economic policies principally encouraged the development of agriculture, of irrigation systems and the processing of agricultural produce. However, in view of the lack of available capital dictated by the weakness of the local bourgeoisie and the limited interest of the tribal landowners in modernization, as well as world market conditions, Iraq's economic progress was very limited. By the end of the 1930s, increasing numbers of high school and college graduates were finding it difficult to obtain employment within Iraq. While it is true that several development projects had been planned and even implemented during the 1920s, most of King Faysal's energies and resources were devoted to ensuring his political survival, maneuvering between rival forces and politicians within Iraq, and constructing the basic organizational infrastructure of the state.

The weakness of the state vis-à-vis the ethnic and tribal forces within it, as well as the weakness of the consciousness of collective identity among its heterogeneous population, brought King Faysal to the verge of despair. The historian Elie Kedourie has accused Faysal of opportunism and weakness. Admittedly, Faysal's political moves were characterized by some degree of opportunism. However, it should be recalled that the task facing him was difficult and extremely complex, given his lack of any practical means of control and power. Political maneuvering and manipulation were the only resources at his disposal in constructing the Iraqi state and fortifying his own position and regime.

The Treaty with Britain and the Iraqi Political Arena in the 1920s

The issue of the treaty with Britain was the central theme of the Iraqi political arena during the 1920s.[16] The contractual relations dictated to Iraq by the British created conditions for constant tension between the two states. Against the background of this tension, opposition to British dominance became the focal point of nationalism in Iraq. The terms of the treaty with the ruling mandatory power were, in effect, what determined the degree of Iraq's independence. Whereas Britain sought, by means of this treaty, to grant only limited independence (with symbols of sovereignty) to Iraq, while preserving British interests and exclusivity, Iraq desired full independence. As noted above, King Faysal I and the ruling elite were embroiled in a contradiction in terms. On one hand, they engaged in a struggle for complete independence and, to this end, exploited and fostered anti-British nationalist unrest; on the other hand, they sought to ensure the continued support and assistance of Britain against Iraq's strong neighbors and against the centrifugal tribal and ethnic forces within. In view of the weakness of the Iraqi Army, which was incapable of coping with the tribal rebellions and securing the integrity of the state, the RAF played a central role in the suppression of Shi'ite and Kurdish tribal revolts and the repulsion of the raids on southern Iraq by the Wahabite Ikhwan from Najd. Iraq was especially in need of British support in overcoming Turkey's objection to its annexation of the Mosul area and the resistance to that annexation by the Kurdish residents of that area.

In 1922, the British formulated a draft treaty between Britain and Iraq. This treaty gave Iraq limited independence—in fact, Iraq became more of an autonomous entity with some characteristics of sovereignty. Britain sought to preserve its interests and to ensure an exclusive role for itself in Iraq, in line with the mandate which it had been given by the League of Nations. According to the treaty, Britain promised to support the independence of Iraq and its acceptance into the League of Nations within twenty years. The government of Iraq initially refused to sign the treaty, but was forced to do so under British pressure. In 1923, the treaty was amended by the British government under the Bonar Law to state that Iraq would be given its independence within four years and that Britain would support its acceptance into the

League of Nations. However, a new treaty, formulated in 1926, deferred the end of the British Mandate for twenty-five years. This change was intended to secure the support of the League of Nations for Iraq's annexation of the Mosul area. In order to allay suspicions concerning Iraq's attitude to its minorities, Britain announced that it would continue to serve as a mandatory power for another twenty-five years.

The nationalist unrest against this treaty, which was exploited and fostered by the Iraqi politicians, increased due to the frustration of the younger, educated members of the effendiyya as a result of their difficulty in finding employment. Early in 1928, violent anti-British riots broke out in Baghdad, with the active participation of high school and college students. The immediate cause of the riots was the arrest and death in prison of Shaykh Dari al-Mahmud, one of the leaders and heroes of the 1920 insurrection, and the visit of British Zionist leader and industrialist Sir Alfred Mond, Lord Melchett. The riots were further fueled by unrest among the populace regarding the treaty and by exploitation of that unrest in power struggles between the Palace, the Sharifian politicians (a group of former Ottoman Army officers who supported the Hashemite-led revolt during World War I), and Prime Minister 'Abd al-Muhsin al-Sa'dun, the scion of an old notable family. King Faysal and the radical club al-Tadamun, which exerted influence on the teachers, also played important (though, obviously, contrasting) roles in the riots. Although the background for the riots, sparked by Sir Alfred Mond's visit, was domestic Iraqi and Iraqi-British in nature, the demonstrations were also marked, for the first time, by anti-Zionist slogans. In the course of the 1920s, anti-Zionist articles had indeed been published in the Iraqi press, and the date of the Balfour Declaration had been mentioned in the Iraqi school system; nonetheless, the importance of the Palestine question in Iraqi politics had been marginal. The riots marked the first time that the Palestine question played a significant role in the Iraqi political arena. Following those riots, the Palestine question became increasingly intertwined with the growth of Iraqi-Arab national identity and pan-Arab ideology in Iraq, as an expression of the common destiny and common cause of pan-Arabism.

In June 1930, during the term in office of the "Sharifian" politician Nuri al-Sa'id as prime minister, a new treaty was signed between Britain and Iraq. According to that treaty, the British Mandate was to come to an end in 1932, following which Britain would support Iraq's acceptance into the League of Nations. Britain retained dominance and exclusivity regarding Iraq's foreign and defense policy, ensuring British control of Iraqi oil. British forces, mainly the RAF, continued to be stationed in Iraq, and Britain retained control of the military bases in Habbaniya and Shu'eiba and of the Basra port, as well as supervision of the Iraqi Army. Iraq was required to coordinate its foreign and defense policy with Britain. Nuri, an intimate of King Faysal, believed that only through close cooperation with Britain could Iraq ensure its continued existence and stability, and only with British assistance could it strengthen its international status and promote its regional aims, primarily the establishment of a large Arab state under Iraqi leadership in the Fertile Crescent.

Opposition to the treaty of 1930 and the demand for the removal of all limitations to Iraq's independence became a central issue among the nationalists. In 1930, Nuri al-Sa'id's rivals organized in a loose structure called al-Ikha al-Watani, the primary objective of which was the struggle to remove the limitations on Iraq's independence established in the treaty with Britain. Among the prominent leaders of al-Ikha al-Watani were Yasin al-Hashimi, an ex-Ottoman general who had based his status on militant anti-British nationalism, and Rashid 'Ali al-Kaylani, a nationalist politician from an old, wealthy notable family, as well as other members of the elite. Nuri and the politicians close to the Palace established their own organization, Hizb al-'Ahd. King Faysal, who viewed the rivalry between Nuri and Yasin al-Hashimi as a personal power struggle, maneuvered between them, trying to prevent unrest and block the rising strength of the latter.

In practice, the politicians of al-Ikha al-Watani took care not to damage Iraq's relations with Britain. Yasin al-Hashimi, during his terms in office as prime minister (August 1924–November 1925; March 1935–October 1936), went out of his way to reassure the British that his anti-British militant statements had been intended for domestic consumption, in order to bolster his own status. When Rashid 'Ali became prime minister in May 1933, he too refrained from taking any steps which could undermine the treaty with Britain. As a result, a rift sprang up between al-Ikha al-Watani and its allies, the nationalist Hizb al-Watani and the Shi'ite Hizb al-Nahda.

In October 1932, the British Mandate came to an end. Iraq received independence and was admitted into the League of Nations. This was not enough to calm the anti-British nationalist unrest in the streets of Iraq, which was exploited and fostered by the elite politicians.

In the summer of 1933, a crisis broke out in the relations between the Iraqi authorities and the Assyrians, a small Christian community (about 40,000 persons), many of whose young men served in the British auxiliaries (Levies). The pro-British attitude of the Assyrians increased the hostility of their Muslim neighbors towards them. Following the crisis between the Assyrians and the authorities, the Iraqi Army conducted a mass slaughter among the small community. The commanders of the Iraqi Army, especially Deputy Chief of Staff Bakr Sidqi, who had been responsible for the slaughter, were viewed as national heroes by nationalist public opinion in Baghdad. This reception reflected the nationalist extremism in Iraqi society and the change that had

taken place with the growth of modern nationalism, as a result of the dominant British role in dictating the relations between the Muslim majority and
Christian minority groups. In the midst of this crisis, which severely de-
tracted from Iraq's international credibility, in September 1933, King Faysal
I died of heart disease and was succeeded by his son, Ghazi.

Social Tensions and Divisions, National Identity, and the Political Arena in Iraq during the 1920s and 1930s

The heterogeneous population of the Iraqi state was devoid of any unifying
consciousness and national identity. The heterogeneity of the population, the
weakness of the collective Iraqi identity, and the traditional local ethnic and
tribal identities and loyalties, together with the various processes of social
change, economic transformation, and Western influence, were the principal
factors forming the social and political conditions within Iraq.[17]

The main "lines of cleavage" in the population of Iraq were between Arabic-speaking Sunnite Muslims (approximately 20%) and Arabic-speaking
Shi'ite Muslims (approximately 55%), and between the combined Sunnite
and Shi'ite Arabic-speaking population (approximately 75%) and the Kurds
(15–18%), most of whom were Sunnite Muslims (though there was also a
Kurdish Shi'ite minority) and whose Kurdish language was close to Persian.
In addition, the population of Iraq included Turkmen (5–6%), Christians of
different sects, Jews, and various other small ethnic minority groups. The
Sunnite Arab ruling elite was capable of absorbing individual Shi'ites and
Kurds who helped preserve the social and ethnic status quo. However, most
of the Shi'ites considered the Iraqi state to be controlled by Sunnites, and
most of the Kurds considered it to be controlled by Arabs. On the other hand,
among the Sunnites, and especially among the ruling elite and the members of
the Sunnite middle class, there was a fear that the Shi'ites would gain in
strength and become dominant in Iraq. The Sunnites suspected the Shi'ites of
having sympathy for and connections with Iran. Despite the Shi'ite and
Kurdish feelings of discrimination and alienation from the "Sunnite Arab"
Iraqi state, most of Iraq's Shi'ite and Kurdish population accepted its existence, although they hoped to change its nature and achieve civil and political
equality. Among the Kurds, who could not identify with Iraqi-Arab nationalism, there were and still are autonomist-separatist movements which incited and still incite revolt against the Iraqi authorities. Among the Shi'ites,
the prevailing currents favored change within the framework of the Iraqi
state. In practice, the extent to which the various Iraqi regimes have succeeded is due, in no small part, to the degree to which they have consistently
neutralized the Shi'ite threat by weakening Shi'ite social frameworks and

centers, integrating various Shi'ite social sectors, leaders, and activists into the Iraqi establishment, and using political maneuvering. Accordingly, the co-optation of Shi'ite tribal landowners into the ruling elite and establishment during the Hashemite monarchy reinforced their own interest in the continued existence of the monarchical regime, which was characterized by Iraqi-Arab nationalism. Such integration assured the status quo of dominance by the Sunnite elite, with the involvement of those Shi'ites who did not endanger the regime. (The integration of Shi'ite activists into the Ba'th Party and Saddam Husayn's regime gave rise to a situation whereby many Shi'ites from the modern middle class have remained loyal to the regime, or at least have maintained a neutral attitude, despite the dominance of Sunnite Arabs among its leaders.)

Contributing factors in the gradual neutralization of the Shi'ite tribal threat during the 1920s and 1930s included a combination of conditions in the region and developments within Iraq:

(1) the change in the balance of power between the Iraqi Army, which gained in strength after 1932, and the tribes (in the 1920s, the RAF's backing had ensured the superiority of the state over the tribes);

(2) the interest and support for the Iraqi state by the Shi'ite tribal notables, which ensured the conditions that enabled them to take over their tribes' lands, thereby becoming major landowners capable of influencing the political system;

(3) the reinforcement of the ties between Faysal and central religious figures such as Muhammad Kashif al-Ghita;

(4) the fostering of Arab-Iraqi nationalism through the educational system and the involvement of Shi'ite members of the effendiyya in the state bureaucracy and political system, thus intensifying the identification with the Iraqi state of Shi'ites from the modern middle stratum;

(5) the gradual diminution, starting in World War I, of the stream of pilgrims, donations, and students from Persia and India to the holy cities, as developments in Persia and in the Shi'ite communities of India reduced the phenomenon of caravans bringing the bodies of the Shi'ite faithful for burial in the holy cities;

(6) the rise to power of Reza Shah in Persia (later Iran) and his moves to secularize the state, which reduced the interest and political assistance offered by that country to the Shi'ites in Iraq;

(7) the decline in the number of students at Shi'ite religious high schools in Najaf and Karbala, coupled with the harassment and deportation of oppositionist religious figures and Persian Shi'ite teachers and

students by the Iraqi authorities. These actions helped to neutralize the Shiʿite urban population in Najaf and Karbala; and

(8) the relative decline of Najaf and Karbala, whose modernization lagged behind that of Baghdad, Basra, and Mosul, making them unattractive to young urban Shiʿites and even to tribesmen, who preferred to seek employment in Baghdad, where they could hope for a better future.

Notwithstanding the strengthening of the cities and the centralist rule of the state, the tribes and tribalism continued to play a role in Iraqi society and to affect the conditions of the Iraqi political arena well into the first half of the twentieth century. (In the last quarter of the twentieth century, tribalism again played a political role, as a manipulative policy of Saddam Husayn's regime.) The intertribal struggles and splits were admittedly rooted in history; at the same time, the growth and outbreak of those struggles in practice generally resulted from concrete economic and social conditions and local or regional political occurrences. In the 1920s and 1930s, tensions among the tribes themselves, and between the tribes and the state, mounted as a result of the political and socioeconomic transformations. Tribal notables who were in the process of becoming landowners became involved in political struggles in Baghdad, and Baghdadi politicians sought to enlist tribal forces for their cause in the power struggles. Another contributing factor was the increasing competition for control of lands and irrigation systems, following the socioeconomic changes by which the latter became means of production to meet the needs of capitalist markets and the economy. The changes in the value of the lands and irrigation canals, and the consequent changes in agrarian relationships, affected and were in turn affected by Iraqi politics and the development of the Iraqi state. However, this process, which was itself fraught with tension and political struggles, aroused tension and struggles within and between the tribes and continued to exacerbate them for some time. In the later 1930s, the tribal and Shiʿite revolts subsided as the army and the state became stronger, thus changing the balance of power and rendering the revolts futile. Another factor which contributed to ending the tribal revolts in southern and central Iraq was the rise of the tribal notables as landowners. As such, they were interested in maintaining a powerful state to secure their own status and the social, political, and land-related status quo convenient for them.

The modernization of Iraq led to the development of social stratification and horizontal socioeconomic gaps between the rich strata, whose members held property and power, and the poor strata with no access to the centers of power. In the villages, the landless or nearly landless fellahin became poorer and poorer, and the gap between them and the landowners (who were becoming richer and richer) widened. The poverty of the rural areas led to migration from the villages to the cities. This process gave rise to growth in the population of Baghdad, Basra, Mosul, and other cities, and slums began to spring up within and on the edges of the cities. The widening of the economic gaps and the abject poverty in which most of Iraq's population—the fellahin, the tribesmen, and the city slum-dwellers—lived were factors contributing to the weakening of traditional social frameworks and the rise of socioeconomic tension. The "new" socioeconomic tensions and contradictions and the social stratification generally became more acute than the ethnic and tribal tensions; nonetheless, at times, they exacerbated those tensions, especially in areas where ethnic-tribal distribution ran parallel to the distribution of wealth and class cleavages. Thus, as noted above, the integration of Shi'ite tribal landowners into the upper socioeconomic class and the ruling elite somewhat neutralized the threat of Shi'ite tribal revolts against the Iraqi state. Still, the social and economic tension between the landowners and the tribesmen who had become fellahin created conditions for violent outbursts on the part of the latter. The great migration of poor tribesmen and fellahin from the southern and central areas of Iraq to the large cities created a kind of parallel between two divisions: that of rich versus poor neighborhoods, and that between the Sunnites, who constituted the majority of Baghdad's well-to-do urban population, and the poor Shi'ites and Kurds (although the poor migrants from the starving villages also included Sunnite Arabs).

Expansion of the modern educational system led to the growth of a modern middle stratum—the effendiyya.[18] (The concept of effendiyya, which developed in Middle Eastern social experience, was used to describe a stratum of persons with more or less modern educations who diverged from traditional patterns of dress, thought, and expression. Although, according to this concept, the son of a rich landowner or the son of an urban notable who had obtained a modern education was also considered an effendi, the concept of effendiyya acquired the meaning of a social stratum whose distinguishing characteristic was modern education, Western dress codes, and modern Western behavior. The grassroots origin of the term left some vagueness. Sometimes it was used to indicate rich westernized landowners; sometimes it was used to describe those with modern educations and dress. To a great degree, the term was in essence parallel to the modern middle class.) The members of this stratum, which expanded with each new graduating class, found it harder and harder to obtain employment which would fulfill their expectations, developed in the course of their deviation from traditional frameworks of society and thought. The slow development of the Iraqi economy and the lack of any significant industrialization gave rise to a situation whereby more and more graduates of high schools and colleges found themselves frustrated and embittered. As early as the late 1920s, a series of strikes and demonstrations broke out in Baghdad, incited by the difficulties graduates encountered in finding jobs. Government bureaucracy, especially the educational system, was the principal source of employment of the effendiyya. However, the expansion of the bureaucracy placed a heavy burden on Iraq's budget and reduced the already limited ability of the government to funnel resources into development. The younger members of the effendiyya, the politically aware high school and college students who had been affected by global and regional political currents, were the principal factor in the demonstrations and riots which took place in Baghdad starting in the 1920s. It was the effendiyya who were not only the readers but also the writers of the modern press, which formulated, to a great degree, the ideological and political climate of Iraq. The acute nature of the identity crises, resulting from their rejection of social and ideological traditions, made this stratum fertile soil for nationalism and radical pan-Arab nationalist ideology. Dissatisfaction with their personal situation, their awareness of Iraq's weakness vis-à-vis the West, and awareness of social and economic distresses made nationalism and pan-Arab ideology attractive to members of this stratum. The pan-Arab nationalist views of the founders of Iraq's modern educational system, who formulated its content, contributed to shaping the world outlook of the effendiyya. Admittedly, by the end of the nineteenth century, the effendiyya had attained a vague awareness of Iraqi identity as "the sons of the Valley of the Two Rivers" (banu wadi al-rafidain). Still, the Arab identity and pan-Arab ideology disseminated by the educational system were more concrete and more attractively formulated.[19] The Arabic-speaking members of the middle class did not consider the Arab identity characterized by the pan-Arab trend and the Iraqi-territorialist identity to be mutually contradictory. Generally speaking, these were levels of identity which were treated as a question of emphasis, or of priorities, in accordance with concrete political conditions and circumstances. Nationalism characterized by a pan-Arab Iraqo-centric trend was the most attractive response to the identity distress of the effendiyya; at the same time, this and other pressures did not threaten the political, social, and economic status quo which was so convenient to the ruling elite. Against this background, politicians from the elite, especially the Sharifian politicians with their nationalist and pan-Arab views, succeeded in building an image of themselves as militant nationalists fighting for the independence of Iraq and for Arab unity. The nationalist politicians of the elite enlisted the support of the effendiyya through the use of a nationalism characterized by anti-British and pan-Arab currents. Although this resonated with the younger members of the effendiyya going through identity transitions, it was of no help in attempting to resolve social or economic problems. Alleviation of the socioeconomic distress of the effendiyya and the poorer strata might have harmed the interests of the major landowners, who were gradually becoming the most important mainstay of the regime, of the elite, and of the Iraqi state, and a counterweight against the threat from Shi'ite tribes and new urban social forces. The effendiyya affected the political climate of the domestic Iraqi political arena, but were incapable of reaching the foci of power and control within the state.

Pan-Arab ideology was especially attractive to the effendiyya—the young men with a modern education who adopted modern political discourse and concepts. Pan-Arab ideology and Arab national identity were extensively reflected in the press, as well as in books and school curricula. At the same time, however, the Iraqi state and some of its politicians also fostered Iraqi territorialist identity (*wataniyya*). Iraqi territorialist identity was also developed and strengthened by day-to-day life within the framework of the Iraqi state, its political arrangements, and direct contact with its institutions.

The currents of pan-Arab and Iraqi territorialist identity were at times contradictory. At other times, however, they became intertwined with each other and constituted different levels of a single identity. The roles of these trends were a function of their political and social context. Thus, for example, Kurds and even many Shi'ites could not identify with Arabism and pan-Arab nationalist ideology. Nonetheless, those who had an interest in and identified with the Iraqi state did develop a degree of Iraqi territorialist identity. Most of the Iraqis saw no contradiction between pan-Arabism and Iraqi territorialism and created a blend of the two currents.

In addition to the modern currents of Iraqi territorial nationalism and supra-Iraqi Arabism with a pan-Arab orientation, there were also tribal, local, and ethno-religious identities among the population of Iraq. On one hand, it was in the interest of the Iraqi state to reinforce its centralized power and control and reduce the strength of the centrifugal ethnic and tribal forces. On the other hand, however, King Faysal I, the ruling elite, and the major politicians considered the support of the tribes, especially of the tribal notables who had become tribal landowners, to be an important bastion of the Iraqi state and the regime. Accordingly, local tribal identities became elements within the Iraqi political arena on the basis of the Iraqi territorialist and Arab identity, which were exploited and nurtured by the state and its politicians during the course of the state-building process. Nonetheless, the reliance of the politicians and the conservative elite on the tribes and the major tribal landowners resulted from the interests of the bureaucratic, landowning, and mercantile stratum. Pan-Arabism and Iraqi territorialist nationalism—the concept of the Iraqi people or the Iraqi nation—were fostered by the state, by King Faysal, and by the ruling elite and its politicians. This policy was intended to assist in the processes of building the state, achieving its regional objectives and preserving the conservative interests of the ruling elite and the wealthy socioeconomic stratum. However, their ability to use these levels of identity resulted directly from the fact that pan-Arabism—and, to a certain degree, Iraqi territorial nationalism—provided a response to the distresses of the effendiyya, the middle stratum which possessed political awareness and was essential to the construction of the state.

Thus, the elite and the effendiyya shared a common interest in reinforcing the strength and power of the Iraqi state and its centralist control as a method of countering the centrifugal ethnic and tribal forces. The elite needed the effendiyya to operate the bureaucratic mechanisms of the modern state. Also, the politicians required the legitimization of the effendiyya as a politically sensitive force concentrated in the cities, especially in Baghdad. However, a contradiction existed between the economic and social interests of the political elite and the upper class in preserving the political-social-economic status quo, and the interests of the effendiyya in changing this status quo so as to modernize, industrialize, democratize, and change the political regime. The regime and the ruling elite found themselves embroiled in this contradiction, which limited their ability to adapt to the new ideological and social conditions. This preoccupation also prevented them from providing either a response to the distresses of the middle and poorer strata or enacting the political reforms which could have given those forces a means of expression within the framework of the regime. Decades later, in 1958, this contradiction contributed to the collapse of the regime and the expulsion of the ruling elite. (However, the weakness of the middle stratum, the weakness of the industrial bourgeoisie and the absence of suitable socioeconomic conditions meant that there was no fertile soil for the growth of liberal-democratic or Socialist political forces.) Under these conditions, no force existed which could have stopped the rise to power, in the 1970s, of the Ba'th Party and Saddam Husayn. The latter successfully exploited the power aggrandized by the Iraqi state since the 1940s and 1950s through its income from petroleum, as well as the weakness, fragmentation, and discord within Iraqi society, to establish a tyrannical, authoritarian regime which survived until the early twenty-first century.

Establishing the Iraqi political entity and setting its borders after World War I created what amounted to a political domestic play yard.[20] The existence of this political domestic arena within Iraq enabled various social and political forces to come into play. Existence of this political arena was an important means by which the ruling elite was able to preserve a cohesive Iraqi state while restraining and weakening the ethnic and tribal centrifugal forces. Still, conditions in that arena—and primarily the indirect, two-stage method of elections, which provided the traditional notables and the "strong men" of society with influence and power, and enabled the regime and the government to determine, to a great degree, the results of the elections— prevented any representation or means of expression for the new social forces and frustrated attempts to bring about reforms within the framework of the regime.

The Development of the Elite and the Ruling Class in the 1920s and 1930s

The Hashemite monarchy was the axis of the regime in Iraq. Admittedly, the attitude of many politicians from the elite toward King Faysal I, his successor, King Ghazi, and the Regent, 'Abd al-Ilah, was reserved and critical. However, in view of the laxity of the Iraqi state, the ethnic and tribal threats, and their own interest in preserving the status quo which was convenient for them, the members of this elite took measures to protect the regime. At the same time, however, in their personal power struggles, the members of the elite did not refrain from exploiting tribal revolts and tensions, even when the latter endangered the stability of Iraq.

The ruling elite that developed in monarchical Iraq and exhibited characteristics of an upper socioeconomic class included three principal components: rich urban notable families, Sharifian officer-politicians, and major tribal landowners.[21] (Notwithstanding the considerable progress which has taken place since the 1920s in research into Iraqi society, basic social and historical questions remain which have not yet been studied.)

Urban Notable Families

As a result of political changes in Iraq, the reforms in the Ottoman Empire and the economic changes which reinforced the ties between the vilayets of Iraq and the outside world, the status of the urban notable families in the cities of Baghdad, Basra, and Mosul, the great majority of whom were Sunnite Arab, improved during the course of the nineteenth century. These families constituted the core of the local-Ottoman elite in the cities of Iraq, which—notwithstanding changes in their composition—succeeded in surviving and adapting to the transformations within the Ottoman Empire in the nineteenth century. Admittedly, the elite of the notable families was supplemented by new families, principally those of successful traders and bureaucrats who had made their fortunes, some replacing other families which had become impoverished and lost their status and power. Nonetheless, in the broader view, the stratum of notable urban families, despite these changes, was still preserved. The Tanzimat reforms enabled the sons of those families to find their place in the new Ottoman bureaucracy and become the owners of large tracts of land in and around the cities. Wealthy urban notable families exploited the conditions which arose following the attempt to apply the Ottoman land laws, as well as the development of the market economy and the increase in production for export, and took over broad stretches of land, especially in the vicinity of the major cities. The development of local trade and trade relations with the West strengthened those of the notable families who were active in commerce and money changing, and gave them the incentive to take over lands, which became means of production for the needs of the local market, and for export as well. Included among the notable families were those whose status came from their religious affiliation; these families as well managed to adapt to the changes and to find their place in trade with the West and in the new Ottoman bureaucracy. The urban notable families were the seed from which the modern bourgeoisie of Iraq grew. However, local and global political and economic conditions and the economic and political dominance of the West prevented rapid industrialization, in which this budding bourgeoisie could have become a cohesive class of industrialists and financiers with political power. Rather, the nature and economic basis of this stratum favored the dominance of conservative interests within it.

The "Sharifian" Officer-Politicians

The expression "Sharifian" applies to a group of former officers in the Ottoman Army who joined the Arab Revolt under the leadership of the Hashemite family during World War I. Some of them joined the administration of the Hashemite King Faysal in Syria only after the surrender of the Ottoman Empire. (According to Muslim tradition, families regarded as descendants of the Prophet Muhammad were referred to by the term *sharif*—roughly, "noble." In monarchical Iraq, the term *Sharifian* was used to describe former Ottoman officers who had joined forces with the Sharifian Hashemite family of Hijaz in the Arab revolt during World War I. These officers did not really belong to Sharifian families; the term was used in the political sense.) Most of the Sharifian officers came from Sunnite Arab families of the traditional middle and lower-middle strata of Baghdad and Mosul, although a few came from the families of urban notables. During Faysal's rule in Damascus (1918–1920), some of them were actively engaged in operations in Iraq (Mesopotamia), which was at the time under British occupation. Following the fall of Faysal's regime in Damascus in 1920, most of them fled Syria. When Faysal came to Baghdad to be crowned as king of Iraq in 1921, he was joined by about 300 of his officers and members of his administration, most of Iraqi origin. The Sharifians, most of whom became senior bureaucrats and politicians, held key positions in most of the governments of Iraq under the

Hashemite monarchy until 1958. The Sharifians were not a cohesive group, and bitter interpersonal struggles often broke out. Although most of them came from the middle or even the lower-middle stratum, they did not seek to advance the interests of that stratum, nor did they attempt to clash with the notable families and the tribal landowners over issues of social and political reforms and accelerated modernization. While it is true that, in the 1920s and early 1930s, considerable tension existed and some conflicts took place between the Sharifian politicians and those from notable families, who viewed them as competitors and treated them with contempt and disdain, the two groups gradually merged. While filling key positions in the Iraqi state, many of the Sharifians became landowners and married into the notable families.

The views held by many of the Sharifians were pan-Arab nationalist in nature. Pan-Arabism thus affected their perceptions of Iraq's regional interests, enabling them to justify Iraq's regional policies with pan-Arab ideological motives. In addition, these views had an impact on legitimizing the regime and on politicians in the domestic Iraqi political arena.

The Major Tribal Landowners

Despite the tendency of the Ottoman state, following the Tanzimat reforms, to limit the power of the tribes and their notables, many of the tribal notables succeeded in maintaining and even strengthening their status by adapting to the new economic and political conditions. The process by which the notables became the owners of their tribal lands accelerated following the British occupation during World War I and continued within the framework of the Iraqi state. Reinforcement of the tribal notables and their takeover of their tribes' lands were favored by British and Iraqi legislation, as well as by their ability to integrate into the Iraqi establishment and political system. The involvement of the tribal notables in the Iraqi political arena strengthened that arena, the Iraqi state and the regime and increased their influence on the development of Iraq.

In 1918, the British authorities occupying Iraq published the Tribal Disputes Regulations, which granted juridical powers to tribal notables on the basis of the local tribal law then in force, the 'urf. These arrangements, the validity of which were ratified in 1925 by the Iraqi Constitution (Articles 113, 114), placed the tribal population outside the authority of the general law and gave governing authority to the tribal notables. King Faysal I, who sought to obtain the support and confidence of the Shi'ite and Kurdish tribal notables, adopted these regulations and ensured their integration into the Constitution. In 1933, shortly after Iraq received its independence, the Iraqi legislature passed a series of agrarian laws which were intended to set forth the rights and duties of the fellahin and the landowners (Law Governing the Rights and Duties of the Cultivators). In practice, these laws helped the tribal landowners and the landowners from among the urban notable families to confirm their control of the tribal lands and the tribesmen themselves, who became, in essence, serfs. The fellahin—that is, the tribesmen who became serfs—were not entitled to leave the lands they worked as long as they owed money to the wealthy landowners. The wealthy landowners could force the fellahin to leave when they no longer needed them as a workforce, and they could prevent them from leaving when they wanted to assure themselves of cheap labor.

The method of taxation customary in Hashemite Iraq, officially intended to provide concessions for the agricultural sector, in practice gave rise to a situation whereby the landowners paid hardly any taxes. In this way, the Iraqi state granted far-ranging benefits to the richest stratum of its population, which controlled the majority of Iraq's lands. The British tribal policy and the agrarian policy of the Iraqi state prevented the development of an independent peasantry.

By giving the tribal landowners, many of whom were Shi'ites, an interest in the existence of the Iraqi state, which facilitated their takeover and control of the lands and their integration into the political system, the state was able to rule the tribesmen-turned-peasants and to neutralize the Shi'ite tribal threat. Although many of the Shi'ite tribal notables who had become landowners and the Shi'ite politicians resented the Sunnites and sought to bolster their own status within the state, on the practical level, their basic interest lay in preserving the status quo.

During the 1920s and 1930s, tensions and struggles sometimes arose between the politicians from the old notable families and the young Sharifian politicians from the middle stratum. Gradually, however, the common interest of the three components in preserving the political and social status quo and maintaining the Iraqi state and its institutions in their current format prevailed. The elite of the notable families, Sharifian politicians, and tribal landowners attained more and more of the characteristics of a conservative ruling class that controlled the state apparatus, owned most of the lands, and maintained dominance in commerce.[22] The overwhelming majority of the Iraqi politicians came from or were related to this social stratum and constituted the ruling political elite, committed to the status quo which served the class interests of the stratum. The tiny industrial bourgeoisie was also connected with the ruling class. At the end of the 1950s, six families owned most of the industrial enterprises in Iraq.

The building of the Iraqi state after World War I and the attempts to crystallize the national identity within it involved complex interactions with the development of an upper social class and the expansion of the effendiyya and the tribesmen, many of whom became peasants and tenants.

Outline of Iraq's Geopolitical Situation and Regional Policy

Iraq's regional policy in the first half of the twentieth century was conducted under conditions characterized by its internal weakness. Composed of a heterogeneous population split by ethnic, religious, and social differences, Iraq was beset by a weak national consciousness. In addition, it suffered threats posed by Iraq's strong and cohesive neighbors, Iran and Turkey, whose relations with Iraq were clouded by unsolved differences, and whose influence on parts of the Iraqi population constituted a potential strategic threat to its existence. King Faysal I had been expelled from Damascus in 1920 with the dissolution of his state by the French. He considered the restoration of his control of Syria to be the duty and historic right of the Hashemites as the implementers and leaders of Arab nationalism. The ambition to achieve a union or federation with Syria was presented as the realization in practice of the pan-Arab vision—unity of the Arabs into a single, strong state. The reinforcement of the "Iraqo-centric" pan-Arab current among those who had developed a national consciousness, as well as the political climate and conditions prevailing in the political arena within Iraq, constituted the political and social background for Iraq's ambition to achieve union with Syria, hegemony in the Fertile Crescent and Arab leadership. Iraq's endeavors toward union or hegemony in Syria had increased steadily since the signing of the treaty with Britain in 1930 and the receipt of independence in 1932.

Iraq's regional foreign policy, which was maintained by the heads of the Hashemite Royal House and the politicians from the ruling elite, was intended to legitimize them within the domestic Iraqi political arena and to ensure the continued existence of Iraq in the face of the threat presented by its neighbors. The shaping of Iraq's foreign policy was influenced by interaction among four forces: (1) the geopolitical situation; (2) social and ideological tensions and contradictions; (3) trends in nation-building which aimed toward defining the Iraqi national identity; and (4) the process of state building. Iraq's weakness and the limited consciousness of its national identity, still in the stages of development and in competition with religious, ethnic, and tribal identities, had a definitive impact on Iraq's regional status, its national security, and its perception of its international interests and the means necessary to protect them.

Iraq's foreign policy was characterized by two orientations which, notwithstanding the differences and contradictions between them, at times ran parallel. One trend favored the establishment of a large Arab state in the Fertile Crescent under Iraqi Hashemite rule and its leadership of the Arab world. The other orientation sought to reinforce Iraq's ties with its northern, non-Arab neighbors, Turkey and Iran.

The Iraqi policy of establishing a large Arab state or an Arab federation in the Fertile Crescent, which would mean Iraqi control of or hegemony in Syria, was nourished by the Sunnite Arab minority's—including the primarily Sunnite ruling elite's—fear of the Shiʿite and Kurdish majority. A union or federation with Syria and the establishment of a large Arab state, in which a Sunnite Arab majority would be ensured, would extricate the Sunnite Arabs of Iraq from the status of a minority which both controlled and feared a Shiʿite and Kurdish majority.

The aim toward union or federation with Syria was also intended to reinforce Iraq's own status vis-à-vis its strong northern neighbors, Turkey and Iran, with which it still had unresolved differences and which embodied a strategic threat. The differences between Iraq and Iran concerned the Shatt al-ʿArab—the confluence of the Euphrates and the Tigris Rivers, which was both Iraq's only outlet to the sea and the maritime route to the large Iranian oil port of Abadan. The fact that Iran was a Shiʿite state and the relations between the Iraqi Shiʿites and their co-religionists in Iran increased the fears of the Sunnite Arab minority and the Sunnite ruling elite that Iran would support the Shiʿite tendency toward challenging the status quo in Iraq, which ensured Sunnite dominance.

The perceived threat from Turkey resulted from the fear that it would attempt to exploit the separatist and autonomist movements among the Kurds in order to take over the petroleum-rich Kirkuk and Mosul areas. Although Turkey, which considered the Kurds as a branch of the Turkish nation, had waived its claims to the Mosul region under strong pressure from Britain in 1926, it did so very reluctantly. Iraq's fears with regard to Turkey's true ambitions concerning the Mosul region continued throughout the monarchical period and even afterward, remaining in effect to this day. Union or federation with Syria was intended to attain additional power for Iraq and to improve the balance of power between it and the neighboring state of Turkey, which was more cohesive, larger in both area and population, and stronger.[23]

The strong Iraqi interest in union or federation with Syria also resulted from Iraq's lack of any outlet to the Mediterranean Sea. Syria, Lebanon, and Palestine were viewed as Iraq's outlets to the Mediterranean. An outlet to the Mediterranean was considered as not only an economic interest but also an important factor in Iraq's international status. The absence of any direct maritime connection to Europe and the West was perceived as a failing which pushed Iraq back to the periphery, from the standpoint of the international global arena, and thus doomed it to weakness and backwardness. Moreover, the Shatt al-ʿArab, Iraq's outlet to the Persian Gulf, was very vulnerable to attack from the Iranian side. In addition to all the reasons stated above, Iraq was in need of an outlet to the Mediterranean Sea for its oil exports.

Iraqi aims in the Fertile Crescent, to dominate Syria under Hashemite rule, also resulted from the ambitions of Iraq's rulers. King Faysal I and his successors, King Ghazi (1933–1939) and the Regent, ʿAbd al-Ilah (1939–1953) aspired to regain the rule of Syria, which they perceived as having been stolen from them in 1920 following France's overthrow of Faysal's regime in Damascus. The aim of ruling Syria under the banner of Arab unity also played a role in legitimizing the Hashemite monarchy in Iraq and in the building of the Iraqi state under Hashemite hegemony. The fact that Faysal and the Hashemites were foreigners who had been set up as kings by the British required them to push for pan-Arab nationalism in order to legitimize their rule within the domestic Iraqi political arena. The drive toward pan-Arab nationalist unity with Syria enabled Faysal and his successors to appear as leaders of the Arab nation, focused on Arab unity and power, and to portray their control of Iraq as the first stage in the achievement of these objectives.

The Arab orientation in Iraq's regional foreign policy was related to the growing dominance of the pan-Arab nationalist trend in the ideological and political climate within Iraq. Under the influence of the Iraqi educational system, which had been shaped by activists with a pan-Arab nationalist worldview, and the weakness of the Iraqi territorial identity, the trend toward Arab nationalist identity and pan-Arab ideology became attractive to the effendiyya and dominated the political climate of Iraq during the 1930s. In light of the above, Iraq's international positions were at times justified by pan-Arab ideological motives. Iraqi politicians, who sought to bolster their own status in the domestic arena, especially in the eyes of the nationalist effendiyya, made frequent and insistent declarations of pan-Arab nationalist attitudes. Iraq's ambition to lead the Arab world and dominate the Fertile Crescent, as well as the weight of pan-Arab nationalism in the domestic Iraqi political arena, led to increasing Iraqi involvement in the Palestine question, starting as early as the late 1920s. Iraq's interests in Syria and the reinforced pan-Arab Iraqo-centric thrust of Iraqi politics gave rise to conditions which encouraged the transformation of the Palestine question into an ideologically and emotionally charged domestic political issue. The first speech made by Iraq's delegate to the League of Nations, upon its acceptance in 1932, expressed Iraq's view of itself and the role which it sought to play as the leader of the Arabs.[24]

The second trend in Iraq's regional foreign policy was to cement its ties with Iran and Turkey. Notwithstanding the unresolved issues and despite the perceived threat posed by those countries, Iraq shared a commonality of interest with them concerning the need to prevent the establishment of a Kurdish state. The establishment of such a state would have ripped extensive land areas away from all three states. An additional common interest resulted from the proximity of the northern states to the Soviet border and their ruling elites' fear of the USSR and of communism. The shared interests in these areas enabled the signing of the Sa'dabad Pact between Iraq, Turkey, Iran, and Afghanistan in 1937.

The Arab and "northern" orientations in Iraq's regional foreign policy did not necessarily contradict each other. Iraq attempted to act according to a combination of both trends. Nuri al-Sa'id, the Iraqi politician who was most active on behalf of union or federation with Syria and the establishment of Arab unity under Iraqi hegemony in the Fertile Crescent, simultaneously aimed at rapprochement with Turkey and Iran. According to his views, Iraq should constitute the link between the Arab states and the non-Arab states to the north. During his term in office as foreign minister under Yasin al-Hashimi (March 1935–October 1936), as prime minister (December 1938–March 1940), and as foreign minister under Rashid 'Ali (March 1940–January 1941), Nuri attempted to promote a tripartite alliance between Iraq, Turkey, and Egypt. Nuri hoped that Iraq, within the framework of that alliance, would play the role of the central Arab power and would obtain the consent of Turkey and Egypt to its own ambitions in Syria.

The Struggles among the Politicians of the Baghdad Elite and the Tribal Shi'ite Revolts Following the Death of Faysal I

The death of King Faysal I in September 1933 undermined the delicate system of balances between the politicians and the political and social forces in Iraq.[25] Faysal, notwithstanding his weaknesses, had the ability to maneuver among the elite politicians, and had acquired a certain degree of trust and personal loyalty among the tribal notables. The young King Ghazi, Faysal's son, had a weak personality, was devoid of any political experience, and lacked any skill in political maneuvering in which his father had been so gifted. There was now no one who could restrain the tensions among the politicians of the mainly Sunnite Baghdad elite, or between the Sunnites and the Shi'ites throughout Iraq. The trust and loyalties of the tribal notables, which had been enjoyed by Faysal, had been given to him on a personal basis, and Ghazi was unable to obtain a similar position for himself.

As Iraq's local market economy expanded and was linked with the world market economy, production and socioeconomic conditions changed. Tribal lands, taken over by tribal leaders, became the means of production for both domestic and foreign markets, and hence the attainment of capital. Thus, the value of the lands increased, leading to increased tensions and struggles between and within the tribes; particularly acute were disputes over lands and irrigation systems. The tensions and struggles between the tribes and their notables, which at times also reflected processes of social stratification and the weakening of traditional frameworks, now spilled over into violent outbursts and revolts against the Iraqi state.

The governments of Iraq during the first years following the death of Faysal I were headed by Jamil al-Midfa'i (November 1933–July 1934, March 1935) and 'Ali Jawdat al-'Ayubi (August 1934–March 1935), moderate Sharifian politicians with links to the Palace, who did not belong to al-Ikha al-Watani. With Faysal's restraining force and manipulative capabilities no longer present, the Sunnite urban politicians now sought to exploit the tribal unrest in order to topple the 'Ali Jawdat and Jamil al-Midfa'i governments.

New elections for Parliament were held in December 1934, as part of the efforts made by the 'Ali Jawdat government to limit the power of the tribal notables. These elections increased the number of urban Sunnite Arab delegates from Baghdad while the number of Shi'ite tribal notables decreased. Among the tribal notables who lost their seats in Parliament was 'Abd al-Wahid al-Sikkar, a notable from the Fatla tribe, who had played an important role in the anti-British revolt in 1920. After losing his seat in Parliament, al-Sikkar began to stress the discrimination against the Shi'ites on the part of the Iraqi state, but was unable to obtain the support of the Shi'ite religious leaders. At the end of December 1934, an extensive tribal revolt led by al-Sikkar broke out, involving connections and negotiations with the heads of al-Ikha al-Watani.[26] These contacts with al-Sikkar were headed by Hikmat Sulayman and Rashid 'Ali. The Iraqi state was incapable of coping with the Shi'ite tribal revolt, which was supported and exploited by the opposition—that is, by politicians from the ruling Sunnite elite. The Iraqi Army, whose chief of staff, Taha al-Hashimi, was the brother of Yasin al-Hashimi, refrained from putting down the revolt. In March 1935, the rebels reached Baghdad without encountering any resistance on the part of the military. In view of the confusion and disorder in the capital and throughout much of southern Iraq, King Ghazi dismissed 'Ali Jawdat, and brought Yasin al-Hashimi back to replace him as prime minister. By exploiting a Shi'ite tribal revolt against the state and the central government, the politicians who supported Iraqi Arab nationalism succeeded in rising to power. The Army did not actually bring about the political change; still, its neutral position and lack of support for the government tipped the scales in favor of al-Ikha al-Watani. The Sunnite politicians from al-Ikha al-Watani had availed themselves of the Shi'ite tribal revolt in order to seize power. They did so even at the price of damage to their own basic interests, as members of the Sunnite elite, in preserving the status quo and the authority of the state over ethnic and tribal forces. Their willingness to adopt a course which endangered the sovereignty of the state is indicative of the shortsighted considerations and political opportunism which characterized Yasin al-Hashimi and other nationalist politicians from the Sunnite ruling elite.[27]

In addition to members of al-Ikha al-Watani, Yasin al-Hashimi's government included Nuri al-Sa'id as foreign minister, and his intimates Ja'far al-'Askari (who had served as prime minister between November 1923 and August 1924 and between November 1926 and December 1927) as minister of defense and Rustum Haydar as minister of finance. The involvement of Nuri and his intimates resulted both from pressure by the British embassy and from Yasin al-Hashimi's fear of Nuri as a member of the opposition. By including Nuri in his cabinet, Yasin al-Hashimi sought to signal the British that his government was not anti-British.

The Yasin al-Hashimi government emphasized its nationalist nature and pan-Arab orientation and took measures to increase the national consciousness and intensify the nationalist ambience. All of the students in Iraq's schools were organized into a national youth movement, al-Futuwwa, which was characterized by fascist proclivities and trends. The nationalist club al-Muthanna was greatly encouraged and in fact transformed into an ideological and political center. Yasin maintained a prominent presence in the club's nationalist activities. In accordance with this line, his foreign minister, Nuri al-Sa'id, launched a campaign intended to reinforce Iraq's regional international status and to promote Iraqi ambitions to control Syria.

Yasin al-Hashimi did not abrogate the 1930 treaty with Britain following his rise to power, despite his image as an anti-British fighter, and the fact that al-Ikha al-Watani had been organized on the basis of opposition to it and especially to demand the elimination of the limitations on Iraq's independence stemming from the treaty. Instead, Yasin al-Hashimi took pains to calm British fears and demonstrate his friendly attitude toward Britain. This was typical of politicians from the Iraqi elite. While they desired to remove the restrictions that had been imposed on Iraq's independence by the treaty with Britain, they also sought to preserve and nurture ties with Britain. They needed to ensure British support of Iraq in the face of the threats posed by its neighbors and as a guarantee of the preservation of the domestic status quo against the threat of the centrifugal Kurdish, Shi'ite, and tribal forces. In addition, under British hegemony, senior politicians and government ministers—some of whom, such as Yasin al-Hashimi, were nationalist extremists—and Shi'ite tribal notables took over lands in the most sought-after areas and transformed themselves into wealthy landowners. The anti-British nationalist fervor was intended to reinforce their nationalist status and image in the eyes of the urban effendiyya, which had become an active nationalistic political element in the streets of Baghdad, and to gain Iraqi public opinion. Yasin al-Hashimi's behavior and that of most of the elite politicians represented the imbalance between the content of the anti-British nationalist radical slogans they voiced to enlist political support when they were in the opposition or in appearances before nationalist supporters, and their inherently conservative, pragmatic tendencies. Their own class interests and their view of the dangers to which the interests of the Iraqi state were exposed directed their essentially conservative behavior.

The Officers' Coups d'Etat and Nationalist Radicalization in Iraq Starting in the Mid-1930s

Two major phenomena were especially prominent in Iraq during the late 1930s: (1) the rise of nationalist and anti-British political unrest, characterized by a pan-Arab orientation among the members of the modern middle stratum, the effendiyya, and the transformation of that unrest into a central element of the political arena; (2) the coups d'etat by army officers and the reinforced status of the officers in Iraqi politics.

The wave of political radicalization, which had increased throughout the Arab world since the mid-1930s among the modern middle stratum and especially among its younger, educated members, took unique shape in each individual state, according to the specific conditions prevailing therein. Political radicalization, the fruit of the social, economic, and ideological distresses and struggles and tensions in relations with the mandatory colonial powers, was expressed in terms of nationalism. Nationalism provided a response to the acute identity distresses and raised hopes that achievement of national power, Arab unity, and equalization of power with the West would resolve the difficulties of individuals and society.

Within the pan-Arab faction in Iraq, two streams existed and maintained a reciprocal relationship. King Faysal, Nuri al-Sa'id, and many "Sharifian" politicians defined pan-Arabism as striving for hegemony within the Fertile Crescent and Iraqi-Hashemite control of Syria. The ideologues of the pan-Arab movement and the shapers of Iraq's educational system, Sati' al-Husri, Fadil al-Jamali, and Sami Shawkat, along with the members of the pan-Arab party al-Istiqlal, defined the Arab nation according to its language and cultural heritage. They strove to achieve a much broader vision of Arab unity, which was intended to include Arabic-speaking areas beyond the Fertile Crescent. Sati' al-Husri, who served as director general and supervisor of the educational system in Iraq during the 1920s and 1930s, recruited teachers with pan-Arabic leanings from Syria and Palestine. (For example, Anis al-Nasuli from Syria and Darwish al-Miqdadi and Aqram Zuʿaitar from Palestine.)

The pan-Arab nationalist and authoritarian trends were intensified by the ideological environment prevailing throughout the world with the rise of nationalist authoritarian fascist movements and regimes in Europe. The wave of radicalization exacerbated the contradiction prevailing among the politicians and the conservative ruling political elites, whose class interests dictated the preservation of the social-economic-political status quo, but who, in order to retain their own status, required the legitimization and political support of the modern middle stratum, which was constantly expanding and whose distresses required a change in the status quo.

The politicians from among the conservative ruling elite in Iraq sought to increase the independence of their country, but at the same time, to ensure the continued support of Britain, retain Iraq's regional status relative to its neighbors, and preserve the social and political status quo within Iraq. This agenda was in conflict with the militant nationalism which they had propounded in order to enlist the support of the modern middle stratum. The Palestinian Arab revolt in Palestine in 1936–39 gave the Iraqi politicians an opportunity to demonstrate nationalist attitudes without being required to adopt an anti-British position which could detract from their personal interests in fostering ties with Britain. The Yasin al-Hashimi government, which adopted an explicitly nationalist line, contributed to increasing the nationalist unrest in the streets. The conservative elite politicians were incapable of providing responses to the distresses and needs of the high school and college graduates, nor to those of the poorer strata of the populace who were undergoing a process of rapid urbanization. Instead, they now exploited and nurtured nationalist approaches and pan-Arab discourse, which had been fostered in the educational system and internalized by the students through nationalist indoctrination since the 1920s.

Politicians from among the conservative elites contributed to the radicalization of nationalism through their efforts to win the support of the effendiyya, in Egypt and Syria as well. In Iraq, however, it was the governments as such, especially those headed by Yasin al-Hashimi and Rashid ʿAli, which played an active role in escalating the nationalist ferment. The extensive involvement of politicians and even prime ministers in the activity of the nationalist club al-Muthanna, the encouragement of the activities of the nationalist paramilitary youth movement al-Futuwwa, which encompassed all students in Iraqi schools, and the nationalist utterances of Yasin al-Hashimi, Rashid ʿAli and other politicians admittedly helped them to preserve their status in the eyes of the nationalist masses. At the same time, these moves and

positions increased the nationalist radicalization of the effendiyya and transformed the politicians from members of an elite to captives of the extremism
which they themselves had fostered.

Political radicalization, characterized by pan-Arab nationalist trends, was
accompanied by great admiration for the army and by reinforcement of the
military. The army, which had constituted the mainstay of the Iraqi state
against the tribal and ethnic threat from within and the geopolitical threats
from without, enjoyed a great deal of prestige among the nationalists and
became a symbol of national power and unity.[28] The weakness characterizing
the modern social and political frameworks, civilian society as a whole (political parties, labor unions), and the legitimacy of the constitutional parliamentary regime made the army, by contrast, even stronger. The expansion of
the army following the activation of the Conscription Law, which had been
passed when Iraq obtained its independence in 1932, as well as admiration
for the army and the militaristic nationalist currents among the modern
middle stratum, created conditions favorable to army intervention in politics
and the launching of military coups.

Military coups in the Arab states in the 1950s and 1960s brought to power
forces from among the modern middle stratum. The result of these coups in
those states was the establishment of radical nationalist regimes with leftist
tendencies, which would achieve social and economic transformations. By
contrast, the coups by the officers in Iraq during the 1930s did not bring
about such transformations and did not change the social status quo which
was so convenient to the ruling elite. The officers who launched the military
coups in Iraq between 1936 and 1941 admittedly came from the middle and
lower middle strata; however, their motives were not based on a desire to
launch a socioeconomic revolution nor on any identification with the social
strata from which they came, but rather, on anti-British nationalism with a
pan-Arab orientation. These officers may be said to have been the nationalist
radical "younger brothers" of the Sharifians. Whereas Nuri al-Saʿid, Yasin
al-Hashimi, Jaʿfar al-ʿAskari, Jamil al-Midfaʿi and others, who had returned
to Iraq upon the coronation of Faysal I in 1921, had already been senior
officers or had held key positions in his Damascus regime, Salah al-Din al-
Sabbagh and other officers who launched the coups between 1936 and 1941
were middle-ranking officers in their twenties. The senior Sharifians had
retired from military service in the 1920s and had become the backbone of
the ruling political elite, working their way—not without friction and conflicts—into the elite of old notable families in Baghdad, Basra, and Mosul.
Their younger comrades were the ones who held the key positions in the
military during the 1930s. Their nationalist leanings were more radical and

were accompanied by a sense of hostility toward the British, who were perceived as interested in keeping Iraq weak in order to ensure its dependency on Britain. The nationalist atmosphere and the admiration displayed for militarism in the streets, the schools and the press throughout Iraq gave the army officers a feeling of power. While they were shaken by the military coups, the ruling elite and the upper class, which gradually coalesced during the 1930s, were not personally affected by them. The elite politicians, notwithstanding their weakness relative to the military officers and despite the radicalization among the effendiyya, succeeded in preserving the socioeconomic status quo. The nationalist atmosphere and the pan-Arab nationalist ideology, which flourished in the streets and under the political conditions prevailing in Iraq, served as a means of enlisting support and legitimization for both the radical nationalist army officers and the conservative ruling elite.

On October 29, 1936, Deputy Chief of Staff Bakr Sidqi launched a military coup that led to the overthrow of the Yasin al-Hashimi government and the establishment of a new government under Hikmat Sulayman.[29] The coup was organized by a loose coalition which included Bakr Sidqi (who was motivated by his personal ambition to become chief of staff and the "strong man" of Iraq), the senior politician Hikmat Sulayman of al-Ikha al-Watani (who had been pushed aside after Yasin al-Hashimi's rise to power), and members of a group called al-Ahali. The latter group was established in 1931 by a number of young Iraqi students, most of them enrolled in universities in Lebanon, who espoused Socialist leanings, reform, and socioeconomic development. Al-Ahali sought to transform Iraq into a modern, democratic state, by means of far-ranging change in Iraqi society. The members of al-Ahali emphasized the need to end illiteracy, develop education, liberate women, enact social security, and initiate limited social reform (distribution of some state-owned lands to farmers). Moreover, they demanded the abrogation of the tribal regulations, which they viewed as an obstacle to the progress of Iraq.

Following the coup, a government was established under Hikmat Sulayman. Among the ministers in the new government were several prominent Shi'ites and Kurds; moreover, Bakr Sidqi himself was of Kurdish descent. The Hikmat Sulayman government was unusual among the governments of Iraq and the dominant political and ideological trends which prevailed in that country during the 1930s. Prominent among its ministers were several personages who, although they constituted part of the upper socioeconomic class and the political elite, supported social reforms, gave a high priority to development and modernization, and even favored moderate, limited agrarian reform, including the distribution of some state lands to the fellahin. By contrast to the pan-Arab nationalist ideological trends which had prevailed in previous governments, this one was characterized by an Iraqi territorialist trend.

The opponents of the Bakr Sidqi–Hikmat Sulayman administration included both Nuri al-Sa'id, the powerful master of intrigue, and the supporters of Yasin al-Hashimi (he himself died in January 1937, in exile). The rivals of the government accused it of not being nationalistic and claimed that its anti-Arab and pro-Kurdish and pro-Turkish approach alluded to the Kurdish origin of Bakr Sidqi and the Turkish descent of Hikmat Sulayman. (Like many members of the Sunnite elite, Hikmat Sulayman came from a family of Ottoman bureaucrats who had settled in Iraq during its rule by the Ottoman Empire and become part of the Baghdad elite.) The government made efforts to dispel these charges by means of political moves in the inter-Arab arena, which were intended to improve Iraq's relations with Saudi Arabia. During its term in office, the government signed a treaty of friendship and cooperation with Saudi Arabia and sent a delegation for a round of talks in the capitals of the Arab states, to reinforce inter-Arab ties. At the same time, the basic trend of this government favored detachment from the pan-Arabism which had been fostered by the Yasin al-Hashimi government.

The aspersions cast by the supporters of Nuri al-Sa'id and of Yasin al-Hashimi against the government found a receptive ear among the effendiyya, imbued as they were with an awareness of Arab identity and pan-Arab ideology. Admittedly, the social policies of the government, and especially those of al-Ahali, served the interests of the modern middle stratum which supported change in the status quo, acceleration of development, and modernization; however, the members of that stratum were more influenced by pan-Arab nationalist motives, which stemmed from the acute nature of the identity crises and the lack of class consciousness among them. Many members of the effendiyya who were employed by the bureaucracy and the corrupt government services feared the new government's intention to wipe out corruption. Although most of the government ministers belonged to the bureaucratic-commercial-landowning elite, most members of that elite began to fear the currents of change, and especially the possibility of agrarian reform, minor though it might be, which was supported by al-Ahali. The fact that the government ministers included Ja'far Abu al-Timman, a Shi'ite politician who was identified with the Shi'ite threat to Sunnite domination, aroused the fears of many members of the Sunnite Arab elite of Baghdad, and even those of the effendiyya, most of whom were Sunnite Arabs. The opposition took pains to inform the major tribal landowners that the government intended to bring about an agrarian reform—that is, to take away their land. The tribes and traditional sectors of the population began to accuse the government of betraying Allah and practicing communism.

In June 1937, the members of al-Ahali, headed by Kamil al-Jadirji, resigned from the government, due to protracted tension between them and Bakr Sidqi following the brutal suppression of the tribal revolt by the army. Bakr Sidqi, who was not popular among the officers even before the coup, was now utterly isolated in the face of intensified pan-Arab nationalist leanings among the officers and the resentment which they felt toward his behavior and the dictatorial patterns of his regime. In view of his isolation in society and in the Iraqi political system, a broad coalition of forces opposed to the Bakr Sidqi–Hikmat Sulayman government now arose seeking to topple it. Britain had displayed a reserved skepticism toward the Bakr Sidqi–Hikmat Sulayman regime. Bakr Sidqi's interest in purchasing arms from Germany had caused severe concern in Britain. A strange coalition, motivated by their shared opposition to Bakr Sidqi, was formed between Britain and Sidqi's rivals among the Iraqi officers, whose own attitudes were pan-Arab nationalist and anti-British in nature.

On August 15, a military coup took place, during which Bakr Sidqi was murdered and the Hikmat Sulayman government resigned. Following the coup, King Ghazi asked the Sharifian politician Jamil al-Midfa'i to head the government. The officers who had launched the coup, under Colonel Salah al-Din al-Sabbagh, became the most powerful force in Iraq between 1937 and 1941. Their power stemmed in part from the weakness of other forces in the political arena and society of Iraq. This power was further enhanced by the militaristic trends that flourished alongside the radical nationalism of the politically aware, rebellious effendiyya, who supported the officers' pan-Arab nationalism. The latter were becoming a significant force in the political and ideological climate of Iraq.

Jamil al-Midfa'i, a man of moderate views, belonged to the central segment of the ruling elite, which—while it did seek to increase Iraq's independence—favored a pan-Arab nationalist outlook. This central group paid lip service to radical pan-Arab nationalism, although its proponents were not anti-British and considered Britain an essential mainstay of Iraq in the regional arena and a guarantor of the socioeconomic status quo within Iraq. Al-Midfa'i was forced to maneuver between the nationalist officers under al-Sabbagh, whose policy demanded the removal of all restrictions to Iraq's independence and the provision of assistance to the Palestinian Arab revolt, notwithstanding Britain's objections, and his own desire to improve relations with Britain in order to secure Iraqi interests and, in practice, his own political interests and those of the ruling elite. The anti-British national sentiments in the streets, which increased against the background of the events in Palestine and the international tension throughout the world, made it difficult to pursue a pragmatic, moderate policy. King Ghazi exploited and helped to intensify the nationalist atmosphere by raising the demand for Iraqi annexation of Kuwait.[30] This demand contributed to the troubled atmosphere that prevailed between Iraq and Britain. Al-Sabbagh, the nationalist officers and oppositionist politicians from the elite, who had taken pains to build up their pan-Arab nationalist image, expressed criticism of the al-Midfaʿi regime, which preferred to avoid tension and conflict with Britain. They were especially critical of Iraq's failure to extend military assistance to the Palestinian Arab revolt, which had become the symbol of the pan-Arab nationalist struggle. Nuri al-Saʿid, who was not a member of the al-Midfaʿi government, resented the new prime minister and strove to overthrow him. In order to convince the British to support him as prime minister, Nuri claimed that al-Midfaʿi was not capable of restraining the anti-British nationalist sentiments in Iraq. At the same time, in order to gain the support of al-Sabbagh and the nationalist officers, Nuri claimed that only he, by virtue of his ties with the British, would be capable of working to achieve the vision of Arab unity.

Al-Midfaʿi attempted to put an end to the involvement of the officers in politics and to return the army to its barracks. With this in mind, he appointed Sabih Najib—an officer who was not close to al-Sabbagh and the nationalist officers—to the post of minister of defense. The attempt to weaken al-Sabbagh and the nationalist officers by replacing key figures in the defense establishment and posting several officers to assignments far outside Baghdad led to an additional military coup in December 1938.

Following the overthrow of Jamil al-Midfaʿi, King Ghazi, at the request of al-Sabbagh, appointed Nuri al-Saʿid as prime minister. This was a strange alliance between Nuri, the explicitly pro-British politician and architect of the 1930 treaty between Britain and Iraq, and al-Sabbagh and the anti-British nationalist officers. This alliance was based on the unwillingness of the officers to seize power directly—possibly because they feared the British reaction to such a move—and on the political skills exhibited by Nuri, who succeeded in retaining popularity among the officers and in convincing them that he was the only one capable, through cooperation with Britain, of promoting Arab nationalist objectives, and primarily those of Arab unity and the Palestine question. (Following the death of King Ghazi on April 3, 1939, ʿAbd al-Ilah, the nephew of King Faysal I, was appointed regent of Iraq.)

The Rashid ʿAli Movement and the Clash between Britain and Iraq in 1941

Following the outbreak of World War II in September 1939, the nationalist, anti-British tension in Iraq increased. The anti-British nationalist currents, which had increased along with the hopes that Britain would be defeated and would withdraw from Iraq, conflicted with Iraq's obligation to assist Britain, pursuant to the 1930 treaty, and with the pro-British trends among the central segment of the ruling elite. In accordance with the British-Iraqi treaty of 1930, which granted independence to Iraq, the latter was supposed to extend all assistance to Britain, to allow it to use Iraqi territory and resources for the purposes of the war effort, and to break off relations with Britain's enemies. Prime Minister Nuri al-Sa'id and other politicians from the central group of the ruling elite viewed the war as Iraq's historic opportunity—and that of the Arabs in general—to achieve what they had failed to achieve at the end of World War I, primarily Arab unity, in the sense of Iraqi hegemony in Syria and the Fertile Crescent. By means of cooperation with Britain, Nuri sought to prove Iraq's importance as an ally and, in return, to gain British support for Iraq's regional ambitions.

Nuri's policies were opposed by army officers under al-Sabbagh, politicians who opposed Nuri among the elite, and the majority nationalist public opinion, which hated Britain as an enslaving colonialist power and supporter of Zionism in Palestine and hoped that Britain would lose to Germany, thereby helping Iraq to achieve total independence. Nationalist politicians and activists fostered and exploited anti-British nationalist sentiments among the members of the modern middle stratum, thereby reinforcing their own status vis-à-vis Nuri and the central group of the ruling elite. Al-Sabbagh and the anti-British nationalist officers and politicians sought, as far as possible, to avoid rendering assistance to Britain and favored only the most minimal of responses to Iraq's obligations pursuant to the treaty.

In October 1939, the Mufti of Jerusalem, Haj Amin al-Husayni, fled to Iraq, where he was welcomed in Baghdad with great enthusiasm by nationalist circles. His arrival in Iraq and activity there contributed to the exacerbation of the anti-British nationalist sentiments already prevailing.[31] Nuri al-Sa'id was trapped between the demands of the British, who insisted that Iraq limit the Mufti's activity, break off diplomatic relations with Italy (relations with Germany had been broken off in September 1939), and comply with the various causes of the British-Iraqi treaty; and the pressure exerted by the officers (headed by al-Sabbagh) and their allies, the nationalist politicians (headed by Rashid 'Ali al-Kaylani), who demanded that Iraq keep its cooperation with Britain to the minimum and refuse to break off relations with Italy. Unable to enlist Iraqi support for Britain, Nuri, in February 1940, made a complicated move which was intended to bring his rival, Rashid 'Ali, to power as prime minister. In this way, Nuri hoped to prevent Rashid 'Ali from becoming the leader of the anti-British nationalists, as the representative of an alternative to his own pro-British policy. Nuri hoped that direct British pressure on Rashid 'Ali would make it difficult for him to object to the proposals to enlist Iraq in support of Britain. Accordingly, Nuri resigned in February 1940 and suggested that Rashid ʿAli be appointed to replace him. The three most senior of the seven officers who constituted the strong center of power in Iraq (Husayn Fawzi, ʿAziz Yamulki, and Amin al-ʿUmari) sought to exploit the opportunity to get rid of Nuri. However, al-Sabbagh and the other three colonels (Fahmi Saʿid, Kamil Shabib, and Mahmud Salman), wished to refrain from a head-on collision with Britain; thanks to their more rapid and more effective organization, they were able to bring about the dismissal of the three senior officers from the army. Following these events, Nuri established a new government; at the end of March, however, he resigned again. This time, in order to convince the four officers headed by al-Sabbagh to appoint Rashid ʿAli in his stead, he enlisted the aid of the Mufti, who held an extremely prestigious position as a pan-Arab hero and who was popular with both Rashid ʿAli and al-Sabbagh. According to al-Sabbagh's memoirs, it was the Mufti who made contact between the officers and Rashid ʿAli. Al-Sabbagh and his fellow officers, who were given the nickname of "Golden Square" because of the golden color of their insignia of rank, agreed to establish a government under Rashid ʿAli, in which Nuri al-Saʿid would serve as foreign minister. Contrary to Nuri's intention, his maneuver not only did not contribute to moderating pro-German leanings among the nationalists, but actually helped to form a tripartite coalition between Rashid ʿAli, the officers of the Golden Square, and the Mufti, which in turn additionally weakened the pro-British politicians within Iraq.

During his term in office as foreign minister under Rashid ʿAli, Nuri attempted to convince the British to take advantage of France's defeat by Germany in order to expel the French from Syria. Nuri sought to involve Iraq in a move against the French in Syria and to convince the British to take the opportunity and transfer Syria to Iraqi control. In this way, Nuri hoped to prove to the anti-British nationalists, and especially al-Sabbagh and the officers, that the alliance with Britain was the way to achieve the vision of Arab unity. At the same time, Nuri launched an initiative of mediation in the Palestine question, in hopes that British concessions to the Palestinian demands would help to change the Mufti's anti-British, pro-German orientation.[32] Britain, however, refused to accede to Nuri's requests. Churchill refused to make any move against the Vichy government in Syria with the cooperation of Iraq, nor was he willing to grant the Mufti's requests with regard to the Palestine question. In view of the disappointment at the British response, and in light of the German victories in Europe and isolation of Britain, Nuri began to send out feelers to the Axis powers, in order to secure his own position, should Germany win the war. The Germans, however, considered him loyal to Britain and did not respond to his initiatives.[33]

Under pressure by the British and the Regent to break off relations with

Italy and to expel the nationalist officers from all positions of power, Rashid 'Ali resigned at the end of January 1941. The new government was headed by Taha al-Hashimi, who had previously served as minister of defense under Rashid 'Ali. Taha al-Hashimi was popular with the Mufti and the nationalist officers, despite his close relations with Nuri al-Sa'id. Although his rise to power had the consent of the Golden Square, it did not take long for him to clash with them over relations with Germany. The policy formed during Rashid 'Ali's term in office had now reached the point where decision was necessary. Taha al-Hashimi was subjected to strong British pressure to break off ties with Italy, to put an end to the activity of the Palestinian refugees and the Mufti, and to restrain the anti-British inclinations among the senior officers in the Iraqi Army. Despite his nationalistic views and his hostile attitude toward British domination of Iraq, al-Hashimi remained loyal to the monarchy and the civil regime.

In the first half of March 1941, Foreign Minister Tawfiq al-Suwaydi visited Cairo, where he met with British Foreign Minister Anthony Eden. At the meeting, the Iraqi minister was apprised of the unequivocal British demand for Iraq to break off relations with Italy, to restrain the anti-British activity of the nationalists in Iraq, and to enable free passage for British forces in the territory of Iraq. Al-Suwaydi attempted to gain certain concessions with regard to the Palestine question—specifically, concerning the implementation of the "White Paper" and the return of exiled Palestinian leaders, in order to make it easier for him to convince the government, the army, and the nationalist circles to agree to the British demands. Eden refused to listen to him. A letter sent by Winston Churchill to the British ambassador to Baghdad, Cornwallis, emphasized the uncompromising British attitude which dictated refusal to accede to any demands for concessions on the Palestine question, even should this be exploited by German propaganda. Taha al-Hashimi, who was caught between a rock and a hard place, attempted to weaken the Golden Square officers by expelling them from Baghdad, thus giving himself a free hand to accede to the British demands. This move led to the launching of a coup against him on April 1 and the establishment of a nationalist government headed by Rashid 'Ali. The establishment of this government, which openly refused to accede to the British demands and sought the assistance of Germany, placed Iraq on an inescapable collision course with Britain. Fearing that al-Sabbagh and the officers would arrest explicitly pro-British politicians, the Regent 'Abd al-Ilah, along with Nuri and other central politicians identified as pro-British or as rivals of Rashid 'Ali, fled Iraq.

In April and May 1941, al-Sabbagh and the Golden Square officers became the major power dictating a shift in Iraq's foreign policy toward a pro-German orientation.[34] Rashid 'Ali, who feared a head-on collision with Britain and sought channels for negotiation and compromise, was forced to comply with the policy dictated by al-Sabbagh and the Mufti. The militant anti-British movement enjoyed the enthusiastic support of a significant proportion of the effendiyya and the popular strata. This was the zenith of the accumulated resentment against Britain: the nationalists from the middle stratum, the nationalist politicians of the elite, and the army officers all blamed the British for all of the ills and troubles of the Iraqi state and Iraqi society. From the social standpoint, anti-British nationalist fervor reflected the personal and collective frustrations of the effendiyya and the economic distress of many members of the middle and poorer strata.

At the end of April, the British Army landed units in Basra without obtaining the consent of the Iraqi government in advance, as Rashid 'Ali had demanded. Churchill was prepared to go as far as a clash with Iraq in order to expel the pro-German entities which threatened the oilfields and the British Army units fighting against the Germans and the Italians in North Africa. In response to the landing of British troops on Iraqi soil, the Iraqi Army attacked the British bases at Habbaniya and Shu'eiba and placed them under siege. A siege was also imposed on the compound of the British embassy in Baghdad.

During May, Iraq was officially and actively at war with Britain. Not all of the Iraqi Army was loyal to al-Sabbagh and the Rashid 'Ali government. At least half the army remained neutral and stayed within its barracks. The British, after assembling forces brought in from India and Palestine, along with units of the Arab Legion from Transjordan, thoroughly defeated the Iraqi Army. The German assistance that al-Sabbagh and the Mufti had anticipated was extremely limited and marginal, from the standpoint of its effect on the Iraqi-British conflict. Occupied in preparations for Operation Barbarossa, the invasion of the Soviet Union, Germany did not render any significant assistance to the revolt, especially as the British control of the Mediterranean prevented the provision of any significant aid. As the British forces approached Baghdad and the Iraqi Army collapsed, so did the Rashid 'Ali government. On May 29, Rashid 'Ali, al-Sabbagh and his fellow officers, and the Mufti fled from Iraq.

In the confusion and disorder during the period between the collapse of the Rashid 'Ali government at the end of May and the British occupation of Baghdad on June 2, outbreaks of violence against the Jews took place in Baghdad and Basra. Nationalist elements led by activists, the last remaining vestiges of the Rashid 'Ali government, denounced the Jews as pro-British and slaughtered them. The British Army stood at the gates of Baghdad during the two days of the slaughter; even though its officers knew what was happening, they refrained from entering the city until the pogrom had come to an end. The outbreaks of violence against the Jews reflected the change in the ideological and social conditions prevailing within Iraq. The relative equilibrium and tolerance which had existed between Muslims and Jews under the Ottoman Empire and in the traditional societal and ideological system were now undermined, as a result of the penetration of modern nationalist ideas. The growth of modern nationalism, in its most radical guise, along with the identification of the Jews and additional minority groups as allies of Britain, coupled with the influence of German anti-Semitic propaganda, led to a violent onslaught against the Jews. These uprisings against the Jews came to be known at Farhud. The shock to the Jewish community accelerated the tendency of young, educated modernized Jews in Iraq to join the Zionist movement or to support communism. Nevertheless, Jews continued to be well integrated into many sectors of Iraqi life and flourished there until the 1948 war in Palestine and the establishment of the state of Israel.

Following the clash and the subsequent open war with Britain, Iraq once again found itself under direct British occupation.

2

Iraq during World War II

Internal Politics and the Economic Situation

Following the British conquest of Iraq and the flight of Rashid ʿAli, the Mufti, and the officers of the "Golden Square" in early June 1941, the regent and the senior politicians from the mainstream of the conservative ruling elite returned to Baghdad. The British preferred not to impose a regime of military occupation on Iraq, so as to preclude arousing nationalist anti-British sentiments and avoid taking on the burden of direct rule. The British, who were now in full control of Iraq, imposed extremely strict limitations on its independence but refrained from undermining the symbols of Iraqi sovereignty. Accordingly, they restored the regent, ʿAbd al-Ilah, to power in Baghdad and reinstated those politicians from the mainstream of the political elite and the higher socioeconomic stratum who chose the path of loyalty to Britain. The prime minister was a moderate Sharifian with a long political record, Jamil al-Midfaʿi. The most pro-British politician, Nuri al-Saʿid, was so identified with them that, on British advice, he remained in Cairo until the autumn of 1941.

The politicians, the elite, and the establishment in Iraq were faced with the need to reestablish their former positions of trust and legitimacy in the eyes of nationalist public opinion. Although Rashid ʿAli and most of his ministers came from the conservative elite, and even Salah al-Din al-Sabbagh and the officers of the Golden Square were related to that elite, the Rashid ʿAli movement was viewed by many in Iraq, and especially by many members of the modern middle stratum with its nationalist leanings, as a popular nationalist movement and the authentic expression of Iraqi Arab nationalism. The politicians who had returned to Iraq with British assistance were now viewed as a corrupt band of lowly servants of British interests. The renewed British occupation and the economic crisis of the war years increased feelings of alienation and hatred among the modern middle and poorer strata vis-à-vis the establishment and conservative ruling elite. The nationalist radical inclination among the modern middle stratum, which reached its height at the time of the Rashid ʿAli movement, had now weakened. However, hatred of the British and feelings of contempt toward members of the conservative ruling elite and the establishment, who were viewed as collaborators with the British, intensified into a state of ongoing unrest. The memory of the Rashid ʿAli movement became a nationalist myth which, along with the myth of the 1920 insurrection, constituted the archetypes of radical nationalism in Iraq. The political elite and the higher stratum were shocked by the outbreak of popular nationalist violence in the spring of 1941, although Rashid ʿAli and the members of his government who had sprung from among them had not intended to bring about a socioeconomic revolution, and their revolt had not led to a change in the existing economic status quo.

The al-Midfaʿi government implemented purges of the Iraqi Army and government offices, removing those officers and functionaries who had been the most active and prominent under Rashid ʿAli, but they refrained from taking drastic action against the supporters of the Rashid ʿAli movement. In his previous term of office as prime minister (August 1937–December 1938) following the fall of the Bakr Sidqi regime, Al-Midfaʿi had attempted to bring about a national reconciliation while restoring the army to its barracks. Now he sought to avoid actions that he felt would deepen the rifts in Iraqi society.

Great Britain took over supervision of the educational system in Iraq. Hundreds of Arab nationalist teachers who had expressed anti-British opinions were dismissed. Changes were made in the textbooks and curricula used in the schools; use of many textbooks was discontinued. Curricula changed from emphasizing history to focusing on society. A shift was made in the teaching of history itself from subjects and figures related to pan-Arabic ideologies and myths, like Muthanna bin al-Kharitha and Khalid bin al-Walid, conquerors of Iraq during the Muslim conquest, to other periods and figures: e.g., pre-Islamic figures like Hammurabi, Sargon, Nebuchadnezzer, and Zinobia or those related to the modernization of Iraq, like Midhat Pasha and Faysal I. In 1941–42, nationalist Arab clubs were closed. The limitations imposed on the pan-Arabic nationalist movement made the spread of Communist influence easier. Many of the teachers who continued to be employed by the British, who were not identified with the pan-Arab nationalist outlooks, were nevertheless affected by the European Left and the Communists. These changes in the outlooks of the teachers and in the educational system contributed to the fact that the ferment among the students, teachers, and educated stratum took on an increasingly leftist and radical nature after the end of World War II. (At the same time, it should be remembered that Arab nationalism continued to play an important role in society, thanks to the impact of students, teachers, and the educated stratum).

In November 1941, al-Midfaʿi was replaced by Nuri al-Saʿid, who served as prime minister until June 1944. Nuri's government launched an extensive purge of Rashid ʿAli and al-Sabbagh supporters among officers and government officials. Hundreds, including intimates of the Mufti, were arrested and incarcerated in prison camps. At the end of 1941, a special tribunal was established that tried the leaders of the Rashid ʿAli regime and the officers who had collaborated with him. The Ministry of Education especially was subjected to extensive purges; many nationalist teachers, supporters of Rashin ʿAli and fans of the Mufti, were fired, including one hundred Palestinians. Yunis al-Sibaʿwi, the minister of economics, who held extremist programmatic views, and Colonels Fahmi Saʿid and Mahmud Salman were sentenced to death and executed. The "strong man" of the Rashid ʿAli movement and most prominent of the Golden Square officers, Salah al-Din al-Sabbagh, was sentenced to death in absentia after having managed to escape to Turkey. In 1945, he was extradited from Turkey to Iraq and executed. (During his imprisonment, he wrote his memoirs, *Fursan al-ʿUruba fi al-ʿIraq* [*The knights of Arabism in Iraq*], which articulated the world outlook of the nationalist officers.)

Upon assumption of his new position, Nuri renewed his efforts to get Iraq into the war on the side of the Allies, in order to ensure that Iraq would have a place among the winning states in future arrangements when the war was over.[1] Nuri attempted to persuade the British that Iraq should declare war against Germany and the Axis powers and that its military forces should be deployed in Syria, replacing the British units posted there, or, alternatively, that they be sent to North Africa. In January 1943, Iraq declared war against Germany; however, Britain preferred that the Iraqi Army be used to keep order in Iraq and to maintain calm in the Kurdish areas.[2] (British consent to the deployment of Iraqi forces in Syria would have aroused the wrath of Egypt and Saudi Arabia and complicated Britain's already complex relations with General Charles de Gaulle, leader of "Free France." De Gaulle, in exile in London, was profoundly suspicious of what he believed to be Britain's attempts to exploit France's weakness by depriving it of its footholds in the Middle East.)

During the course of the war, Iraq experienced a grave economic crisis. Its petroleum output shrank from 3.9 million tons in 1939 to 1.5 million in 1941. As a result, the income earned by the government of Iraq from petroleum dropped from £2.2 million to £1.4 million.[3] Inflation between 1939 and 1945 totaled 495 percent. Basic commodity prices rose 525 percent. Although salaries of state employees rose by about 300 percent, the actual purchasing power of their wages was eroded by 50 percent.[4] According to one source, between August 1941 and January 1944, the prices of principal food products consumed by the Iraqi population rose by 514 percent.[5] The presence of a large British army, purchasing most of its supplies in Iraq, gave rise to severe inflation to a degree that Iraq had never known before. Between 1941 and 1944, expenditures of the British army in Iraq totaled about £64 million. While it is true that jobs were created in and around the major cities, the high cost of living led to severe deterioration in the standard of living and nutrition experienced by most of the population. In remote areas, food shortages were so grave as to amount to famine. The government took several measures aimed at imposing price controls, but success was limited at best. Among other factors, the trend to rising prices was fostered by several government ministers and many among the elite who stood to gain from galloping inflation. Key figures in commerce, major landowners who sold agricultural produce, and owners of light industrial plants prospered.[6] Thus, against a background of inflation and food shortages, the gaps widened and social tensions worsened between the ruling elite and the poorer and modern middle strata. However, as long as the war continued and the state of emergency remained in force, social tensions remained trapped beneath the surface and were not manifested in politics. Nuri's government failed to find a solution for the severe economic distress, which intensified as the war progressed. Nuri himself devoted most of his time to foreign affairs and paid only minor attention to the economic and administrative problems of his regime, and the situation deteriorated as a result.

Starting in 1943, ferment and revolt among the Kurds resumed. In June 1943, the Kurdish leader Mulla Mustafa al-Barzani escaped from Suleimaniyya, a Kurdish city in northern Iraq. He and other leaders of the Barzani clan had been exiled to Suleimaniyya from their native area of Barzan, after the failure of their revolt in 1931–32 (which had been led by Sheikh Ahmed Barzani, Mulla Mustafa's brother). After returning to Barzan, al-Barzani organized an armed force that began to attack Iraqi Army posts in the area. Barzani demanded that the government of Iraq release the remaining Barzani leaders and allow them to return to their homes. In addition to the demands of his own clan, Barzani made a number of demands on behalf of the Kurdish nation, including the integration of Kurds into the regional administration and economic assistance to the Kurdish area.[7] Against the background of the famine in Kurdistan, the revolt gained support from outside the Barzani clan, but did not amount to an all-Kurdish national uprising. The fragmentation of the Kurdish people into tribes, the weakness of their national consciousness, and the fact that some of the Kurds were linked to the government of Iraq prevented the development of a broad-scale Kurdish nationalist revolt. Due to the weakness of the Kurdish national movement's modern leadership, the revolt remained a traditional tribal uprising led by clan notables.

The Iraqi Army, which had difficulty functioning in the mountainous terrain of Kurdistan, was unsuccessful in suppressing the revolt in 1943. Given the difficulty involved in ending the revolt and the fear that it would spread to other Kurdish areas and even to the oil fields of Kirkuk, Nuri, with British encouragement, attempted to reach an agreement with Mulla Mustafa al-Barzani. In December 1943, Majid Mustafa, a Kurd serving as a minister without portfolio in the government, was put in charge of Kurdish affairs. Majid Mustafa came to an understanding with Mulla Mustafa al-Barzani and submitted to Nuri a series of proposals for compromise that would satisfy the rebels. Among his proposals, acceding to Mulla Mustafa al-Barzani's demands, were pardoning of Kurdish prisoners, appointment of Kurdish liaison officers in the government offices in Kurdistan, adoption of a liberal policy toward the Kurds, distribution of food, and employment of Kurds in road-paving projects.[8] Majid Mustafa's proposals, while acceptable to Nuri, aroused widespread opposition. The heads of the army objected to the compromise and demanded that the revolt be eradicated by armed force. Leading politicians, such as Minister of the Interior 'Omar Nadhmi, were opposed to any cooperation in the appointment of Kurdish liaison officers. Kurdish politicians and members of Parliament whose clans were rivals of the Barzani feared any improvement in the status of the latter, while also seeking to prevent any reinforcement of Majid Mustafa's own position.[9] The regent also objected to these proposals. However, opposition to the agreement with the Barzani tribe proved decisive for another reason. Its main achievement was the fact that it gave so many Iraqi politicians a common cause for the removal of Nuri al-Sa'id from office as prime minister.

During World War II, Nuri made frequent changes in his government; these, however, chiefly involved replacing personnel from a small pool of mainstream politicians belonging to the ruling elite. Early in July 1944, Nuri al-Sa'id resigned in the face of the severe opposition to his policy in Kurdistan and justifiable arguments concerning his neglect of domestic affairs and the Iraqi economy. Appointed as his replacement was Hamdi al-Bajhaji, who, like his predecessor, was conservative in domestic affairs; however, his attitude differed from Nuri's regarding inter-Arab relations. Mulla Mustafa al-Barzani's revolt continued well into 1945, but it did not become an all-Kurdish revolt. In the autumn of 1945, the Iraqi government succeeded in convincing several Kurdish tribal leaders to cease cooperating with Barzani, thus effectively isolating him. That isolation and his military inferiority—he had no more than one thousand combat troops at his disposal at the time—forced Mulla Mustafa al-Barzani to flee to Iran with a handful of his followers; from Iran he went on to the USSR. He would return to Iraq in 1958 to head the struggle for Kurdish national rights, which would continue until his death in 1978. (The Kurdish Democratic Party, or KDP, was founded in 1946 and expressed its support for Mulla Mustafa al-Barzani's leadership. The party was established by educated Kurds, and its activists primarily consisted of urban Kurds with nationalist leftist views. The establishment of the party gave the Kurdish struggle, which until then had been tribal in nature, a modern political dimension. Admittedly, the tribes and tribalism continued to play a major role in the Kurdish struggle until the twenty-first century, but these were now augmented by a modern national aspect. In 1953 the name of the party was changed to the Kurdistan Democratic Party.)

Iraq's Regional Foreign Policy and Its Role in Establishing the Arab League

During World War II, Iraq was the most active state in the inter-Arab arena. Nuri al-Sa'id devoted most of his time and energy to exploiting the conditions of the war in order to achieve Iraqi dominance in Syria, hegemony in the Fertile Crescent, and leadership in the Arab world.[10] Nuri's intensive activity resulted, inter alia, from the need to restore his own nationalist legitimacy and that of the mainstream of the conservative ruling elite, which had been severely damaged within Iraq.

In addition to the Iraqi Hashemite ambitions for dominance in the Fertile Crescent and control of Syria, Nuri, the royal palace, and the mainstream of the conservative ruling elite had another powerful motive for rehabilitating their nationalist status and image within Iraq by means of activity in the inter-Arab arena and achievements of pan-Arab significance. Nuri had a personal motive as well. As a result of the Rashid 'Ali movement, a change was made in the Iraqi constitution, reinforcing the status and powers of the regent and making it easier for him to dismiss prime ministers. Thus, the prime minister's status relative to that of the king or the regent was considerably weakened.[11] Quite possibly, through his pan-Arab activity, Nuri was seeking to reinforce his status as the most senior Iraqi statesman whose power extended beyond the borders of Iraq.

France's weakness as a result of the German occupation, as well as the expectations that a new world order would form at the end of the war, encouraged Nuri and other Arab politicians to hope that a golden opportunity was arising for realization of the dream of Arab unity. From Nuri's point of view, this meant establishing a union or federation between Iraq and Syria and the establishment of a large Hashemite state, under Iraqi domination, in the Fertile Crescent. Nuri hoped to reach an arrangement for the division of the Arab world into spheres of influence. According to this concept, Egypt would become the dominant Arab power in North Africa and would receive pan-Arab support in its endeavors to accomplish the unification of the Nile

Valley—that is, union with Sudan. Ibn Sa'ud would achieve complete recognition of his role as the major power in the Arabian Peninsula. The Hashemites would receive inter-Arab recognition and support as the dominant force in the Fertile Crescent. Nuri sought to divert the efforts of Emir 'Abdallah of Transjordan toward Palestine, leaving Syria free for Iraqi activity.[12] (At the same time, Nuri considered rapprochement with Iraq's non-Arab northern neighbors, Turkey and Iran, as an important component in building a significant regional status for Iraq and as the link between the Arab and non-Arab states in the area.)

In January 1943, in a letter to Richard Casey, the British minister for Middle Eastern affairs, Nuri al-Sa'id proposed a plan to redesign the Arab world. The first stage would involve the unification of Transjordan, Syria, Lebanon, and Palestine. In a second stage, Iraq would join them and create an Arab League between Iraq and this enlarged Syria. Other states would join it later.[13]

Integration of Egypt and the other Arab states into his plan was intended to provide pan-Arab legitimacy for the takeover of Syria and Iraqi Hashemite hegemony in the Fertile Crescent. Nuri hoped to obtain the support of Egypt, in order to neutralize the anticipated objections of Ibn Sa'ud, who viewed the Hashemite plans and Iraqi ambitions as an existential threat to his kingdom. (The relationship between the Hashemite and the Saudi royal houses was characterized by profound hostility, which had taken the form of a life-and-death struggle from the beginning of the rise of the Saudi state, in the Nejd area in the heart of the Arabian Peninsula, early in the twentieth century. An additional chapter in the long-standing hostility between the Hashemites and the Saudis began in 1925, when Ibn Sa'ud expelled the Hashemites from their homeland of Hijaz.) As Nuri saw it, Egypt had no explicit interest in the Fertile Crescent, and its support of his plans would assist in their realization. (It should be recalled that Nuri had already aimed for rapprochement between Iraq and Egypt when he was foreign minister (1935–36), prime minister (1939), and foreign minister (1940). In 1939–40, Nuri had proposed to Egypt a plan for cooperation involving the tripartite strengthening of relations between Iraq, Turkey, and Egypt. In this way, he had hoped to achieve Egyptian consent to Iraq's ambitions in Syria and the Fertile Crescent.)

The relations between the two branches of the Hashemite dynasty—specifically, between Emir 'Abdallah of Transjordan, who considered himself the senior member of the Hashemite family and had the right of primacy in Syria, and the regent, 'Abd al-Ilah, and the Iraqi royal house—was problematic and sensitive. Therefore, Nuri preferred to give top priority to the unification of Jordan and Syria, in order to prevent 'Abdallah from voicing any objections. This was based on his assumption that, following 'Abdallah's death, Transjordan would unite with Iraq.

Nuri's initiative and activity fostered wide-ranging inter-Arab activity, in which Egypt attained leading status. The prime minister of Egypt, Mustafa Nahas, had since 1942 been devoting himself to the inter-Arab arena with a view to achieving a leadership position for his country and reinforcing his own status as a nationalist leader. Nahas, the ruling Wafd party, and the Egyptian elite also needed to rehabilitate their nationalist image and status. They had been restored to power through British intervention; the British had forced King Farouq, in February 1942, to dismiss a government that had been suspected of pro-German tendencies. Through his inter-Arab activities, Nahas sought to rehabilitate his nationalist status with the nationalist middle stratum as well as with Farouq. The king had also increased his activities in the inter-Arab and Islamic arena. Nuri's plan impelled Nahas to take the initiative and convene a conference of Arab states, with the aim of establishing a League of Arab States. Egypt's intention was to frustrate the Hashemite plans and to become the primary force among the Arab states.

In the winter of 1943–44, Nuri al-Sa'id held talks with the heads of the Nationalist Bloc (al-Kutla al-Wataniyya) in Syria, in order to persuade them to request Iraq's assistance against France, whose position in Syria had weakened, and to agree to establish a federation with Iraq even before the expected inter-Arab conference convened. Nuri encouraged the Syrians to adopt a militant attitude with regard to the French, and proposed that, should conflict develop between France and Syria, Iraq would send its army to assist Syria. However, President Shukri al-Quwatli and most of the Syrian nationalist leaders (especially the heads of the "Nationalist Bloc" whose power was centered in Damascus), were not interested in Iraqi dominance or in a Hashemite monarchy, although they did request assistance from the Arab states in order to drive out the French and achieve independence for Syria.[14]

The Iraqi effort to exploit the conditions of a world war in order to achieve Iraq's plans regarding Syria and the leadership of the Arab world did not lead to the desired outcome. Moreover, Egypt's entry into inter-Arab activity, which was intended to block the Hashemites, led to the establishment of the Arab League, which in practice granted legitimacy to the political fragmentation of the Arab world and reduced the chances for realization of Iraq's plans and ambitions. When representatives of the Arab states met in Alexandria in October 1944 for the preliminary conference in preparation for the establishment of the Arab League, it was Egypt, and not Iraq, which was the prominent leading force. Egypt was named as the official home of the League, and the Egyptian politician 'Abd al-Rahman 'Azzam was selected as secretary of the League. Egypt had a definitive influence on the formation and ongoing activities of the organization. Moreover, the Arab League Convention, which took final form at the founding conference of the organization in March 1945, became an additional obstacle on the way to realization of Iraq's ambition in Syria and in the Fertile Crescent. Section 8 of the League Convention stated: "Each member state shall honor the regimes in force in other states and shall relate to them as to an exclusively internal matter. Each of the members of the League shall undertake to refrain from any activity aimed at changing other regimes existing in other member states." An additional section stated that any union between Arab states had to be approved by the League. These sections were in direct conflict with Iraq's ambition to change the republican regime of Syria and to establish therein a Hashemite monarchy, in the framework of a union with Iraq. The legitimization given by the League to the existence of the Arab states within their respective existing borders created an inter-Arab political obstacle for Hashemite Iraq and Transjordan, but also adversely affected the pan-Arab ideological argument fostered by those states. Pan-Arab ideology contended that existing borders between the Arab states, which had taken shape after World War I, were temporary, pending the establishment of the great Arab state that would unite the entire Fertile Crescent. The Egyptian-Saudi line favored the preservation of the territorial states in their existing borders throughout the Arab world, as well as Syria's intention to preserve its independence and its republican regime, while avoiding federation with Iraq or Transjordan. This spelled failure for Iraq's foreign policy efforts during the war. However, notwithstanding that failure, Iraq continued to strive to establish a union or federation with Syria, as a basis for achieving hegemony in the Fertile Crescent and a central status in the inter-Arab arena.

3

Iraq after World War II

Domestic Economic Crisis and Sociopolitical Tensions
and the Struggle for Seniority in the Inter-Arab Arena

Following World War II, political ferment and social tensions in Iraq rose, due to the economic crisis and the exacerbation of the socioeconomic gaps and ideological contradictions between the conservative ruling elite and those of upper socioeconomic class and the modern middle and the poorer strata of the population. The anti-British struggle in Egypt and the tensions regarding the Palestine question added to the internal tension within Iraq and became charged issues in domestic politics. The nationalist radicalism of the younger members of the effendiyya began to adopt leftist, anti-Establishment attitudes directed at socioeconomic change. These trends grew stronger with the beginning of the cold war. Socialist messages had even greater impact due to the increased prestige of the USSR following its victory over Germany. Another factor was the rise of Social Democratic parties in Western Europe, primarily the British Labour Party victory in 1945.

During World War II and the first year thereafter, the regent, ʿAbd al-Ilah, and members of the ruling elite availed themselves of emergency laws to prevent the formation of any political organizations and to frustrate social reforms which, they felt, could undermine the existing sociopolitical status quo. This group of politicians was riddled with personal rivalries. The regent constantly interfered in domestic and foreign policy, and his personal involvement in intrigues disturbed nearly all Iraqi politicians.[1] Even those who were intimate with the regent and supported the Hashemite dynasty were upset by his behavior.

The political agenda of Iraq at the time included four elements that incensed public opinion—that is, the opinion of the modern middle stratum, or the effendiyya:

1. Iraq's relations with Britain and the question of the treaty between Britain and Iraq.
2. Change in the method of elections from two-stage, indirect elections to one-stage, direct elections.

3. The Palestine question.
4. The economic crisis and the food supply.

The method of elections and relations with Great Britain and the British Petroleum Company were viewed as essential to Iraq's social, political, and economic development. Accordingly, they became a prime subject for public debate and political conflict after World War II.

Iraq's relations with Britain were viewed as critical to Iraq's future, in view of the balance of forces between it and its powerful neighbors, Turkey and Iran, and the imagined or real threat posed by the Communists and the USSR. Admittedly, Iraq had signed the 1937 Sa'dabad Pact of friendship and co-operation with Iran, Turkey, and Afghanistan, and the four states shared a common interest in preventing the establishment of a Kurdish state. None-theless, relations between them were characterized by suspicion. Iraq felt threatened by the superior strength of Iran and Turkey and the unresolved border issues and disputes, especially around the question of the Shatt al-'Arab, Iraq's sole outlet to the sea. As a general rule, Iraqi politicians aimed to increase Iraq's independence by ensuring the removal of the limitations to which it had been subjected by the 1930 treaty with Britain. However, many such politicians were ambivalent: Along with their aim of complete inde-pendence, as members of the conservative elite they also desired to ensure Britain's support of the regime and Iraq's status with regard to its neighbors and the Soviet Union.

In 1945, the question of the British-Iraqi treaty preoccupied the Iraqi press and the Iraqi Parliament.[2] The nationalists, the leftists, and those conserva-tive politicians who wished to benefit from the nationalist climate among the effendiyya repeatedly raised the need for changes in the 1930 treaty, demand-ing the withdrawal of the British Army from Iraq and the rescission of the limitations imposed on Iraq by the treaty. The regent and the politicians close to the Palace, who favored continued reliance on Britain, were not happy about entering into deliberations that would subject them to nationalist de-mands. However, Egypt set an example by appealing to Britain to negotiate with it so as to modify the treaty between them, demanding withdrawal of the British Army and deliberations on the future of Sudan. Following Egypt's move, even those in Iraq who had not wanted to renew deliberations on the treaty were forced to look for ways to satisfy the nationalists or gain popular-ity through the use of this theme.

The question of the treaty with Britain and the Palestine question, both of which were emotionally and ideologically charged, became catalysts and fo-cal points of nationalist ferment among the effendiyya. The distress and frustration that resulted from the socioeconomic situation were utilized by members of the nationalist al-Istiqlal party and politicians from the elite. Seeking to bolster their own status by means of nationalist positions, they channeled their anger into nationalist activity, manifested in anti-British and anti-Zionist terms. The regent proposed holding negotiations on military matters. Other politicians, who sought to avoid resuming these deliberations, proposed that Britain demonstrate flexibility within the framework of the existing treaty by removing the limitations that had been imposed on Iraq and easing its policies toward Iraq in military matters.[3]

In 1947, Iraqi prime minister Salih Jabr attempted to exploit the impasse in British-Egyptian relations to conclude a new treaty with Britain that would rescind the limitations on Iraq's independence while ensuring economic and military assistance for Iraq and support of its central status in the region. This attempt, however, gave rise to a wave of rioting that shook the regime and led to rejection of the treaty.

The Economic Crisis

While the end of the war did slow the rate of inflation in Iraq, the economic crisis worsened. British forces were withdrawn from Iraq and other Middle Eastern states. As a result, local industries and workshops, whose output had supplied the needs of the British forces, were damaged, and the number of Iraqi employees holding jobs in British Army camps declined.

The erosion of wages as a result of inflation and price increases during the war had severely affected the standard of living of civil servants and members of the middle and poorer strata. (Between 1939 and 1945, the Consumer Price Index climbed to 595 points—indicating an inflation of 495 percent.)[4] The state had difficulty paying the salaries of its civil servants. Growth in the size of government and ever-expanding state services from the 1930s on placed a heavy burden on Iraq's budget, in which the wage component amounted to more than 50 percent (the number of clerks and teachers increased from 10,000 in 1939 to 18,000 in 1948; the number of policemen increased from 7,000 in 1930 to 25,000 in 1948).[5]

Economic stagnation and the government's inability to finance continued expansion of the bureaucratic apparatus and public services created unemployment among educated Iraqis. More and more high school and college graduates were unable to find jobs.

Several consecutive years of drought, accompanied by a plague of locusts, grievously damaged harvests and reduced the food supply. The wheat harvest dropped from 370,000 tons in 1946 to 235,000 tons in 1947.[6] Despite food shortages, Iraq continued—under pressure by major landowners from the elite, who desired the dollar currency unavailable from the government—to export food, principally grain and dates.

The weakness of the pound sterling and the crisis that had affected the British economy prevented Britain from providing assistance and hard currency, as Iraq demanded. Iraq had accumulated a credit of about £65–70 million, in consideration of services, goods, and petroleum purchased by Britain during the war for its troops. This money was being held in London, and its release depended upon Britain. The British, however, were not prepared either to release the full amount or to convert it into dollars. Financial negotiations between the two states continued intermittently between 1944 and 1947 and had a disruptive effect on the relations between them.[7] Due to Iraq's financial distress and inability to make use of the funds on deposit in Britain, the government of Iraq found itself unable to allocate resources for development and accelerated economic activity.

Economic and social tensions and the frustrations of the modern middle stratum, the effendiyya, led to increased agitation by Communist activists. Thus, the social sensitivity of Iraqi high school and college students increased. Intense activity on the part of the National Democratic Party and al-Istiqlal activists, whose positions were more radical than those of their leaders, as well as by Communist Party activists, fostered the translation of social tensions and economic distress into workers' strikes. Between 1945 and 1947, strikes broke out in large workplaces, including the port of Basra and the Iraqi Petroleum Company. During the Petroleum Company strike in Kirkuk in June 1946, the police opened fire on demonstrators, killing ten.[8]

The social unrest, the increasingly wide socioeconomic gaps, and the severe economic distress gave rise to a political ambience fraught with tension. Among the middle class, the prevailing sentiment was that the state was being controlled by a gang of corrupt, reactionary politicians who sought to hinder development and feared losing their economic advantages as the ruling elite and the upper class.

Conservatism and Liberalization in Iraqi Politics

In June 1944, the regent accepted the resignation of Nuri al-Sa'id. The reasons for his resignation included his shaky relationship with the regent, who envied Nuri's inter-Arab status; criticism voiced against Nuri for having neglected Iraq's domestic problems; objections to his efforts to reach a compromise with the Kurds; conflicts between Nuri and the Iraqi politicians; and the state of his health. The task of forming the new government was assigned to Hamdi al-Bajhaji, who served as prime minister of Iraq until the end of January 1946—a rather long period in Iraqi history. During his term in office, a number of highly important events with ramifications for Iraq occurred: the end of World War II, the dropping of the atom bomb on Japan, the founding of the United Nations, the beginning of the cold war between the USSR and the West, and the further polarization of the Arab world.

During this period of events and changes, the Iraqi government was headed by Hamdi al-Bajhaji, a conservative, loyal to the regent, and pro-British politician, with a personality that was far from dominant. He endeavored to preserve the status quo that had existed in Iraq during the war. Utilizing the emergency laws that he refused to rescind, he prevented the organization of any political parties, halted demands for reform, and quelled social unrest. The nationalists suspected him of having reservations about pan-Arabism; accordingly, when he assumed office, he was forced to allay these suspicions. As his foreign minister he appointed Arshad al-ʿUmari, a conservative politician who objected to any liberalization and was felt to be unenthusiastic regarding pan-Arabism and Nuri's pan-Arab activities. In fact, both men leaned toward cooperation with Egypt and Saudi Arabia in the framework of the Arab League, rather than toward competition for dominance in the inter-Arab arena and in Syria.[9] Al-Bajhaji's success in staying in office for a relatively long time resulted from the regent's desire for a loyal, weak prime minister who would enable him to maintain his own status, as well as from the fact that Nuri al-Saʿid retained his influence on foreign policy, which he felt to be the most important sphere of political action.

The al-Bajhaji government was forced to deal with increasing political unrest, nourished by nationalist politicians and leftist political forces. Echoes of the worldwide wave of sympathy for the USSR were heard in Iraq and were manifested by a surge of Communist and leftist activity; this, in turn, aroused anxiety among the elite, out of any proportion to whatever real threat to the regime may have existed. The fear of communism and the USSR increased in light of the Soviet military presence in northern Iran, near the Iraqi border. Establishment of an independent Kurdish Republic under the protection of the USSR, in Mahabad in western Iran near the border with Iraq, increased Iraqi fears of a combined Communist-Kurdish threat.

Through all this, as noted, the government attempted to retain control using emergency orders dating from the war that barred any political organization. This was a time of worldwide admiration for democratic ideals—liberty, equality, and social justice—which were echoed among the educated members of the effendiyya and some of the politicians in Iraq. Pressure for repeal of the emergency laws, resumption of political life, and certain economic and social reforms came not only from the effendiyya but also from Parliament and the elite politicians. They believed that, unless steps were taken toward political liberalization and certain socioeconomic reforms were introduced, Iraq would fall into a state of social unrest and would lag even further behind the West and the other Arab states. The internal pressures within Iraq were augmented by external pressure on the part of British diplomats, who believed that, in order to maintain political stability in Iraq and successfully cope with the Communist peril, it would be necessary to institute controlled political, social, and economic reforms. These diplomats were influenced by the views of the new British foreign minister, Ernest Bevin, a member of the Labour Party, who believed that, without an alliance between Britain and the effendiyya and without controlled development and modernization, Britain would have difficulty maintaining its influence in the region. This concern came from Britain's identification with the old elite, which desired to preserve the status quo and to prevent the modern middle stratum and its nationalist ideas from achieving any political expression.

In December 1945, the regent, in a surprising speech, called for the resumption of political life and the establishment of political parties and promised socioeconomic reforms.[10] The regent's declaration augmented the expectations of free elections that had arisen with the end of the war, when there was no longer any reason for the emergency laws to continue. In the wake of the regent's declaration, a government was established in February 1946 under Tawfiq al-Suwaydi. This awakened hopes for political liberalization. Al-Suwaydi, a conservative Sharifian politician who nevertheless entertained some liberal views, understood that, in order to preserve the regime, it would be necessary to bring about political liberalization and moderate, controlled economic reforms.[11]

The British diplomats hoped that al-Suwaydi and Salih Jabr would be the type of progressive politicians who, despite their roots in the old elite, would be able to enlist the support of the nationalist anti-British effendiyya.[12] In April 1946, the government announced limited renewal of political activity. The parties that began their activity within the framework of this law were oppositionist in nature but loyal to the regime—in other words, they demanded economic, social, and political reforms and removal of the limitations on Iraq's independence imposed by the 1930 treaty with Britain. The senior conservative politicians from the mainstream of the ruling elite refrained from establishing parties in 1946, preferring to continue utilizing traditional leadership and social networks.

The parties that began or renewed their activities were al-Istiqlal, the National Democratic Party, the Liberal Party, and two radical leftist parties: the National Unity Party and the People's Party. Al-Istiqlal was a nationalist party that had been active as early as the 1930s. Among its members were nationalists who had supported the Rashid 'Ali movement in 1941. The party principally focused on nationalist demands for the complete independence of Iraq and cancellation of the treaty with Britain, on the Palestine question, and on Arab unity. Social and economic issues were given only marginal consideration. The National Democratic Party, led by Kamil al-Jadirji, Muhammad Hadid, and Husain Jamil, embodied a moderate Socialist approach. Its activities and demands centered on domestic economic and social reform. The party supported accelerated modernization and industrialization, social legislation, and limited agrarian reform. The party proposed allocating state lands to landless peasants and imposing limitations on the growth of huge estates. Its moderate approach, aimed at preventing violence and disturbances, avoided demanding any widespread agrarian reform that would include expropriation of lands privately owned by the major landowners and their distribution to peasants with little or no land holdings. The National Democratic Party was actually the continuation of al-Ahali, a reformist Socialist group founded in 1932 that had played a role during the Bakr Sidqi regime, when Kamil al-Jadirji had served as minister of economics under Hikmat Sulayman (December 1936 through March 1937). The party enjoyed the support of the middle class, especially that of the educated members of the effendiyya. Its declared intention of hastening Iraq's transformation into a liberal capitalist country while reducing poverty and socioeconomic gaps won it the support of the weak bourgeoisie of Iraq.[13]

The Liberal Party was a loose organization of politicians with moderate liberal views, all of whom were more or less close to Tawfiq al-Suwaydi. Beyond a general inclination toward support of political liberalization, its positions were vague and its importance was extremely limited. It did not succeed in coalescing into a real party.

The three parties were led by politicians from, or affiliated with, the conservative ruling elite and activists from among the effendiyya. The National Democratic Party, whose younger activists were forced to compete in the streets with Communist activists, on one hand, and nationalist al-Istiqlal activists on the other, attempted to move beyond the middle stratum and the bourgeoisie and gain a foothold among the working class, but with only limited success.

The radical left was represented by the People's Party (Hizb al-Sha'ab) and the National Unity Party (Hizb al-Ittihad al-Qawmi). They adopted radical positions with regard to agrarian reform and economic, social, and political change. The People's Party was established by the Communist Party as a means to circumvent the prohibition against communism. Grievously persecuted by all Iraqi governments, the Communist Party remained limited in scope. Its members were mostly students, teachers, noncommissioned officers, and skilled workers from lower-middle-class or humble families. Despite the party's small size, these determined activists played a major role in creating unrest among laborers and students and in organizing the strikes between 1946 and 1948.[14]

The three governments that were in power between the regent's declaration and the elections of March 1947 were supposed to prepare for the elections. Established in February 1946, the government headed by Tawfiq al-Suwaydi had aroused hope among the effendiyya and the politicians who favored reform and political liberalization. It fell at the end of May as the result of differences with the regent and with Nuri al-Saʿid on matters of foreign policy. Although no longer officially in the cabinet, Nuri had remained extremely influential behind the scenes.[15] Nuri and the regent were also interested in ousting al-Suwaydi because they feared that his liberal leanings would lead to reinforcement of the oppositionist and radical forces and would thus endanger the regime. A government headed by Arshad al-ʿUmari was established in June 1946, and it remained in power for five months, suppressing the political forces that had begun to organize under Tawfiq al-Suwaydi. Arshad al-ʿUmari took action not only against the outlawed Communist Party but also against the legal oppositionist parties: the National Democratic Party and al-Istiqlal. Their newspapers were closed, and their leaders were put on trial, including Kamil al-Jadirji, a man of moderate Socialist views.

Al-ʿUmari's policy aroused unrest among the younger members of the effendiyya, opposition among the politicians, and criticism among the British diplomats. His isolation, as well as his failure to prepare for the elections adequately, led the regent to dismiss him. In November, a new government was established under Nuri al-Saʿid, who succeeded in organizing the March 1947 elections in such a way that the results favored the conservatives. The elections proved a disappointment to both al-Istiqlal and the National Democratic Party.[16] The failure of the oppositionist parties was the result of the two-stage, indirect method of elections. The modern middle stratum, with its political awareness, social sensitivity, and nationalist views, was a major source of support for both al-Istiqlal and the National Democratic Party. However, the effendiyya constituted a minority. Most Iraqis still lived in traditional frameworks, and their voting patterns were affected by the instructions of the traditional leaders and by their ethnic and tribal identities. This ensured an overwhelming majority for politicians from among the conservative ruling elite, the major tribal landowners, and the upper socioeconomic class. Moreover, not all members of the effendiyya necessarily acted in accordance with their ideologies or social interests. Their voting patterns and political behavior at times expressed their nationalist views and support of social and political reforms; at other times, however, they reflected their loyalty to the politicians of the ruling elite, to whom they were linked by traditional loyalties and identities, economic dependency, and/or the desire for personal advancement.

Iraq and Polarization in the Inter-Arab Arena after World War II

Hashemite ambitions in Syria and the Fertile Crescent and the efforts made by Egypt and Saudi Arabia to frustrate those ambitions led to polarization in the inter-Arab arena during the establishment of the Arab League in 1944–45. The issues on which the inter-Arab arena focused, which was polarized between the Hashemite states of Iraq and Transjordan and the opposing bloc of Egypt and Saudi Arabia, included the future of Syria, dominance within the Arab League, and handling of the Palestine question.[17]

At the beginning of 1945, Iraqi-Transjordanian cooperation increased, as a counterbalance to Egypt's dominance in the Arab League and the rapprochement between Egypt, Saudi Arabia, and Syria. The strong relationships between these three countries was manifested in a summit conference in January 1945 between King Farouq, King Ibn Saʿud, and Syrian president Shukri al-Quwatli. The regent and Nuri al-Saʿid were the prime promoters of increased Hashemite cooperation to oppose Egypt and Saudi Arabia.

With the departure of the French from Syria in April 1946, the disappointment of both Iraq and Transjordan increased, due to the clear tendency of Syria's leaders to preserve the republican regime and continue to rely on Egypt and Saudi Arabia against Hashemite ambitions. Iraqi politicians expressed their frustration at what they viewed as the "ingratitude" of the Syrian leaders toward Iraq, which had for years supported Syria's struggle for independence.[18]

Disappointment with Egypt's dominance in the Arab League led Iraq to adopt oppositionist attitudes critical of the League's policies and orientations; according to both Iraq and Transjordan, the League served the interests of Egypt and Saudi Arabia.

Two main approaches existed among Iraqi politicians regarding its regional foreign policy and the issues facing the Arab states, in view of Egypt's dominance within the inter-Arab arena and the Arab League. Nuri adopted an aggressive line intended to give Iraq leadership in the inter-Arab arena and dominance in Syria, even at the price of exacerbating the polarization and increasing the tension. Nuri accused Egypt and the secretary of the Arab League of having transformed the organization into a tool of Egyptian policy and a means of serving Egypt's interests in its relations with Britain, at the price of abandoning and sacrificing the interests of the other Arab states. Nuri was even heard by British diplomats to threaten that Iraq and

Transjordan might withdraw from the League. At the same time, Nuri promoted intensive activity in Syria and intended to impose Iraqi dominance on that country.[19]

The other approach among the Iraqi politicians, manifested by the policies practiced by Prime Ministers Hamdi al-Bajhaji (June 1944–December 1945), Tawfiq al-Suwaydi (February 1946–May 1946), and Muzahim al-Bajhaji (June 1948–December 1948), sought to integrate Iraq into the League and its activities, while reducing tensions in the inter-Arab arena and increasing cooperation with Egypt. These politicians endeavored to relieve tensions with Syria, claiming that, in order for Iraq to be able to reinforce its own status in Syria, mutual understanding and dialogue with Egypt would be necessary. The conservative Hamdi al-Bajhaji displayed limited activity in foreign affairs, but succeeded in blocking Nuri's tendency to intensify the conflict with Egypt. At the same time, al-Bajhaji evaded the pressure tactics of Emir ʿAbdallah, who sought to enlist Iraq in his own cause, an effort to pressure Syrian leaders into agreeing to establish a union or federation with Transjordan.

In June 1945, Hamdi al-Bajhaji rejected the proposal of Transjordan's ʿAbdallah, that Iraq and Transjordan jointly raise the issue of the establishment of "Greater Syria" at a special session of the League or at a special conference convened for the purpose. In ʿAbdallah's view, such a "Greater Syria" would include Transjordan, Syria, and Iraq under Hashemite rule— or, specifically, under the rule of ʿAbdallah himself (who believed that the Syrian throne was his by right, as the senior member of the Hashemite Dynasty). Tawfiq al-Suwaydi, during his term in office as prime minister, attempted to persuade the regent to weaken ties with ʿAbdallah, reduce the extent of Iraq's commitment to him, and improve relations with Egypt and Syria. In his conversations with the regent, al-Suwaydi argued that the tension created by ʿAbdallah on the question of "Greater Syria" was damaging Iraqi-Syrian relations. Iraq, as he put it, was forced to bear the consequences of ʿAbdallah's policy without being able to exert any influence on that policy. He even proposed that the regent set aside the Iraqi-Transjordanian agreement of 1945 regarding federal union between the two states.

At a meeting of the Arab League Council in March 1946, Tawfiq al-Suwaydi attempted to improve Iraq's relations with Egypt. Before leaving for that meeting, he had proposed to the regent that he invite King Farouq of Egypt to visit Iraq. Al-Suwaydi's position, however, was not strong enough to affect the rigid attitudes of the regent and Nuri al-Saʿid.

The differences in attitude regarding regional foreign policy were not translated into struggles between groups with different orientations. All of the groups in question belonged to the same conservative elite. They sought ways of preserving the political, economic, and social status quo within Iraq. At the same time, they wanted to obtain a central role for Iraq among the Arab states, the Middle East in general, regarding the Western powers, whose assistance they wished to ensure. The reality of the inter-Arab and the internal political arenas, as well as the interrelationship between the two arenas, made political leaders aware of the necessity of adopting one of the two approaches. Politicians whose approach was different from that of Nuri, while unable to succeed against him, did manage to restrain his overtures, or perhaps to offset his verbal threats to take action, which could have further worsened inter-Arab tension. Yet even when he was not serving as a minister or prime minister, Nuri succeeded in dictating the agenda of the government of Iraq and bringing about the replacement of prime ministers whose policies were not to his liking. During the terms in office of Hamdi al-Bajhaji and Tawfiq al-Suwaydi, Nuri—who was then only a senator and a member of the Regency Council—conducted complex political processes in order to cement relations with Turkey, thus placing a fait accompli before the government in Baghdad.

In the summer of 1945, Nuri launched an initiative for rapprochement with Turkey. In September 1945, the regent and Nuri visited Turkey and discussed intensifying and deepening their cooperation to prevent Communist and Kurdish activity. Nuri proposed strengthening the relations between Turkey and the Arab League. (Even during his term in office as prime minister in 1939–40, Nuri had proposed establishing an alliance between Iraq, Egypt, and Turkey.) In his 1945 proposal, Nuri hoped to create a counterweight to the regional status of Egypt and obtain an advantage for Iraq on the basis of its special relationship with Turkey, in the framework of the Sa'dabad Alliance, as a mediator between the Arab and non-Arab states in the northern Middle East. In November 1945, Nuri again visited Turkey, where he proposed a treaty that would bring Turkey into the League and create a Mediterranean Alliance combining the Arab League with the Sa'dabad Alliance. Turkey, however, had reservations with regard to Nuri's grandiose plans. Turkey was not eager to become overly involved in inter-Arab relations and the Arab League, preferring bilateral agreements and treaties with individual Arab countries.

When Tawfiq al-Suwaydi was appointed prime minister in February 1946, Nuri was granted special powers to negotiate an economic, administrative, and cultural agreement with Turkey. However, when visiting Turkey in March, Nuri exceeded his authority and signed a draft treaty for broadbased cooperation that included politics as well. Nuri's moves embarrassed al-Suwaydi, who had not wanted to sign the proposed treaty without deliberations and coordination with the Arab League. He was afraid that rejection

of the treaty would adversely affect relations between Iraq and Turkey, especially because he suspected that Nuri was supported by Britain. (The ratification of the treaty was delayed and only came about in June 1947 under the
Salih Jabr government.) In his attempts at rapprochement with Turkey, Nuri
attempted to act as a mediator between that country and Syria. Nuri was
hoping to exploit the Syrian leaders' fears of Turkey and of a strategic Turk-
ish-Hashemite-Zionist outflanking, in order to convince the Syrians of the
vital nature of the alliance and engagement with Iraq, which could protect
Syrian interests. As Nuri saw it, Iraq's regional power and connection with
Turkey would move the Syrians to understand the advantages of cementing
relations and so establish a federation with Iraq. Tawfiq al-Suwaydi's policy
of alleviating tensions between Iraq and Egypt while accepting Egypt's dominance in the League, along with his tendency to reduce Iraqi activity in Syria,
met with objections on Nuri's part. Together with the regent, Nuri pressured
al-Suwaydi to concentrate on domestic matters and to leave foreign affairs
alone. Al-Suwaydi and Nuri clashed on the question of whether the regent
should participate in a conference of rulers of the Arab states that was to be
convened by King Farouq of Egypt at the end of May 1946 in Inshas, Egypt.
This conference was originally intended to address the dangers of communism and the threat posed by the USSR in view of the heightening of the
global interbloc cold war. Instead, the conference eventually focused on Palestine, following the publication of the Anglo-American plan for the solution
to that problem. Al-Suwaydi urged the regent to participate in the planned
conference, despite Nuri's objections. Eventually, the regent accepted al-
Suwaydi's position; however, the delegation that accompanied the regent included not al-Suwaydi but Nuri, who was not well liked by the Egyptians.
The regent's decision and the differences with Nuri led al-Suwaydi to resign
his office as prime minister.

As a consequence of its struggle against Egyptian dominance and its ambition for dominance over or union with Syria, Iraq became the flagship of
the Arab struggle against Zionism and the establishment of a Jewish state.
(From the 1930s on, Iraq had exploited the Palestine question in order to
realize its own ambitions regarding Syria and to promote its aims of Arab
leadership and hegemony in the Fertile Crescent. Using the Palestine conflict
to promote Iraq's foreign policy was also well in line with the tendency to
weave the Palestine question into domestic politics and ideology in Iraq.)[20]

As early as 1944, Iraq had proposed establishing Arab information offices
in London, Geneva, and New York to explain the Arab position on the Palestine conflict. When the Arab League was founded, its secretary, 'Abd al-
Rahman 'Azzam, demanded that the planned offices be subordinate to the
Secretariat of the League and be involved in public relations in all matters

concerning the League and the interests of the Arab states. Iraq, which had intended to control the offices and to act as the flagship of the struggle in Palestine, claimed that the offices should focus on the most acute and central subject affecting the Arab nation—that is, the Palestine question. Iraq demanded that the central office should not be in Egypt, adjacent to the League institutions, but in Jerusalem, and that it should be headed by Musa al-ʿAlami, a Palestinian activist with a strong link to Iraq. As Iraq was capable of allocating the requisite financial resources, the offices were established in accordance with Iraqi wishes, and Musa al-ʿAlami was placed in charge of them. Iraq also financed a Palestinian Fund, established at the initiative of al-ʿAlami, which was intended to compete with the Jewish National Fund and the Palestine Foundation Fund (Keren Hayesod)—both of them Zionist funds—for the purchase of lands in Palestine, development of the Palestinian economy, and its villages.

At Arab League conferences between 1945 and 1948, Iraq—in contrast to the moderate approach adopted by the League secretary and by Egypt—took extreme militant positions regarding the Palestine question. Under the influence of Nuri al-Saʿid and given the importance of the Palestine question in domestic Iraqi politics, Iraq transformed its own extremism with regard to the Palestine conflict into a means of undermining Egypt's status and that of the secretary of the Arab League. According to Iraqi accusations, the League and its secretary were neglecting Palestine and refraining from taking any definitive stand in its defense, due to excessive weight placed by the League on Egyptian interests. In this way, Iraq was able to substantiate its argument to the effect that it was the staunchest supporter of the Arab nationalist cause.

Despite the united Hashemite front shown by Iraq and Transjordan toward their rivals, Egypt and Saudi Arabia, the relations between the two branches of the Hashemite royal house were charged with covert rivalry concerning Syria and with differences in their approaches regarding Palestine. King ʿAbdallah of Transjordan believed he should rule Syria. The Iraqi politicians had difficulty in taking an overt stand against ʿAbdallah's moves in Syria, although they considered them dangerous and repellent to the Syrians themselves. According to the Iraqis, the only circumstance under which Syria would agree to the establishment of a federation was precisely with a strong country possessed of resources, such as Iraq, and not with Transjordan. The Hashemite states were attempting to achieve a special status, or exclusivity, regarding the handling of the Palestine question—but in different ways. While Iraq adopted an extremist militant position, based on considerations involving the struggle for nationalist prestige and status and power in the inter-Arab arena, King ʿAbdallah of Transjordan viewed himself as having not only the right of rule in Palestine but also the ability to achieve a solution to the Jewish-Arab conflict. He sought ways of reaching a dialogue and arrangement with the Zionist Movement and the Jewish community in Palestine.

The militant position adopted by Iraq on the Palestine question stemmed from the reciprocal relationship between the roles of that issue in Iraqi domestic and foreign politics. Domestically, the Palestinian issue was used as a pan-Arab nationalist symbol by which the ruling elite sought to build up their nationalist image. The instrumental use of the Palestine question in foreign policy was intended to achieve Iraqi hegemony of the Fertile Crescent, Iraqi rule in Syria, and Iraqi leadership in the Arab world. Nuri promoted Iraq's militant attitude as a means of substantiating its inter-Arab status; yet, on several occasions, Nuri expressed pragmatic resignation to the partition of Palestine.[21] Behind the militant nationalist jargon, Nuri was prepared to accept the establishment of a Jewish state in part of Palestine, provided that no Palestinian state would be established that could lean on Egypt. Such dependency on Egypt would threaten the Hashemite regime in Transjordan, and constitute an additional obstacle to the realization of Nuri's ambitions in Syria and the Fertile Crescent. Nuri's attitude toward the establishment of the Jewish state in Palestine depended on whether this would further frustrate his aims for dominance in Syria and the establishment of a federation under Iraqi dominance in the Fertile Crescent.

4

The Earthquake of the Iraqi Regime

The Wathba Crisis and Iraq's Role in the 1948 War in Palestine

The Salih Jabr Government and Its Trends

Following the elections to Parliament in March 1947, a government was formed under Salih Jabr.[1] This was the first time that a Shi'ite had headed the government of Iraq. Jabr was one of the members of the *effendiyya* who had come from the middle and lower strata and had succeeded, by ascending the ranks of bureaucracy and by marriage, in joining the upper class and the ruling political elite. Jabr, the scion of a humble family of craftsmen, acquired a modern education, found employment, and continued to advance in civil service. He married the daughter of Sheikh Rabi'a, one of the major Shi'ite tribal landowners. Although he was a protégé of Nuri al-Sa'id, he differed from his conservative patron in that he favored limited political, social, and economic reforms within the existing regime. A technocrat with liberal, re-formist tendencies, Jabr sought to accelerate modernization in his country; he was aware of the need to create jobs for the educated members of the effendiyya, and he sought to integrate them into the political system. At the same time, he exploited his Shi'ite identity and family connections to gain the trust of Shi'ite tribal notables. Inspired by Foreign Minister Ernest Bevin, a member of the British Labour Party, British diplomats were looking for allies among the new social strata and political forces. They considered Jabr a "new politician" capable of becoming popular with the effendiyya.[2] None-theless, despite his reformist tendencies, Jabr continued to limit the activity of the radical political parties.

The Jabr government had to cope with an acute economic crisis as well as with growing unrest. Between 1939 and 1947, the cost of living index rose by 800 percent, whereas the unskilled wage increased by only 400 percent. In other words, the standard of living of the majority of the population dropped by 50 percent. The salaries of lower-level civil servants, which rose by only 50 percent during that period, were even more seriously eroded. As a result of several consecutive years of drought and a plague of locusts, Iraq suffered a severe food shortage. Unable to pay the major landowners in hard currency, the government continued to allow them to export grain and other food products, in exchange for which the landowners received dollars. In the autumn of 1947 and the winter of 1948, the food shortage reached unprecedented levels, and famine was rampant. The government did not have the money to purchase and import food. It even had trouble paying the salaries of its civil servants.[3] Iraq demanded that Britain release the monetary assets that were frozen in banks in London and repay its debts for the Iraqi oil it had purchased during the war. However, Britain was prepared to pay its debt only in pounds sterling, a currency which was gradually weakening and which the government of Iraq refused to accept.

The failure of the opposition parties to win the March 1947 elections to Parliament increased the unrest of the effendiyya, who had supported them. Most of those elected were representatives of the establishment and the conservative movement. Despite the intensive activity and overall euphoria of the political party activists, the results of the elections were determined, to a great degree, by the two-stage, indirect method of elections and by the political behavior patterns of most of Iraq's population. These two elements together ensured that the majority of those elected would come from among the conservative elite and the major tribal landowners. The political unrest of Iraq's high school and college students was magnified by the fact that graduates had little chance of finding suitable employment. Iraq's stagnating economy and financial shortages prevented the government from continuously expanding its bureaucracy and thus creating new jobs.

Many politicians shunned Jabr because he was a Shi'ite and a friend of Nuri. The conservative ruling elite had co-opted and integrated Shi'ites and even Kurds into its ranks, and the Iraqi state constantly argued that it did not discriminate against Shi'ites. That said, however, in practice the Sunnites feared and despised Shi'ites, and the fact of a Shi'ite prime minister was enough to arouse anti-Shi'ite feelings among the primarily Sunnite ruling elite.

In January 1947, the Palestine crisis and the tensions that prevailed in relations between Transjordan and Syria were exacerbated by the actions taken by King 'Abdallah aimed at bringing Syria under his rule. Since January 1947, tensions had increased between Transjordan and Syria following an attempt by the government in Damascus to impose sovereignty on Jebel Druze (Mt. Druze), thereby undermining the status of the al-Atrash family, a prominent Druze family that was closely linked to King 'Abdallah. In March, the Transjordanian consulate in Damascus was closed, after thousands of posters calling for unification of Syria with Transjordan under

'Abdallah's rule were found in the building. In May, the "Jordanian White Paper" (*al-kittab al-abyad al-urduni*) was published, containing historical justification for 'Abdallah's right to rule over united Syria.

'Abdallah increased his pressure on Syria, following his disappointment at the results of the Syrian elections. In those elections, held in July, 'Abdallah's supporters (or those who were considered his supporters) failed to obtain the results for which he had hoped, which would have constituted proof of his arguments that most Syrians wanted him as their king.

In August, he wrote to the Syrian leaders, asking them to meet with him concerning unification. At the same time, he appealed directly to the citizens of Syria, calling for union between Syria and Transjordan. On August 5, in a radio broadcast, 'Abdallah called for the establishment of a preliminary council in preparation for the unification of Syria and Transjordan, and he sent letters to that effect to President Shukri al-Quwatli and members of the Syrian Parliament.[4]

These actions embarrassed the Iraqis. They were obligated to support 'Abdallah, but many believed that his crass pressure was damaging the Hashemite cause, since the anti-Hashemite elements regarded Iraq and Transjordan as a single front threatening Syria.

Although Nuri al-Sa'id was identified with the ambition to achieve union or federation with Syria, his protégé was an Iraqi territorialist. Although Jabr paid "lip service" to pan-Arab rhetoric and did not actually reject Iraq's ambitions in Syria, he also did not devote any special efforts to those ambitions. Domestic concerns and the regional status of Iraq headed his priority list. He had no interest in being dragged into an inter-Arab crisis by 'Abdallah, which would hinder him in his efforts to reach a new treaty with Britain. Accordingly, when the crisis between Transjordan and Syria worsened in August 1947, Jabr attempted to "calm the waters" by placing the Palestine question at the center of Arab activity and attention.

Iraq and the Inter-Arab Dynamics Concerning the Palestine Question

In the autumn of 1947, during the United Nations debate on the partition plan for Palestine and the exacerbation of the Jewish-Arab conflict, Iraq was the militant activist Arab country leading the Arab states to increase their commitment to rigid positions opposing the partitioning of Palestine. Thus, Iraq was the chief contributor to the inter-Arab dynamics that led to the 1948 war in Palestine. As noted in chapter 3, Iraq's militant policy in the autumn of 1947 stemmed from a combination of domestic and international factors. Internationally, Iraq used the Palestine question to reinforce its status and promote its ambitions for regional leadership. Domestically, the issue was used to enlist support by focusing on the issue of Palestine and nationalism, thus distracting the populace from problems the regime could not solve, particularly social and economic problems. On August 31, the United Nations committee that had investigated the Palestine question submitted its recommendations for the partition of Palestine into a Jewish state and a Palestinian Arab state while retaining its economic unity. Immediately upon the publication of those recommendations, Salih Jabr launched an initiative to convene the Arab heads of state. He circumvented the secretary of the Arab League and its institutions, which were actually responsible for handling the situation. This was the beginning of intense Iraqi activity concerning the Palestine question, which was to last throughout the autumn of 1947. This activity continued the Iraqi policy of exploiting the Palestine question as a means of bolstering Iraq's status as a leader of the Arab world and undermining the status of Egypt and the Arab League. At the inter-Arab conferences that took place in Sofar (September 1947) and ʿAley (October 1947) in Lebanon, and in Cairo (December 1947), Iraq adopted militant radical positions and demanded the military involvement of the Arab states, in order to frustrate the partition plan and the establishment of a Jewish state.[5] Iraq pressed for a military committee to plan and coordinate military activity of the Arab states in Palestine. Whereas Egypt, Saudi Arabia, and Syria sent relatively junior officers to that committee, the Iraqi delegation consisted of senior officers. Egypt and Saudi Arabia sought to take action by diplomatic means and not intensify the crisis; by contrast, Iraq's positions were militant in the extreme. Iraq demanded the implementation of the secret resolutions of the June 1946 Bludan Conference, calling for the Arab states to use the "oil weapon" and impose restrictions on the franchises of Western oil companies, in order to exert pressure on Britain and the United States to accept the Arab positions. Somewhat cynically, Iraq could allow itself to demonstrate militant attitudes and propose use of the "oil weapon," which was liable to have grave effects on its own economy, because it knew that Saudi Arabia and Egypt would block its proposals. Although Saudi Arabia and Egypt did not want to be dragged into the conflict by Iraqi militancy, they could not avoid participating in the military conference. The role of the Palestine question as an emotionally charged and weighty topic in domestic politics and inter-Arab relations required them to stick to the Iraqi line, at least on the level of declarations.

Jabr's motives resulted from considerations of inter-Arab foreign policy as well as from domestic Iraqi concerns. He sought to end the crisis (which, from Iraq's point of view, was quite inconvenient) in Transjordanian-Syrian relations. Moreover, this was a golden opportunity to reinforce Iraq's own status and image as the Arab leader in a pan-Arab nationalist issue of unparalleled importance. However, Jabr's principal motive was to create a militant nationalist image for himself and to set up a smoke screen in the domestic political arena of Iraq, so that he could conclude the new treaty with Britain. Jabr was aware that the issue of the treaty was charged with nationalist sentiment that would be exploited by his political rivals. Hoping to obtain economic and military assistance from Britain and remove the restrictions on Iraq's independence, he knew he would not be able to achieve a treaty that accomplished both aims: to satisfy nationalist anti-British demands and obtain the required assistance and status for Iraq. To bring about acceptance of the treaty in Iraq, he promoted himself as a nationalist by demonstrating militancy concerning the Palestine question. He stressed Iraq's militant position under his leadership in his public appearances. In so doing, he contributed to the nationalist fervor in Iraq.

The Wathba Riots and the Foiling of the Portsmouth Treaty

Through the conclusion of a new treaty with Great Britain, intended to reduce restrictions on Iraq's independence, Jabr sought to dissolve one of the causes of the nationalist tension in Iraq, which was threatening domestic stability. He hoped that removing the stumbling blocks in Iraqi-British relations would ensure that Iraq received military and economic assistance, thereby strengthening its regional status and enabling the government of Iraq to promote essential reforms. Jabr sought to exploit the tendency of Britain's ruling Labour Party to dismantle the old colonial empire and replace it with bilateral treaties with its former protectorates (through the broad framework of the British Commonwealth).

In May 1947, intermittent negotiations commenced. The British officials proceeded with caution, however, and were unwilling to rush into signing the new treaty, hoping to avoid further difficulties with Egypt. The British Foreign Office, late in 1946, suffered a severe blow to its prestige when a draft of the treaty with Egypt, which had been arranged with Egyptian prime minister Isma'il Sidqi, was rejected following pressure by the opposition and a wave of anti-British rioting. The identification of nationalist public opinion in Iraq with the Egyptian position, especially following the rejection of the draft treaty in December 1946, made it difficult for the government of Iraq to exploit the crisis in Egyptian-British relations and move forward on signing a treaty with Britain.

In the spring of 1947, Egypt brought the differences between it and Britain before the United Nations. This move did not give rise to the desired results from the Egyptian point of view, however, and relations between the two states reached an impasse. In view of the impasse in the negotiations between

Egypt and Britain, Jabr took steps intended to lead rapidly to the signing of a treaty between Britain and Iraq and thus, by preceding Egypt, to give Iraq the status of the most important Arab ally of Britain and the West, thereby ensuring precedence in receiving assistance. The impasse in British relations with Egypt, as well as the image that British diplomats and Foreign Minister Bevin had of Jabr as a new kind of Arab statesman, capable of forming a connection between Britain and the new social forces and thereby weakening their anti-British tendencies, led the British government, in the autumn of 1947, to agree to accelerated negotiations with Iraq.[6]

On January 6, 1948, a delegation headed by Jabr set out for Britain. Among the delegates were Nuri al-Saʿid, Foreign Minister Fadil al-Jamali, and Defense Minister Shakir al-Wadi. While the talks were going on in the city of Portsmouth in southern England, tension increased in Iraq. The nationalist demonstrations and expressions of identification with the Palestine question, which had been encouraged by the government during the autumn, intensified and took on strong anti-British tones, under the influence of activists from al-Istiqlal and the Communist Party. Following conflicts with the police on January 5, in which a number of students were injured and arrested, a strike of high school and college students broke out over the demand to release their colleagues from detention.

On January 15, the Iraqi delegation and the British representatives signed a draft treaty that removed some of the restrictions on Iraq's independence. However, Britain preserved its own status and strategic and economic interests. Britain retained control of its military bases in Habaniya and Shuʿeiba, its right to move its troops throughout Iraq, and its right to sail its warships up the Shatt al-ʿArab without obtaining prior approval from the Iraqi government.

News of the Portsmouth treaty set the streets of Baghdad on fire. On January 16, strikes and demonstrations broke out among college and high school students, who demanded the rejection of the new treaty and an end to the British presence in Iraq. Nationalist anti-British sentiments that had been incited by activists from al-Istiqlal and the National Democratic and Communist Parties, fueled by political unrest and economic distress, led to the outbreak of riots and demonstrations, soon termed the *wathba* (the sudden leap). The students and younger members of the effendiyya were joined by masses from the poorer strata protesting food shortages and the rising cost of living. (The Consumer Price Index had risen from 463 points in March 1947 to 629 in March 1948.)[7]

The policy that had been adopted by Jabr from September 1947 on, of highlighting the Palestine question and using it to create a smoke screen to help him conclude the treaty with Britain, had backfired. The nationalist atmosphere, which had been encouraged by the Jabr government, of placing the Palestine question at its focal point had now become a factor leading to violent outbursts against his own government.[8]

The demonstrations reached their zenith on January 19, 20, and 21. When the demonstrators rushed to the bridges over the Euphrates River, on their way to storm the Palace, the police opened fire, injuring dozens. The city fell into confusion, and imminent revolution was anticipated. Some of the demonstrators screamed slogans in favor of a republic and against the monarchy. Although the activists of the National Democratic Party and al-Istiqlal played a role in inciting the riots, the leaders of both parties became frightened at the intensity of the outbreak and lost control of their activists. The frustrations and moods that had given rise to the events of 1941—called "the spirit of 1941"—returned to the streets of Baghdad in January 1948.

The rioting also had a generational aspect. Some of the demonstrating students were sons of the conservative ruling elite. A feeling of common cause and experience with the effendiyya from poorer socioeconomic backgrounds led these students to participate in demonstrations that threatened their fathers' very existence.

The Palace was seized with panic. The vehemence of the riots, inept police protection, and widespread use of anti-Hashemite slogans brought the regent, 'Abd al-Ilah, and his family to the verge of hysteria. Before their eyes danced the macabre vision of the fall of the czar of Russia and his family in the Russian Revolution of 1917. (Nor was this vision a mere illusion: Ten years later, in 1958, most of the Iraqi branch of the Hashemite dynasty would be executed on the Palace steps by one of the officers who launched the revolution.)[9] On January 21, 'Abd al-Ilah called a group of senior politicians and party representatives to a meeting in the Palace, at which it was decided to reject the draft treaty. Repudiation of the treaty was caused by public pressure and the frightened regent. Another strong factor was the politicians' desire to see Jabr's premiership end. Publication of the regent's announcement rejecting the Portsmouth treaty embarrassed both the Iraqi delegation, which was still in Portsmouth, and the British Foreign Office. Salih Jabr and Fadil Al-Jamali hurried to Baghdad to defend the treaty, but to no avail.

Upon Salih Jabr's return to Baghdad on January 26, the riots grew all out of proportion. Hundreds were injured in clashes with police; according to estimates, 100 were killed. Jabr asked 'Abd al-Ilah to allow him to suppress the riots and impose order. The regent refused, whereupon the ministers of his government submitted their resignations. On January 27, Jabr himself resigned.

In addition to the general confusion prevailing in Baghdad, the Shi'ite tribes threatened to storm the city and suppress the riots. Shi'ite tribal leaders claimed that the demonstrations were provoked by the Sunnites and Communists.[10]

As a replacement for Jabr, the regent appointed Muhammad Sadr, a religious, conservative senior Shi'ite politician. In the eyes of the effendiyya, Sadr enjoyed nationalist prestige as one of the participants in the anti-British revolt of 1920 and was popular among the Shi'ite tribal leaders as a Shi'ite and conservative. Sadr now faced the difficult and complex task of stabilizing the situation and ensuring a source of food supply. In order to "calm the waters," Sadr announced that preparations were being made for new elections. He also sent an urgent request to Britain for food. The British responded by diverting two ships full of wheat, en route from Australia to Britain, to the port of Basra. Although the demonstrators had achieved most of their goals—specifically, preventing ratification of the treaty and overthrowing the Jabr government—they continued to riot for another three months. On February 22, the regent decided to dissolve Parliament and hold new elections, yielding once again to the demands of the demonstrators. The National Democratic Party and al-Istiqlal were capable of using students to incite riots, and they even succeeded in gaining some tactical concessions. However, once these had been achieved, they were incapable of putting the genie back into the bottle. Although the party leaders had won over members of the effendiyya through either nationalist slogans (al-Istiqlal) or calls for social change (National Democratic Party), they themselves belonged to the ruling elite and the regime abhorred by the younger effendiyya. The activity of the Communists further limited the ability of al-Istiqlal and the National Democratic Party to control the demonstrators.

Nuri al-Said, whose status had also declined sharply as a result of the repudiation of the treaty he had coauthored, drew his own self-serving conclusions: As early as the end of January, he proposed to the British that the regent should resign and be replaced by another Hashemite figure. He proposed (and referred repeatedly to the proposal during later periods of tension between himself and the regent) that Emir Zayd, brother of Faysal I and 'Abdallah and at that time the Iraqi ambassador in London, should take 'Abd al-Ilah's place. Nuri held the regent responsible for the failure to ratify the treaty and the situation that this had created. Trying to goad the British into taking action, he asserted that only 'Abd al-Ilah's resignation could save the Hashemite dynasty in Iraq. Nuri acted not only from mistrust of the regent but also from the fear that, to save his own skin, the regent would dismiss him from his positions as speaker of the Senate and member of the Regency Council. Nuri had grounds to believe that the regent would turn against him and, to get rid of the nationalists' most hated target, replace him in the Senate and on the Council with Emir Zayd.[11]

The British strongly urged the regent to persuade the government to take stringent measures to restore order and halt the demonstrations. In late March, the British embassy in Baghdad and the Foreign Office in London coordinated a pressure campaign on the regent to put an end to the unrest. At the request of the British ambassador in Baghdad, Emir Zayd was invited to the Foreign Office and asked to convey to his government a demand that the demonstrations be halted at once.[12] At the same time, the ambassador in Baghdad used strong words and even threats in his talks with the regent and the politicians.

Nonetheless, 'Abd al-Ilah and the prime minister hesitated to take severe measures, lest they lead to wider unrest and complete loss of control. The regent felt trapped. He feared the loss of British support, but had neither the strength nor the courage to force the government to adopt unpopular ways of putting down the riots. He considered replacing the government, but was afraid that, should Sadr resign, it would be difficult to find another candidate. No politician was likely to forget the precedent of Jabr's losing the regent's support when on the point of implementing the Portsmouth treaty upon which they had jointly agreed.[13]

The wathba riots constituted a traumatic shock for the Hashemite regime and the ruling elite in Iraq. Jabr's rivals from among the elite, who sought to oust him because of his Shi'ite origin or his connections with Nuri al-Sa'id, contributed to a downward-spiraling process that threatened their own status as well as the entire sociopolitical status quo in Iraq. Politicians from the conservative elite who had objected to the Portsmouth treaty in order to undermine the Jabr government, although their basic position favored close relations with Britain, raised a tempest that they had not meant to raise.

Iraq and the Invasion of Palestine by the Arab Armies

In March 1948, demonstrators again shouted about Palestine. The aggressive tone taken by the press and the nationalist politicians—calling for the rescue of Palestine by military force—made the regent apprehensive of what might occur following Britain's withdrawal from Palestine and creation of the Jewish state of Israel. Furthermore, these actions, with an agreement or understanding between the Jews and King 'Abdallah of Transjordan, were likely to cause further Iraqi anger and anti-Hashemite feelings. Another wave of rioting and civil disorder might hasten the end of the regent's rule and perhaps even end the Hashemite dynasty's reign.

During this time of internal instability within Iraq, the crisis regarding the Palestine question grew as the date approached for termination of the British Mandate in Palestine and the establishment of a Jewish state. Prime Minister

Muhammad Sadr showed relatively little interest in the Palestine question. In order to repel nationalist pressure, he suggested, at one of the demonstrations held in Baghdad over the Palestine question, that the enthusiastic demonstrators volunteer for the Army of Rescue (Jeysh al-Inkadh), under the command of Fawzi al-Qawuqji, which had been established pursuant to the resolutions of the Arab League. On the other hand, the regent, who previously had not paid any special attention to the Palestine question, now began a period of intense activity on the subject. The regent's increased preoccupation with Palestine was intended to rehabilitate his own status and image. In meetings in February, March and April, he urged King 'Abdallah to invade Palestine with the assistance of Iraqi military forces. The two Hashemite states differed in their approaches. The regent and other politicians from the Iraqi elite pushed for military involvement in Palestine, hoping that this would divert the internal ferment within Iraq to an external nationalist topic. 'Abdallah, by contrast, was still seeking the possibility of reaching an arrangement with the Zionist leadership of the Jewish community in Palestine. Admittedly, Iraq's representatives were the loudest and most forceful objectors to the partition of Palestine and the establishment of a Jewish state. Nonetheless, it was not the idea of partition itself that disturbed them. Rather, they feared that the establishment of a Palestinian state under the Mufti, Haj Amin al-Husayni, would threaten Iraq's ally, 'Abdallah of Transjordan. Also, they were concerned that the establishment of a Jewish state would give rise to a new wave of nationalist riots against the Hashemites. Haj Amin al-Husayni was perceived as Enemy #2 of the regime in Iraq (Enemy #1 being Rashid 'Ali). The regent, the royal house, and the Iraqi elite feared that an additional wave of riots would undermine the stability of the Iraqi government even further and pose a grave risk to them. In view of 'Abdallah's demand for control of Palestine and the rivalry between him and Haj Amin al-Husayni, a new Palestinian state would probably become the ally of Egypt and Saudi Arabia. This would have undermined 'Abdallah's status and constituted an additional obstacle to the Iraqi and Hashemite aim of achieving dominance and control throughout the Fertile Crescent.

Just as Iraq's policy, in the autumn of 1947, had played a role in creating a dynamic that pushed the Arab states into rigid and intransigent positions, making it difficult for them to conduct pragmatic policies, Iraq's moves in April 1948 accelerated the developments that led to war in Palestine. Arab leaders became committed to military intervention, although most of them, despite their tough rhetoric, hoped to avoid all-out war and involvement of regular armies. As a result of its regional ambitions and its internal socio-political situation, Iraq, which had no common border with Palestine, became an important catalyst in exacerbating the crisis and the outbreak of war.[14] The Iraqi politicians were trapped in their own declared militant positions with regard to the Palestine question, due to the domestic conflict between the conservative interests of the ruling elite and its inability to find answers for the economic and social distress of the effendiyya. The elite politicians had wooed the effendiyya through the adoption of nationalism, which at least provided a response to the identity crisis of the effendiyya. Thus, Fadil al-Jamali, a nationalist politician with militant ideological views on the Palestine question, expressed his reservations to the British in March 1948 regarding military involvement or war in Palestine, but noted that, given the atmosphere prevailing in the streets of Baghdad, it was difficult to express a moderate position in public.[15]

With the escalating Jewish-Arab conflict and the expected British withdrawal from Palestine at the beginning of May, the Council of the Arab League met in Cairo on April 10. The representative of Transjordan announced that the Legion would enter Palestine when the Mandate had expired and the British had left. In response, King Faruq declared that the invasion of Palestine by Arab armies would be temporary and that Palestine should eventually be handed over to its Palestinian residents. This statement clearly delineated the opposing positions of two blocs: Transjordan, with Iraqi support, demanded control of Palestine, or at least of those parts which would be conquered by the Arab armies, whereas Egypt sought to prevent Hashemite conquest and annexation of Palestine and demanded the establishment of a Palestinian state. Notwithstanding these declarations, the Arab politicians and generals hoped that there would eventually be no intervention by the regular armies and no war in Palestine.

Realizing that his own position within Iraq was tenuous, the regent launched an initiative intended to bring about the military intervention of the Arab states in Palestine. On April 24, accompanied by Lebanese prime minister Riad al-Sulh and the commander in chief of the Iraqi Army, 'Abd al-Ilah went to Amman and met with King 'Abdallah to discuss the invasion of Palestine. 'Abd al-Ilah made it clear to 'Abdallah that there was no longer any possibility of avoiding war. Granted, the Hashemite states and their rulers shared a common interest, to prevent the establishment of a Palestinian state headed by the Mufti. Still, unlike 'Abdallah, who sought to reach this objective through negotiations with the Jews, 'Abd al-Ilah viewed war as essential to his status and that of the Hashemites; he considered avoidance of war an existential threat. Accordingly, he pressed for armed conflict between the regular Arab armies and the Jews, in which Iraq and its leadership would prove their nationalist position. From Amman, 'Abd al-Ilah continued to Cairo, where he met with King Faruq twice, on April 25 and 26. Apparently, the invasion of Palestine by regular Arab armies was agreed upon at those meetings.[16] Following the talks with ʿAbd al-Ilah, Faruq ordered the Egyptian Army to prepare for immediate war. In so doing, Faruq bypassed the Egyptian Army command, who had reservations. Faruq's move met with the disapproval of the Egyptian prime minister, Mahmud Fahmi al-Nuqrashi, and senior army officers. From Cairo, ʿAbd al-Ilah sent an order to the Iraqi Army to move all of its forces into Transjordan and to invade Palestine immediately upon the expiration of the British Mandate. He returned to Amman, where he again met with ʿAbdallah in the presence of the Lebanese prime minister and secretary of the Arab League, ʿAbd al-Rahman ʿAzzam. At that meeting, ʿAbd al-Ilah clarified Faruq's commitment to the invasion of Palestine as soon as the British left and a Jewish state was declared. (At the end of April, King ʿAbdallah himself concluded that only through a limited war against the Jews, in which he would appear as the savior of the Palestinians, could he succeed in taking over the Arab section of Palestine.)

The Arab foreign ministers continued tentative discussions of possibly avoiding war until the very eve of the invasion, and even the chiefs of staff still hoped that war would be averted. Nonetheless, ʿAbd al-Ilah's diplomatic moves in late April 1948 and his meetings with the rival kings stimulated the Arab heads of state to make the crucial decision to invade Palestine.

Iraq's Military Policies during the 1948 War in Israel

On May 15, 1948, immediately following the declaration of the establishment of the state of Israel, units of the Iraqi Army seized the power station in Naharayim in the Jordan Valley and attacked adjacent Kibbutz Gesher. ʿAbd al-Ilah watched the attack through binoculars and ensured that his presence near the battlefield would be widely publicized in Iraq. The objective of the attack reflected Iraqi interests, which had been expressed even earlier, in the war plans worked out by the Military Committee of the Arab League in the autumn of 1947. According to those plans—drawn up with decisive involvement of Iraqi officers—the armies of Iraq and Transjordan were to conquer the hills surrounding Nazareth and the Jezreel Valley and to proceed from there to Haifa. It should be recalled that Haifa, as the outlet of the Iraqi oil pipeline to the Mediterranean Sea and the terminus of the planned railway line from Baghdad, embodied a concrete interest for Iraq. Iraq's involvement in this theater of war reflected another aspect of its interest: Conquest of the northern part of Israel would have constituted a Hashemite outflanking of Syria. (Since the 1920s, various proposals had been made to pave a road and build a railway from Baghdad to Haifa, which would have become a port serving the interests of Iraq's economy and its connections with Europe.)

However, when war actually broke out, 'Abdallah preferred to concentrate his military efforts in the area of Jerusalem, in order to initially ensure his control of the Holy City and the surrounding hilly areas. Thus, 'Abdallah's military actions reflected his own interest: He wanted to prevent the establishment of a Palestinian state. Such a state would have constituted a threat to the stability of his continued rule. Accordingly, after the failed attack on Kibbutz Gesher and the seizure of the power station in Naharayim, the Iraqi expeditionary force was transferred to the Samaria region, in accordance with 'Abdallah's interests. The presence of the Iraqi Army in the Samarian hills, while it did put pressure on the Israel Defense Forces and the Israeli "bottleneck" on the coastal plain, actually strengthened 'Abdallah's control of the Palestinian population and of the areas allocated by the United Nations resolution to the Palestinian state.

The Iraqi expeditionary force against Israel, which included more than 16,000 troops, fifty artillery guns, and twenty assault aircraft, was reinforced at the end of 1948 to a total of 20,000 troops. However, except for a few limited local actions, most of the Iraqi force remained idle. The basic presence of the Iraqi Army was intended to serve the Hashemite interests—that is, the interests of King 'Abdallah—in first taking control of the areas which had been intended for the Palestinian state, in order to annex them to Transjordan.[17]

In July, as a result of Arab military failures, the Iraqi Parliament appointed a parliamentary Board of Inquiry to examine the Palestine problem and the moves made by the Iraqi and Arab armies.[18] The report of this parliamentary committee was exploited by Iraqi politicians for mutual accusations. The objectives of the report were related to Iraqi politics; however, it proved to be of benefit to historians as well, thanks to its exposure of political and military documents and moves on the part of the Arab states in general and Iraq in particular.

Iraq continued to take a militant public stance, intended to reinforce its status in the inter-Arab arena and the image of the Iraqi government within the country. Iraqi representatives objected to the first truce in June 1948. When asked by British diplomats to explain the reason for Iraq's objection, Prime Minister Muzahim al-Bajhaji explained that, as it was obvious that the truce would take place in any event, this provided Iraq with an opportunity to demonstrate its militant nationalist position. This position was also intended to deflate the opposition in Baghdad and especially that of al-Istiqlal, which had threatened to provoke demonstrations against any cease-fire in Palestine.

The state of emergency that had been declared in Iraq upon the outbreak of war helped the authorities to restore order, by pursuing party activities and preventing demonstrations in the streets. The force of the demonstrations in Baghdad had decreased gradually since February. The National Democratic Party and al-Istiqlal were careful not to provoke riots that they could not control. Organizational and financial difficulties of the opposition parties and restraint of their activities by the authorities led to an additional reduction in the scope of party activity. Communist Party activists were persecuted, arrested, and put on trial. Their leader, Yusuf Salman "Fahed," was executed in 1949. At the same time, an improvement in the food supply helped to restore order among the poor.

In June 1948, the Iraqi government, under Prime Minister Muhammad Sadr, held elections for Parliament. The state of emergency facilitated the elections and helped to ensure that the results would serve the interests of the ruling elite and the royal house. As expected, the two-stage indirect method of elections, as well as the weight and influence of the traditional tribal leadership, secured a majority for the conservative delegates.[19]

In the summer of 1948, the conservative senior politicians who had fled the city during the wathba riots and sought shelter with tribal landowners and notables returned to Baghdad. Backed by the tribal landowners and the tribes, the conservative elite was able to regain control of the political system and to stabilize the police force.

Following the June elections, a government was set up with Muzahim al-Bajhaji as prime minister. From the standpoint of its composition, this government was no different from previous governments and included the conservative senior politicians. However, by contrast to the policies promulgated by Nuri al-Sa'id, Muzahim al-Bajhaji took action aimed at intensifying Iraq's cooperation with Egypt and reducing the tension concerning Syria. Al-Bajhaji attempted to improve military coordination between the armies of Iraq and Egypt in Israel and to reinforce the relationship between those two countries. When King 'Abdallah of Transjordan began to take measures aimed at annexing the West Bank to his kingdom, which in practice meant accepting the partition of Palestine and the establishment of the state of Israel, al-Bajhaji declined to support him. In October, Iraq recognized the "All-Palestine" government that had been established in Gaza, at the initiative of the Mufti, Haj Amin al-Husayni, the enemy of the Hashemites. This move was met with marked displeasure by both King 'Abdallah and 'Abd al-Ilah. They viewed it as demonstrating the prime minister's disloyalty to the Hashemite royal house. Al-Bajhaji's efforts to relieve inter-Arab tensions and foster closer ties with Egypt were viewed by the Hashemites and by Nuri al-Sa'id as de facto recognition of Egypt's dominance in the Arab League and renunciation of Iraq's interests in Syria and the Fertile Crescent. Al-Bajhaji had difficulty controlling the maneuvers of the Iraqi Army in Israel, as its commanders were loyal to the regent and to Nuri al-Sa'id, who thus managed to sabotage the intentions and actions of the prime minister himself. The basic lack of confidence in the prime minister and the disputes between al-Bajhaji and the regent led to the fall of the government early in January 1949. The new government, headed by Nuri al-Sa'id, remained in power until December of that year.

At the end of the fighting in Israel, Iraq was the only Arab state (of those which had taken an active part) which did not participate in the talks in Rhodes and did not sign the armistice agreement with Israel. This was perfectly in line with the Iraqi pattern of behavior which had prevailed regarding Palestine since the 1930s: obvious and declared adoption of a rigid, uncompromising position, exploiting the Palestine conflict to reinforce Iraq's status in the inter-Arab arena as the champion of the pan-Arab nationalist struggle and to strengthen the nationalist image of the politicians and governments of Iraq in the eyes of domestic nationalist public opinion. The Iraqi Army, which was encamped in Samaria, was the only force which had not concluded an agreement with Israel and was therefore exposed to the possibility of a concentrated attack by the Israeli Army. However, the government of Iraq hesitated to recall its expeditionary force, in view of the unrest which had broken out among its troops, who felt that they had been used more for the manipulation and securing of Hashemite objectives than for fighting against Israel. After the coup launched in Syria in March 1949 by the Syrian chief of staff, Husni al-Za'im, Nuri proposed posting Iraqi Army units on Syrian soil, in order to protect Syria against Israel. Nuri's proposal—which was intended both to promote Iraq's ambitions in Syria and to delay the return of the Iraqi expeditionary force to its own country—was rejected. Eventually, the Iraqi expeditionary force was returned to Iraq, and its units were dispersed far from Baghdad, in order to frustrate the rise of any antigovernment sentiments among its ranks.

The governments headed by Nuri al-Sa'id (January–December 1949), 'Ali Jawdat al-Ayubi (December 1949–February 1950), and Tawfiq al-Suwaydi (February–September 1950) were forced to cope with the effects of the 1948 war on the inter-Arab arena and the domestic situation within Iraq.

Tawfiq al-Suwaydi was forced to deal with the crisis that arose in the inter-Arab arena caused by King 'Abdallah's efforts to annex the West Bank of Palestine to Jordan. This placed al-Suwaydi in an uncomfortable position. The increased tension between the Hashemite states and Egypt and Saudi Arabia ran counter to his intentions of restoring tranquility while reconciling Iraq and Egypt. Loyalty to the Hashemites obligated Iraq to support 'Abdallah. When a proposal was raised in the Arab League for the expulsion of Jordan from the organization as a consequence of its unilateral steps toward annexing the West Bank, Iraq proposed compromises intended to rescue its ally from isolation and prevent its expulsion from the League.

The Historical Consequences of the Wathba and the 1948 War

The events of the wathba and the 1948 war had long-term effects on the political processes and ideological climate of Iraq between 1948 and 1958. Undeniably, in the second half of 1948, the politicians and the conservative establishment succeeded in bringing about some degree of calm in Baghdad and regaining control of the situation. Nonetheless, the wathba riots eroded the strength of the regime. The wathba intensified the feelings of alienation and hostility directed by the modern middle and poor strata toward the regime and the ruling elite; the latter were seen as responsible for the misery affecting individuals in particular and Iraqi society in general. The wathba reinforced the tendency of the ruling political elite to lean on the major tribal landowners as a counterweight offsetting the new urban forces. The co-optation of the tribal landowners by the upper socioeconomic stratum and its ruling political elite, based on their common interest in preserving the political and social status quo, strengthened the conservative trends among the ruling elite and the regime. While this co-optation appeared to reinforce the regime and the ruling elite, the dominance of the conservative trends reduced their capacity for flexibility and ability to bring about reforms, vitally needed to cope with the challenges of modernization and provide a response to the distress of the new social forces.

The weakness of the opposition political forces aided the survival and relative rehabilitation of the elite and the conservative politicians. The legal opposition parties, al-Istiqlal and the National Democratic Party, most of whose leaders came from the upper stratum and the political elite, or from the bourgeoisie which lacked any strength of its own and clung to the elite, were shocked by the events of the wathba. They felt they had lost control of the young activists. The leadership of these parties, while aiming at reform and political, economic, and social change, preferred to achieve these changes within the framework of the existing regime and avoid revolutionary violence. Given the strength of the major tribal landowners and their influence on the tribes and traditional sectors of the population, these parties were incapable of constituting an alternative to the regime or of forcing the adoption of any far-ranging reform within it. The illegal Communist Party had an impact on the ideological climate among the young, educated members of the effendiyya and contributed to increasing the unrest of the students and the working class; activists from the Communist and other political parties were a factor in the outbreak of the strikes and riots. Nonetheless, they did not have the power to launch an actual revolution.

Whereas the wathba was a shock that undermined the status and strength of the senior politicians and the ruling elite, the 1948 war in Israel destroyed their nationalist image and legitimacy. Because the conservative politicians, who required the support of the effendiyya but were incapable of responding to its distress, had treated the Palestine question as a central nationalist issue, the failure in Israel did grievous harm. The shock waves resonating from the failure of the war were almost immediately reflected in the series of military coups d'état that took place in Syria in the autumn of 1949. Syria was the weakest of the Arab states and had only limited control of its army; extreme social division prevailed among its elite. In Iraq and Egypt, stronger than Syria, several years were to pass before similar coups occurred. In those two countries, the generation of young officers who had experienced the war in Israel and were personally aware of the weakness, helplessness, and corruption of the regimes later rose to positions of power in the armed forces and acquired the consciousness that impelled them to topple the governments and remove the conservative elites from power. The results of the 1948 war reduced the ability of the politicians and the conservative elites to obtain support and achieve legitimacy using pan-Arab nationalist rhetoric and ideology. Instead, this nationalist rhetoric and ideology became the banner and the battle cry of the revolutionary political forces that were to arise from among the officers and the modern middle stratum starting in the second half of the 1950s.

The Immigration to Israel of the Iraqi Jews

The movement of Jews from Iraq to Israel increased significantly between 1950 and 1952. As a result, the Jewish community in Iraq, which had existed for some 2,500 years, completely disappeared. The Jews had always been part of the ethnic-religious mosaic of the Tigris-Euphrates Plain. Long before the appearance of modern national identity, the Jewish ethnic religious identity was recognized by the Ottoman authorities and by the traditional Islamic cultural, legal, and social systems.

At the end of World War I, some 88,000 Jews lived in Iraq, constituting 3.1 percent of the population of 2.85 million. Most were urban. The Jews formed 25 percent of the Baghdadi population. After the British conquest and then in the new Iraqi nation, the Jews enjoyed economic wealth, and Jewish cultural life flourished. Their relatively high level of education, their concentration in large cities, and their commercial contacts eased their integration into the state apparatus. They were appointed and even elected to positions in the state bureaucracy.

The Jews had a tremendous impact on the Iraqi economy. They owned 75 percent of import companies, and in the 1930s, the biggest transport and trucking firm in Iraq was Jewish-owned. Three banks owned by Jews fulfilled a critical role in the country's finances. Until 1939, most of the board of directors of the Baghdad Chamber of Commerce were Jewish. Even in 1948, of the fifteen board members, six were Jewish; of 2,450 Chamber of Commerce members, 826 were Jewish. The first Iraqi minister of finance, Yehezkiel Sasson, was Jewish. Many Jews worked in the Ministry of Finance, the majority in the currency department. The director of the National Bank of Iraq was Jewish. Jews held pivotal positions in the Iraqi Railroad Company, particularly as members of the board of directors.

The Iraqi Constitution of 1925 allocated four places for Jews in the Parliament and one seat in the Senate. During the 1920s and 1930s, a sense of identity with the state of Iraq developed among the country's modern, educated Jews. However, at the same time, the equilibrium and the relative tolerance in the dynamic relationships between Muslims and Jews that had existed in the Ottoman Empire and traditional Islamic societies began to be undermined. The introduction of ideas and attitudes reflecting a modern collective national identity changed the traditional interethnic relationships. The growth of a modern nationalist identity with a pan-Arab orientation, together with concomitant social tensions and economic distresses, led to stronger anti-Jewish tendencies in Iraq. The image of Jews as a minority enjoying wealth and economic abundance, despite the fact that many Iraqi Jews were poor, created the socioeconomic background that gave rise to anti-Jewish feelings. The nationalists, for whom Britain was the focus of hatred, were also the core of anti-Jewish feelings in Iraq. This was further provoked by the fact that the Jews were identified as supporting Britain. These anti-Jewish feelings were reinforced by entwining the Palestine conflict in the growth of Arab national consciousness and pan-Arab ideology, both as a symbolical and as a concrete manifestation of Arab unity.

Budding Zionist activities made it easier for the pan-Arabic nationalists and the politicians who were trying to prove themselves as pan-Arabic nationalists to accuse the Jews of disloyalty. The Iraqi Jews were also accused of being Zionists, despite the fact that during the 1930s and even the early 1940s, only a very small number were drawn to Zionism.

The growth of the modern nationalism, which took on chauvinist characteristics, combined with the identification of Jews as allies of Great Britain and supporters of Zionism (an identification that was very imprecise), along with the anti-Semitic propaganda emanating from Germany, brought about an explosion of violence against Jews at the end of May 1941, the Farhud (during the clash between Iraq and Britain, when Rashid 'Ali was prime minister). The disturbances against Jews in Baghdad and Basra by the remnants of the 'Ali Rashid movement shocked the Jewish community and shook the confidence that many Jews had had concerning their ability to be integral members of the Iraqi country and society. As a result, starting in 1941, many young, educated Jews became increasingly involved in Zionist and Communist activities. At the same time, the greater part of Iraqi Jews continued to enjoy the benefits of the state and see themselves as members of Iraqi society. The tendency to continue to see the Iraqi Jews as an integral part of society was still strong among the educated middle stratum and even among traditional Jewish circles.

After World War II, with the increased tensions brought about by the question of Israel and increased sociopolitical agitation in Iraq, the governments of Iraq increasingly took an anti-Jewish tack. Up until then, most of the governments of Iraq, with the exception of that of Rashid 'Ali in 1941, had tried to prevent discrimination against the Jews. This traditional line of Iraqi governments stemmed from two elements. One was the close relationship and mutual interests of the politicians and ruling elite with economically powerful Jews; the two groups were economically and even socially tied. The other was the fear that harming the Jews would raise the interethnic tensions in Iraq in general, thus endangering the state's stability. Such instability would run counter to the interests of the government, the ruling elite, and even of the Sunnite Arab minority in maintaining the status quo. However, after World War II, the role of Jewish Communist activists in the wathba demonstrations and in underground Zionist activities, which the Iraqi rulers were unable to prevent, aroused the anger of politicians from the elite and boosted their tendency to utilize incitement against the Jews as demonstrating their nationalist loyalty in their conflict with the populist radical nationalist forces. In 1948–49, during the governments of Muzahim al-Bajhaji and Nuri al-Sa'id, most Jewish government employees were dismissed. Severe restrictions were placed on the Jewish banks. The governments, utilizing various pretexts, imprisoned Jewish merchants and intellectuals.

In September 1948, Shafiq 'Adas, a very rich businessman and a pillar of the Jewish community in Basra, was arrested, convicted, and executed. This and the trial of Reuven Batat, a former member of the Iraqi Parliament and former judge, who was a respected expert on Iraqi jurisprudence, shocked the Jewish community. Physical harm to Jews in the streets continued.

During 1949, newspapers and politicians increasingly called for the expulsion of the Jews and expropriation of their property. In the summer of 1949, proposals for exchanging populations were raised. Prime Minister Nuri al-Sa'id proposed that 100,000 Jews would emigrate from Iraq, and in exchange Iraq would absorb 100,000 Palestinian refugees. Such suggestions simultaneously served the pan-Arabic image of Iraq, satisfied nationalist public opinion within Iraq, and addressed the Israeli question, a cause of agitation which was troubling and dangerous to the ruling elite. Proposals for the exchange of populations were also raised as feelers in settling the Israeli-Arab conflict after the end of the 1948 war in Israel.

On March 2, 1950, Salih Jabr, the interior minister in Tawfiq al-Suwaydi's government, proposed a law that would strip Iraqi citizenship from those Jews who wanted to emigrate or who had left the country already (to study or do business abroad). The law was designed to encourage emigration. Jabr and al-Suwaydi relied on those Iraqi politicians who predicted that only some of the Iraqi Jews would emigrate to Israel as a result of the law. According to their assessment, primarily the poor and lower-middle-class Jews who had Communist and Zionist leanings would leave, and most of the rich and middle-class Jews would remain. However, the prevailing anti-Jewish atmosphere and schemes against the Jews, combined with feelings of personal insecurity on the part of the Jews and the encouragement of Zionist emissaries, all led to one result. Most Jews wanted to move to Israel.

With the establishment of Nuri al-Saʿid's government in September 1950, the government's propensity to encourage the Jews to leave was reinforced. Simultaneously, incitement against the Jews increased. Nuri al-Saʿid and other conservative politicians now saw the Jews as a cause of disturbance, and they seized on the violence against the Jews as a means of diverting Iraqi sociopolitical agitation. Those politicians who were concerned that harming the Jews and forcing them out of Iraq would lead to domestic instability and damage Iraq's economic interests and international image did not dare oppose the nationalism which now took on anti-Jewish coloration.

On March 10, 1952, the Iraqi Parliament passed a law freezing the property of Jews who left Iraq. In this way, the economic foundation of both the rich Jews and the lower-middle-class Jews was destroyed.

From 1950 to 1952, 112,000 Iraqi Jews moved to Israel, leaving behind fewer than 6,000 Jews in Iraq.

This created employment opportunities and advancement for the young effendiyya, many of them Shiʿite, who replaced the Jews, primarily in government as low-level clerks and in commerce. The loss of thousands of Jewish merchants made it easier for many young Shiʿites, who had come to Baghdad and Basra seeking employment, to integrate into commerce. However, the emigration of the bureaucrats and experienced high-level Jewish government administrators impaired the level of public services provided and damaged the quality of financial management. An educated element, which had fulfilled a principal role in the economic life of the country and was one of the major components in the growth of the civil society and Iraqi territorial identity, was excised from Iraqi society.

The Economic Development of Iraq and the Social Processes of the 1950s

Petroleum and the Recovery of the Iraqi Economy

After the protracted depression of World War II and the profound crisis of 1947–48, the year 1949 marked the beginning of economic recovery for Iraq, with a dramatic improvement in the financial situation of the Iraqi government. Income earned by the government of Iraq from petroleum royalties increased from £2.3 million in 1945 to £4,388,000 in 1949, constituting 11.8 percent of state income.[1] (Note: Between 1949 and 1968, 1 pound sterling = 2.8 U.S. dollars.) During the 1950s, the increase in income from petroleum royalties accelerated from £5,285,000 in 1950 to £73.8 million in 1955 and 84.6 million in 1958.[2] (According to other data cited by Dr. Jalal Ferhang, CEO of the Industrial Bank of Iraq, based on publications by the Central Bank of Iraq and a report by the Iraq Petroleum Company, the income earned by the government of Iraq amounted to about £40 million in 1952, £58.3 million in 1953, £73.7 million in 1955, and £79.8 million in 1958.)[3]

The rapid increase in the Iraqi government's income was based on two factors:

1. Expansion of Iraq's petroleum output due to the increase in world needs, following the recovery of the global economy and the application of the United States' Marshall Plan for the rehabilitation of Europe.
2. New agreements between the government of Iraq and the Iraq Petroleum Company (IPC), which obligated the company to expand its output and increase Iraq's share in its profits from petroleum as well.

In 1950, an agreement was reached between the government of Iraq and the IPC and its components (the Mosul Petroleum Company and the Basra Petroleum Company), according to which the government's petroleum royalties were increased from four shillings to six shillings a barrel.[4]

Despite the increase in Iraq's income, this agreement did not satisfy its demands of the petroleum company. The feeling that Iraq was exploited by the IPC contributed to increasing nationalist anti-British unrest in Iraq. Demands to nationalize Iraq's petroleum resources were voiced by opposition politicians from the nationalist al-Istiqlal Party, the National Democratic Party, and the Communists and were sympathetically received by public opinion within the middle stratum.

In March 1952, following protracted negotiations, a new agreement was signed between the government of Iraq and the IPC. The IPC adopted more flexible positions and accepted some of the demands made by the Iraqi government. The agreement stipulated, inter alia, that:

1. The government of Iraq would receive 50 percent of the profits made by the IPC (the "fifty-fifty" principle).
2. The IPC undertook to produce at least 30 million tons of petroleum per year and promised that the income earned by the government of Iraq from petroleum royalties would be at least £20 million per year in 1953 and 1954, increasing to at least £25 million starting in 1955.
3. Iraqi citizens would be added to the various managerial levels at IPC.[5]

The IPC adopted the new, more flexible position due to pressures and constraints on the Western petroleum companies starting in the early 1950s. The nationalization of petroleum by the Mossadeq government in Iran in 1950 and the strengthening of nationalist anti-Western trends in the Middle Eastern states with emphasis on demands for national control of petroleum resources, put pressure on the IPC to reach an agreement with the conservative government of Iraq. The agreement between the American petroleum company Aramco and Saudi Arabia in 1950, according to which petroleum profits were distributed on a fifty-fifty basis, created a precedent that made it difficult for the IPC to object to similar demands advanced by Iraq.

Notwithstanding the significant achievements attained by Iraq in the framework of the new contract, the IPC continued to maintain control of petroleum in Iraq, with its franchise covering almost the entire territory of Iraq. Although petroleum accounted for about 49 percent of the income earned by the Iraqi government in 1953, the government had no control over petroleum prices or company policy. Unsettled issues and disagreements concerning the method of computing IPC's profits soured the relationship between the company and the government of Iraq, and they continued to be disputed by the parties throughout the 1950s.

IPC's impact on the economy of Iraq was primarily felt in the financial sector. The agreements with the company brought considerable financial resources to the government of Iraq, which it could apply to development and modernization. Above and beyond the financial aspect, however, the direct effect of Iraq's progress toward industrialization and modernization was marginal. Granted, the IPC established a center for training administrative and technical personnel and employed 12,000 Iraqi workers.[6] Nevertheless, the tremendous scope of poverty in Iraq and its backwardness meant that even such a large workforce had a marginal effect on the country's economy.

The Development Board during the 1950s

From the standpoint of industrialization, modernization, and the standard of living of most of its population, Iraq was a backward state with an economy based on agriculture and petroleum. The number of persons employed in industrial plants and small workshops with more than four employees was about 46,000 in 1941 (including employees in IPC facilities) and about 55,000 in 1954. Of these, only 2,000 were employed in advanced industry.[7] Most of the industrial plants and workshops operated at a low technological level; primarily, agricultural produce was processed, and building materials, cigarettes, matches, and simple consumer goods were manufactured for the domestic market. Of Iraq's industrial plants and small workshops, 93 percent employed five or fewer workers and were, in fact, no more than cottage industries. The share of industry in the national product (exclusive of petroleum) was 8.1 percent in 1953 and 9.9 percent in 1958.[8] According to another source, industry's share of the national income was 7.5 percent in 1953 and 11 percent in 1961.[9]

In order to promote industry and development and raise the standard of living, in 1948 the Iraqi government under Muzahim al-Bajhaji established a Development Board (Majlis al-ʿAmar). In March 1950, ʿAbd al-Karim al-Uzri, minister of finance in the Tawfiq al-Suwaydi government, presented the Development Board Law to Parliament for approval. Initially, all of the income earned by the government of Iraq from petroleum royalties was allocated to the Board.[10] In 1951, the Nuri al-Saʿid government reduced the resources at the disposal of the Board to 70 percent of petroleum royalties.[11] The remaining royalties were allocated to financing current government expenses. The Ministry of Development, which was entrusted with implementing development plans, was established in 1953. (The Board's responsibilities were basically limited to planning and budgeting.)

Between 1951 and 1958, three multiyear development and investment plans were formulated. The first plan, for the years 1951–56, entailed expenditures of 155.4 million Iraqi dinars. In 1955, a new plan was formulated, and expenditures were set at 304 million dinars. As a result of the anticipated increase in income from petroleum royalties, a third plan (intended to replace the second plan), formulated late in 1955, set expenditures at 500 million dinars.[12]

The Board's policy was prudent and conservative, allocating priority to agriculture and planning for long-term development in transportation and water. Foreign experts and consultants—primarily a committee headed by Lord Slater—recommended that Iraq concentrate its principal investments on agriculture and criticized the imbalance between the long-term development plans and failure to place sufficient emphasis on investments to improve the living conditions of the population in the short term.[13] In the first plan, 42.5 percent of the budget, amounting to 155.4 million dinars, was dedicated to agriculture and water development; 20 percent to industry, 13.3 percent to housing and construction, and 18.7 percent to developing the transportation infrastructure. In the second plan, 37.6 percent was allocated to agriculture, 14.3 percent to industry, and 20 percent to housing and construction. In the third plan, agriculture and water development received 33.6 percent, housing and development 29.9 percent, and industry 13.4 percent.[14] Although the third plan incorporated the conclusions of a committee headed by Arthur Little, a consultant employed by the Development Board, regarding the establishment of chemical and steel industrial plants and date processing plants,[15] industrialization was not a high priority for the Board.

The Development Board had difficulty implementing its plans, some of which never advanced beyond the paper stage and others of which were applied slowly and almost reluctantly. In reality, only about one-third of the planned investments were actually put into practice in 1951. In 1955, only 68 percent of budget allocated for development was actually used to execute plans.[16] The greatest difficulties encountered in actualizing the plans was in industrialization. Unquestionably, industrial plants were established between 1951 and 1958, primarily to manufacture building materials, shoes, and textiles and to process agricultural produce. Nonetheless, no breakthrough in industrialization occurred at a scope capable of transforming Iraq's economy and society.

The state had problems actually realizing its development plans and in locating investing partners or entrepreneurs from among the private sector, the local bourgeoisie, or foreign companies. The local bourgeoisie was of limited scope, with limited equity capital and no motivation for taking risks; it was linked to the dominant conservative interests of the elite. The low standard of living of the great majority of the population prevented the development of a local market that could have served as a catalyst for developing industry. International trade conditions did not permit the Iraqi economy to expand its markets, with the exception of petroleum and dates. The weakness of the industrial bourgeoisie kept it from affecting the social and political conditions in Iraq or promoting its industrialization.[17] This weakness prevented the bourgeoisie from offering an alternative to the dominant conservative policies of the regime and the ruling elite. These dominant policies reflected the outlook and interests of the upper stratum of landowners, bureaucrats, and merchants who wished to preserve what was for them a convenient status quo.

Investments in agriculture and water development did contribute to improving the food supply, but the benefits accrued principally to the major landowners.[18] Iraq sought to improve the living conditions of its population as a whole, but without a concomitant negative impact on the major landowners, who constituted an important source of support for the regime and the ruling elite. The combination of political and social conservatism, bureaucratic inefficiency, and the structural limitations of the Iraqi society and economy prevented the Iraqi state—despite the vast amounts of financial resources at its disposal—from transforming Iraq into a modern industrialized country.

The Economic Situation and Social Processes and Their Effect on Political Conditions

Despite the high income earned by the Iraqi state in the 1950s, most Iraqis lived in poverty. While it was true that inflation of the prices of consumer goods had been stopped as early as 1948 and the cost of living had even begun to decline, living conditions remained miserable.[19] Per capita income in 1953 was only £46.[20] In 1956, 80 percent of residences in Iraq had neither running water nor electrical power; most houses were made of mud, cloth, or improvised materials in poverty-stricken neighborhoods.[21] Despite the advances in sanitation, infant mortality in poor areas was still as high as 25 percent.[22] In education, Iraq was severely underdeveloped. In 1947, only 8 percent of Iraqis were literate. Although the number of schools and pupils grew steadily (in 1951, Iraq had 1,451 elementary schools with 258,000 pupils, and 134 high schools and teachers' colleges with 35,000 pupils); by 1957, still only about one-third of the children of elementary school age were actually enrolled in schools—that is, two-thirds of Iraq's younger generation remained illiterate.[23]

Without industrialization and/or agrarian reform, Iraq had no possibility of bringing about any significant transformation in the living conditions of the majority of its population, nor of achieving modernization of its society. Maintaining the social status quo and the prerogatives of the major landowners meant that nothing would change. The growing dependence of the regime and the elite on the tribal landowners prevented any attempt at agrarian reform or changes in the regime. Thus, adapting to the new social, economic, and ideological conditions which had begun to prevail in Iraq and throughout the world was impossible.

The takeover by tribal notables of the lands belonging to their tribes had begun in the nineteenth century, with the formation of the link between the economy of Iraq and the global capitalist market economy, following the Tanzimat reforms in the Ottoman Empire. Those reforms included the application of a law requiring registration of tribal and community lands. In practice, the lands were registered in the name of tribal or urban notables. In the 1950s, 1 percent of landowners held more than 50 percent of arable land, compared to 73 percent of the *fellahin* who owned only 6 percent of the land. According to one source, the forty-nine richest families held 16.7 percent of private land.[24] Some 600,000 fellahin households (that is, the majority of the fellahin) were landless or almost landless. This process, by which the tribal notables became landowners, had far-ranging social consequences: The regressive taxation system created a situation whereby most of the major landowners paid almost no taxes.

Enrichment of the tribal notables and their transformation into landowners, along with their involvement in the political and bureaucratic systems of the Iraqi state, had an adverse effect on tribal structure and created alienation between the landowners and members of the tribes, who became landless serfs or nearly landless farmers. The reinforced status of the tribal landowners within the state's structure, as well as their reliance on a system of laws that favored them (the Tribal Disputes Regulations and the Law Governing the Rights and Duties of Cultivators of 1933) and their increasing wealth, dialectically led to erosion of their social status and weakened the effectiveness of their support for the regime and the ruling elite. The ability of the tribal notables-turned-landowners to enlist the support of the tribesmen-turned-fellahin for the regime decreased, as a result of the economic gaps that accelerated development of social stratification and alienation, with a concomitant adverse effect on tribal frameworks and loyalties. Starting in the last days of World War II, migration from villages to cities constantly increased. Rural and tribal populations flowed into the cities to escape the natural population increase and poverty of the villages, hoping to find work and improved living conditions in the urban centers.[25] The influx of the poor rural population to the cities was not accompanied by urban industrialization, which could provide them with jobs; their lives were not improved, nor did a class of urban workers result. The poverty-stricken fellahin and tribesmen were illiterate and devoid of any vocational training, and they lacked the skills required for an industrial state. Instead, the migration of fellahin and tribesmen to the cities led to the growth of poor neighborhoods characterized by extremely difficult living conditions. Most of this population lived without running water, electricity, or even minimal social services. This wave of migration resulted in a spurt in Baghdad's population of over 50 percent in just a decade, from 515,500 in 1947 to 795,000 in 1957.[26]

Conspicuous consumption emphasized the gaps between the rich members of the upper socioeconomic stratum and certain sections of the middle stratum, which had succeeded in accumulating some measure of wealth, and the majority of the population, which was living in abject poverty. At the same time, the modern middle stratum expanded, and some parts of it— primarily members of the liberal professions—found their way into government and civil service and enjoyed a high standard of living. Nonetheless, the middle stratum as a whole was characterized by shame, frustration, alienation, and contempt for the elite and the regime. This stratum, whose members had acquired a secondary or higher Western-style education and had adopted modern Western dress codes and political language, expanded further with each new graduating class. However, notwithstanding the increasing political and social sensitivity that characterized its younger members in the 1950s, this stratum did not develop class consciousness, and its political expression was that of nationalism—which, in the 1950s, was increasingly radical in nature. Most members of the middle stratum expressed hostility toward the ruling elite and the regime, but also felt contempt and condescension toward the traditional, uneducated majority of the population. While this stratum had some influence on the country's ideological climate and political atmosphere, it was unable to bring about any real political or social change due to the political conditions prevailing in Iraq within the framework of the Hashemite monarchy.

Thus, despite the grinding poverty suffered by most Iraqis and the growth of the politically aware modern middle stratum, no way was found to bring about a change in the socioeconomic conditions of Iraq within the framework of its regime.

6

The Political Conflict in Iraq between 1950 and 1954

Failed Attempts at Reform within the Regime

The Political and Social Struggle in Iraq, 1950–1952

Between 1950 and 1954, the conflicts marking Iraqi politics remained within the ruling political elite, played out between the supporters of the dominant conservative line and those who supported limited socioeconomic reform and political liberalization.[1] The socioeconomic and ideological transformations and processes in Iraq, the ramifications of the global cold war, and the beginning of the radical revolutions within the Arab world were all contributory factors to these conflicts. The political atmosphere in Iraq was affected by the anti-British outbursts in Egypt and the protracted crisis in Egyptian-British relations between 1950 and 1952. The political press and public opinion in Iraq identified with Egypt and followed developments of its relations with Britain closely. The political unrest and nationalist anti-British sentiments were intensified by the echoes of events and the crisis in Iran, following the nationalization of that country's petroleum resources by Prime Minister Mohammad Mossadeq. Younger members (students) of the modern middle stratum experienced increasing unrest, directed against the government, the establishment, and Britain. The anti-British nationalism of Iraq's students assumed a leftist radical character against the background of the cold war and as a result of activity by Communists and National Democratic Party activists. In rural areas, outbreaks of violence occurred among the poor and landless fellahin. Given the domestic sociopolitical unrest and the threat posed by radical revolutionary forces and movements throughout the Arab world, the various conservative governments of Iraq sought to bolster the regime and the political and social status quo by developing connections between Iraq and the West; they sought to establish a regional defense treaty under Western auspices. At the same time, political awareness and involvement at the national level were still limited, strong only among the modern educated middle stratum and the few educated workers—the effendiyya. The vast majority of Iraq's population remained outside political life during the 1950s.

At the head of the political agenda between 1950 and 1952 was the method of elections. The opposition parties, as well as those politicians who sought to bring about reform and accelerate Iraqi development, viewed the two-stage, indirect method of elections as their principal obstacle. The electoral system for Parliament entailed a two-stage process. In the initial stage, the citizens of Iraq voted for electors from their electoral precincts. Generally speaking, the electors were local traditional notables or persons loyal to them. In the second stage, the electors or secondary voters elected representatives to Parliament. The Elections Law, promulgated in 1924, granted the right to vote to all men in Iraq who had attained the age of twenty and paid taxes. Originally, in the first stage of the elections, every 250 primary voters elected one elector. In 1946, when Tawfiq al-Suwaydi was in power, the Elections Law was amended to read that 100 primary voters would elect one elector. (Women did not have the right to vote throughout the years of the monarchy in Iraq. Only in March 1958 did the Parliament decide to grant suffrage, within one year, to women who could read and write. This condition did not apply to men. In practice, this amendment to the Elections Law was not implemented, because the monarchy was overthrown in July 1958.)

The indirect method ensured that the electors would be loyal supporters and protégés of the traditional notables who were candidates for Parliament. In certain areas, most of them tribal, election was by way of tazkiya, or "consent"—meaning that the local notables gave their common consent to a single candidate, who was elected without competition. This method gave Prime Minister Nuri al-Saʿid and the regent, ʿAbd al-Ilah, the ability to maintain a majority in Parliament and perpetuated the dominance of conservatism among the political elite. The politicians who headed the opposition parties contended that the existing method of elections prevented them from obtaining proper representation within the new urban social strata and caused them frustration and alienation vis-à-vis the regime. Nuri and the regent, notwithstanding the rivalry between them at the personal level, joined forces in the effort to preserve the existing method of elections as a means of maintaining the social and political status quo. The major tribal landowners, the most conservative part of the ruling stratum, on which the political elite and the monarchy had become increasingly dependent, were interested in preserving the indirect method of elections. In this way, the laws were retained that granted them legal status relative to the fellahin—the members of their tribes—and helped them preserve their own status and interests.

Additional issues at the forefront of the political conflicts included the negotiations with the IPC and the question of Iraq's international orientation vis-à-vis the cold war. The debates and conflicts on those issues also reflected interpersonal rivalry between various politicians of the Iraqi elite—principally between Nuri al-Sa'id and Salih Jabr, who attempted to challenge the dominant status of his rival.

Toward the end of 1952, the struggle over the method of elections was settled; as the opposition had demanded, a direct electoral system was adopted. It then transpired, however, that even when the direct method of elections was implemented, Nuri, 'Abd al-Ilah, and the elite conservatives within the regime gained control of Parliament and state institutions. In 1954, the conservatives assumed definitive control of the domestic arena, and Nuri increased his efforts toward establishing a regional defense treaty in cooperation with the West.

The Struggle within the Elite and the Regime: Nuri vs. Salih Jabr and the Demands for Reform

In 1949, Nuri began to organize a political party. Notwithstanding his own distaste for party politics, Nuri understood that the establishment of a political framework would be of value to him in his maneuvers within the political arena and would strengthen his own position. Included in the new Constitutional Union Party (Hizb al-Ittihad al-Dusturi) were senior conservative politicians who supported Nuri and were linked to the Palace, major tribal landowners, and minor tribal notables. Other party members included wealthy members of the liberal professions and senior bureaucrats who were now seeking positions of political influence and possibly government employment by joining the party.[2] On December 23, 1949, the founding conference of the new party took place, and an executive board was nominated, which included a remarkable number of tribal landowners and notables: twenty-three, as against twenty-two urban members. This was not a "mass party" in the modern sense. Instead, it was a political body by means of which Nuri sought to adapt traditional political patterns of tribal loyalty and patron-client relationships to a parliamentary political structure characterized by the increasing importance of the modern urban middle stratum and by a political climate that reinforced radical nationalist and leftist movements. The party line was definitely conservative and pro-Western in its attitudes toward the global interbloc polarization. The Constitutional Union Party held an absolute majority in Parliament, with 83 out of 135 members. Nuri and the regent ensured the almost automatic support of delegates from among the tribal landowners, who represented more than 30 percent of the members of Parliament, as well as of conservative politicians from the urban elite. The two-stage method of elections produced a bilateral system, with Nuri and the regent assisting in the election of loyal conservative urban and tribal delegates according to their loyalty, and the elected delegates giving their patrons parliamentary support in return for their backing. This symbiosis preserved the status quo and helped the elite to maintain its own economic and social status.

Among those who played a central and active role in the establishment and organization of the Constitutional Union Party was Salih Jabr. Nonetheless, differences rapidly arose between Jabr and Nuri. The relationship between the two politicians had been charged ever since the wathba of January 1948. Jabr resented Nuri for not coming to his assistance. Nuri, who saw Jabr as a protégé, did not want him to become too strong and shake off the bonds of his patronage. In 1950, Jabr left the Constitutional Union Party and began to take action aimed at becoming the alternative leader to Nuri, including adopting terminology attractive to the younger members of the middle stratum.[3]

Under the government headed by Tawfiq al-Suwaydi (February–September 1950), a triangle of tension arose within the government. The vertices of that tension were the prime minister, Salih Jabr (then minister of the interior), and the supporters of Nuri al-Saʿid, who—while not himself a government minister—had facilitated the formation of the al-Suwaydi government through support by his party in Parliament. Although Jabr had organized the Constitutional Union Party, his supporters were in the minority; Nuri controlled the party. In April 1950, most of the opposition delegates resigned to protest a violent incident between one of them and a delegate who supported the government.[4] This incident bore witness to the increasing tensions within the Iraqi Parliament and the frustration of the oppositionist delegates at the absolute control exercised by the Constitutional Union Party delegates loyal to Nuri al-Saʿid. Paradoxically, this move had the effect of helping Nuri and his party strengthen their control over Parliament.

Salih Jabr's attempt to promulgate a new Press Law that would extend and confirm the freedom of the press met with objections from ministers of the Constitutional Union Party and deepened the rift between Jabr and Nuri. Jabr and his associates were accused of having illegally profited from the emigration of Iraq's Jews. Sunnite politicians—possibly inspired by Nuri—charged that Jabr had issued 400 passports to wealthy Iraqi Jews and, in so doing, had made himself a tidy profit. The number of Shiʿite ministers in government (five ministers) gave rise to bitterness and fear on the part of the Sunnites. The Shiʿite ministers held several important portfolios: Salih Jabr was minister of the interior; ʿAbd al-Karim al-Uzri was minister of finance; Diya Jaʿfar was minister of economic affairs; Saʿd Salih was minister of education; and ʿAbd al-Mahdi was minister of transportation and labor. Salih Jabr, who considered himself to be the most senior Shiʿite and Iraqi politician, tried to dominate the Shiʿite ministers. Some of them, however, were not eager to accept his leadership, preferring to retain their independent status while cooperating with senior Sunnite politicians such as Nuri al-Saʿid and Tawfiq al-Suwaydi.

Given the important role played by the Shiʿite cabinet ministers, Shiʿite bureaucrats, and educated people holding government posts hoped for rapid personal promotion and improvement in the status of Shiʿites in general. These ambitions on the part of Shiʿite officials and educated people, who felt deprived and discriminated against, aroused the anxiety of Sunnite bureaucrats and politicians and exacerbated tensions between Sunnites and Shiʿites. Nonetheless, it was actually the differences in outlook between Nuri and al-Suwaydi concerning Iraq's regional foreign policy that led to the overthrow of the government. Nuri, who disagreed with al-Suwaydi's policy of reconciliation and intensified cooperation with Egypt, brought about the resignation of the government in September 1950.[5]

The struggle between Salih Jabr and Nuri assumed a central role in the political and parliamentary arena during the terms in office of Nuri himself (September 1950–July 1952) and Mustafa al-ʿUmari (July–November 1952). In June 1951, Jabr established the People's Socialist Party (Hizb al-Umma al-Ishtiraqiyya). Through this party, Jabr sought the support of widely different social circles and sectors with conflicting interests: the effendiyya, or modern urban middle stratum, which was composed primarily of Sunnites; the traditional Shiʿite population; the Shiʿite and Kurdish tribes; and the tribal landowners.[6] The inclusion of the term "Socialist" in the name of his party reflected his desire to win the heart of the radical nationalist effendiyya. Periodicals under the influence of his party, al-Umma and al-Naba, reflected his sharp criticism of the conservative establishment and published radically worded articles. Jabr endeavored to represent himself to the urban Sunnite modern middle stratum as an all-Iraqi, progressive, reform-oriented leader; to the landowning tribal notables as a person capable of preserving their status; and to the Shiʿites as a champion in their fight against discrimination. Nuri and his supporters spread rumors to the effect that the Sunnites had rejected Jabr because of the preponderance of Shiʿites among his supporters. At the same time, in order to gain popularity among the Shiʿites, Nuri enlisted several Shiʿite tribal landowners to the leadership of his party. Jabr, on the other hand, emphasized that his camp was characterized by the complete integration of Sunnites, Shiʿites, and Kurds.[7]

Jabr claimed that young Sunnites were turning away from Nuri as a result of his reactionary positions. Despite the radical rhetoric, the fundamental orientation shared by Jabr and most of the members of his party was based on moderate, cautious reform. Jabr took pains to explain that the reforms which he sought to carry out would not harm tribal landowners.

The regent, who hoped to gain more room for political maneuvering, gave his discreet support to the establishment of Jabr's party, believing that this would create a counterweight to Nuri's power. The party eventually turned out to be one of loyal opposition, which sought to preserve the existing regime while implementing moderate change and reform. Despite the considerable support given to the party by the Shi'ite and Kurdish tribes and the modern middle stratum, Jabr proved unable to challenge Nuri, who not only enjoyed the support of the tribal landowners and the traditional sectors of the populace but also maintained control of the bureaucracy and the establishment within Iraq. The fact of Jabr's Shi'ite origin aroused the suspicion of many Sunnites. His identification with the Portsmouth treaty with Britain, his past history as an intimate and protégé of Nuri himself, and his vague and moderate reformism made it difficult for him to attain the status of an alternative opposition leader to Nuri. These factors also prevented him from obtaining the support of the younger and more radical members of the effendiyya, whose bitterness against the establishment and the elite was constantly increasing. Jabr and his party were considered by those young people and students part of the ruling elite. (The rivalry between the two leading political personages continued until Jabr's sudden death in Parliament, in the midst of an antigovernment speech, in 1957.)

In April 1951, an additional political organization was established: the United Popular Front (al-Jabha al-Sha'biyya al-Muttahida). This was a loose organization of senior conservative politicians who hated Nuri al-Sa'id and could not accept Salih Jabr.[8] Even though their basic worldview was essentially conservative, due to tactical considerations aimed at creating concern for the future of the regime, they gave their support to moderate reform. Aware of the need for reform and hoping to weaken Nuri's position and that of the Constitutional Union Party, the United Popular Front gave its backing to the demands for change in the method of elections and for moderate political and socioeconomic reform. In response to the prevailing sentiments among the younger members of the middle stratum, the party adopted the demand for a neutralist policy regarding the interbloc cold war. In private conversations, some of the party leaders articulated their preference for an alliance with the West. The leading members of the party differed in their attitude toward Iraq's regional policy. On one hand, Taha al-Hashimi, a prominent party leader with pan-Arab nationalist views, supported dynamic Iraqi activity aimed at achieving union or federation with Syria. On the other hand, Muzahim al-Bajhaji tended toward an Iraqi territorialist orientation and sought to increase inter-Arab cooperation and achieve rapprochement with Egypt while reducing the scope of Iraqi activity in Syria. (As prime minister in the first half of 1948 and as foreign minister under 'Ali Jawdat al-

Ayubi in the winter of 1949–50, al-Bajhaji had sought to reduce Iraqi involvement in Syria and had been prepared to reach an agreement with Egypt regarding Syria, in contrast to the positions adopted by Nuri and the regent.) These differences in approach regarding Iraq's regional policy and status did not prevent the Iraqi politicians—who were primarily motivated by interpersonal power struggles—from forming a tactical alliance against Nuri. The United Popular Front cooperated with the older opposition parties, al-Istiqlal and the National Democratic Party; still, notwithstanding the rhetoric and inflammatory statements, its leaders attempted to find common ground with the Constitutional Union Party, and their positions were actually somewhat more moderate than their rhetoric would indicate. United Popular Front politicians took part in governments established by Nuri or his associates. While a member of Parliament, Taha al-Hashimi himself was appointed in 1951 to serve as chair of the Development Board.

Both al-Istiqlal and the National Democratic Party—which had been officially founded in 1946 but whose roots may be traced to the period preceding World War II—expressed unequivocal opposition to the dominant conservative line adopted by Nuri and his government.

The nationalist rightist al-Istiqlal headed its list of demands with an urgent call to abrogate the treaty with Britain and an appeal to Iraq to maintain a pan-Arab policy. It became a rightist, anti-Communist party that abhorred the Soviet Union but supported the adoption of a neutralist position in the interbloc conflict. During the 1950s, al-Istiqlal began to emphasize its demands for social and economic reform. At the fifth conference of al-Istiqlal, which took place in Baghdad on November 3, 1950, the deputy secretary of the party, Faiq al-Samarrai, called for social and economic reform, a progressive tax on lands, and a limitation on the size of private estates. Al-Samarrai called for the institution of democratic socialism in the Arab states, in order to launch reforms and improve the standard of living. However, the party's socioeconomic platform remained clouded.[9]

The National Democratic Party had a liberal Social Democratic ideology and accordingly focused its activities on demands for political, economic, and social reforms. Its demands included moderate agrarian reform involving assistance to nearly landless peasants, reform of the regressive taxation system, which granted far-ranging concessions to the large landowners, accelerated development, creation of jobs for high school and college graduates, improvement of social conditions, and greater Iraqi involvement in the control of the country's petroleum resources. The party also demanded the expulsion of all foreign (i.e., British) forces from Iraq, repudiation of the treaty with Britain, and a neutralist policy with regard to the cold war.[10]

Notwithstanding the differences and even the antagonism between the

two parties, during the 1950s their common interests enabled them to cooperate. The obviously socialist platform of the National Democratic Party and
increasing social awareness among the effendiyya and the working class led
al-Istiqlal to begin considering social issues and to join the demands for social
and economic reform. For both parties, changing the electoral system was
essential; under the status quo, they were doomed to remain in the minority,
unable to overthrow the conservative Constitutional Union. Both parties
called for agrarian and tax reform and expressed criticism of the laws that
gave legal status and power to the tribal landowners but not to the tribesmen
and fellahin. They shared a common belief that, without political democratization, which would give the modern middle stratum and particularly the
students a means of expression, unrest was liable to lead to outbreaks of
violence that would undermine or topple the regime. Both parties demanded
limits on the political powers of the Palace, which, under the regent, 'Abd al-
Ilah, had become an important conservative center of power.

Both parties focused their activities on the modern middle stratum and
gained the support of the students. They also enjoyed a certain degree of
support among the bourgeoisie, which was interested in economic and social
reforms so as to create conditions favorable to industrialization and commerce. (The Iraqi bourgeoisie, however, was extremely weak and dependent
upon the state and the ruling elite.) The National Democratic Party was also
active among the working class. Al-Istiqlal had difficulty in pursuing any
activity in that sector, due to its lack of an attractive social platform.

Despite the real differences between the two parties, most of their leaders
came from the ruling elite and the upper socioeconomic stratum.[11] Kamil al-
Jadirji himself, the leader of the National Democratic Party, was the son of a
rich landowning urban family. Despite their radical positions and the fact
that their activists in the street enlisted the support of the students and
younger members of the effendiyya, whose hostility toward the ruling elite
was constantly increasing, the leaders of both parties feared the outburst of
revolutionary violence and took measures to ward it off. Although both parties were legal and most of their members came from the elite, al-Istiqlal and
the National Democratic Party suffered from the severe attitudes and harsh
treatment shown to them by the conservative governments, which limited
their activity and harassed their leaders.

The illegal, radical opposition, the Communist Party and the Ba'th Party,
were persecuted by the authorities, and their activists were imprisoned.[12]
Although they were incapable of directly affecting the struggles among the
parties, the ideological climate allowed them some influence over the sentiments prevailing among young, educated persons. Communist activists
played a role in stirring up unrest and organizing labor strikes and riots in the

prisons, starting in 1945 and more intensively between 1952 and 1954.[13] The radical parties were involved in the violent antigovernment outbursts of the intifada in November 1952 and October 1956.

Nonetheless, the radical forces were incapable of translating the violent riots of January 1948 and November 1952 into political achievements or of undermining the existing status quo. The legal opposition parties were unable to bring about any change through Parliament itself, thanks to the solid majority ensured by the indirect method of elections and the structure of Iraqi society, as well as to Nuri, the regent, and the conservative forces in Parliament. Due to the strength of the conservative Iraqi establishment, with its vast economic resources and the support given to it by the tribal landowners and the army, the opposition parties could not achieve any significant reforms; nor were they able to frustrate Nuri's moves, such as the new agreement with the IPC, ratified by Parliament in the spring of 1952.

The political struggles and increasing inequality and socioeconomic gaps between the rich and the poor were at times even stronger than the tensions between Sunnites and Shi'ites. Among the Shi'ites from the modern middle and poorer strata, the feelings of deprivation and discrimination grew steadily. Although more and more Shi'ites were involved in the political system and could be found in the lower levels of civil service and among the merchants, they continued to feel deprived. The Shi'ite politicians took pains to deny any ethnic motive for their activity; however, they took action to ensure the support of their own ethnic community. Nonetheless, in the 1950s, social gaps and tensions, fed by economic inequality between the upper class and the ruling elite, on one hand, and the modern middle and poorer strata, on the other, were no less acute than the tension between Shi'ites and Sunnites. Moreover, the central interest of the Shi'ite tribal landowners, politicians, and bureaucrats lay in preserving the existing regime and the socioeconomic status quo.

The Intifada of November 1952

In the spring of 1952, Nuri al-Sa'id succeeded in obtaining a new agreement with the Iraq Petroleum Company (IPC). This agreement increased the government's share of petroleum income and gave the government some degree of influence over IPC policies. The agreement was ratified over the severe objections of the opposition parties, which demanded nationalization of Iraq's petroleum resources or at least greater government control over the company. Despite the echoes raised in Iraq by the Iranian crisis, following the nationalization of Iran's petroleum by the Mossadeq government, the opposition was unsuccessful in enlisting broad and effective public support to a degree which would have interfered with ratification of the agreement.[14]

In 1952, as the parliamentary elections approached (scheduled for the autumn), political tensions increased over the way the elections were conducted, and the rift between Nuri and Jabr deepened. Attempts at reconciliation, initiated by various politicians and encouraged by British diplomats, proved futile. In addition to the fear that the conflict between Nuri and Jabr would be exploited by radical opposition forces seeking to undermine the stability of the regime in Baghdad, there was increasing concern that this rivalry would fan the flames between Shiʿites and Sunnites.

The cold war, which reached a peak in 1950–53 with the Korean War and the palpable threat of a third world war, exacerbated internal tensions. These tensions were exploited by an organization called the "Partisans of Peace," which was established and operated with the support of the Soviet Union and the Communist parties. The protracted crisis in neighboring Iran and the tensions between Iran, on one hand, and Britain and the United States, on the other, stirred the students and younger members of the effendiyya.[15] The coup launched by the "Free Officers" and the fall of the monarchy in Egypt in July 1952 aroused both fear and hope in Iraq. Even though the characteristic traits of the revolutionary regime in Egypt had not yet coalesced and its radical Socialist trends had not begun to develop in 1952, the toppling of the monarchy caused anxiety among the ruling elite in Iraq. Jabr and his party nurtured that anxiety and emphasized that, without political, economic, and social reform, the danger of a military coup in Iraq would only increase. The hopes of those who sought to achieve reform within the framework of the regime were excited by the downfall of Bishara al-Khoury in Lebanon in September 1952, ousted in a bloodless coup by Camille Chamoun. The Iraqi reformers hoped such examples would help them in their efforts to reduce the powers of the Palace and undermine the dominance of Nuri al-Saʿid.[16]

Events in Egypt, Iran, and Lebanon intensified political tensions. These were manifested in sporadic labor strikes and occasional violent demonstrations, against the background of economic distress and widening social gaps. Due to the lack of suitable employment for college and high school graduates, unrest among the students increased. The Colleges of Law and of Pharmacy and Chemistry became focal points of unrest, and Communist and Baʿth activists achieved considerable success among the students; they were even able to compete with the activists of al-Istiqlal and the National Democratic Party.

Given these conditions, many members of the ruling elite hoped that the crowning of King Faysal II in the spring of 1953 would breathe new life into the state, improve the chances for a solution for the economic and social distresses, and reduce the alienation and hostility of the young people and students. It became more and more important that the elections give solid legitimacy to Parliament, so that the government to be established following the elections would be able to ensure that the coronation would be followed by political stability and tranquility.

In order to refute the arguments of the opposition and to reassure British diplomats, without changing the existing method of elections, certain amendments to the Elections Law were introduced in the summer of 1952.[17] The existing election method, however, remained unchanged. These amendments, intended to prevent irregularities in the elections and to limit the ability of local functionaries and notables to interfere with the electoral process and affect its results, were basically cosmetic in nature and did not satisfy the opposition parties. Those parties threatened to boycott the elections if they were run by Nuri's government using the existing indirect method. Jabr contended that, if direct elections were held without the interference of tribal notables and loyalist officials, his party would defeat Nuri.[18]

Given the real fear that if the elections were managed by Nuri, rioting would result and the stability of the regime would be undermined, the regent was faced with two alternatives. Either Nuri and Jabr would reach an understanding and prepare lists of candidates from tribal areas for the regent's approval, or Nuri's government would resign, leaving the elections to be managed by a "neutral" government. As it proved impossible for Nuri and Jabr to agree, the regent opted for the second alternative.[19] In July, Nuri's government resigned and a new government was established under Mustafa al-'Umari, with the primary mission of preparing and conducting the elections to Parliament, according to the amended law that had been rejected by the opposition. The conservative al-'Umari, who had served as minister of the interior in the Muhammad Sadr government in the first half of 1948, was viewed by the opposition as the obedient servant of 'Abd al-Ilah and Nuri al-Sa'id.

Late in October, when the regent returned from a protracted visit to Europe, the opposition parties—al-Istiqlal, the National Democratic Party, and the United Popular Front—presented him with a list of demands. Heading the list was their insistence that the upcoming elections be conducted directly, using a one-stage method.[20] Salih Jabr and the People's Socialist Party did not directly join this offensive, not wishing to be identified with the radical opposition parties; however, they exerted extreme pressure to change the method of the elections.

On November 3, the regent called a meeting of former prime ministers, former senior ministers, and heads of parties in order to discuss the elections. In a spirited debate, Nuri al-Sa'id, Tawfiq al-Suwaydi, the regent, and other politicians defended the existing method of elections, claiming that direct elections were not appropriate to the conditions prevailing in Iraq. By calling that meeting, the regent intended to quell the fervor of the opposition leaders by involving them in the discussion in which they could express themselves and make their positions known, but in which the majority would support the existing indirect method. (The convocation of a forum of former prime ministers, former senior ministers, and senior politicians, a common practice in times of crisis in Iraq, was one of the means the regent used to strengthen his own position. These conferences, held in the Palace, had no official authority. Nevertheless, they had some degree of political importance and reflected both the common consent and the internal contradictions within the elite and the regime.) A tense atmosphere marked the meeting, with the opposition politicians insolently making strong accusations and demanding direct elections and political, social, and economic reforms. The meeting did not achieve any positive results; in fact, it broke up during a heated confrontation between Taha al-Hashimi, the leader of the United Popular Front, and the regent, who hated one another.[21] The positions adopted by the regent and Nuri, who supported holding elections utilizing the existing method (with certain amendments, as stated above), were antithetical to the positions of the opposition leaders, who vigorously demanded change in the method of elections and significant reforms in the regime. The rigidity displayed by Nuri, the regent, and the conservative politicians prevented any possibility of compromise among the elite.

Salih Jabr announced his party's intention of boycotting the elections. The Palace and the British embassy both pressured him to compromise and reconcile with Nuri. Jabr was warned that the tensions between him and Nuri and his insistence on changing the election process were liable to lead to rioting, destabilization, and heightened tensions between Sunnites and Shi'ites. Jabr countered by referring to the coup by the Free Officers that had toppled the Egyptian monarchy and warned the ruling elite that, unless political, economic, and social reforms were instituted, the regime in Iraq would be endangered.

On November 18, a dispute broke out between the students and the dean and faculty of the College of Pharmacy and Chemistry. The next day, the students of all the colleges in Iraq declared an apolitical strike in sympathy with their colleagues. However, when the government met on November 22 to set a date for the elections, the student strike became a wave of riots and demonstrations that were joined by laborers and masses from the poorer strata. Communist activists, as well as young activists from the opposition parties, played a role in provoking the strikes. This was the beginning of a brief period of violence (November 22–24) known as the intifada.[22]

Prime Minister Mustafa al-'Umari submitted his resignation. After an emergency conference with a group of senior Sunni politicians and former prime ministers—Nuri al-Sa'id, Jamil al-Midfa'i, Tawfiq al-Suwaydi, and

'Ali Jawdat al-Ayubi, all Sunnites—the regent assigned Jamil al-Midfa'i, an old, sick Sharifian politician, to the task of establishing a new government.

Later on November 22, the government lost control of the streets of Baghdad. In several places, the demonstrators called for the establishment of a people's government headed by Kamil al-Jadirji, leader of the National Democratic Party. This call came at the initiative of activists of that party, joined by the Communists, who sought in this way to enlist the support of the hesitant opposition parties and contradict the government's claims that the demonstrations resulted from provocation by a tiny group of Communists.

The demonstrators attacked police stations and set fire to them. Policemen were wounded and killed. An angry crowd led by Communist activists burned down the American Library and the offices of the British airline. Masses of demonstrators thronged to the bridges over the Euphrates, which connected the two halves of the city, where bloody clashes between demonstrators and police had taken place during the wathba riots of January 1948. The mayor of the city, who had lost control of the situation, called on the army to intervene and restore order. On the afternoon of November 23, after hearing that the riots had spread to Basra, Kut, 'Amara, Najaf, and other cities, and after Jamil al-Midfa'i had failed in his attempts to establish a government, the regent ordered his chief of staff, Nur al-Din Mahmud, to establish an emergency government and impose order. Nur al-Din Mahmud imposed a partial curfew on Baghdad, forbade any activity by political parties, and closed the newspapers, schools, and colleges. This was not a military coup but the active intervention by an army loyal to the Palace and the regime, which had been called in by the regent to rescue the regime and the ruling elite. Nur al-Din Mahmud had no personal political ambitions, and he clearly understood that his new government, consisting of senior politicians and technocrats, was only temporary, intended solely to restore order and conduct elections.

On November 24, mass arrests of the organizers and participants in the demonstrations began. The heads of the opposition parties were also arrested, including Kamil al-Jadirji, Faiq al-Samarai, deputy chairman of al-Istiqlal, and key politicians from the People's Socialist Party headed by Salih Jabr. At the same time, in order to restore calm, Nur al-Din Mahmud announced that his government would establish a committee to examine the election process, with a view to adopting direct elections. At first glance, this appeared to be an achievement by the opposition. However, it rapidly transpired that, even under direct elections, Nuri, 'Abd al-Ilah, and the conservatives were able to preserve their dominance and keep the majority in Parliament in the hands of their conservative supporters.

The elections for Parliament were held on January 17, 1953.[23] The opposition parties boycotted the elections, claiming that any election under a military government, with strict censorship of the press and prohibition of party activities, was worthless and that the results of such an election were known in advance. Despite the boycott, the lax structure of the political parties enabled some of their members to run as independent candidates. Due to their total control of the state apparatus, their connections with the tribal notables, and the boycott, the Constitutional Union Party and the supporters of Nuri and the regent were assured an absolute majority.

Nuri al-Saʿid enjoyed the support of 90 of the 135 elected delegates, most of whom (77) were automatically elected, with no one from their areas running against them (66 of the delegates were major landowners and tribal notables). This majority, however, could not ensure stability, given the political and social ferment that had been encouraged and exploited by the opposition.

The intifada of 1952, like the wathba of 1948, was a violent outburst by young members of the effendiyya, especially by angry and frustrated students desperately seeking political and social change and by the masses from the poorer strata. The personal frustration and economic insecurity experienced by the effendiyya, due to the shortage of employment opportunities for college graduates, along with the difficult economic conditions of the working people and the poorer strata, constituted the background for the outbreak of riots. The leaders of the legal opposition parties were dragged into the events but were unable to lead or transform the riots into political achievements. Even the one major achievement—the change in the method of elections—did not yield the anticipated results for the opposition.

The intifada stressed the dependence of the regime and the ruling elite on the army, the tribal landowners, and the tribes in general. The regime, assisted by the army, coped with the riots relatively easily, but its conservative tendencies increased, reducing its ability to adapt to new conditions requiring far-ranging changes and reforms.

The task assigned to the new government headed by Jamil al-Midfaʿi was to enable the peaceful, orderly transfer of authority from the hands of the regent, ʿAbd al-Ilah, to those of the new king, Faysal II.[24] The coronation in May 1953 was met with limited, short-lived enthusiasm, which could not diminish the rising alienation of the effendiyya vis-à-vis the regime and the ruling elite. Al-Midfaʿi was asked to continue in office until the young king could find a candidate who had a chance of setting up a government that could cope with Iraq's complex problems. His weak government had difficulty dealing with the continued political and social tensions and unrest among the young people and in the prisons where radical political activists and participants in the intifada had been sent. Finding a strong prime minister who could stabilize the situation and calm the populace became more and more urgent.

The Fadhil al-Jamali Government, 1953–1954: Attempts at Reforms within the Framework of the Monarchy and Their Frustration by the Conservative Forces

The young king was surrounded by a band of conservative politicians and Palace officials, headed by his uncle, Crown Prince ʿAbd al-Ilah, who had remained the "strong man in the Palace." Faysal had difficulty finding a suitable prime minister who could function despite the rivalry between Nuri al-Saʿid and Salih Jabr. Assigning the task of forming the government to Nuri might have led to escalation of that tension and, as a result, to riots in Baghdad. It was obvious that, in such a case, Jabr would adopt an extremist stance and would raise the level of tension so far as to risk the outbreak of violence both in Baghdad and among the Shiʿites. On the other hand, Nuri's majority in Parliament and the support given to him by the tribal landowners would enable him to frustrate any moves by Jabr, should the task of forming the government be assigned to the latter. The depth of the rift between them meant that the two could not possibly be expected to serve in the same government. The other candidates—Hikmat Sulayman, Ahmad Mukhtar Baban, ʿAli Mumtaz, Tawfiq al-Suwaydi, and the Shiʿite Nasrat al-Farisi—had only minimal chances of succeeding in establishing a government.

On September 15, in a surprising move, King Faysal II designated a relatively young (52) Shiʿite politician, Fadhil al-Jamali, as prime minister.[25] Al-Jamali, a man who combined pan-Arab nationalism with rightist-liberalist views, had held several key positions in Iraq's education system during the 1930s and had helped to shape the nationalist content of that system. In 1940 and 1941, al-Jamali had held the post of inspector-general of education in the Rashid ʿAli government. Notwithstanding his cooperation with Rashid ʿAli, Nuri had adopted him as his protégé and had enabled him to return to politics. After World War II, al-Jamali had held a number of posts in foreign service and had served as foreign minister in the governments headed by Nuri and Jabr between 1946 and 1948.

Al-Jamali was arguably the most intellectual of the Iraqi ministers. He had acquired his academic education in the United States, at Columbia University, where in 1932 he had earned a Ph.D. on the subject of "The New Iraq: Its Problem of Bedouin Education." Al-Jamali was one of the members of the ruling elite who understood the need for development, modernization, creation of jobs for high school and college graduates, and integration of members of the effendiyya into state institutions and the political system. However, his liberal reformist tendencies were quite moderate, and despite the differences in their outlook, he was close to Nuri al-Saʿid and belonged to the conservative sector of the ruling elite. Al-Jamali tried to find the golden mean between Arab nationalism and conservative liberalism, while supporting development and moderate reforms. On the basis of his nationalist anti-British attitude and in accordance with his belief that the development of Iraq should be accelerated, he sought to reinforce the ties between Iraq and the United States and ensure American military, economic, and political assistance to Iraq.

Between 1951 and 1953, al-Jamali tried to bring about a reconciliation between Nuri and Jabr. In the summer of 1953, following Faysal's coronation, al-Jamali's own status increased; he served as a member of the delegation that accompanied the young king on his first visit to Jordan. By designating al-Jamali prime minister, Faysal hoped to reassure and gain the trust of the younger, educated members of the middle stratum as well as the Shiʿites. Indeed, the government established by al-Jamali was characterized by a large number of relatively young technocrats among its members. Eight of the seventeen ministers in his government were Shiʿites—the largest number of Shiʿites in any government in the history of Iraq.

The principal weakness of that government lay in its lack of parliamentary support. Nuri showed reservations about al-Jamali's appointment and feared that his tendency toward political liberalization would be exploited by the opposition and Communist parties to incite riots and undermine the stability of the regime. While it is true that four of the ministers in al-Jamali's government were members of the Constitutional Union Party, they were appointed on a personal basis and not as party representatives. The opposition parties, the National Democratic Party and al-Istiqlal, objected to al-Jamali's appointment and demanded disbandment of Parliament and the holding of new elections. Salih Jabr displayed a moderate attitude toward the government; however, beginning in December 1953, his party began to make more stringent demands and increased its opposition to the government. On the other hand, the al-Jamali government included two ministers from the United Popular Front, which was a loosely structured organization of conservative, opportunist politicians united by a common hatred of Nuri al-Saʿid.

The first measures adopted by the government included cancellation of the state of emergency and the censorship that had been imposed on the press. As part of the ensuing process of political liberalization, the penalties which had been imposed on students and teachers who had participated in the intifada were reduced or canceled entirely. In an effort to bring about a change in the economic situation of the poorer strata and to calm the student population, immediate measures were taken in several areas:[26]

1. One million dinars was allocated to construction projects for the benefit of the homeless.
2. Thirty thousand dinars was allocated for vocational retraining and advanced study courses for students and graduates of the College of Law who had difficulty finding employment and constituted a constant focus of antigovernment unrest.
3. Rent on small residential units was reduced.
4. Postal fees were reduced.

At the same time, social security programs were implemented for industrial workers, widows, and orphans. Plans were made for the expansion of Basra Port, the construction of an additional port in Umm Qasr, the extension of Iraq's road network, and the construction of dams.

The government's objectives included developing Iraq's resources; economic and social development and modernization; and improvement of the living conditions and economic situation of the general populace:

1. Expansion of the stratum of minor landowners by allocating some state lands to landless or nearly landless fellahin.
2. Changes in the taxation system, so as to achieve a more progressive distribution of the tax burden.
3. Preservation of the value of salaries paid to employees in civil service and the public sector.
4. Expansion of social services.[27]

The motivating force behind the economic and social programs and attempts at their implementation was the minister of finance, ʿAbd al-Karim al-Uzri. A talented Shiʿite technocrat who played a central role in setting up the Development Board of Iraq, Al-Uzri had already served as minister of finance in the Tawfiq al-Suwaydi government in 1950.[28]

The programs of the al-Jamali government aroused the opposition of the tribal landowners, who were afraid of any move that could be interpreted as an attempt at agrarian reform; they considered even a limited distribution of state lands to be threatening. The tribal landowners, as well as the landowning urban notables, wanted to prevent a precedent involving the distribution of lands and to continue to benefit from the cheap labor of landless fellahin. The plans for changes in the taxation system caused the major landowners to fear that the generous provisions from which they benefited would be reduced.

Nuri al-Saʿid expressed severe criticism of the programs and policies of the al-Jamali government and stated his fears that the changes in taxation and the distribution of lands to the landless fellahin would arouse the wrath of the major tribal landowners, most of whom were Shi'ites. Such a situation would alienate them from the regime, thus undermining one of its mainstays. Nuri's fears reflected not only his personal views but also the quandary affecting the ruling elite, which had become more and more dependent on the major landowners, precisely when it should have been able to show flexibility, given the rising modern social forces.

The al-Jamali government was in a "no-win" situation. It was under attack by Nuri and the conservative majority in Parliament and among the ruling elite. In addition, the younger members of the effendiyya and the opposition parties considered al-Jamali to be a protégé of Nuri al-Sa'id and did not trust his plans for reform. Nor did the weak Iraqi bourgeoisie grant its support to al-Jamali. Most of Iraq's industrialists and entrepreneurs belonged to or were related to the elite; they did not constitute an independent political force that could have supported the changes in line with their interests in creating appropriate conditions for development and industrialization.

While Shi'ites responded favorably to the appointment of one of their own as prime minister, in this case his ethnic origin was less important than his class interests and class identity. The Shi'ite tribal landowners who were linked to Nuri (a Sunnite) and the conservative sectors of the political elite felt that al-Jamali's planned reforms were liable to harm their own interests and undermine the status quo. Although his liberal and reformist tendencies were genuine, al-Jamali wanted to avoid confrontation with the tribal landowners and did not try to take away their status or the privileges accorded to them under law.

Not even the young king could save the al-Jamali government. Like all of the elite, Faysal was dependent upon extremely conservative elements.

In February 1954, a controversy broke out between Nuri and al-Uzri with regard to financing the construction of new army camps. Al-Uzri demanded that the defense budget be used to finance the military construction, whereas Nuri insisted that the financing should come from the development budget. This dispute over the budget forced the al-Jamali government to resign on March 8, 1954, whereupon the king asked al-Jamali to form a new government.

His second government was even weaker than its predecessor. Under pressure by Nuri and 'Abd al-Ilah, al-Jamali moved al-Uzri to the Ministry of Development, which was dependent upon the Ministry of Finance. Immediately following its establishment, the second al-Jamali government was forced to contend with inter-Arab tension, dealing with Egypt's allegations that Iraq intended to become a party to a treaty signed between Turkey and Pakistan. The Egyptian allegations, which set off a conflict between Egypt and Iraq that was to last from 1954 to 1958, found a sympathetic audience among the young, nationalist, radical members of the effendiyya in Baghdad.

Al-Jamali did not succeed in actually promoting any significant reform. The only area in which he managed to realize his policies to some degree concerned Iraq's relations with the United States, which had agreed to supply arms to Iraq. However, although Secretary of State John Foster Dulles was prepared to accede to some of al-Jamali's requests, the United States was not yet ready for full involvement and responsibility for Western interests in the Middle East. Accordingly, the United States was not prepared to become Iraq's chief ally. This was especially true in light of the fact that such a move could have provoked the mistrust of Britain, then Iraq's major ally within the Western bloc.

The second al-Jamali government resigned on April 29, 1954. The direct reason for the resignation was Parliament's refusal to approve the government's request for a special budget to cover activity in Syria. Al-Jamali, in accordance with his pan-Arab nationalist views, attempted to maintain active Iraqi involvement in Syria for the purpose of establishing a federation or union with it. Nuri—who considered a regional treaty with the West to be a central element in his political strategy—viewed allocation of funds for the support of pro-Iraqi elements in Syria as a dangerous waste of money. The al-Jamali government (as well as al-Jamali personally) was also accused of having failed in its handling of the heavy spring floods that had swept over Baghdad and caused considerable damage. (Since the dawn of history, the seasonal floods each autumn and spring, with the melting of the snows from the Zagros Mountains, had been one of the challenges weighing heavily on all of the regimes governing the Mesopotamian plains.) However, the basic reasons for the failure of the al-Jamali government were the objections of the major tribal landowners to any reform and the dominance of conservative attitudes among the ruling elite. This was the last attempt by liberal reformist entities within the elite to bring about moderate and controlled reforms within the framework of the regime.

Nuri's Return as Prime Minister: A Victory for Conservative Forces

Despite the majority held by Nuri and the Constitutional Union Party in Parliament, which enabled them to bring about al-Jamali's resignation as prime minister, the new government was established, at the end of April 1954, by Arshad al-'Umari, an associate of Crown Prince 'Abd al-Ilah. The relationship between 'Abd al-Ilah and Nuri was a complex one, involving both rivalry and mutual dependency. 'Abd al-Ilah, still the "strong man in the

Palace" even after the coronation of Faysal II, used intrigue and pressure on key politicians to prevent Nuri from establishing a government.

Arshad al-ʿUmari clearly understood that his government was being established for the purpose of holding new elections. In preparing for the elections, the National Democratic Party and al-Istiqlal set up the National Front as an electoral bloc. The Front was joined by additional organizations, such as the "Partisans of Peace," the Bar Association, the Medical Association, and various labor unions, all of which had been established by activists of the Communist Party, whose activity was prohibited under law.

The elections took place on June 9, under the new one-stage direct method. Thirty-eight of the delegates were elected by consent (*tazkiya*), meaning that they were the sole candidates in tribal electoral areas, and ninety-seven delegates were elected by majority vote. The Constitutional Union Party received fifty-one seats, the People's Socialist Party twenty-one seats, the National Bloc nine seats (seven of them belonging to the National Democratic Party and two to al-Istiqlal), and the United Popular Front a single seat. In addition, fifty-four independent delegates were elected.[29] This was an achievement for the opposition parties, especially the People's Socialist Party (led by Salih Jabr) and the National Democratic Party—both of which, notwithstanding efforts by the authorities, had succeeded in significantly increasing their strength and power.

Despite the change in the method of elections, the Constitutional Union Party succeeded in maintaining its status as the largest party in Parliament. Although it did not receive a majority (51 out of 135 members of Parliament), the influence exerted by Nuri and ʿAbd al-Ilah on most of the independent delegates, who represented tribal and rural areas, ensured that Parliament would remain under their control. Nuri viewed the results of the elections as unacceptable. He was unwilling to content himself with a majority based on the independent delegates, some of whom maintained close ties with ʿAbd al-Ilah; he expressed his fury and disgust at party politics and at the failure of the Constitutional Union Party to secure an absolute majority.[30] Nuri was afraid that, in light of the growing rivalry between them, ʿAbd al-Ilah would attempt to detract from his power by supporting other conservative politicians.

The elections did not liberate the Iraqi political system from its "no-win" situation. Nuri was not prepared to establish a government without an absolute majority in Parliament, whereas Salih Jabr was incapable of forming a government because of the strength of Nuri's supporters. Other politicians might have been able to establish a government, but only if they could win the support of both Nuri and ʿAbd al-Ilah. The structure of Iraqi society and the support given to Nuri by the tribal notables, especially the tribal land-owners, as well as Nuri's influence on the state apparatus, enabled him and the conservative forces to retain dominance even under the direct method of elections.

In such a situation, with the threat of renewed rioting and the possible collapse of the regime hovering over Iraq and its ruling elite, 'Abd al-Ilah attempted to establish a dialogue with Nuri. Faysal II and 'Abd al-Ilah were also subjected to British pressure to restore Nuri as prime minister. The British saw the danger clearly: The regime depended on one older politician, Nuri, who, while capable of establishing a stable government, was despised by many members of the middle stratum and the elite alike. Nonetheless, they believed that there was no other choice.

'Abd al-Ilah met with Nuri, who was vacationing in Paris.[31] (During the summer months, when the heat of Baghdad was most oppressive, Nuri frequently took vacations in London and Paris.) Nuri agreed to return as prime minister, provided that the recently elected Parliament was disbanded and new elections were conducted, in order to ensure that he would receive an absolute majority. (An additional condition raised by Nuri was that 'Abd al-Ilah would cease to be involved in Syrian affairs. Nuri believed that this could only harm Iraq's status in Syria and lead to dangerous entanglements. As he saw it, reinforcing Iraq's regional status and internal stability would lead Syria to strengthen its ties with Iraq or even to establish a federation.)

Immediately following the formation of the new government in August, Nuri disbanded the Constitutional Union Party. Nuri, disappointed at the failure of the Constitutional Union Party to obtain an absolute majority and contemptuous of party politics, believed he would be able to organize such a majority without having recourse to a party, by adopting a political course that relied on the notables and on traditional patronage. The disbandment of the party allowed him to approach Salih Jabr and propose that his People's Socialist Party disband as well. The talks held between Nuri's intimates and the People's Socialist Party leaders led to a rift between those party figures who were prepared to cooperate with Nuri and those who insisted on continued party activity. Eventually, some of the People's Socialist Party leaders actually announced that they were disbanding. In response, those leaders who opposed cooperation with Nuri and did not agree to participate in the elections decided to expel any politicians who did. This included Salih Jabr himself, who had decided to take part in the elections. The party collapsed.

Following a decision by al-Istiqlal to take part in the elections and a decision by the National Democratic Party to boycott them, the National Front, which had been established in preparation for the June elections, also disbanded. This action resulted from the belief that there was no justification for the disbandment of Parliament and that the holding of elections by Nuri's government would guarantee the results of those elections in advance.[32] (Al-Istiqlal leader Muhammad Mahdi Kubba had already gained Nuri's support and knew that his own place in Parliament was automatically ensured.)

As the elections approached, Nuri took steps to limit the activity of the opposition parties, and he intensified suppression of Communist activity. By order of the government, eighteen newspapers were closed. The license of the National Democratic Party was revoked, and its periodical, *Sawt al-Ahali,* was closed for a year.[33]

The election results were a foregone conclusion. One hundred and thirteen members of Parliament were elected without opposition as the sole candidates in their areas. Potential opposing candidates had withdrawn after receiving threats. Of the delegates elected, forty-eight had previously belonged to the Constitutional Union Party. A majority of the remaining delegates, who were elected as independents, were supported by the government and supporters of Nuri. Nine were associates of Salih Jabr, who had been expelled from the People's Socialist Party, and two were representatives of al-Istiqlal. Al-Istiqlal leader Muhammad Mahdi Kubba was elected by consent, with no competing candidate in his area.[34] The National Democratic Party boycotted the elections, but one of its members, Mas'ud Muhammad al-Jalabi, was elected as an independent candidate in an area with a largely Kurdish population, Koysanjaq, near Irbil.

The opposition was but weakly represented in the new Parliament. In this way, the conservative forces of the regime prevented those politicians within the elite who wished to implement reform within the regime from achieving any effective means of expression. Even more important, it denied any political voice to the modern middle stratum; increasing numbers of this stratum viewed the regime with hostility and alienation. Following the elections in September 1954, Nuri's absolute control of Parliament was assured until the fall of the regime in July 1958.

Despite the coordination between Nuri and 'Abd al-Ilah and their common conservative interests, the relations between them continued to be tense. Nuri, seeking a way to remove 'Abd al-Ilah from the political arena of Iraq, again toyed with the idea (which he had originally raised in 1945 and again in 1948) of appointing him as Iraqi ambassador to Britain or the United States. Meanwhile, 'Abd al-Ilah endeavored to bolster his own status within Iraq as the "strong man in the Palace."

Nuri, 'Abd al-Ilah, and the conservative politicians hoped that Iraq's large income from the export of petroleum would enable solutions to the country's socioeconomic distress without detracting from the status, economic, and social advantages of the tribal notables and landowners and without having to implement agrarian reform. Nuri believed that the support of the military and the tribal notables, combined with Western assistance in the framework of a regional defense treaty, would enable the regime to survive without implementing any real reforms or transformations.

However, suppression of the opposition and freezing of political life in Iraq prevented the new social and ideological forces—and particularly the new middle stratum—from achieving political expression or representation in the framework of the existing regime. At the same time, the regime's growing reliance on the conservative tribal landowners limited its ability to adapt to the new social and ideological conditions and prevented the launching of the reforms intended to adjust the regime to the changes taking place in the Middle East and throughout the world. Thus the incompatibility between the regime and the political system, on one hand, and the social conditions and ideological climate, on the other, not only persisted but continued to grow.

The Monarchy in Iraq versus the Radical Revolutionary Forces in the Arab World, 1954–1958

Now, after guaranteeing the automatic support of the absolute majority in Parliament, neutralizing the political parties, and robbing them of the ability to interfere with his moves, Nuri al-Saʿid could devote most of his energies to foreign policy. Primarily he wished establish a pro-Western defense treaty to reinforce Iraq's international status and help maintain its political regime and domestic status quo. He sought a central role for Iraq as the link between the Arab and non-Arab states in the area and the Western powers. The regional defense treaty was intended to secure Western backing and support for Iraq and its regime, replacing the bilateral treaty with Britain, which was about to expire. That treaty had become a political issue within Iraq; it was the focus of nationalist irritation and antigovernment criticism in the political arena and among the politically aware segments of the Iraqi public. Initially, Nuri attempted to reach his goals while cooperating with Egypt, hoping that by doing so, he would succeed in reinforcing Iraq's status in the inter-Arab arena while weakening domestic opposition to his moves within Iraq. At the same time, however, Nuri was taking measures of his own that were intended to lead to the signing of the treaty, even at the price of conflict with Egypt.

Between 1950 and 1958, with the global cold war and the rise of the radical revolutionary political forces in the Arab states, the upper strata and the ruling elite in Iraq became increasingly fearful of communism and pan-Arab radicalism. Under these conditions, the complex nature of the link between Iraq's regional foreign policy and the state of the Iraqi upper strata and ruling political elite became clear. Iraq's weakness, stemming from the heterogeneous composition of its population, its geopolitical position, the situation of its ruling elite in the face of rising social tensions, and its fear of the Soviet Union and the radical forces were the main motivations guiding Iraq's regional policy, especially its desire to create regional defense treaties: the Saʿdabad Pact of 1937 and the Baghdad Pact of 1955.

The Conflict between the Neutralist and the Pro-Western Orientations and Its Social Context, 1949–1954

The debate regarding international orientation within the reality of the global cold war was one of the central topics on Iraq's political agenda between 1949 and 1954. The dominant orientation among the elite and the regime, whose major supporters included Crown Prince 'Abd al-Ilah, Faysal I (1921–33), Faysal II (1953–58), Prime Ministers Nuri al-Sa'id, Tawfiq al-Suwaydi, Fadhil al-Jamali, Jamil al-Midfa'i, Arshad al-'Umari, and others, traditionally supported alliance with the West, maintaining ideological sympathy and a feeling of common destiny with the conservative forces. This was the traditional approach of the regime and the conservative trend among the political ruling elite, who viewed Britain as Iraq's ally against its strong and threatening neighbors, Iran and Turkey, and against the perceived threat from the Soviet Union and the Communists. Members of the upper socioeconomic stratum and the ruling elite considered Britain the mainstay of the regime, protecting it from external threats and maintaining the domestic status quo in the face of ethnic, Shi'ite, and Kurdish forces and the new social forces with their radical political orientation.

At the end of World War II, Nuri, 'Abd al-Ilah, and the conservative politicians began to fear the possibility of Soviet cooperation with the Kurds and a Soviet invasion of Iraq through Kurdistan. The fears of the upper stratum and its political elite increased following the war, with the development of the cold war and the threat of World War III on one hand, and on the other, the increased social and political tension and the reinforcement of the radical currents and social unrest within Iraq. These fears reached a zenith at the time of the Korean War (1949–53), and following the contemporaneous Iranian crisis under Mossadeq marked by the Iranian Communist Party's growing strength between 1949 and 1952.

Nuri al-Sa'id, with his conservative, dogmatic political and social views, saw communism and the radical movements as threats to Iraq, its regime, and the Arab nation in general. From the beginning of the cold war, he repeatedly argued that the Arabs were incapable of remaining neutral in the interbloc struggle and that they must throw in their lot with the West. In the last half of 1950, against the background of the Korean War, the development of the nuclear balance of terror and reinforcement of the neutralist orientations in Asia and the Arab states, Nuri gave a series of public lectures. He argued that Iraqi and Arab national interests called for identification and alliance with the Western bloc and rejected neutralism as an orientation in the interbloc conflict.[1] Nuri sought to prepare Iraqis to accept an alliance with the West and to block the neutralist sentiments that had been steadily increasing among the modern middle stratum. These neutralist positions became an inseparable part of Arab nationalist trends, which had begun to assume a leftist radical nature. The threat of Soviet invasion of Iraq in the framework of a third world war and the risk of a nuclear holocaust reinforced not only the pro-Western leanings of the ruling elite and the regime in Iraq, but also the leanings toward neutralism as well. This neutralist orientation gained the support of those politicians from among the elite who headed opposition parties and proved popular as well—primarily among students and the modern middle stratum.

Neutralism as an approach—or, rather, as the common factor in a variety of ideological and political approaches—resulted from the growth of anticolonialist national movements in Asian and African countries. These movements, which led the struggle for independence and against poverty and backwardness, were actually capable of distinguishing between the anticolonialist trends of the United States and the Soviet Union and the veteran colonialist trends of Britain and France. Nonetheless, under the conditions of the cold war and faced with the threat of a nuclear world war, they maintained an attitude of alienation and reservations vis-à-vis both blocs.

The roots of neutralism went back to the alienation experienced during and after World War I by Westernized, educated population segments in the Asian and African colonies. Dominated by the Western powers, the Asian and African communities felt disconnected from international power struggles and ideological conflicts between primarily European and American forces. After World War II, and principally from the late 1940s, with the exacerbation of the cold war and the threat of a global nuclear disaster, neutralist trends developed rapidly among national anticolonial movements in the Asian countries and gradually spread to British and French colonies in Africa as well. The neutralist concept held that most people, living in poverty in colonies or postcolonial states in Asia and Africa, had no interest in the struggle between the Great Powers and the ideological debate between communism and capitalism. Accordingly, the independent states of Asia and the national movements of Asia and Africa should unite, in order to prevent the risk of nuclear holocaust and to put an end to the dangerous interbloc struggle that was wasting the resources essential to modernization, development, and solutions for the poverty and backwardness of most of the world.

In April 1955, a conference of neutralist or nonaligned states took place in Bandung, Indonesia. The participants in this conference—which constituted an important milestone in the development of the neutralist or nonaligned bloc—included Asian states, Arab states, and Yugoslavia. (The conference was also attended by delegates from several states identified with one or the other bloc, such as Communist China and Iraq, with its explicit pro-Western orientation.) Prime Minister Nehru of India (who, more than any other leader, was identified with neutralism as an approach and contributed to its development), President Sukarno of Indonesia, President Tito of Yugoslavia (which had withdrawn from the Soviet bloc in 1948), and President Gamal 'Abd al-Nasir of Egypt played central roles in the conference.

In the United States and the Soviet Union, attitudes toward the neutralism policy varied. Following Stalin's death in 1953 and Khrushchev's rise to power in 1954, a transformation had taken place in the Soviet Union's rigid ideological doctrine, accompanied by a willingness to compromise and thaw the cold war. Accordingly, the Soviet Union now developed a flexible, sympathetic approach to the neutralist states. The rulers and elites of the postcolonial states in Asia and Africa, forced to contend with poverty and backwardness, as well as with the weakness and undeveloped national character of their states, were attracted by the centralist, etatist model presented by the Soviet Union. The Soviet willingness to supply arms and assist in the development and construction of large infrastructural projects, unaffected by considerations of economic feasibility, helped the USSR to develop ties with the neutralist states. By contrast, the reinforcement of rigid conservative, anti-Communist trends in the United States under Harry Truman (1945–52) and Dwight D. Eisenhower (1952–60) cast a shadow over the relations between the United States and the neutralist countries, which was to dissipate only following the election of John F. Kennedy in 1960.

Against the background of the central role played by Iraq in the establishment of the pro-Western Baghdad Pact in the Middle East in 1955 and in light of Iraq's explicit pro-Western image, the debate that took place in Baghdad on the question of neutralism and international orientation has not been given appropriate historical coverage.

From the beginning of the interbloc conflict and the cold war, the modern middle stratum of Iraq, and especially its student population, was increasingly affected by neutralist sentiments, rooted in nationalist anti-British tendencies, feelings of disgust and alienation toward the ruling elite and the regime, and the reinforcement of leftist attitudes. The West was perceived as the mainstay of the despised elite and the hated rulers, who were collectively blamed for Iraq's backwardness, poverty, and social misery.[2] The anticolonial wars in Southeast Asia—the Viet Minh against French rule in Indochina, the Indonesian struggle against Holland, and the Malay revolt against Britain—gained Iraqi sympathy. The United States, despite its anticolonialist tradition, was perceived as the ally of hated Britain and a supporter of Israel; accordingly, the feelings of nationalist hatred were directed against the United States as well. With the rise in interbloc tension as a result of the Korean War, articles appeared in the Iraqi press in 1950 and 1951 which stressed the need to establish a third, neutralist power, with which the Arab states could ally themselves.[3]

The political forces that supported neutrality were those of the veteran opposition parties, the National Democratic Party and al-Istiqlal. The position adopted by the National Democratic Party stemmed from its social-democratic, anticolonialist ideological concepts. In the case of the nationalist rightist, anti-Communist, and anti-Soviet al-Istiqlal, the support of neutralism was derived from its nationalist anti-British position. The demand for a neutralist policy was one of the main slogans of the United Popular Front, which called for absolute neutralism in the conflict between West and East.[4] This definitive stand resulted both from the nationalist outlook of Taha al-Hashimi and other party leaders and from the need to compete with al-Istiqlal and the National Democratic Party in winning over the modern middle stratum and the students. In actual practice, its position was less definitive than the public pronouncements of its leaders. Some of its foremost politicians noted, in conversations with British and American diplomats, that Iraq's basic interest lay in an alliance with the West and that neutralism was impractical. Taha al-Hashimi even attempted to find a strange compromise, claiming that there need be no contradiction between Iraq's neutralist orientation and the presence of British military forces on Iraqi soil.

Salih Jabr and the People's Socialist Party, seeking to represent the main alternative to Nuri al-Sa'id and the Constitutional Union Party, but without identifying with the radical oppositionist parties, adopted an ambivalent position regarding neutralism. Although the People's Socialist Party supported the nationalist demand for the expulsion of all foreign (i.e., British) forces from Iraq, it refrained from joining the opposition parties in their support of a neutralist policy. Jabr endeavored to adopt a radical image when dealing with the young members of the effendiyya, while representing himself to Western diplomats, tribal landowners, and the ruling elite as reliably pro-Western.

The supporters of the neutralist orientation in Iraq had little chance of success, since the debate on Iraq's foreign policy was part of a political and social conflict focusing on the issue of the electoral system and attempts to present an alternative to Nuri al-Sa'id and the most conservative elements of the elite and the regime. The liberal-reform politicians and political forces who had tried to promote reforms by changing the method of elections had not succeeded in undermining the dominance of Nuri al-Sa'id, 'Abd al-Ilah, and the conservative forces. Since pro-Western politicians headed the Iraqi government between 1950 and 1954 when the question of neutralism started appearing on the political agenda, in fact, the debate on the orientation of Iraq's foreign policy was settled in favor of the treaty with the West. Supporters of neutralism expressed their opposition to this policy in newspaper articles, in the demands of the opposition parties, and in the mood of the young effendiyya. However, Nuri al-Sa'id's reelection as prime minister in August 1954 and his suppression of the opposition parties put an end to domestic objections to complete identification with the West, enabling accelerated Iraqi activity toward drawing up a pro-Western treaty. This activity bore fruit in 1955 when the treaty between Iraq and Turkey was signed; later in the same year, the Baghdad Pact was established.

Iraq and the Establishment of the Baghdad Pact, 1954–1955

The question of the orientation adopted by the Arab states in the global interbloc conflict following the end of World War II had been one of the main points of dispute between Iraq and Egypt ever since the establishment of the Arab League. The dispute on interbloc orientation and the question of which of the two states would lead the Arab states in the global arena reflected their rivalry for dominance of the Arab world.

Iraq's aim to establish a pro-Western regional defense treaty resulted from its geopolitical status, the social and political conditions prevailing within it, and the reality of the interbloc conflict and the cold war in the 1950s and their effect on the international and regional arena. Iraq aimed for the integration of members of the Arab League into the Western bloc and the conclusion of an alliance with the non-Arab states of the northern Middle East, Turkey and Iran, which had signed the Sa'dabad Pact with Iraq in 1938. Turkey and Iran shared with Iraq a common interest in blocking the national separatist movements among the Kurds and a common fear of the Soviet Union and communism. Iraq's role in the regional defense organization based on the Arab Collective Security Pact combined with its position in the Sa'dabad Pact was intended to give Iraq a leading role among the Arab states and to reinforce its status in the eyes of its neighbors and future partners in this alliance, Turkey, Iran, and Pakistan. By attaining a key position in a regional defense alliance, the Iraqi heads of state sought to strengthen its position as a counterbalance to the Egyptian dominance of the Arab League. The establishment of a regional defense alliance was intended to assuage the anxiety of the elite and the regime in Iraq regarding the threat posed by communism and the radical forces. Nuri also hoped that the centrality of Iraq in the regional defense alliance would reinforce Iraq's status in Syria. He believed that, if Iraq could demonstrate internal stability and power in the international arena, Syria would be more willing to cement relations between the two states and create conditions allowing a union between them. By establishing a regional defense alliance with the participation of Britain, Nuri and the supporters of his program sought to solve the problem of the treaty signed in 1930 between Britain and Iraq. Scheduled to expire in 1957, this treaty had constituted a constant strain on the relations between the two states and on Iraqi domestic politics. In this way, the Iraqi heads of state hoped to find a way out of the despised British-Iraqi treaty and thus to put an end to the nationalist unrest provoked by it, without losing continued British strategic support and assistance to Iraq or changing the status quo.

Whereas Iraq hoped to achieve an alliance among the Arab states, the Western powers, Turkey, and Iran, and retain room for maneuvering concerning bilateral treaties and arrangements, Egypt insisted that no Arab state should sign any treaty with any state that was not a member of the League. According to Egypt, the Arab states were expected to maintain a coordinated, united policy, which would give them power and bargaining strength under the conditions of the interbloc struggle. The Egyptian position was intended to reinforce the power of the Arab League and the status of Egypt itself as the central force within the League, while strengthening its position and bargaining ability in the framework of the problematic negotiations between Egypt and Britain.

In the autumn of 1949, Egypt launched the initiative for a collective security agreement among the Arab states (Mithak al-Diman al-Jama'i al-'Arabi—the Treaty of Joint Defense and Economic Cooperation, or Arab Collective Security Pact).[5] The initiative arose against the background of Egypt's rivalry with Iraq for leadership in the Arab world, which at the time was expressed in terms of acute competition for influence in Syria. Following the rise to power of pro-Iraqi forces in Damascus, the chances for establishing a federation or union between Syria and Iraq increased. The Egyptian initiative was intended to weaken the argument, advanced by Iraq and its supporters in Syria, to the effect that federation with Iraq was essential to Syria in light of the threat posed by Israel.[6]

Iraq expressed its objection to Article 10 of the pact, which stated that "every signatory undertakes not to conclude any international agreement which contradicts this Pact and not to adopt, in its international relations, any position counter to the spirit hereof." Iraq feared—and, from its point of view, justifiably so—that this article would adversely affect its ability to maintain an independent policy vis-à-vis establishing an alliance with the Western bloc and the non-Arab states in the region. As an alternative, Nuri suggested a treaty between the Arab states and the West (in addition to his proposal for reorganizing the League, intended to limit the powers of the Egyptian secretary of the League, 'Abd al-Rahman 'Azzam). Eventually, following the introduction of certain amendments to the Pact, Iraq signed it in 1951, out of a desire to prevent its isolation in the Arab world.

Starting in the last half of 1950, in light of the Korean war, the crisis in Iran, the breakdown in British-Egyptian negotiations, and the heating up of the cold war, Britain and the United States began establishing a regional defense alliance in the Middle East. In September 1951, they proposed creating the Middle East Command, the founding members of which were to be the United States, Britain, France, Turkey, and Egypt. The proposal was deleterious to Iraq's status, as Egypt was included as the senior Arab state and the only Arab founder of the organization. This was a slap in the face for Nuri, who had believed that Iraq should be the senior Arab ally of the Western bloc and had invested efforts to achieve this goal. Nonetheless, when Egypt rejected the Western proposal, Nuri attempted to mediate between Egypt and Britain to reinforce Iraq's status.[7]

Following the rejection of the Middle East Command by Egypt and the member states of the Arab League, who insistently repeated that the Arab Collective Security Pact must constitute the basis for any undertaking between the Arab states and the Western bloc, Britain and United States proposed a new plan for establishing the Middle East Defense Organization (MEDO) in June 1952. Again, Egypt rather than Iraq was slated to play the role of Arab founder and senior Arab partner. This situation, in turn, raised Iraqi reservations about the new plan. Nuri, who in 1953 was serving as minister of defense in the Jamil al-Midfaʻi government, proposed to the commander of the British forces in the Middle East, General Brian Robertson, that if Egypt refused to join MEDO, Iraq would sign a defense agreement with the United States and Britain. At the same time, he emphasized that, given the prevailing sentiments of public opinion in the Arab states in general and Iraq in particular, the desirable solution for the defense of the Middle East should be based on the Arab Collective Security Pact. Nuri's approach reflected his desire to forge an Arab-Western alliance with Iraq as its leading force and his fear of the anti-Western sentiments prevailing in the Arab states. The latter could be aggravated and exploited by Egypt in order to adopt an aggressive position toward the West. It was in Iraq's interest to lead Egypt and the remaining Arab states to participate in a regional defense organization under Western auspices, in which Iraq would play the role of coordinator and motive force.

The MEDO proposal was also rejected by Egypt and the Arab League, which issued a statement in May 1953, shortly before John Foster Dulles's visit to the Middle East, to the effect that the Arab Collective Security Pact was the proper basis for the defense of the Arab states.[8] The failure of the two Western defense plans, MEC and MEDO, paved the way for a new plan, the "Northern Tier," which was based on Turkey and Iran (the northernmost states of the Middle East, which shared a border with the Soviet Union), the Western powers, Pakistan, and Iraq.

In February 1954, a treaty of defense and cooperation, constituting the cornerstone for the new regional organization, was signed between Turkey and Pakistan. The treaty led Egypt to fear the establishment of a pro-Western defense organization that would be joined by Iraq and the Arab states of the Fertile Crescent, thus weakening the Arab League and its Collective Security Pact and isolating Egypt. Egypt attacked the treaty, presenting it as a move by the Western powers to force a defense alliance on the Arabs, and warned Iraq not to join. The matter of the treaty and the possibility that Iraq would sign it aroused unrest among the students and nationalist public opinion in Baghdad. At the same time, suspicion and tension increased between Iraq and Egypt, with the fall of the Adib al-Shishakli regime in Syria and the renewed struggle for control of that country. Prime Minister Fadhil al-Jamali, whose views combined a pan-Arab nationalist approach with a pro-Western, pro-American orientation and who sought to secure American assistance for Iraq, unofficially expressed his support of the treaty. Nevertheless, on March 6, he informed the governments of Turkey, Britain, and Pakistan that Iraq would not sign the treaty. (On March 21, the government of Iraq published an official statement to this effect.)[9] This position was based on a desire to avoid increasing domestic political unrest and on Iraq's dissatisfaction with the format of the organization, which was to include only Iraq, Iran, Turkey, and Pakistan. Iraq wanted to establish a comprehensive organization on the basis of the Arab Collective Security Pact, in coordination with Egypt and with its consent. Only in that way could Iraq ensure itself a central role in the regional defense organization, relative to the larger and stronger Northern Tier states, and a position of leadership among the Arab states.

In June 1954, Britain launched a series of moves intended to resolve the issue of the British-Iraqi treaty of 1930. Crown Prince 'Abd al-Ilah told the British that amending the treaty was vital but that it would be necessary to establish a strong government that could unite the "anti-Communist" forces of Iraq.[10] Nuri al-Sa'id told 'Abd al-Ilah that he would be prepared to serve as prime minister of Iraq, provided that new elections were held for Parliament which would assure him an absolute majority, and he demanded that 'Abd al-Ilah stop intervening in Syria. (Nuri feared that 'Abd al-Ilah's actions would lead to an entanglement in Syria that would have a "boomerang effect" against Iraq itself, especially given that this type of activity could only harm Iraq's status in Syria.) Nuri proposed to the British that the British-Iraqi treaty be replaced by an alliance between Iraq, Iran, and Pakistan, which would later be joined by Britain and Turkey. This type of arrangement, according to Nuri, was intended to constitute a basis for a regional defense alliance based on the Arab League and would include Egypt. However, should Egypt refuse to join this alliance, Nuri was determined to establish the alliance without it, hoping that Iraq would succeed in persuading Syria, Jordan, and Lebanon to join the alliance, thus isolating Egypt.[11] Upon his return as prime minister in August 1954, Nuri launched a program of intensive activity aimed at achieving this objective. In order to neutralize the expected resistance in the inter-Arab arena and within Iraq, Nuri sought Egypt as a partner in setting up the alliance. In this way, Nuri hoped that Iraq would enter into an alliance with the West and the Northern Tier states, as the leader of the Arab states (or at least of the Fertile Crescent states), and not as an isolated Arab state.

In mid-August 1954, at the resort of Sarsanq, Nuri met with a delegation headed by the Egyptian minister of national guidance, Salah Salam.[12] Nuri was a sophisticated politician with great experience and skill in maneuvering, while Salam was a naive and enthusiastic type with no real political or diplomatic experience. Salam articulated Egypt's strong objections to the Turkish-Pakistani pact and rejected the idea of Arab states joining that alliance. Nuri proposed that the Arab Collective Security Pact be extended to include Turkey, Iran, Pakistan, Britain, and the United States.

At the press conference that concluded the visit, Salam and Nuri presented different versions of what had been decided. According to Nuri, Egypt had agreed that Arab states could join a pro-Western alliance together with the non-Arab states of the Northern Tier. Apparently, what was perceived as Egyptian consent to the moves proposed by Nuri resulted from the unequal abilities and status of the negotiators. In response to a journalist's question, Salam announced that Egypt did not object to union agreements between Arab states. This was taken as implying that Egypt did not object to a union or federation between Iraq and Syria.

Nuri later claimed that the Egyptians had agreed that the Pact would provide that the Arab states would assist non-Arab states in the event of any aggression—specifically, aggression on the part of the Soviet Union and the Communist bloc. In addition, proposals would be submitted by Iraq and Egypt for study by Britain and United States. Another area of agreement, according to Nuri, concerned the willingness of the Arab states to prepare for peace with Israel, in the spirit of the United Nations resolutions.

Although Nasir did not rule out cooperation with the West, he was not prepared to accept the format proposed by Nuri, who claimed that Salam had consented. Nor was Nasir prepared to deviate from the Egyptian policy rejecting the idea of a federation between Syria and Iraq. This ran counter to the traditional Egyptian interests in preventing the establishment of a strong

Arab state under Iraqi dominance in the Fertile Crescent. Indeed, the establishment of such a state would have resulted in the isolation of the revolutionary regime in Egypt. Shortly after Salah Salam returned to Egypt, Nasir fired him.

On September 15, Nuri arrived in Egypt for talks with Nasir, to coordinate defense arrangements and the establishment of the regional defense alliance. In July, Egypt had signed an agreement with Britain without consulting the Arab states. One clause in that agreement permitted the British to operate military bases in the Suez Canal region in case of aggression against an Arab state or Turkey. Given that background, Nuri may have believed that Nasir would find it difficult to object to the moves proposed by Iraq concerning the inclusion of the Western powers and the Northern Tier states in the framework of the Arab Collective Security Pact. Nuri emphasized that Iraq, given its proximity to the Soviet border, was liable to be exposed and vulnerable in the event of an interbloc world war. According to Nuri, the Collective Security Pact, in its current format, was effective against Israel. However, in order to ensure regional and Arab security under the conditions of the global interbloc struggle, the pact should be integrated into an effective defense organization with the participation of Turkey, Iran, Pakistan, and Britain. The gap between Nuri's position and Nasir's was ideological, political, generational, and personal in nature, but also reflected conflicts of interest between their respective states. Nuri and Nasir could not reach an agreement, and in the months and years to come, each was to accuse the other of fraud.[13]

At the Twenty-second Conference of the Arab League in November and December 1954, Egypt continued its efforts to prevent Iraq and other Arab states from joining the Turkish-Pakistani treaty or any other alliance outside of the Arab League.[14] In fact, the resolutions adopted at that session of the League prohibited Arab states from joining any alliance outside of the Arab Collective Security Pact. They were countered by the Iraqi foreign minister, who expressed reservations regarding Iraq's right to sign any agreement that was vital to its defense. Egypt, which had signed the secret version of its treaty with Britain in October 1954, had difficulty objecting to the inclusion of the Iraqi reservations, which were presented in the minutes of the League as referring to the relations and the treaty between Iraq and Britain. On the basis of his reservations, which were entered into the minutes, Nuri was later to claim that Iraq's moves to establish an alliance with Turkey and a regional defense organization did not violate the resolutions adopted by the League. This was an Iraqi trick, intended to prove that Iraq was not deviating from the Arab Collective Security Pact, and thus to enable Iraq to continue striving toward establishing a regional defense organization under Iraqi leadership.

During the autumn of 1954, Nuri conducted intensive negotiations with

Turkey and Britain regarding the proposed regional defense organization, so as to enable Egypt and the other Arab states to join that organization. However, during the course of a visit to Baghdad by Turkish prime minister Adnan Menderes in January 1955, under Turkish pressure, the two states published a joint announcement of their intention to sign a cooperation agreement and a defense treaty.[15] Egypt's response to the Turkish-Iraqi statement was acutely negative. The idea of the defense treaty seemed to constitute part of the British plot to isolate Egypt and force it to join a pro-Western alliance in which Iraq would be dominant and would succeed in promoting its own interests in Syria and the Arab world.

Despite the agreement with Britain, which was signed in October 1954, Nasir and the Free Officers remained insecure. The legitimacy of their regime was uncertain; they lacked experience in foreign affairs, and so they feared international isolation and its possible consequences for the continuation of their rule. Criticism of the Egyptian government embarrassed the Free Officers, who were embroiled in a struggle against the Muslim Brotherhood and desired to preserve their nationalist, anti-imperialist image, important to the legitimacy of their regime. In the political reality of the international arena in 1954, Nasir's attempt to find a way to gain Arab support without entering into an alliance with the West or adopting an unequivocal pro-Western position in the cold war required both skill and daring.[16] It should be recalled that, in 1954 and early 1955, the neutralist bloc and the concept of "positive neutralism"—which were later, following the Bandung Conference in April 1955, to give Nasir and the Free Officers a sense of security and support—had not yet been formulated.

Egypt, aghast at Nuri's move, attempted to torpedo the Iraqi-Turkish agreement by appealing to Arabs through an unprecedented propaganda campaign. Nasir sought to isolate Iraq. As soon as the Iraqi-Turkish statement was published, Egypt convened a conference of the prime ministers of the Arab League states. Despite the extreme pressure exerted on Iraq to desist from concluding the alliance with Turkey, Egypt was unable to force Nuri to abandon his intention. Egypt threatened to withdraw from the Arab Collective Security Pact if Iraq signed an alliance with Turkey and demanded that the Arab states adopt an uncompromising position. Egypt was closely supported by Saudi Arabia. Syrian prime minister Faris al-Khuri and his foreign minister, Faidi al-Atasi, both of whom were pro-Western and pro-Iraqi, sought to relieve the inter-Arab tension and prevented the adoption of the unequivocal anti-Iraqi position. Faris al-Khuri attempted to reach a compromise between Egypt and Iraq, in order to give Syria the status of an intermediary without having to actually decide on the issue—a decision that could have grave consequences in the Syrian domestic arena.

On February 24, Iraq and Turkey signed the alliance and invited additional states to join them. On April 4, a special agreement was signed between Britain and Iraq, which replaced the previous treaty between them; two days later, Britain joined the Turkish-Iraqi alliance, thus laying the foundation for the regional defense organization, the Baghdad Pact.

Several days after the conference of Arab prime ministers in Cairo, Iraq's status in the inter-Arab and regional arena was dealt a blow by the collapse of Faris al-Khuri's government. The situation which had arisen in January had increased the pressure on Syria from several directions. The day after the conclusion of the Iraqi-Turkish talks, Turkish prime minister Menderes visited Damascus and on January 14 informed the Syrians that Turkey was capable of arousing civil disobedience in the Aleppo area and along the Turkish-Syrian border if Syria did not join the alliance.[17] Meanwhile, in the Foreign Affairs Committee of the Syrian Parliament, the majority denounced the Turkish-Iraqi alliance. Faris al-Khuri hastened to declare that Syria would not join the alliance. The opposition, including the Syrian Ba'th Party, independent delegates, and many of the National Party delegates, exploited the Egyptian propaganda campaign against Iraq in order to undermine al-Khuri. Recalling the pro-Iraqi positions adopted by al-Khuri and Faidi al-Atasi at the Cairo conference, which prevented the passing of the anti-Iraqi resolutions demanded by Egypt, the Ba'th Party delegates to the Syrian Parliament began to form a majority that would condemn the Turkish-Iraqi alliance. Such action would obligate the Syrian government to join the opposition to that alliance. Syria's limited room for maneuver within the inter-Arab arena and the need to choose between Egypt and Iraq rendered al-Khuri incapable of conducting a policy that would preserve the option of rapprochement with the Western bloc and cooperation with Iraq while maintaining orderly relations with Egypt. The growing strength of the powerful and vociferous leftist opposition, which was backed by the military, left al-Khuri unable to rely on the conservative pro-Iraqi and pro-Western forces to keep him in power.

The primary cause of the fall of Faris al-Khuri's government was its failure to obtain parliamentary approval for the draft budget submitted by it. This failure, however, resulted from the formation of a parliamentary bloc that strove to topple the government, on the basis of its position on the Iraqi-Turkish alliance. The coalition consisted of conservative politicians from the National Party, who sought to reinforce their own status in light of the radicalization of public opinion and the political climate prevailing in Syria, and delegates from the Ba'th Party and the Democratic Bloc, headed by leftist politician Khalid al-'Azm. This coalition had the encouragement and support of the army, which had increased its involvement in Syrian political life. The glue holding this strange coalition between left and right together was their opposition to the ruling People's Party. Although the reason for the collapse of the government was domestic and economic in nature, given the changes in conditions prevailing in the inter-Arab arena and their ramifications on domestic Syrian politics, the breakdown was only a matter of time.

A new government was established in Syria under Sabri al-'Asli of the National Party. He was also pro-Iraqi and had enjoyed the political and financial support of Iraq in the early 1950s. However, by the time he became prime minister in February 1955, he believed that his only chance of establishing a durable government was by acting in accordance with the pro-Egyptian, anti-Iraqi trends. The change in Sabri al-'Asli's orientation was in line with the transformation which had occurred in Syria between 1954 and 1956, following the increased strength of the nationalist radical and leftist forces and dominance of the pro-Egyptian, anti-Iraqi orientation in the politics and political climate of Syria. The conservative pro-Iraqi politicians from among the old, rich elite found themselves on the defensive, faced with rising radical and leftist tendencies. Sabri al-'Asli, always an opportunist, chose to adopt a radical anti-Iraqi line. At the same time, however, both he and President Hashim al-Atasi, in talks with Iraqi leaders, repeatedly expressed their support of increased Iraqi involvement in Syria, in order to strengthen the forces that would eventually be able to halt the rise of radicalism among the officers, the Ba'th Party, and the Democratic Bloc.[18] Hashim al-Atasi, who secretly desired the assistance of Iraq, admitted that he could not allow himself to say so in public, for fear that he would be ousted by the Syrian Army.

After the failure to frustrate the Iraqi-Turkish alliance at the conference of Arab leaders in Cairo, Egypt turned its efforts to establishing a new organization for cooperation and defense, to prevent the Arab states from joining the organization that Iraq was setting up. On March 2, after a series of talks conducted by an Egyptian emissary in Damascus, a joint Egyptian-Syrian statement was published, followed by an Egyptian-Saudi-Syrian statement on March 6, both of which strongly rejected any action by an Arab state in joining any alliance outside the Arab League, including the alliance between Iraq and Turkey. Egypt, Syria, and Saudi Arabia declared their intention of establishing an organization for joint defense and economic cooperation, to be known as the Tripartite Alliance. However, despite this pro-Egyptian turn in Syrian policy, Syrian politicians—including some who openly supported this turn—continued trying to maintain Syria's ability to maneuver between Egypt and Iraq. The Syrian minister of defense, Khalid al-'Azm, who enjoyed the backing of some of the radical officers nonetheless feared that the Syrian Army would become too strong to manage and that an alliance would be concluded between the Ba'th Party and the radical officers. Al-'Azm, who sought election as president of Syria, also feared the candidacy of Shukri al-

Quwatli, who had Egypt's support. Considerations resulting from the complex political situation within Syria and the desire to maintain room to maneuver within the inter-Arab arena led al-'Azm and the Syrian chief of staff, Shawkat Shukair, to attempt to find a way to reconcile the pro-Western Iraqi-Turkish regional defense organization with the organization that Egypt was endeavoring to establish. The Syrians tried to convince Iraq that there was no conflict of interest between the Tripartite Alliance and the Baghdad Pact.[19] However, the attitude adopted by Nuri al-Sa'id, 'Abd al-Ilah, and Faysal II remained uncompromising. They demanded that Syria refrain from allying with Egypt and Saudi Arabia, and pressed publication of a joint statement to the effect that the alliance between Iraq and Turkey did not contradict the Security Pact of the Arab League. Understandably, the Syrian politicians were unable to agree to this.

Iraq failed to bring Syria into the pro-Western regional defense organization; moreover, even Iraq's Hashemite partner, Jordan, refused to join the organization. Despite the kinship between Faysal II of Iraq and his cousin, King Husayn of Jordan, and the feeling of common destiny shared by the elites of both states, Jordan did not support Iraq in this matter. The young King Husayn was maneuvering for the survival of his regime—and even for his life. In the face of the nationalist radical currents within Jordan and among the officers of the Jordanian Army, King Husayn chose to avoid challenging the anti-Iraqi, anti-Western movements that were growing in strength and momentum.

Immediately after signing the treaty with Egypt, the Syrian government, headed by Sa'id al-Ghazi, made an effort to reconcile with Iraq. A Syrian delegation, headed by Syrian defense minister Rashad Barmada, proposed that Iraq sign a bilateral treaty similar to the one concluded between Syria and Egypt. The Syrian initiative had the blessing of the new president, Shukri al-Quwatli, who—notwithstanding his connections with Egypt, which supported him—returned to the tactics that he had adopted during his previous term in office (1945–49): to rely on Egypt, while preserving the ability to maneuver between it and Iraq, in order to prevent Egyptian dominance in Syria. The moves made by al-Quwatli and al-Ghazi reflected the situation of the conservative elite and its politicians in Syria. To ensure their own survival, they cooperated with the radical forces while desperately seeking to keep them from becoming stronger.[20] Nuri, however, was suspicious of the abilities of the Syrian prime minister and defense minister to sign the treaty with Iraq, and he insisted on conditions that Syria was unable to accept. The attempt at reconciliation by the Syrian government provoked an extreme response by the radical officers and leftist forces within Syria. The Syrian defense minister was forced to deny that he had proposed a military agreement with Iraq, and the prime minister withdrew from his initiative and announced that he did not intend to visit Baghdad for the purpose of signing any kind of treaty or alliance. This, however, did not end the conflict between Egypt and Iraq over the issue of the Baghdad Pact, the question of leadership in the Arab world, and the future of Syria.

The Baghdad Pact, which included Iraq, Turkey, Iran, Pakistan, and Britain, was signed in September 1955. In October, bilateral agreements were concluded between Egypt and Syria and between Egypt and Saudi Arabia, thus establishing the Tripartite Alliance.

Egypt failed to prevent the establishment of the Baghdad Pact. While Iraq admittedly succeeded in establishing a pro-Western regional defense alliance, in which it was the leading Arab state, it failed in its efforts to bring in additional Arab states, especially Syria and Jordan. During the course of its conflict with Egypt, Iraq became isolated within the inter-Arab arena, as well as in public opinion and among the social and political forces that had come to dominate the domestic political arenas and the ideological climates of the Arab world. In the eyes of those forces, Iraq and its political leadership became the detested symbol of reactionism and capitulation to the West.

The Iraqi-Egyptian conflict over the Baghdad Pact may be viewed as an additional chapter of the struggle between those states for control of the Arab world and the future of Syria and Jordan. This conflict took on intergenerational, ideological, and social dimensions during the 1950s.

Hashemite Iraq versus the Radical Nasirist Wave Following the Suez-Sinai Crisis, 1956

The attack launched by Britain, France, and Israel against Egypt in October 1956, aimed at toppling the regime of the Free Officers led by Gamal 'Abd al-Nasir, placed the Baghdad Pact, and primarily Iraq as the sole Arab member, in an extremely difficult position. The attack on Egypt gave rise to a vast wave of sympathy and identification with Egypt and its regime throughout the Arab and Muslim states. Iraq's close ties with Britain, the affinity of its leaders with British interests, and its opposition to the radical revolutionary regime in Egypt transformed Iraq into a target for nationalist radical attacks and brought down upon it anger throughout the Arab world.

The demonstrations and riots that erupted throughout the cities of Iraq shocked the regime and was perceived as a threat to its stability and even its existence. Demonstrations in Baghdad, Mosul, and the Shi'ite city of Najaf on October 29 and 30, 1956, led to the imposition of martial law on November 1.[21] In Baghdad, with the help of large military and police forces, the authorities managed to maintain control of the situation. By means of extensive arrests, they frustrated attempts to establish coordination and joint leadership between the illegal opposition parties (Communist and Ba'th) and activists from the National Democratic Party. However, in light of the protracted tension, Nuri expressed his fears that if the fighting against Egypt continued, the situation in Iraq could deteriorate to the point that the government would lose control of the situation. When the unrest continued, the government of Iraq ordered the closure of all schools on November 3. Nuri appealed to the Shi'ite religious leaders to restore order, while emphasizing the role played by the Communists in the organization of the riots. (The Shi'ite religious leaders, as early as 1952–53, had expressed their concern at the rise in Communist activity among the members of their community, and the Shi'ite religious leader, Mujtahid Muhammad Kashif al-Ghita, had gone so far as to meet with American diplomats in order to suppress this activity.)

Although Nuri al-Sa'id considered Nasir to be the mortal enemy and the greatest possible threat to the existence of Iraq and other Arab states, he could not allow himself, under the conditions created by the attack on Egypt, to approve the operation intended to oust his rival. In order to repel the accusations and attacks on Iraq and its leadership as alleged partners in the Western-Zionist plot to overthrow the revolutionary Arab nationalist regime and restore Western colonial control of Egypt and other Arab states, the government of Iraq submitted a strong protest to Britain. At a meeting of the Muslim members of the Baghdad Pact—that is, all of the member states except Britain—which took place on November 3 in Teheran, Nuri submitted draft resolutions demanding that the independence and territorial integrity of Egypt be preserved, that Israel withdraw beyond the armistice line, and that actions be taken toward finding a solution to the Palestine question. But the government of Iraq, fraught with anxiety and subjected to internal and external pressure, issued an appeal on November 13 for the destruction of the state of Israel and the return of the Palestinian refugees.[22] As had been the case innumerable times in the history of Iraq, the conflict with Israel was adopted by the Iraqi policy makers as a means of attaining other objectives or distracting attention from the Baghdadi regime's distress. In order to demonstrate that Iraq's membership in the Baghdad Pact did not make it the ally of Britain, France, and Israel, all of whom were perceived as the enemies of the Arab world, Iraq announced the severing of its diplomatic relations with France on November 6. On November 9, an official Iraqi statement proclaimed the transformation of the Baghdad Pact into an Islamic alliance.[23] On November 17, a conference of the Muslim members of the Baghdad Pact—Iraq, Turkey, Iran, and Pakistan—took place in Baghdad. The conference only increased tensions within Iraq and led to an additional wave of demonstrations and riots, which continued until early December.

At the beginning of the attack, Saudi Arabia, Syria, and Jordan proposed sending expeditionary forces to assist Egypt. Since Nasir asked that they refrain from doing so, Saudi Arabia and Syria then suggested sending their military units to Jordan to assist in its defense. In line with these proposals, Iraq hastily reached an agreement with Jordan, providing for the dispatch of an Iraqi division to Jordan to help defend it against Israel.[24] This Iraqi force, which encamped around Mafraq in the east, was actually sent to protect the Hashemite Jordanian regime against the Syrians and Saudis. This force may also have been intended to back up the conspiracy by various Iraqi elements, chief among them 'Abd al-Ilah, to overthrow the regime in Syria, by preventing the radical forces from increasing in strength.

The demonstrations in Iraq, which continued until January 1957, aroused the anxiety of the Iraqi politicians and elite, as well as that of Western diplomats, regarding the continued stability of the regime. 'Abd al-Ilah sent a missive to British foreign minister Anthony Eden, emphasizing the dangerous situation in which the friends and allies of Britain found themselves. Nonetheless, despite the new disruptions—a logical continuation of the wathba of 1948 and the intifada of 1952—Nuri, 'Abd al-Ilah, and the conservative ruling elite succeeded in preserving their own status and the integrity of the regime. Any revolution powerful enough to cause the collapse of the regime and to bring about profound changes in the social structure of Iraq would have required a well-organized political force. In the autumn of 1956, there was no such force in Iraq.

The Defeat of Iraq's Supporters in Syria, 1955–1957

Iraq's policy regarding Syria resulted both from the geopolitical status of the region and from the social, political, and ideological conditions prevailing within Iraq. Iraq's aims at dominance over or union with Syria were the practical political outcome of pan-Arab nationalist attitudes. Iraq's policy was justified by means of pan-Arab nationalist rhetoric. This rhetoric also constituted a means of political recruitment and granted legitimacy to the regime and the politicians within Iraq. Thus, this policy and its failures affected the domestic political conditions and climate in which the Iraqi politicians and the ruling elite had to function. In addition, the ruling elite began to fear the rise to power of radical revolutionary (or perhaps even Communist) forces in Syria.

Among the Iraqi politicians involved in Syrian affairs, a wide range of opinions and approaches existed. 'Abd al-Ilah supported constant activity within Syria, with a view to establishing a pro-Iraqi regime in Damascus, which would eventually lead to union with Iraq. Nuri al-Sa'id—who, as stated above, had actively supported the establishment of a union or federation in the Fertile Crescent and unification with Syria—began to show more caution in the late 1940s. Although Nuri clung to the vision of Arab unity under Iraqi dominance and control in the Fertile Crescent and in Syria given the political instability in Syria, the pragmatic, conservative politician was willing to consider the union with Syria only under conditions that would ensure that Syrian instability did not infect Iraq. Nuri instinctively mistrusted Syria and the Syrian politicians and wanted to prevent Iraq from being dragged into entanglement in mercurial Syrian politics, which could adversely affect Iraq itself. Nuri believed that the chances of realizing Iraq's interests in Syria would increase after Iraq had acquired a sound regional and international status, and that this would increase Syria's tendency to rely on Iraq in order to escape external threats and the risk of internal chaos.

In the winter of 1955, after the Syrian rapprochement with Egypt and the weakening of the pro-Iraqi politicians in Syria, Iraq increased its conspiratorial activity aimed at organizing a coup in Syria and bringing the pro-Iraqis back to power. 'Abd al-Ilah was the Iraqi most actively involved in this conspiracy. Nuri, although consulted and peripherally involved, displayed a lack of enthusiasm and apparently no small amount of pessimism concerning its chances for success. The clandestine organization in Syria involved politicians and notables from among the conservative Syrian elite, members of the pro-Iraqi People's Party, some army officers who felt endangered by leftist and radical officers, and politicians who hoped to improve their own status following the coup. This was a weak, conflict-ridden alliance of forces and personages whose status had declined as time went by and who felt constantly endangered by the rise of radical forces, namely, the Ba'thists and the army officers. Of the army officers who joined the organization, some were related to old notable families and shared conservative interests, while others feared the rise of the radical officers. The conspiracy was uncovered by the Syrian security services, headed by Colonel 'Abd al-Hamid Seraj, a radical officer who maintained close ties with Nasirist Egypt. Seraj took advantage of the Suez-Sinai crisis of November 1956, Nasir's popularity, and hatred of the West and Iraq to announce on November 23 that the plot had been exposed.[25] Some of the conspirators managed to escape from Syria; others were arrested and tried. This was a grave blow to the supporters of Iraq in Syria and to Iraq's image in Syrian public opinion. Many Syrians decided that Iraq constituted a threat to their independence. The remaining pro-Iraqi politicians did not dare to express any sympathy for Iraq. The tension increased when Radio Damascus, the Sawt al-Arab radio station in Cairo, and the Egyptian press called for the fall of the regime in Iraq and the ouster of Nuri al-Sa'id.[26]

Thus, in 1957, Iraq's supporters in Syria had lost their positions, whereas the Ba'th Party and the nationalist radical army officers had acquired more and more power. Iraq continued to put pressure on Syria, while attempting to coordinate with Turkey and the United States, which feared that the Communists would rise to power in Damascus. Nuri sought to ensure that Iraq would retain a central role in the framework of Iraqi-Turkish-American pressure on Syria. Iraqi policy on this issue embodied a contradiction: on one hand, Iraq sought Turkey's assistance, although it feared that a clash between Turkey and Syria would have grave consequences for Iraq and its regime. A collision between Turkey and Syria would have given rise to severe domestic pressure on the Iraqi government to support Syria in the name of Arabism.[27] In October 1957, politicians from al-Istiqlal and the National Democratic Party demanded that Iraq support Syria against Turkey, which was amassing military forces on the Syrian border.[28] The common Iraqi-Turkish interest in overthrowing the Syrian regime and halting the rise of pro-Nasirist radical forces could have led the Iraqi regime into a dangerous trap. Accordingly, Iraq required an anti-Egyptian, pro-Western front, with the participation of additional Arab states. This conflicted with the radical pro-Egyptian and anti-Western trend increasingly dominating public opinion in Iraq and the entire Arab world. The situation in which the Iraqi regime now found itself accelerated the rapprochement with Saudi Arabia and the settling of a historical conflict.[29]

Iraq against the Nasirist Wave: The Iraqi-Saudi Reconciliation and the Effects of the Defeat in Syria on the Regime in Baghdad, 1957–1958

It was precisely the wave of pan-Arab leftist radical fervor which rose throughout the Arab world and the prestige ascribed to the revolutionary Nasirist regime in 1956 and 1957 that brought about a certain improvement, in favor of Iraq, in the balance of forces in the inter-Arab arena. The joint threat posed to the conservative monarchies of Iraq and Saudi Arabia impelled them to reach a historic rapprochement and reconciliation and motivated King Husayn of Jordan to intensify his cooperation with Iraq. Saudi Arabia, the traditional rival of the Hashemites and Iraq, continued to maintain close ties and cooperation with Egypt even after the overthrow of the monarchy by the Free Officers in 1952 and the establishment of the revolutionary regime under Nasir. In the autumn of 1955, in response to the establishment of the pro-Western Baghdad Pact, Egypt and Saudi Arabia signed a cooperation agreement which, together with the agreement between Egypt and Syria, became the Tripartite Arab Alliance.

The fear of Iraq and the desire to prevent it from taking over Syria were the cohesive forces in this strange alliance between the radical revolutionary regime in Egypt and the conservative monarchy in the Saudi Arabia. However, in 1956, following the rapprochement between Egypt and the Soviet Union and the transformation of Gamal 'Abd al-Nasir and his regime into a source of inspiration for revolutionary forces throughout the Arab world, Saudi Arabia began to develop fear and hostility toward Egypt and its leaders. These fears, arousing simultaneously with the threat posed by radical forces (with the backing of Egypt) to King Husayn's regime in the spring of 1956, enabled the beginning of a thaw in the relations between Iraq and Saudi Arabia. Starting in early 1957, Iraq and Saudi Arabia found themselves sharing a positive approach to the Eisenhower Doctrine promulgated by the United States, whereas Egypt and Syria responded to that doctrine with severe censure. (The Eisenhower Doctrine was a resolution by the U.S. House of Representatives, based on a proposal by President Eisenhower, according to which the United States would call in its military forces to protect any state in the Middle East needing assistance against a state under Communist influence.) The attitude toward the Eisenhower Doctrine became a bone of contention between its conservative supporters (Iraq, Saudi Arabia, Morocco, Libya, and Lebanon) and its opponents (Syria and Egypt).[30]

The movement toward rapprochement continued between Iraq and Saudi Arabia and among the conservative states of the Arab world, based on the perceived threat posed to their regimes by Nasirist Egypt, which was assisting radical revolutionary forces in other Arab countries. Nasirist Egypt had become a source of inspiration for the wave of revolutionary nationalist fervor that had pervaded public opinion in general, and the younger and urban sections of the populations in particular, throughout the Arab world. In February 1957, 'Abd al-Ilah met with King Saud in Washington. In May, King Saud came to Baghdad, where he met with King Faysal II of Iraq. In the spring of 1957, King Husayn of Jordan intensified his cooperation with Iraq, after having ousted his nationalist, pro-Egyptian prime minister, Sulayman al-Nabulsi, and suppressed an attempted coup by the Jordanian chief of staff. Thus, in mid-1957, despite the sympathy and prestige inspired by the radical-revolutionary Nasirist regime throughout the Arab world, Egypt and Syria found themselves isolated from almost all other Arab governments. Nevertheless, despite the improvement in Iraq's favor in the inter-Arab balance of forces, the Iraqi ruling elite feared the rising wave of sympathy for Nasir and its effect on Iraq. This was accentuated by the fact that the Iraqi heads of state had become a target for attacks and hatred, not only in Egypt but in public opinion throughout the entire Arab world. The anti-Iraqi propaganda and personal attacks launched by Egypt against Nuri al-Saʿid and ʿAbd al-Ilah, as well as the counterpropaganda aimed by Iraq against Egypt, added to the tension between the two states.

To alleviate this tension and improve Iraq's image, Nuri al-Saʿid, who had become the symbol of reaction and cooperation with the West, resigned in June 1957. He was replaced by ʿAli Jawdat al-Ayubi, a relatively moderate politician who supported the improvement of relations with both Egypt and Syria. The appointment of ʿAli Jawdat was based on a complex reality within Iraq. In the confusion created by Nuri's resignation, it was hard to find a politician who was acceptable to the elite politicians and could form a stable government without arousing strenuous opposition and whose personal status was not too strong for the taste of Nuri and ʿAbd al-Ilah.[31]

ʿAli Jawdat had only very limited room to maneuver, due to the continued control exerted by Nuri and ʿAbd al-Ilah over Parliament, the state apparatus, and the senior officers, as well as the tension in Iraqi relations with Egypt and the profound crisis within and around Syria. Nuri and ʿAbd al-Ilah continued to make independent political moves, over the head of the Iraqi government. For example, an initiative by ʿAli Jawdat, aimed at stopping the propaganda broadcasts from Baghdad, encountered intense opposition in the Iraqi Committee for the Control of Propaganda Broadcasts, because most of its members received their orders from the Palace, Nuri, and the army.

The differences between ʿAli Jawdat's approach and that adopted by ʿAbd al-Ilah and Nuri continued to grow as tensions between Turkey and Syria became more acute during the summer of 1957. King Faysal II, ʿAbd al-Ilah, and Nuri al-Saʿid met with an American emissary to the Middle East and with Turkish leaders in August and September to unite against the Soviet Union and the rising radical forces in Syria, whereas ʿAli Jawdat adopted a policy of conciliation toward Egypt and Syria. He declared that Iraq would support Syria in the event of aggression against it. On September 28, ʿAli Jawdat visited Damascus, where he met with President Shukri al-Quwatli and Prime Minister Sabri al-ʿAsli, as well as with King Saud of Saudi Arabia.[32]

Despite his efforts, ʿAli Jawdat was unsuccessful in improving Iraq's image and relations with Syria and Egypt because neither believed ʿAli Jawdat could pursue an independent policy unaffected by Nuri and ʿAbd al-Ilah.

Both Nuri and ʿAbd al-Ilah were prepared to accept ʿAli Jawdat's moves on a short-term basis because he was useful to them as a "fig leaf" for their continued activity, in cooperation with the United States, aimed at overthrowing the regime in Syria and halting the rise of the radical forces in that country. The 'Ali Jawdat government gave Nuri and 'Abd al-Ilah the time they needed to prepare for continued activity in Syria and within the inter-Arab arena, and helped them to prove that, despite Iraq's efforts, it was not possible to achieve understanding or improve relations with Syria. Although he criticized 'Ali Jawdat's "soft" policy toward Syria, Nuri did not express any objections to his trip to Damascus. Nevertheless, Nuri subsequently used that trip to hurt him. The objections that both 'Abd al-Ilah and Nuri had to 'Ali Jawdat's policy in Syria and in the inter-Arab arena, and their fear that he was not determined enough to maintain tranquility and stability within Iraq, led to his resignation in December 1957. 'Ali Jawdat's inability to present an alternative to the political line adopted by Nuri and 'Abd al-Ilah reflected the situation of the ruling elite and the monarchy in Iraq, which had reached a blind alley in their foreign and domestic policies.

Following 'Ali Jawdat's resignation, a new government was formed under 'Abd al-Wahhab Mirjan, a Shi'ite politician and supporter of Nuri al-Sa'id. His appointment was intended to ensure the continuation of Nuri's own policies and increase Shi'ite support for the regime.

The protracted pressure placed on Syria by Iraq, Turkey, the United States, and Britain, as well as their support of the attempted conspiracy in Syria to establish a pro-Western regime, increased the perceived threats and the fear of internal collapse in Syria. This fear pushed Syria toward Egypt. The activities of the Ba'th Party prepared the political atmosphere and the ideological background for the move made by the radical army officers to establish a union with Egypt under Nasir early in 1958. The resulting United Arab Republic was a historic defeat for Hashemite Iraq. All of Iraq's efforts, starting in the 1920s, toward the achievement of a federation or union with Syria had actually driven Syria to unite with Iraq's rival. The establishment of the UAR and the nationalist, pro-Nasirist euphoria throughout the Arab world created a threat to the regimes of both Iraq and Jordan. This euphoria isolated the Iraqi regime and trickled down into public opinion within Iraq, affecting even the army officers. The radical Nasirist threat in 1957 pushed Iraq and Jordan toward closer cooperation, and at the end of that year King Husayn proposed a union between Jordan and Iraq, with the possibility that Saudi Arabia might join later. Following the establishment of the United Arab Republic on February 1, 1958, talks on the subject of union between Iraq and Jordan were launched in Amman. However, King Husayn refused to join the Baghdad Pact and insisted that Iraq withdraw from it. He remembered well that public opposition to the Baghdad Pact had given rise to riots and demonstrations in Jordan in December 1955, when Jordan was pressured by both Britain and Iraq to join the pact. After a compromise was negotiated that enabled Iraq to stay within the Baghdad Pact without forcing Jordan to join it, the union agreement between Iraq and Jordan was signed on February 14, thus establishing the Arab Federation.[33]

On May 19, the first government of the Arab Federation was established, under the leadership of Nuri al-Sa'id; at the same time, a new Iraqi government was formed in Baghdad under Prime Minister Ahmad Mukhtar Baban, a Kurdish politician with close ties to the Palace.[34] Nuri demanded that Britain ensure that Kuwait would join the Arab Federation. The Iraqi claim to Kuwait was renewed by Nuri in order to give Iraq and the Federation more economic power and nationalist prestige.[35] Nuri and Tawfiq al-Suwaydi, the foreign minister of the Arab Federation, attempted to convince both Britain and Sheikh Sabah, the ruler of Kuwait, that Kuwait should join the union. Britain, however, refused to accept this demand on the part of Iraq. The British position caused Nuri intense frustration, and he publicly voiced his disappointment.[36]

In the spring of 1958, inter-Arab tension over Iraq's relations with the Egyptian-Syrian union increased. The government of Iraq went so far as to consider the possibility of invading Syria, in order to prevent an Egyptian takeover. However, for that purpose, Iraq would have required the support and assistance of the Western powers, which were obviously not forthcoming.

In July 1958, a difference of opinion arose between Nuri, prime minister of the Federation, and Baban, prime minister of Iraq. Desiring to strengthen the Arab Federation, Nuri asked that Iraq's financial resources be made available to the Federation and allocated by him as its prime minister. Baban, who refused to waive his own powers, objected strenuously and submitted his resignation.[37] In view of the increased unrest, fear of the UAR, and the crisis in Lebanon in July 1958, Nuri, acting as prime minister of the Arab Federation, ordered Iraqi forces to enter Jordan. This order was exploited by a group of officers led by 'Abd al-Karim Qasim and 'Abd al-Salam 'Arif, who brought their troops into Baghdad and launched the revolution that put an end to the Hashemite monarchy in Iraq on July 14, 1958.

The 1958 Revolution and the Qasim Regime

The 1958 Revolution and the Fall of the Hashemite Monarchy

In the midst of the blazing Iraqi summer, on the morning of July 14, 1958, units of the Iraqi Army, commanded by Brigadier General 'Abd al-Karim Qasim and Colonel 'Abd al-Salam 'Arif, took control of the centers of government in Baghdad. The revolutionary officers exploited the order that had been given them to move with their units into Jordan. Officially, they were to reinforce the Jordanian Army against Israel. In truth, they were to strengthen the regime of the Hashemite King Husayn against the threat posed by the United Arab Republic (UAR) under Nasir and the wave of pan-Arab radicalism that had swept over the cities of Jordan. But they didn't move into Jordan. Instead, they entered Baghdad and attacked the Palace.[1]

The weakness of the monarchy and laxity and negligence of its security services created an opportunity that the revolutionary officers succeeded in exploiting. The heads of the regime and its security services did not heed the warnings that had reached them regarding the organization of cells of radical officers. Generally speaking, no ammunition was issued to the Iraqi Army units, and any movement by a military unit required the approval of the high commanders, in order to prevent the risk of a military coup. However, in July, in preparation for the transfer to Jordan, ammunition was issued to the units commanded by 'Abd al-Karim Qasim and 'Abd al-Salam 'Arif, which were ordered to move from their bases in northern Iraq toward the Jordanian border.

The Royal Guard surrendered, and the Palace and all government centers fell into the hands of the army. The royal family, headed by the young king, Faysal II, and his uncle, 'Abd al-Ilah, were cut down by a submachine gun fired by one of the revolutionary officers as they descended the steps, hands raised in surrender. The revolutionary regime later claimed that one of the officers had run amok.[2] It is also possible, however, that the commanding officers had received orders from Qasim and 'Arif to kill the

Hashemite family.[3] Nuri al-Sa'id, a senior politician who had served as prime minister thirteen times and who, for many, symbolized reactionary conservatism and subservience to the West, attempted to escape disguised as a woman. But he was identified and lynched by an angry crowd.[4]

No forces and no political entities attempted to defend the ruling regime. The three mainstays on which the Hashemite monarchy had relied—the tribal landowners, the army, and the regional defense alliance involving the West—could not prevent a revolution launched by the army officers. The officers enjoyed widespread support.

The support of the tribal landowners for the regime was shown to be a slender reed. The transformation of the tribal notables into major landowners and their integration into the ruling class strengthened their social standing and gave them power over the political system and the regime. At the same time, it reinforced the class stratification of Iraqi society and alienated the tribal landowners from their own tribesmen, who became poor peasants or migrated to the slums.[5] Tribal identities and loyalties did not dissipate; however, the change in social relationships and resulting alienation reduced the ability of the tribal landowners to enlist the support of their tribes. Thus, their ability to serve as a strong, effective body of political support for the regime, which in turn would preserve the sociopolitical status quo which the landowners sought to maintain, was significantly reduced.

The army had constituted the second pillar of support for the monarchical regime since the post-1941 purge of the officers who had been involved in or sympathized with the Rashid 'Ali movement and the Salah al-Din al-Sabbagh group. The existence of a strong army was vital to the Iraqi state, given the strength of ethnic and tribal forces within Iraq and the external strategic threats resulting from Iraq's geopolitical situation. From World War II on, the army had also provided support for the regime against the new urban social forces and radical political movements. In this framework, the army was called upon to defend the regime against the student riots during the intifada in November 1952. Fostering and expanding the army by the conservative elite created a contradiction in terms. Most of the Iraqi officers came from the middle or even lower middle class, shared its frustrations, and were influenced by the ideological currents which were attractive to that stratum.

The belief by senior conservative politicians that it would be possible to preserve the army's loyalty to the regime by paying its officers high salaries and providing them with economic benefits was proven wrong. The radical and leftist ideas that had become attractive to younger members of the middle stratum penetrated the army; the politicians were incapable of halting this development. The officers who launched the revolution shared the belief held by many members of the modern middle stratum that the Iraqi regime was no more than the degenerated, corrupt servant of the narrow-minded, exploitative, reactionary elite, itself in the service of foreign interests, and that the social transformation vital to the survival of Iraq and its extrication from the swamp of backwardness could not be accomplished from within the regime. The ruling political elite, the upper class, and the Hashemite monarchy were perceived by the officers as obstacles to be removed in order to bring about the essential political, social, and economic changes that would rescue Iraq and the Arab nations from weakness, backwardness, and dependency on the West and would provide a response to its economic and social distress.

The third mainstay of the regime—Iraq's involvement in a regional defense alliance with the Western powers, the Baghdad Pact—turned out to be worthless. The defense alliance was incapable of defending the regime from a domestic military coup. The coup enjoyed domestic social backing and a supportive political and ideological climate in the Arab world. The Baghdad Pact, intended to block the Soviet Union and the radical forces in the Middle East, was ineffective against leftist radical nationalist ideologies, outlooks, and movements that infiltrated Iraqi public opinion and the Iraqi Army. It was precisely the struggle over the Baghdad Pact and the threat posed by Nasirist Egypt—a threat which reinforced the image of the Iraqi regime and its leaders as reactionary servants of the West—which weakened their prestige in the eyes of nationalist public opinion throughout the Arab world and particularly in Iraq.

The regime and the ruling elite failed to adapt themselves to social and ideological changes. Nor did they provide a means for political expression and response to the distress of the new social forces, which had sprung up in the course of the modernization of Iraq. These failures gave rise to the domestic conditions which favored a political and social revolution and the fall of the Hashemite monarchy.

The fact that the ruling political elite was chained to the conservative interests of the upper socioeconomic class frustrated attempts by those politicians within the elite who sought to effectuate reform within the framework of the regime. The ruling elite increasingly depended on the tribal landowners, most of them Shi'ites, who had found their place within the bureaucratic structure of the Iraqi state, in the upper socioeconomic class, and within the ruling political elite. This dependence did neutralize the Shi'ite tribal threat and create a temporary counterweight to the new social forces and their reformist and revolutionary movements. However, these policies only reinforced the conservative character of the regime and further reduced the possibility of controlled, directed reform.

The fall of the Hashemite monarchy was one link in the chain of collapse of the political elites and socioeconomic classes which had constituted the dominant force within the states and societies of the Fertile Crescent since the seventeenth and eighteenth centuries and in Egypt since the nineteenth century. The elites, who had demonstrated an impressive ability to adapt to changes in the social and political conditions that had taken place in the region and throughout the world since the eighteenth century, now became embroiled in internal contradictions and found themselves unable to adapt to the conditions of the twentieth century, especially after World War II. The economic, political, and ideological dominance of the West, along with the absence of conditions conducive to the development of modern industry (e.g., domestic immaturity and backwardness) prevented the old elites of notables from developing into a powerful industrial-commercial-financial bourgeoisie. They could not cope with the rise of the educated modern middle stratum nor with the poverty and misery of the poorer strata. Any solution to their distress would have run counter to the basic conservative interests of the elites and the upper classes.

Given the fact that traditional elites and their politicians had headed the Arab states and the nationalist movements within them since World War I, their interests lay in building strong states and powerful nations. However, this required rapid modernization, industrialization, agrarian reform, and opportunities for the new social forces to express themselves politically. Intent on maintaining their own status, the conservative elites would not countenance such modernization. Instead, politicians from among the conservative elites who headed their national movements enlisted the support of the modern middle stratum by means of militant nationalism, directed against British and French dominance, and by exploiting the Palestine question as an expression of the nationalist Arab struggle. However, the politicians' ability to do this was exhausted in the late 1940s. Their nationalist image was damaged during World War II and following the failure of the 1948 war. Militant nationalism fostered by the conservative politicians turned into a boomerang, giving rise to waves of violence, increasingly directed against the ruling elite themselves. Militant nationalism in its leftist radical version became the battle cry, the political expression, and the banner of the revolutionary radical forces that bitterly opposed the conservative elites and upper classes. This was coupled with increased social and political unrest and the rise of Nasir's regime in Egypt and the Ba'th Party in Syria. The regimes and the ruling elites of the Arab states were unable to respond to the revolutionary nationalist radical messages of Nasirism and the Ba'th, which became attractive to the younger educated and semieducated members of the modern middle stratum.

Weaknesses of the bourgeoisie, of the middle stratum's class consciousness, and of the political parties and civilian organizations gave rise to a situation in which the army officers found a sense of mission. Aware of Iraq's weaknesses and the distress of its population and affected by the radical ideological movements in the Arab world, they emerged as the only force capable of changing the regime.

Qasim and ʿArif were members of the generation which had launched the revolution in Egypt in 1952. The formative experience of that generation was nationalist radicalization among the effendiyya in the 1930s, when they were in high school or enrolled in the military academies that had been opened for sons of the middle and lower social strata. Many of the Iraqi officers of this generation felt sympathy toward al-Sabbagh and the Rashid ʿAli movement of 1941, regarding it as a national popular movement opposed to the conservative establishment and British imperialism. For the Free Officers in both Egypt and Iraq, the 1948 war against Israel was a traumatic experience that intensified their sense of duty. They saw their mission as bringing down the corrupt regimes that had weakened the Arab nation and thrown their countries into distress. The success of the Free Officers in overthrowing the Egyptian monarchy and seizing power in 1952, and the success of the Nasirist regime in withstanding the combined forces of Britain, France, and Israel in the Suez-Sinai Campaign of 1956, transformed Nasir and his regime into a source of inspiration and a shining example for the Iraqi officers.

The underground organization of army officers in Iraq apparently began as early as 1952. Inspired by the Egyptian example, the officers in Iraq also called themselves Free Officers. However, they did not develop a core of leadership acceptable to all.[6]

Qasim and ʿArif carried out the revolution by utilizing military forces under their direct command. To prevent their plans from being revealed to the authorities, they did not disclose the date of the revolution even to their own comrades in the underground organization. Several of the officers maintained connections with politicians from the opposition parties; however, the planning, timing, and implementation were entirely in the hands of Qasim and ʿArif, along with a handful of their closest associates. Motivated by their admiration for Nasir, as well as by fear of a reaction from members of the Baghdad Pact to the overthrow of the regime in Iraq, the Free Officers sought to ensure Nasir's support and the assistance of the UAR. As early as the winter of 1957—that is, even before the establishment of the UAR—Nasir, at the time engaged in a life-and-death struggle with Nuri al-Saʿid and the Hashemite regime, secretly informed the Free Officers of Iraq that he would support their revolution. What Nasir offered, however, was only moral support, whose practical significance remained vague.[7] Egypt did not play a practical role in the Iraqi revolution. Nevertheless, the inspiration provided by Nasir and the impact of his success and the revolutionary regime in Egypt on the determination of the Iraqi officers and the success of the revolution in Iraq cannot be ignored.

Socially, most of the Free Officers came from the middle and lower middle classes, but some of them were sons of wealthy landowning notables and others belonged to poorer families. The latter included ʿAbd al-Karim Qasim and ʿAbd al-Salam ʿArif. ʿAbd al-Karim Qasim was of mixed Sunnite-Shiʿite origin, and his father was a carpenter who owned a small farm. ʿAbd al-Salam ʿArif was from the Sunnite al-Jumayla tribe, the son of a draper who owned a small shop. As a group, however, the Free Officers were from the modern middle stratum. Most of them were Sunnite Arabs, with only two or three Shiʿites.

On July 15, Nasir declared his support for the revolution in Iraq and announced that any attack on Iraq would be considered an attack on the UAR.[8] The summer and autumn of 1958 were the height of success of revolutionary radical pan-Arab nationalism, with Nasir extolled as its admired leader. The time seemed ripe for the start of a new era.

The Political System, the Nationalist Movements, and the Foreign Policy of Iraq upon Establishment of the Revolutionary Regime

The revolution was enthusiastically welcomed by large sections of Iraqi society. During the first months, the revolutionary regime established by Qasim and ʿArif enjoyed the widespread support of the modern middle stratum, the urban poor, and the fellahin (small landowners and landless peasants), who looked forward to agrarian reform. The new regime also raised the expectations of Iraq's rather limited bourgeoisie, which hoped for the creation of conditions that would favor industrialization and development. Politicians from the parties that had opposed the old regime, organized since 1957 in the framework of the United National Front (which included the National Democratic Party, al-Istiqlal, the Communist Party, and the Baʿth Party), supported the revolution, and key figures in those parties were integrated into the new regime.[9] The revolutionary regime also enjoyed the support of most of the Kurds, although the notables and the major tribal landowners, who stood to lose the benefits they enjoyed under the monarchy, feared the policies of the new regime. In contrast to the major landowners, whose status was adversely affected by the change in the status quo and agrarian reform, the small and medium-sized landowners were strengthened and so lent their support to the regime.

The declared approach of the regime, which recognized the national rights of the Kurds, constituted a major change from the traditional Iraqi approach;

in practice, only the civil equality of the Kurds as individuals had been recognized. Paragraph 3 of the Provisional Constitution, published on July 27, stated that the Arabs and Kurds were partners in the Iraqi homeland and that the Kurds' national rights were recognized.[10] The placement of Paragraph 3 immediately after Paragraph 2, which states that Iraq constitutes part of the Arab nation, is significant. The two sections together reflect the complexity of defining national identity in Iraq as well as the attempt to reconcile Arab national identity and its pan-Arab tendencies with territorial Iraqi national identity. A demand by Ibrahim Ahmad, secretary of the Kurdistan Democratic Party (KDP), to include in the Constitution a clause recognizing the Kurds' right to autonomy, was rejected, apparently under pressure by 'Arif.

The atmosphere of mass enthusiasm following the revolution gave rise to a dramatic increase in the influence of the radical political forces: the Communists and the pan-Arab nationalists. During the euphoria aroused by the revolution, they helped create a political climate characterized by unrest and radicalism.

The government established by Qasim included personages from both the legal and underground opposition parties which operated during the monarchy. (Let us recall that, ever since the return of Nuri al-Sa'id to power in the autumn of 1954, all party activity was actually prohibited in Iraq, so that even those parties which had previously operated within the framework of the law, the National Democratic Party and al-Istiqlal, were forced to cease their official activity.) The government was not composed of a coalition of parties, because political party activity had officially not yet been allowed to resume; rather, ministers from the various political parties were appointed to the government on an individual basis. This included the secretary of the National Democratic Party, Muhammad Hadid, who was appointed minister of finance, and Hudeib al-Haj Hmud, who was appointed minister of agriculture. Sadik Shanshal, one of the leading figures in al-Istiqlal, was appointed minister of guidance. Fuad al-Rikabi, secretary of the Ba'th Party, became minister of development. The position of minister of economic affairs was filled by Dr. Ibrahim Kubba, an economist with Marxist views who was linked to the Communist Party.

Qasim served as prime minister and minister of defense, in addition to his position as commander in chief of the army. 'Abd al-Salam 'Arif was appointed deputy prime minister and minister of the interior, in addition to his role as deputy commander in chief of the army. The government included only one other officer, Naji Talib, as minister of social affairs.[11] The small number of officers and the appointment of Naji Talib, one of the most senior of the Free Officers, to a relatively minor position reflected the dominance of

Qasim and ʿArif among the officers and within the revolutionary regime. Beginning in September of that year, a few more officers—all personal associates of Qasim—were appointed as ministers.

The Council of Sovereignty (Presidential Council), established immediately after the revolution, was to be the supreme authority within Iraq. The Council—which was devoid of any real power—included Lieutenant General Najib al-Rubaʿi, a Sunni Arab retired senior officer with links to the Free Officers but with no political ambition; Mahdi Kubba, a senior Shiʿite politician and leader of the nationalist al-Istiqlal; and Khalid al-Nakshbandi, a Kurdish administrator and notable from a family of high religious status.

In contrast to the majority of revolutionary regimes in Arab states, Qasim's regime did not establish a political party that would enlist social support, assist in controlling society, and reinforce the legitimacy of the regime. Qasim preferred to operate by maneuvering between the existing political forces and by appealing directly to the people without involving political parties.

In early August, the government established a militia (al-Muqawama al-Shaʿbiyya—the People's Resistance) to control the streets and neighborhoods of the large cities.

A special military tribunal (Mahkamat al-Shaʿb—the People's Court), headed by Colonel Fadhil ʿAbbas al-Mahdawi, began its operations on August 16. Politicians, heads of the monarchical establishment, leading figures in the security services, and senior army officers were tried by this tribunal. Most of them were sentenced to imprisonment; the death penalty was imposed on some, but in practice it was carried out in only four cases. All of the others sentenced were released within a few months or years. With the exacerbation of the conflict between Qasim and his rivals within the revolutionary regime, and following the exposure of attempts to overthrow the regime, persons accused of conspiracy against the revolutionary regime were also brought before the tribunal. The testimony heard by the tribunal and the documents submitted to it as evidence were compiled into twenty-three volumes of protocols that were published by the government of Iraq; these protocols constitute a very important source for studying the history of Hashemite Iraq in the 1940s and 1950s and Iraq under Qasim.[12]

Following the fall of the monarchy, a dramatic shift took place in Iraq's foreign policy and international status. Proclamation Number One of the revolutionary regime expressed complete support of the principles of Bandung—that is, of a policy of positive neutralism and nonalignment in the global interbloc struggle.[13] Iraq was no longer the pro-Western state par excellence, the only Arab member of a regional defense alliance under the auspices of the West and directed against the Soviet Union; rather, it had become a neutralist state with close ties to the USSR. As early as August 16, the Soviet Union and Communist China recognized the republican regime in Iraq.[14] Diplomatic relations between the Soviet Union and Iraq resumed immediately. Although the United States and Britain officially recognized the new regime at the beginning of August, the heads of the regime considered the Western powers as rivals who sought its downfall. The revolutionary regime put a stop to Iraqi activity in the Baghdad Pact, and Iraq officially withdrew from the Pact in March 1959. From the standpoint of the Soviet Union, the fall of the pro-Western monarchy in Iraq was an important strategic achievement. It dealt a severe blow to the anti-Soviet Baghdad Pact, which constituted a link between NATO and SEATO, both of which had been established by the Western powers in order to outflank and contain the Soviet Union, Communist China, and the Communist bloc. The important role played by the Communists in the revolutionary regime raised the USSR's hopes that Iraq would become its most important ally among the Mediterranean and Arab countries.

In October 1958, Iraq and the Soviet Union signed a commercial development and cooperation agreement.[15] The USSR agreed to assist in the industrialization of Iraq and in constructing infrastructure plants. Iraq immediately began to receive military equipment from the USSR—initially on a limited scale, which increased as the months went on. In March 1959, the USSR granted Iraq a loan in the amount of 550 million rubles (about $150 million) for the purpose of purchasing Soviet-made products, especially machinery. In May 1959, Iraq signed additional agreements with other Communist countries in Eastern European; in August 1959, the USSR and Iraq signed an agreement for nuclear cooperation.[16] Although Qasim was glad to avail himself of the aid offered by the USSR, he remained cautious and did not give the USSR any real influence over Iraq. Qasim's fear of a Communist coup never entirely subsided.

The revolution led to a change in the regional and inter-Arab status of Iraq. Iraq switched from the conservative, pro-Western camp to the radical revolutionary neutralist-oriented camp and strengthened its ties with the Soviet Union.

The revolution and the shift in Iraq's policy marked the end of a chapter in the history of inter-Arab relations, which had focused on the struggle between the conservative states and forces, led by Iraq, and the radical states and forces, led by Nasirist Egypt. The revolution and the subsequent radicalization of Iraq were major victories for the radical revolutionaries throughout the Arab world and a marked waning of conservative forces and regimes.[17]

On July 19, five days after the revolution, a delegation headed by 'Abd al-

Salam ʿArif set out for Damascus. In the course of that visit, ʿArif met with Nasir and agreed to sign a mutual assistance pact with the UAR.[18] (You will recall that Egypt and Syria had been united in the United Arab Republic since February 1958.) Within a few days, small shipments of arms from the UAR began to reach Iraq. In October, a unit of the UAR Air Force, including Soviet-made MiG-17 combat aircraft, landed at Habaniyya Air Force Base in Iraq. The Iraqi minister of economic affairs, Dr. Ibrahim Kubba, and the minister of social affairs, Naji Talib, met with their opposite numbers in the UAR. At the end of October, a convention for cultural union was signed in Baghdad, and the rector of Asyut University in Egypt was chosen to serve as president of Baghdad University.[19] Nasir apparently did not pressure Iraq to join the UAR at once; however, he did act with determination to cement ties between the two states and enlist Iraq in the camp of "progressive" revolutionary states under his leadership and Egyptian dominance.

Socioeconomic Policy and Relations with the IPC under the Qasim Regime

The radical nationalist, authoritarian etatist regimes during the 1950s and 1960s were established by nationalist officers. In launching the military coups that put an end to the conservative regimes, the ruling elites, and the prosperous upper classes in the Arab states, these officers clearly declared their motives. They wanted to end their countries' relative backwardness and weakness, compared with the West and Israel, and to build up their national power. The revolutionary officers in Egypt, Iraq, Syria, Libya, and Sudan, notwithstanding the differences in specific conditions prevailing in each of those states, shared an awareness that building national power and military forces required economic development, industrialization, social modernization, and a drastic improvement in the standard of living, especially in the level of education. Accordingly, the radical regimes established during the 1950s and 1960s placed special emphasis on agrarian reform and fostering higher education, industrializing, and constructing infrastructure projects, as well as on efforts toward building up military power.

The characteristics of the revolutionary regime in Iraq under Qasim were similar to those of other nationalist radical regimes in the Arab world, but with the addition of a special social sensitivity.[20] The special emphasis placed by the regime on social legislation and improving the living conditions of the poorer strata resulted from a combination of Qasim's personal approach and the important role played in the regime by the Communists and the National Democratic Party, with its well-established liberal social democratic concepts. During the first months of its existence, the revolutionary regime passed a number of important social laws and augmented enforcement of the existing laws.

Immediately after the establishment of the revolutionary government, Finance Minister Muhammad Hadid announced that the government would act as a welfare state.[21] The prices of bread and flour were reduced. Rents were lowered. The working day was reduced from nine hours to eight. Salaries of civil servants in the lower and middle grades were raised by 20 percent. Economic companies and manufacturing plants were required to construct housing for their workers. Directives regarding old age insurance were issued. The Ministry of Social Affairs began to formulate plans for establishing orphanages and sheltered housing for the physically and mentally disabled. Plans were developed to reduce prostitution and juvenile delinquency. The Social Security Law, passed in 1958, was now scrupulously enforced, emphasizing compulsory savings for employees and required participation by the state and employers. Control of food prices was established, along with penalties for merchants who raised their prices without cause.[22]

In accordance with the developments elaborated by Hadid, himself an industrialist with liberal social democratic views, the government made changes in the tax structure. Indirect taxes were reduced, and direct taxes were raised. The agricultural sector, which had not paid any taxes at all during the monarchy due to the pressure of the major landowners, was now subjected to progressive taxation.

On July 27, with the publication of the provisional constitution, the revolutionary regime abrogated the laws which had given special legal status to the tribes. This revolutionary move ended the struggle that had been led, since the 1930s, by personages and forces who sought to bring about the modernization of Iraq. The tribal jurisdiction had been the legal basis for the preservation of the agrarian status quo, had prevented any progress in liberating women, and had posed a serious obstacle to the socioeconomic and political modernization of Iraq.

The intention of the regime to solve the problems of abject poverty was expressed in the emphasis placed on improving residential conditions in the poor neighborhoods on the periphery of the large cities. The scope of residential construction initiated by the revolutionary regime in Iraq was unprecedented and unequaled by any other regime throughout the Arab states. On the eastern and northeastern outskirts of Baghdad, a huge residential project, Madinat al-Thawra ("Revolution Town"), was erected for evacuees of slum neighborhoods.[23] The Provisional Economic Plan elaborated in 1959 devoted 191 million dinars, close to 50 percent of the development budget, to construction and housing. At the same time, considerable resources were invested in improving the health system. In 1959, 6.26 percent of the development budget was invested in health.

In the five-year economic program of 1960, 13.7 million dinars were allocated to the Ministry of Health. Thus, between 1957 and 1960, the number of hospital beds in Iraq increased by 25 percent, to 8,596 beds; in 1963, the number of hospital beds totaled 14,000 (2.1 beds per 1,000 residents).[24] At the same time, many clinics and child care centers were established. These measures contributed to a significant decrease in mortality. The social welfare policy of the Qasim regime brought about constant improvements in the living conditions of the poorer strata.[25]

Improvement in secondary and higher education was viewed by the revolutionary officers of the Arab states as an important means of achieving modernization of society and building national power. Accordingly, the revolutionary regimes invested vast resources in this field and attained significant achievements, which contributed to far-ranging social change. Thus, the 1960 budget doubled the amount that had been devoted to education by the monarchy in 1958. The number of primary and secondary school pupils increased from 520,000 in 1958 to 930,000 in 1960.[26] During the four and a half years of Qasim's revolutionary regime, the number of students tripled, compared with the period of the monarchy.

The progressive social characteristics of the regime were evident in its attitude toward the status of women. In 1959, the government passed the Personal Status Law, which set forth equal rights for women and men in the areas of inheritance, in contrast to the religious law. The new law set the marriageable age at eighteen and up, restricted men's right to divorce their wives, and prohibited polygamy. In view of the legal status of women and their social situation in practice, the great majority of Iraqi society at the time considered this to be an extremely radical revolutionary move.

The law encountered criticism and objections on the part of the Islamic clergy. The senior Shi'ite religious leader in Iraq, Muhsin al-Hakim, published a religious ruling that indirectly censured the law. The ruling condemned the antireligious policy shown by Nasir, but it was obvious to its readers that it was actually directed against Qasim. (Shi'ite religious leaders' opposition to this law was a catalyst in the Shi'ite awakening in Iraq.)

In January 1960, for the first time in the Arab world, a woman was appointed as a government minister. Dr. Naziya Dulaymi, head of the League for the Protection of Women's Rights (Rabitat al-Difa'i a'n Huquq al-Maraa), established in 1952 by Communist activists, was appointed as minister for municipal affairs. Dr. Dulaymi, who was affiliated with the Communist Party, served until the autumn of 1960. (She was then dismissed as part of a series of changes made by Qasim in his government, in order to reduce the influence of the Communist ministers.)

Agrarian reform was one of the first measures enacted by the revolutionary regimes established in the Arab states. In practice, ownership of most agricultural land throughout the Arab world was held by a small number of affluent notable families. These tribal landowners and urban notables had become part of the upper class from whence the ruling political elite had sprung and whose interests they served. On the other hand, the overwhelming majority of the population consisted of poor, landless, or nearly landless fellahin. This system was perceived by the new political and social forces and the revolutionary officers as both a cause and a manifestation of the weakness and backwardness of the Arab states. Agrarian reform was intended to shatter the economic basis of the social stratum of major landowners, which had become one of the mainstays of the political regime and of the ruling elite. In the long term, the agrarian reform was intended to create conditions for modernization, industrialization, and the buildup of national power.

On the eve of the revolution, most of the private land in Iraq was owned by a very few rich families. Forty-nine families held title to 5.4 million dunams,[27] constituting 16.7 percent of private land. A total of 2,480 people held title to 17 million dunams, or 55 percent of arable land. According to other data, 2,803 major landowners controlled 18 million dunams. At the same time, 71 percent of fellahin owned less than 10 dunams, and 43 percent owned less than 4 dunams.[28] Most of the fellahin in Iraq were either entirely landless or owned tiny plots of land too small for their families' subsistence. The landless fellahin and small farmers suffered from severe exploitation and grinding poverty, in a situation which amounted to serfdom. The method of distributing harvests was profitable for the major landowners, at the expense of the poor fellahin, sharecroppers, and agricultural workers. On the eve of the revolution, there were 1.4 million farm workers; 4.5 million people were landless or almost landless with no permanent means of earning a living.[29]

The Agrarian Reform Law, published on September 30, 1958, limited the amount of private land that could be owned by one person to 1,000 dunams of irrigated land and 2,000 dunams of unirrigated land.[30] The law provided for expropriation of larger privately owned areas by the state, to be distributed to fellahin in plots of 30 dunams of irrigated land and 60 dunams of unirrigated land. The major landowners whose lands were to be expropriated would receive compensation in the form of government bonds. The revolutionary regime abrogated the Constitution of 1925, thereby revoking the laws and arrangements which had granted legal status to the tribal notables and enabled them to take control of their tribes' lands (Rights and

Duties of Cultivators, dating from 1933, and Tribal Disputes Regulations, British regulations dating from 1918 and ratified in the Iraqi Constitution in 1925). One of the clauses of the new law changed the terms of the relationship between the landowners and the sharecropping fellahin. Another clause dealt with establishing cooperatives, intended to assist the fellahin in the provision of credit, seeds, and fertilizers, the organization of irrigation, the maintenance of irrigation systems, and the introduction of agricultural machinery.

Application of agrarian reform encountered tremendous obstacles, including resistance from landowners, illiteracy of the fellahin, and complexity of the government bureaucracy. The vast differences in the various areas within Iraq required flexibility and adaptability. The attempt to establish cooperatives progressed extremely slowly. The fellahin were suspicious, and the major landowners exploited the illiteracy and fears of the fellahin in order to stifle the reforms and prevent the establishment of cooperatives. Despite the many errors and difficulties, agrarian reform in Iraq attained certain achievements. By August 1961, 4.8 million dunams of land had been expropriated, and more than 2 million dunams of expropriated and state land had been distributed to the fellahin. Between 1958 and 1962, 6 million dunams were expropriated, of which about 1.4 million dunams were distributed to 28,000 fellahin. According to the data of the Iraqi Ministry of Agriculture, as cited by researcher Hanna Batatu, by September 1963, 1.8 million dunams had been distributed to 35,000 fellahin families. In addition, some 2.8 million dunams were expropriated and, along with 4.2 million dunams of state-owned land, were leased to 244,700 fellahin families on a temporary basis.[31]

Although the agrarian reform was not completed under the Qasim regime, and notwithstanding the limited improvement in the living conditions and standard of living of most fellahin, this policy brought about basic social changes. The stratum of major landowners lost its economic and legal basis and its social and political status. Although the distribution of lands to the fellahin progressed extremely slowly, it prepared the ground for continuation of the reforms following the overthrow of the Qasim regime. Despite the achievements in connection with a more egalitarian and equitable distribution of lands and improvement in living conditions for the fellahin, the reform caused great difficulties and reduced harvests. The bureaucratic system that had been set up to replace the brokers between the fellahin and the market, who had supplied the fellahin with grain and loans, had difficulty operating effectively. The upheavals and changes in the agrarian system, the lack of sufficient financial backing for the fellahin, and the difficulties encountered in modernizing agriculture and adapting irrigation systems to the new conditions led to decreased harvests between 1959 and 1963.[32] However, thanks to the financial resources at the disposal of the government, an adequate supply of food was assured.

The revolutionary regime considered rapid industrialization to be the key to modernization and achievement of national power for Iraq. The Development Board, which had been established in 1950, was disbanded and replaced by the Planning Board and the Ministry of Planning. The centralistic Development Board had emphasized the development of agriculture, irrigation systems, and dams, to which it had devoted most of its resources. In contrast, the Planning Board was intended to serve as a technical coordinator, with various ministries implementing the development programs. The result of the change, while eliminating the bureaucracy of the Development Board, gave rise to confusion and contradictions in the activities of the various ministries and resulted in an even more complex bureaucracy, which hampered industrialization and development.[33] The emphasis of the revolutionary regime on industrialization was evident in its diversion of development budget funds from agriculture to industry. Whereas the Development Board, under the monarchy, had allocated 39 percent of the development budget to agriculture (according to the 1956 plan), the revolutionary regime reduced the resources devoted to agriculture to 12 percent, while increasing the housing and industrialization budget from 9 percent to 49 percent.[34]

The revolutionary regime attempted to promote industrialization on two parallel levels: industrialization by the state itself, and industrialization by encouraging the bourgeoisie and private capital. Thanks to the oil revenues and the economic assistance granted to Iraq by the Soviet Union and other Communist countries, the government of Iraq was able to allocate significant resources to industry. At the same time, with the support of the ministers belonging to the National Democratic Party, the government took steps intended to encourage the bourgeoisie and private capital to invest in industry.[35]

The development plans prepared by the government, the Provisional Economic Plan of 1959 and the Detailed Economic Plan (for the years 1961–62 to 1965–66), suffered from deficiencies, internal contradictions, and a lack of clarity. They amounted to a disorganized collection of various plans that were not always mutually compatible. Admittedly, between 1959 and 1963, industrial plants were established and plans were launched for the establishment of additional plants. Most of these plans, however, had been initiated during the monarchy by the Development Board. The growth of private investment in industry was slow, amounting to about 21 percent throughout the entire Qasim regime, for a total of 23 million Iraqi dinars.[36] The efforts made toward industrialization under Qasim were characterized by an etatist trend, as supported by the Communists and by those entities who considered industrial infrastructure plants and heavy industry to be fundamental for continued industrialization and who were cognizant of the weakness and limitations of the bourgeoisie and private capital.

Despite the diversion of resources to industry, the elaboration of plans, and the encouragement given to the bourgeoisie and private capital, no significant breakthrough occurred in the industrialization of Iraq. The Iraqi economy remained dependent on oil and agriculture, and no headway was made in reducing the gap between Iraq and the rich industrialized states. The share of industry in the GNP of 1961 did not exceed 11 percent; in 1963, it totaled 12.7 percent.[37] The flow of oil profits into the hands of the state gave it great power and potential; nevertheless, industrialization by the state, with a certain degree of encouragement to the bourgeoisie and private capital, did not bring about a change in the structure of the Iraqi economy. Nor was a modern industrial society established in Iraq. Still, despite the limited achievements in modernizing agriculture and in industrializing, the Qasim regime laid the foundations for continued reform and accelerated change in the structure of Iraq's agricultural sector and in the scope of the modern middle class.

Nationalization of oil—Iraq's most important natural and economic resource—had been suggested by various radical nationalist leftist politicians and political forces even during the monarchy. More moderate forces and politicians, as well as the various governments of Iraq, had concentrated their efforts on negotiations with the Iraqi Petroleum Company to increase Iraq's share in oil profits and improve oil output.

In light of the anxiety experienced by the IPC following the fall of the monarchy, Qasim hastened to proclaim on July 18, 1958, that the revolutionary government would comply with all of Iraq's commitments. On July 23, the government officially announced that Iraq would continue the orderly production of oil.[38] Government officials repeatedly announced that Iraq had no intention of nationalizing oil.[39] Of course, Qasim and the heads of his regime were interested in transferring oil to state control; however, they were more influenced by pragmatic considerations of ensuring the flow of oil and increasing government income. They may also have taken into account the lessons learned as a result of the failed attempt by Iran's Prime Minister Mossadeq to nationalize oil between 1950 and 1952. While the IPC was not nationalized during the Qasim regime, the relationship between the IPC and the Iraqi government was characterized by crises, tensions, and suspicion.

Under pressure from the Iraqi government, and fearful that the question of nationalization would be raised, the IPC acceded to some of the government's demands. Government oil revenues increased from $224 million in 1958 to $353 million in 1963.[40] Nonetheless, this increase in income did not satisfy

the government, which considered the IPC to be an imperialist entity exploiting Iraq. In July 1960, the government raised the tax on oil exports through
Basra Port by a factor of 12: from 24 fils per ton to 280 fils per ton.[41] In
response, the IPC temporarily halted the export of oil through Basra. The
demands made by the Iraqi government on the IPC included 50–50 division
of profits, change in the method of calculating profits, transfer of 20 percent
of shares in the company to government ownership, employing Iraqi workers
instead of foreigners, and waiving the IPC's concession on those areas where
no oil had been produced to date. The IPC refused to expand and intensify oil
prospecting in most of this area; the Iraqi government, which wanted to raise
its oil revenues, had been demanding an increase in oil production for years.
During the course of negotiations in 1960, Iraq demanded that the IPC waive
60 percent of the concession areas. The negotiations continued intermittently
until October 1961, when Iraq demanded a waiver of 90 percent of the concession areas.[42]

In October 1961, after a period of turbulent negotiations, during which
the Iraqi government progressively increased its demands, the negotiations
were halted. In the domestic arena, the Qasim regime exploited the negotiations with the IPC and the crises that characterized them for the purpose of
arousing nationalist fervor and mass support of the regime. In December
1961, following the cessation of talks with the IPC, the government promulgated Law no. 80, according to which 99 percent of the concession areas
were expropriated from the IPC; in practice, the IPC was left holding only the
active oilfields.[43] (This took place after the IPC had already agreed to waive
75 percent of the concessions, whereas the government of Iraq demanded a
waiver of all of the inactive concession areas.) Parallel to the negotiations
with the IPC, the government accelerated its plans for the establishment of
the Iraqi National Oil Company (INOC).[44]

In the international arena, Iraq played an active role in establishing the
Organization of Petroleum Exporting Countries (OPEC), intended to reinforce the status of those countries vis-à-vis the oil companies and the West.
OPEC began at a conference in Baghdad in August 1960, with the participation of Iraq, Iran, Kuwait, Saudi Arabia, and Venezuela; its official purpose
was to discuss the decrease in oil prices.[45] The Iraqi initiative resulted from
Iraq's desire to increase its oil revenues; another contributing factor was
Iraq's ambition to bolster its international status, in view of the struggle in the
inter-Arab arena between Iraq and the UAR under Nasir.

Although the Qasim regime did not actually nationalize the IPC, its status
was severely weakened, with Iraq (by means of Law no. 80) regaining control
of all national oil resources except for the active oilfields. Although Qasim's
negotiations with the IPC were chaotic and inefficient, Iraq managed to at-

tain certain achievements without real crisis and without stopping the flow of oil.

The Confrontation between the Ideological Trends of the Revolutionary Regime and the Struggle between Qasim and ʿArif

A few days after the revolution, a pattern of political differences and personal rivalry began to evolve between the two heads of the revolutionary regime, ʿAbd al-Karim Qasim and ʿAbd al-Salam ʿArif. As often happens in political life, the disputes between the two regarding politics and policies, their differences in outlook, and their personal rivalry each aggravated the other element and led to a forceful confrontation that essentially amounted to a struggle between political and ideological orientations. As long as the Iraqi officers who launched the coup remained underground, facing the threat of execution if the conspiracy was discovered, and as long as their common goal remained the overthrow of the despised monarchy, the political disputes and differences in world outlook were suppressed. However, once the revolutionary regime had risen to power, it became necessary to choose between various courses of operation and to reach concrete political decisions. In August and September 1958, a conflict arose between Qasim and ʿArif, leading to the expulsion of ʿArif . This conflict was the first stage in the struggle between Qasim, who represented the Iraqi territorialist approach and was supported by the Communists and the Kurds (and, to some degree, the Shiʿites), and his nationalist rivals (with ʿArif as their hero and champion), whose common denominator was support for Arab unity and unification between Iraq and the UAR.

In the euphoric atmosphere prevailing in the streets of Iraq following the revolution, two different radical ideological and political trends arose, reflecting the two main political forces and orientations in Iraq's national identity. The struggle between these orientations was manifested, during the first months of the revolutionary regime, by the confrontation between Qasim and ʿArif. The two ideological orientations had joined forces to achieve the revolution but could not continue to cooperate over time. One of them was the orientation toward pan-Arab nationalism. Supporters of pan-Arabic policies immediately sought to realize the vision of Arab unity by unification between Iraq and the UAR under Gamal ʿAbd al-Nasir, who had become the leader and symbol of radical nationalist revolutionary forces throughout the Arab world. This movement gave rise to the slogan "complete and immediate unity" (al-wahda al-fawriyya al-shamila). The other was the Iraqi-territorial approach, which primarily sought to fortify the revolutionary regime in Iraq, to achieve domestic social and economic reform, and to preserve and strengthen Iraq as a sovereign state. This approach, while not actually rejecting the slogan of Arab unity, interpreted it in terms of close relations, or even the establishment of a loose federation, between the radical regimes of the Arab world, but without subordinating Iraq to the sovereignty of Nasir. The historical development of the collective consciousness of identity in Iraq's heterogeneous society involved both the orientation toward Arab national identity (with its pan-Arab orientation) and that toward Iraqi-territorial national identity. At times, these two orientations complemented each other; at other times, as a function of the prevailing political conditions, they opposed each other. During the period of Hashemite rule, the "Iraqocentric" pan-Arab orientation, which aimed at Arab unity centered around Iraq, was more dominant and more ideologically cohesive. During the Hashemite monarchy, only the Bakr Sidqi-Hikmat Sulayman government in 1936–37 adopted an Iraqi territorialist orientation.

The radical pan-Arab nationalist euphoria, which had been aroused throughout the Arab world in 1958 following the establishment of the UAR and the overthrow of the monarchy in Iraq, empowered pan-Arab nationalism. This movement, in its radical version—at least in the initial stage of enthusiasm—amounted to a call for unification of Iraq with the UAR to form a single, powerful Arab state under the leadership of Nasir. Opposed to the pan-Arab orientation were the forces of Iraqi territorialism: the National Democratic Party, the KDP, most of the army officers, and the Communists— the most ideologically cohesive force on the Iraqi scene, who succeeded in dramatically increasing their influence over the Iraqi public.

Qasim's inclinations were to mediate between integrative Iraqi territorialism, which favored the preservation, reinforcement, and development of the Iraqi state and the integration of the various ethnic communities into the Iraqi nation, and Iraqi Arabism, intended to preserve Iraq's status among the separate Arab states, each of which maintained its own independence. This trend opposed unification between Iraq and the UAR, abandoned the traditional Hashemite policy which had favored unification with Syria under Iraqi dominance, and turned its back on the vision of Arab unity manifested by merger of Arab states into a single entity. Qasim's supporters who favored the Iraqi territorial approach did not publicly reject the slogan of Arab unity; rather, they changed the emphasis of that slogan by calling for the establishment of an Arab federation. This federation would foster inter-Arab cooperation while preserving the separate existence and identity of the various states and preventing any real unification between Iraq and the UAR. Qasim's approach placed its highest priority on resolving the economic distresses of Iraqi society, promoting development and modernization within the Iraqi economy, and building the Iraqi nation through the integration of Iraq's heterogeneous population.

A hasty unification with the UAR in the name of Arab nationalism could well have resulted in the alienation of the Kurds, who remained one of the primary mainstays of the revolutionary regime. Fearing that, as part of a large Arab state, they would be marginalized into a negligible minority and that the oil resources in their territory would be exploited, the Kurds were liable to withdraw their support of the regime and to renew their national struggle against the Iraqi state. Qasim personally feared that, if and when unification of Iraq and the UAR took place, he would lose his status as the leader of the revolution and of Iraq in favor of 'Arif, who would depose him by virtue of his close ties with Nasir and willingness to recognize Nasir's supreme leadership. Qasim was not prepared to accept Nasir as his leader and did not want Iraq's oil resources to be placed at the disposal and under the control of a united Arab state dominated by Egypt and led by Nasir. Qasim and the officers associated with him feared a takeover of Iraq by the Egyptian regime, which would leave them with no government and no state.

On July 19, 'Arif departed for Syria, as part of a delegation sent by the revolutionary regime. In Damascus, he met with Nasir and the Syrian president, Shukri al-Quwatli.[46] In the course of the visit, a friendship and cooperation agreement was signed between Iraq and the UAR, and the two states—both governed by revolutionary nationalist radical regimes with similar slogans, and both headed by army officers with nationalist radical views—agreed on cementing ties between them. The meeting with Nasir, the hero and champion of many of the revolutionary officers in Iraq, and the enthusiastic reception which he was given in Damascus made 'Arif even more convinced that the historic opportunity of realizing the vision of Arab unity had arrived. Upon his return, 'Arif launched a campaign throughout Iraq, to enlist public support for the revolutionary regime and for himself as the leader who would bring Iraq to Arab unity via unification with the UAR.[47] 'Arif was swept up by the wave of pan-Arab nationalist and pro-Nasirist enthusiasm which washed over the streets of Iraq's cities, encompassing the younger members of the effendiyya and the poorer strata. In his impassioned public appearances, 'Arif contributed to empowering that trend.

On July 24, Michel 'Aflaq, the leader and ideologue of the Syrian Ba'th Party, came to Baghdad to accelerate the process of unification between Iraq and the UAR. It is possible that 'Arif was inspired by the revolutionary regime of the Free Officers in Egypt and accordingly sought to remove Qasim and to take his place, just as Nasir had removed Muhammad Nagib, his senior partner in both rank and age.[48]

To counter the mass demonstrations of support for 'Arif throughout Iraq and the calls for support of his leadership and of Nasir as the leader of the Arab nation, other mass demonstrations were organized in support of the existing regime and the establishment of an Arab federation.[49] At first glance, there was no great difference between the slogans of the two varieties of demonstrations; the seemingly minor difference in emphasis, however, concealed contrasting orientations and a steadily mounting personal rivalry. The slogans that called for an Arab federation (*ittihad*) embodied rejection of the slogans that supported immediate unity with the UAR (*wahda*). Qasim succeeded in having his name identified with the revolutionary regime in Iraq, so that the expression of support of the regime had the additional meaning of support for his leadership. Qasim was extremely popular among the poor, whose standard of living had been improved by the regime and who looked to him and to the revolutionary regime identified with him in hopes of improving their economic situation. The poor were less exposed than the educated middle class to the influence of Arab nationalist ideology and Nasirist slogans. Still, Qasim also enjoyed the extensive support of the middle class and the educated members of the effendiyya. Although most of that stratum subscribed to nationalist views and pan-Arab discourse, its members also had strong feelings of Iraqi or Iraqi-Arab identity and maintained an interest in the continued existence of Iraq. Accordingly, many of them supported the movement for strengthening the revolutionary regime and preserving Iraq as a sovereign state. Other groups that supported Qasim included the Communists, the Kurds, members of the National Democratic Party, and most of the army officers.

In order to strengthen his position with regard to Qasim, 'Arif issued an appeal on September 10 for the establishment of the Revolutionary Council. However, Qasim exploited his public status, his position in the eyes of the officers, and his control of the Council of Sovereignty, which had been established as the supreme governing body after the fall of the monarchy, in order to oust 'Arif from his positions as deputy chief of staff and deputy prime minister. On September 30, 'Arif was fired from his post as minister of the interior and from all his government positions. An attempt by 'Arif to organize his supporters in government and among the senior army officers was frustrated by Qasim, who appointed him ambassador to West Germany.[50] Qasim also took steps to weaken 'Arif's pan-Arab nationalist supporters by removing Fuad al-Rikabi, the leader of the Ba'th Party, from his position as minister of development and appointing him minister of state—a position devoid of any actual authority.

'Arif, who could not accept his ouster, returned to Baghdad on November 4. He was arrested at the airport and imprisoned. (Qasim refrained from having him executed. During 'Arif's imprisonment, Qasim frequently visited him and held conversations and debates with him. He eventually released him, thus making it easier for 'Arif to organize the coup that led to Qasim's fall in 1963.) Qasim had succeeded in fortifying his personal leadership and had dealt a severe blow to the supporters of the pan-Arab nationalist movement. The struggle within the revolutionary regime, however, was far from over.

The Struggle between Qasim and the Nationalists: The Rashid 'Ali Conspiracy and the Shawwaf Revolt in Mosul

Early in December 1958, the Iraqi security services exposed a conspiracy to overthrow the Qasim regime. The plot was organized by senior nationalist politician Rashid 'Ali al-Kaylani.[51] Rashid 'Ali had been a key figure in the conservative ruling elite in the 1920s and 1930s. In the early 1930s, he and Yasin al-Hashimi had jointly founded a political organization called al-Ikha al-Watani, a loose association of nationalist politicians who built their political nationalist status by opposing the 1930 treaty between Iraq and Britain and demanding the removal of all restrictions on Iraq's independence. In the early 1940s, he allied himself with a group of nationalist officers led by Salah al-Din al-Sabbagh, who established him as prime minister in April 1940. Rashid 'Ali served as prime minister until June 1941, when anti-British, pro-German leanings in Iraq led to a deterioration in the relationship between Iraq and Britain and eventually to war between the two states. Following the British occupation of Iraq in 1941, Rashid 'Ali fled to Nazi Germany. At the end of World War II, he was granted asylum by King Ibn Saud; since 1953, he had lived in Egypt and Syria. The Hashemite regime considered Rashid 'Ali to be a traitor to the kingdom and the Iraqi state. However, many of the nationalists viewed him as a hero by virtue of his role in leading the anti-British nationalist revolt in 1941. Due to this image, and despite the fact that he had belonged to the reactionary conservative elite of the monarchy, he was permitted to return to Iraq after the revolution. Rashid 'Ali, with his pan-Arab nationalist views, attempted to reinforce his personal status by supporting the unification between Iraq and the UAR. He was rapidly surrounded by a strange coalition of revolutionary radical nationalists who supported 'Arif, officers and activists whose personal ambitions had not been realized in the new regime, and the few remaining supporters of the Hashemite monarchy—namely, landowners who objected to agrarian reform and feared the increasing strength of the Communists. Among the major tribal landowners who supported this organization was 'Abd al-Rida al-Haj al-Sikkar of Diwaniyya, whose family had been affiliated with Rashid 'Ali back in the 1920s and

1930s. (His relative, 'Abd al-Wahid al-Sikkar, had led the great tribal revolt that had brought al-Ikha al-Watani to power in 1935, culminating in the establishment of a government under Yasin al-Hashimi, with Rashid 'Ali as interior minister.)

Many senior officers were involved in, or at least aware of, the developing conspiracy, but they preferred to keep silent and await its results. The conspirators planned to provoke riots and confusion in the streets of Iraq and then demand Qasim's resignation. The organization received financial support from the embassy of the UAR and a promise for help by way of Syria when the coup actually took place.[52] However, the security services and officers loyal to Qasim exposed the plot, which had been sloppily organized, and arrested its leaders. The heads of the conspiracy were tried by the revolutionary tribunal headed by Mahdawi—which, in addition to prosecuting the leaders of the old regime, had begun to try persons suspected of conspiracy against the revolutionary regime. At the same time, at least on the surface, the relations with and cooperation between Iraq and the UAR continued.

The fact that the Communists were the most organized and most cohesive force among Qasim's supporters transformed them into the principal rival of the pan-Arab nationalists in the competition for control of public opinion and the streets. The tension between the nationalists and the Communists, which had prevailed since the revolution, now became open conflict. This conflict was exacerbated by the crisis between Nasir and the Communists, which had erupted following his speech of December 23 in Port Said, in which he had attacked communism and defined it as the enemy of Arab nationalism and Arab unity. Nasir's attack on the Communists had been engendered by their skeptical attitude toward the establishment of the UAR and toward pan-Arab nationalism and by their new role as the principal ideological and political rival of the nationalists in Iraq. Nasir may also have attacked the Communists as an attempt to improve relations between the UAR and the United States. Reinforcement of communism in Iraq and the Communists' status as an important mainstay in the Qasim regime gave rise to the combination of circumstances whereby Nasir was in conflict with the Communists and with Qasim and his regime in Iraq.

On February 5, 1959, the Mahdawi tribunal condemned 'Arif to death (although he was not actually executed). Publication of the sentence sparked a crisis in the Qasim government, and six ministers submitted their resignations.[53] The resigning ministers belonged to the pan-Arab nationalist parties, al-Istiqlal and the Ba'th. Among them were Minister Without Portfolio Fuad al-Rikabi, who was also secretary of the Ba'th Party; Foreign Minister 'Abd al-Jabbar Jumurd; and Minister of Guidance Sadik Shanshal, a leading member of al-Istiqlal.

The ministers of the National Democratic Party, who did not support immediate union with the UAR, also submitted their resignation, in protest against the undemocratic procedures of the trial and their unwillingness to remain the sole partners of the Communists in the government. However, under pressure by Qasim, they withdrew their resignations. The other three ministers who actually resigned were Minister of Social Affairs Naji Talib, Minister of Transport and Public Works Shaykh Baba 'Ali, and Minister of Health Muhammad Salah Mahmud.

The ministers appointed to replace them included army officers, associates of Qasim, members of the National Democratic Party, and men affiliated with the Communists.

During the government crisis in February, a clandestine organization of nationalist officers arose in an attempt to block the Communists by limiting Qasim's powers and eventually deposing him. The conspirators considered establishing a new Revolutionary Council, headed by Brigadier General Nadhim Tabaqchali. They included the head of military intelligence, Col. Rif'at al-Haj Sirri, Brigadier General Naji Talib (who had resigned from the government), the commander of the Fifth Brigade (posted in Mosul), Colonel 'Abd al-Wahhab al-Shawwaf, and other officers. The official—and perhaps even the real—motive of these officers was their criticism of Qasim's government, stemming from their pan-Arab nationalist outlook. Several of them, scions of notable families, were also motivated by their objections to agrarian reform and their fear of communism. Some of them were disappointed in their ambitions to attain cabinet posts or other positions of influence in the revolutionary regime. In preparing for the revolt, close ties were forged between the Ba'th Party under Fuad al-Rikabi and the army officers.

A coalition of forces supporting pan-Arab nationalism and unification between Iraq and the UAR now arose against Qasim in a joint attempt to depose him. Among Qasim's rivals were those of his partners in the revolution who entertained pan-Arab nationalist and revolutionary radical views, and who considered unification with the UAR to be the fulfillment of the vision of Arab unity. These, however, were joined by conservative elements as well—tribal landowners who opposed agrarian reform and feared the increasing strength of communism. It is doubtful whether the tribal landowners and the conservative elements were really willing to accomplish Arab unity by means of unification between Iraq and the UAR under the radical regime headed by Nasir. However, their hostility toward Qasim and their fear of communism created the necessary common denominator for a coalition of opposing forces. Fear of communism was also exploited in order to arouse resistance to Qasim among Islamic circles and within the traditional popular strata. Among the Shi'ites, especially from the popular and traditional strata,

Qasim's new laws and secular leanings aroused resistance and opposition. At the same time, however, pan-Arab slogans and calls for immediate Arab unity were also met with suspicion and resistance. Many Shi'ites feared that, in the case of Iraqi union with Egypt and Syria, the resulting state would have a vast Sunnite majority, and the Shi'ites would lose any importance and become a marginal minority.

The plans made by the conspirators for an organized revolt were not implemented in practice, due to an independent, uncoordinated move by Colonel Shawwaf, commander of the garrison in Mosul, who sought to secure for himself the senior position in the coup against Qasim.

The city of Mosul was characterized by social conservatism and pan-Arab nationalism, both attitudes popular among the Sunnite Arabs The relationship between the Sunnite Arab majority and the Christian and Kurdish minorities within the city, as well as the Kurdish and Turkmen majority in the surrounding area, was complex and fraught with tension. Following the revolt against the Qasim regime in Mosul and among the army units posted there, the Partisans of Peace—an umbrella organization that carried out activities initiated by the Communist Party—held a mass rally in support of the regime and of Qasim. The rally, on March 5, was attended by about 250,000 people, most of whom had come from out of town. After the rally ended and most of its participants had left Mosul, anti-Communist demonstrations broke out in the city, fanned by fears inspired among the urban Sunnite Arab population by the presence of thousands of Kurds and Turkmen at the rally.

On March 8, the military commander of Mosul, Colonel Shawwaf, called for Qasim's ouster.[54] Shawwaf was joined by additional senior army officers, including the commander of the Air Force base outside Mosul. Other officers from remote areas of Iraq adopted a position of sympathetic expectancy.

The revolt was supported by landowners, wealthy merchants, and tribal notables, but most of its military leaders came not from those classes but from the middle class (characterized by pan-Arab nationalist views), which had supported the revolution against the monarchy and now considered unification with the UAR to be essential to complete the revolution. The rising strength of the Communists and the tension between them and Nasir aroused the fears of those officers and increased their desire for the immediate realization of Arab unity.

The revolt in Mosul inspired Qasim's opponents throughout Iraq. On the outskirts of Baghdad, demonstrations in support of the revolt broke out. In and around Mosul itself, bloody clashes took place between army units and various social groups. The resulting confusion was fueled by the complex interplay of ethnic, tribal, and class-related tensions.

The events in Mosul were breathtakingly described by Hanna Batatu, a scholar of Iraq and its revolutionary social and political movements:

> The events of March at Mosul illumined with a flaming glare the complexity of the conflicts that agitated Iraq and disclosed its various social forces in their essential nature and in the genuine line-up of their life interests. For four days and four nights Kurds and Yezidis stood against Arabs; Assyrian and Aramean Christians against Arab Moslems; the Arab tribe of Al-Bu Mutaiwit against the Arab tribe of Shammar; the Kurdish tribe of al-Gargariyyah against Arab Al-Bu Mutaiwit; the peasants of the Mosul country against their landlords; the soldiers of the Fifth Brigade against their officers; the periphery of the city of Mosul against its center; the plebeians of the Arab quarters of al-Makkawi and Wadi Hajar against the aristocrats of the Arab quarter of ad-Dawwasah; and within the quarter of Bab al-Baid, the family of al-Rajabu against its traditional rivals, the Aghawat (Kurdish notables). It seemed as if all social cement dissolved and all political authority vanished. Individualism, breaking out, waxed into anarchy. The struggle between nationalists and Communists had released age-old antagonisms, investing them with an explosive force and carrying them to the point of civil war.

What added to the acuteness of the conflicts was the high degree of coincidence between the economic and ethnic or religious divisions. For example, many of the soldiers of the Fifth Brigade were not only from the poorer layers of the population, but were also Kurds, whereas the officers were preponderantly from the Arab middle or lower middle classes. Again, many of the peasants in the villages around Mosul were Christian Arameans, whereas the landlords were, for the most part, Moslem Arabs or Arabized Moslems.

Where the economic and ethnic or confessional divisions did not coincide, it was often not the racial or religious, but the class factor, that asserted itself. The Arab soldiers clung not to the Arab officers, but to the Kurdish soldiers. The landed chieftains of Kurdish al-Gargariyyah sided with the landed chieftains of Arab Shammar. The old and affluent commercial Christian families such as the Baituns, Sarsams, and Rassams did not make common cause with the Christian peasants. When acting on their own initiative, the peasants, whatever their nation, poured their wrath upon the landlords indiscriminately and without regard even to political alignment: they killed among others, 'Ali al-'Umari, a Moslem Arab and an anti-Qasimite; Qasim Hadid, a Moslem Arab and the uncle of Muhammad Hadid, Qasim's most trusted minister; and Yusuf Namrud, a fence-sitter and a notorious Christian Aramean landed usurer. For their part, the poor and the laborers of the Arab Moslem quarters of al-Makkawi, al-Mashahadah, and at-Tay-yanah stood shoulder to shoulder with the Kurdish and Aramean peasants against the Arab Moslem landlords. In all three quarters, and especially in al-Makkawi, the influence of the Communists was widespread: al-Makkawi was the home of 'Abd ur-Rahman al-Qassab, a member of the Local Party Committee and the most authoritative Communist in Mosul. But there were Moslem Arabs from the poorer classes on the other side too: they were either attracted to the pan-Arab cause of Nasir or of the left-inclined Ba'th—the effective leader of the Ba'th in Mosul, Fadil ash-Shagarah, was a humble construction worker—or were clients of traditionally dominant families such as al-Aghawat in the quarter of Bab al-Baid or of established bullies—qabadayat—such as the Kashmulas in the Manqushah quarter and the Sinjaris in Ra's aj-Jadah.

The tribal, ethnic, and class conflicts had been ripening for years. The ill feeling between the settled cultivating tribe of Al-Bu Mutaiwit and the originally warring mobile tribe of Shammar went back at the latest to 1946, when a dispute over land led to a bloody encounter in which 144 men from both sides met their death. The Assyrians, a foreign and unassimilable people, whom the English had employed as mercenary troops and whose very name still irritated Iraqis, had nursed a bitter hatred against Arab Mosul ever since 1933, when officers from this town played a prominent role in the crushing of a forlorn Assyrian rebellion. The Kurds, for their part, had long regarded Mosul as a thorn in their flesh—an Arab rampart projecting into territory which they considered their own. Moreover, they as yet remembered the murder of Shaikh Sa'id of Barzinjah, father of the famed rebel Shaikh Mahmud and leader of Sulaymaniyyah's mystic Qadiri order and eighteen of his retainers by angry Mosul crowds in 1909.[55]

Notwithstanding the support shown for the revolt in Mosul by many army officers and nationalists throughout Iraq, who considered it as exemplifying the conflict with the Communists and heralding the overthrow of Qasim, most of the army units and extensive segments of the public remained loyal to his leadership. The Communist Party, acting through workers' organizations and the sympathetic militia (al-Muqawama al-Sha'biyya), enabled Qasim to retain control of the streets of Baghdad. The loyalty evidenced by officers of the air force and of many army units enabled launching an offensive against the rebelling units in Mosul. Within the rebelling units themselves, a social, class-related rift, which at times involved ethnic elements as well, now came into play. The rebellious officers who supported Shawwaf, most of them Sunnite Arabs from the middle or lower middle classes, were opposed by the enlisted men and NCOs from the poorer strata, most of them Shi'ites and Kurds. Whereas the officers, staunch supporters of pan-Arab nationalist ideology, were influenced by Nasirism and Ba'th ideology, the enlisted men—mainly sons of fellahin and residents of slum neighborhoods—believed in the social messages of the Qasim regime and viewed Qasim himself as their leader and great hope. In the course of the revolt in Mosul, situations arose in which enlisted men refused to carry out their officers' orders to revolt against the regime. Soldiers, NCOs, and those officers who wished to remain loyal to the regime or who supported the Communist Party rose up against their senior officers who were trying to overthrow Qasim.

Colonel Shawwaf himself was wounded in a bombing raid by aircraft belonging to the loyalist forces; upon evacuation to hospital, he was murdered by an orderly. Given the strong resistance and failure to undermine Qasim's hold on Baghdad, the revolt among the military and even in Mosul itself began to subside. Supporters of Qasim and pro-Communists regained control of Mosul. Members of the poorer strata, the Kurds, and the Communists took to the streets, murdering nationalists and those considered wealthy.[56]

Ethnic, class-related, ideological, and personal tensions and hatred combined in an outburst of cruel violence, both on the part of the nationalists at the beginning of the revolt and on the part of Qasim's supporters at its end. Qasim succeeded in putting down the dangerous revolt in Mosul, but the rift between him and the nationalists had become irrevocable. The Communists now remained the only strong and well-organized force among Qasim's supporters in the political arena. The officer-conspirators Sirri and Tabaqchali, who had enjoyed nationalist prestige among the officers, were executed. While their execution was a severe blow to Qasim's nationalist enemies, it inspired a number of officers who had not been expelled from the army to make clandestine contact with the Ba'th Party, which had gone underground.

Despite the chill in the relationship between the UAR and Iraq following the exposure of the Rashid 'Ali conspiracy, both states and their leaders refrained from overt conflict until March 1959. Various UAR newspapers published articles that expressed criticism of the rise of communism in Iraq. At the end of January 1959, the senior Egyptian journalist Hassanein Heikal published an open letter to Qasim, in which he expressed his astonishment at the freedom of action given to the Communists in Iraq.[57] The deliberations of the revolutionary People's Court headed by Mahdawi, which tried both 'Arif and Rashid 'Ali, received hostile and mocking coverage in the UAR press. Mahdawi himself openly attacked the UAR on various occasions, starting in mid-December. However, Qasim and Nasir themselves refrained from overt conflict. Nasir attempted to meet with Qasim several times, but Qasim avoided such a meeting. (In fact, the two men, who had headed the most significant revolutions of the Arab world, never met face-to-face.) The conspirators against Qasim had been in contact with the UAR, which had expressed its willingness to support them. In practice, however, when the revolt broke out in Mosul, the UAR press expressed its enthusiastic support, but no real assistance of any type was rendered.[58]

Following the revolt and the public support given to it by Radio Damascus and other UAR media, the tensions between the states became an overt rift. Qasim was accused of betraying the Arab nation and was portrayed as the servant of communism. Military, economic, cultural, and educational cooperation was suspended. Hundreds of Egyptian expert consultants, who had come to Iraq following the revolution, returned to Egypt. The plans for continued cooperation were frozen and eventually terminated.[59]

Within seven months after the fall of the monarchy in Baghdad, which had marked the end of the struggle between the conservative regime of Iraq and radical revolutionary Egypt, the conflict between those two states—both of which were now controlled by revolutionary nationalist radical regimes with similar slogans and ideological principles—was renewed. The ideological affinity and the similarity of the social and political conditions under which the heads of both regimes had developed their world outlook and pursued their courses of action did not prevent the renewal of rivalry between the states, now in the guise of a struggle between two radical entities which drew their strength from similar social forces. Although Qasim admired Nasir, he was not prepared to accept his leadership unquestioningly and did not wish to acquiesce to Egyptian domination under the banner of Arab unity. Although Qasim did not aspire to leadership of the Arab world and did not give a high priority to Iraqi ambitions for dominance in Syria, the very fact of the rivalry between him and the nationalist forces which supported unification and considered Nasir to be the leader of Arab unity transformed him into an enemy from Nasir's point of view. As Nasir saw it, the existence of a radical revolutionary regime in Iraq, which made use of slogans similar to those of the UAR but was not prepared to accept his leadership, constituted a threat to his status and dominance and that of Egypt in the Arab world, especially among the forces of radicalism.

Despite the crass attacks launched by Nasir and the Egyptian press, Qasim maintained some degree of restraint until the attempt on his life by members of the Ba'th Party on October 7, 1959.[60] (Among the participants in the failed attempt at assassination was a young, determined Ba'th leader named Saddam Husayn.) Following the failure of the assassination, Fuad al-Rikabi, secretary of the Ba'th Party, fled to Syria, along with those conspirators who managed to get away. A wave of arrests was launched against the Ba'th Party, but did not succeed in putting it entirely out of action.

At this point, tensions between the UAR and Iraq reached unprecedented heights. Qasim began to appeal to the Syrian people to secede from the UAR.[61] In Baghdad itself, an anti-Nasirist radio station began a series of attacks against the UAR and Nasir himself.

As part of the struggle that developed between Iraq and the UAR, the conflict with Israel was used as a vehicle for mutual accusations, in order to reinforce the status of nationalism. Starting in March 1959, Egypt, within the framework of the Arab League, began to raise the Palestine question and propose that the League renew its activities on that question, including recognition of a Palestinian entity (*kiyan*).[62] In November 1959, Iraq issued a memorandum calling for the establishment of a Palestinian army; in December, Qasim advocated the establishment of a Palestinian republic.[63] During the course of 1960, the conflict with Israel and the Palestinian problem were frequently used for the purpose of mutual accusations and recriminations between Iraq and the UAR. Qasim accused Israel, Egypt, and Jordan of taking over Palestine and claimed that the only way to remedy this injustice was to establish a Palestinian state in Gaza and the West Bank.[64] Qasim, who in practice was only nominally interested in the conflict with Israel and showed no particular empathy toward the Palestinians, made his proposals in order to repel the Nasirist offensive.

The Rise and Fall of the Communists under the Qasim Regime

The deeper the rift between Qasim and the nationalists became, the stronger the Communists became as the only organized political bastion of his regime. The dramatic reinforcement of the Communists following the overthrow of the monarchy in Iraq is a striking historical phenomenon, especially given the weakness of the Communist parties in the other Arab states and the limited effect exerted by Marxism and Communist ideology in Middle Eastern societies.

Ever since its establishment in 1939, the Communist Party of Iraq had operated illegally and underground. During the monarchy, its leaders and activists were arrested and imprisoned from time to time, and some of them were even sentenced to death and executed. Thus, in the autumn of 1948, the legendary party leader Yusuf Salman ("Fahed") was executed; he had been arrested with other party leaders following the wathba riots in January of that year. As to the number of party members after World War II, several estimates indicate figures between a few hundred and four thousand.[65] These fluctuations were at least partly occasioned by the changes in the underground operating conditions of the party. In some years, the Communists were actively persecuted by the authorities; in others, liberal leanings within the regime enabled the expansion of Communist activity, with party leaders using various political, social, and professional organizations as fronts for their actions.

The difficulty of promulgating atheist Communist ideology in a traditional-religious society, the nature of the Hashemite monarchy and the political arena within Iraq, and the absence of those conditions which had enabled the development of Communist parties in Europe made it difficult for Iraq's Communists to become a popular force that enjoyed extensive support of the public.

Although the number of Communist Party members remained small (0.4 percent of the population of Iraq in 1947), they played an active role in labor strikes and outbursts of violence involving young members of the effendiyya—high school and college students—in January 1948, November 1952, and October 1956. Although never achieving the dimensions of a mass movement, in the 1940s and 1950s the Communists did manage to win a certain level of support not only among college students (about 3.8 percent of students) but also with teachers and lawyers, and to exert considerable influence on the political and ideological climate prevailing among those groups.[66]

The relative success of the Communists in affecting the political moods and attitudes among the younger members of the effendiyya during the monarchy, and their dramatic rise after the fall of the Hashemite regime, resulted (among other factors) from the weakness of the nationalist radical forces. The pan-Arab nationalist radical forces—which had arisen in Iraq from the mid-1930s on and had manifested themselves in the al-Muthanna club, the al-Futuwwa youth movement, the orientation of the educational system, and the attitudes of the army officers who became a strong force behind the scenes in politics—lost some of their power following the suppression of the Rashid 'Ali revolt in 1941.[67] It should be recalled that pan-Arab nationalist radicalization was not accompanied by the fostering of any programs or messages that supported radical social change. This was a nationalist radicalism that retained a socially conservative point of view. The pan-Arab nationalist party, al-Istiqlal, which represented the legitimate political expression of the pan-Arab nationalist movements after World War II, never developed any cohesive program or messages in support of radical social or economic change or any drastic solution to the prevailing social and economic distresses.

The relative attraction felt by young, educated Iraqis toward the Communist messages resulted from a combination of social radicalism and a revolutionary political attitude with a national concept based on Iraqi territorialism. The Communists (and, to a certain degree, the Nationalist Democratic Party as well) represented a combination of the Iraqi-territorialist trend in the national consciousness of identity and demands for radical social and political change. Within the Iraqi Communist Party, members of ethnic minorities played a significant role. The supranational and supra-ethnic messages of communism were attractive to young, educated Kurds, Shi'ites, Jews, and others who identified with Iraq but had difficulty identifying with pan-Arab nationalism and whose sensitivity to social injustice motivated them to desire revolutionary change within Iraq.

The success of the Communists in increasing their influence following the revolution resulted from a combination of two major factors. One was the effective tactics and determination of their activists, who had gained strength during the period of persecution by the monarchy. The other, the conditions which had arisen as a result of the conflict between the various inclinations in the collective consciousness of identity of Iraqi society, as expressed in the conflict between Qasim and the pan-Arab nationalists.

Immediately following the overthrow of the monarchy, the Communists launched an extensive campaign of public activity, utilizing three front organizations: the Federation of Democratic Youth, the League for the Defense of Women's Rights, and Partisans of Peace.[68] These were Iraqi branches of worldwide organizations which had been established during the 1950s with the support of the Soviet Union, as means of expanding Communist influence over the intelligentsia and the workers, as part of the overall conflict with the capitalist West during the cold war.

When the revolutionary regime, early in August 1958, began to establish its militia to retain control of the streets, the organized enlistment of Communists in the new organization transformed them into the dominant entity within its ranks.[69] At the same time, the Communists endeavored to attain control of workers' unions and other civilian organizations. In the first months after the revolution, the Communists played a pivotal role in establishing many trade unions and professional organizations, becoming dominant within them: the Teachers' Union, the Journalists' Union, the Bar Association, the General Union of Fellahin Societies, the Printers' Union, the Basra Port Workers' Union, the Association of Engineers, the Railway Workers' Union, the General Union of Iraqi Students, and other organizations. In 1959, Communist activists established the General Federation of Trade Unions.

Communist Party membership increased to 26,000; however, their activity within the various unions and associations extended their influence to hundreds of thousands. Thus, for example, the General Union of Fellahin

Societies claimed to represent 250,000 members; the General Federation of Trade Unions boasted 275,000 members.[70] More than 84,000 members were registered in the Federation of Democratic Youth in the summer of 1959. At the same time, the Communists expanded their influence within the army and enjoyed support among the officers. Of course, National Democratic Party activists attempted to oppose the Communist activists in various organizations; still, in 1958–59, the Communist Party had no objection to the representation of other "progressive" and "democratic" forces in the various organizations and associations—provided, of course, that those forces did not endanger Communist dominance. The expansion of the Communist Party in Iraq in 1958 and 1959 was unprecedented throughout the Arab world. In no other Arab state was Communist influence so strong.

The increased strength of the Communists, along with the crisis in the relations between Egypt and the Soviet Union, temporarily gave Iraq the status of principal Arab ally of the USSR. In March 1959, a series of cooperation and economic assistance agreements were signed between the Soviet Union and Iraq.

The strengthening and increased self-confidence of the Communist Party led its leaders, in the spring of 1959, to increase their demands for participation of Communist representatives in the government.[71] (Dr. Ibrahim Kubba, minister of economic affairs, was not a member of the party, despite his Marxist views.) Qasim, however, rejected that demand and began to take steps toward limiting the power of the Communists in Iraq. The anxiety aroused within the regime and in some portions of Iraqi society by the growth and empowerment of the Communist Party following the Shawwaf revolt set the stage for Qasim to introduce a series of measures designed to restrain the Communists. Nonetheless, the turning point regarding both the reinforcement of the Communist Party and Qasim's attitude toward them took place only after the events in Kirkuk in July 1959.

The riots that broke out in Kirkuk on the anniversary of the Revolution, on July 14, 1959, and the repercussions of those riots marked the point at which the Communist momentum was checked, the party leadership was frustrated, and the party itself became weak, isolated, and effectively powerless. During the course of the riots in Kirkuk, which lasted three days, Kurds identified with the Communist Party wrought havoc and slaughter among the Turkmenian residents of the city, many of whom were well-to-do landlords and homeowners and constituted a central element of the local bourgeoisie.[72] The Turkmen of Kirkuk were also an important element among the conservative political forces and represented a counterweight to the influence of communism among the intelligentsia and the poor workers, many of whom were Kurds. Thus ethnic, class, economic, and political tensions combined in an outburst of terrible violence. The Communist Party leaders were unsuccessful in controlling Communist sympathizers in Kirkuk; against their will and in defiance of their ideological beliefs, they were dragged into a violent ethnic confrontation that did not serve the party's objectives. The events in Kirkuk shook all of Iraq and increased anti-Communist sentiments. Although the events were really more of an ethnic clash between Kurds and Turkmen, Qasim preferred to cast the blame on the Communists rather than on the Kurds.

Qasim sought to prevent a Communist threat to the dominance of his regime and to avoid any identification with the Communists. While the Communists were, in fact, an important mainstay in his conflict with the Nasirist pan-Arab nationalists, the accusations to the effect that his regime was dependent upon the Communists were exploited by the nationalists within Iraq and by UAR propaganda in the inter-Arab arena. Allegations made by Nasir himself and by the pro-Egyptian press found a sympathetic audience among many Iraqis, whose fears of communism drove them to support the pan-Arab nationalists, considered to constitute the national alternative to a regime viewed by many as relying upon the Communists.

Between 1960 and 1962, Qasim adopted a policy intended to neutralize the Communist Party. Qasim aimed to fortify his position as a one-man leader by relying on the support of the masses and maneuvering among the various political forces in Iraq. Starting in 1960, the authorities began to limit the distribution of newspapers and periodicals linked to the Communist Party and, in some instances, even to close them down.[73] Journalists identified as Communists or leftists were persecuted and arrested. Nationalist gangs were responsible for murdering a number of Communist activists. The political atmosphere, which had favored the Communists in the first year of the revolutionary regime, now turned against them, with the regime's encouragement. Shi'ite and Sunnite religious leaders—who, since 1959, had attempted to persuade Qasim to block the Communists—now increased their activities in that direction. The Shi'ite leaders were concerned by the influence exerted by communism among educated Shi'ites, particularly among working-class Shi'ites employed in places where labor unions operated under Communist influence. The Shi'ite religious leader Muhsin al-Hakim promulgated a fatwa against the Communists and demanded the abrogation of the civil liberties law, which, according to his interpretation, violated the Islamic rules of inheritance.[74] Against the background of the suspicion and resistance aroused in traditional Shi'ite circles by the Communists and the secular trends of the regime, the activity of radical young Shi'ite religious leaders increased. These leaders were organized in a group known as al-Da'wa ("The

Call"), which gradually, during the 1960s and 1970s, became a highly influential force, inciting the Shi'ites in Iraq.

By 1961, the Communists had lost all control and influence among a considerable portion of the trade unions. Thus, during the course of 1960, the Communists lost control of the General Union of Fellahin Societies, the Teachers' Union, the Bar Association, the Printers' Union, and other unions. Between 1961 and 1962, the Communists lost their leading status in the General Federation of Trade Unions (which they had established in 1959), the Journalists' Union, the Medical Association, and the Association of Engineers, and the last remaining Communist activists were expelled from the Teachers' Union. Starting in 1960, the Communist front organizations were subjected to increasing limitations, and they were gradually closed down.[75] In February 1960, at the explicit request of Qasim himself, the minister with the greatest affinity to the Communists, Dr. Ibrahim Kubba, who had served as minister of petroleum and minister of agrarian reform, resigned.

Notwithstanding these restrictions and persecutions, the Communist Party continued to support the Qasim regime. The rift between them and the nationalists was absolute, and they realized that, should a coalition of nationalist and conservative forces rise to power, the social and international policies of such a coalition would be further from their own positions than the policies of the Qasim regime. Such a coalition would take action to deprive the Communists of any power whatsoever.

The events in Kirkuk embarrassed the leadership of the Communist Party, which adopted a moderate position and continued to support Qasim following internal deliberations. The party believed that conditions in Iraq were not yet ripe for the establishment of a Communist regime, and accordingly, the Communists would have to cooperate with the "democratic patriotic forces" and the "national bourgeoisie"—in other words, with Qasim's regime and the National Democratic Party.

The Communist Party held out great hopes that the Association Law, promulgated in 1960, would enable them to operate legally and to translate their public influence into political power. However, when a party delegation sought to register and obtain an official license, the members of the delegation were told, to their great surprise, that another delegation had already registered as the "Iraqi Communist Party."[76] Qasim had surprised the Communist Party by establishing a rival "Communist" party, headed by Dawud al-Sa'igh, a Communist activist who had left the ranks of the party as early as 1943; other former party members joined him.

Having no other choice, the Communist Party applied to register under the name Ittihad al-Sha'b (the People's Union), but its application was rejected. This gave rise to an absurd situation whereby a party that represented a small minority of ex-Communists but bore the name of the Iraqi Communist Party held a license according to law, whereas the real Communist Party was not granted a license or officially recognized. While the party founded by al-Sa'igh included a number of ex-Communists among its ranks, it could not possibly compete with the strength and influence of the Communist Party.

The status of the Communist Party was also damaged by the position adopted in the summer of 1959 by the KDP, which, under pressure by Mulla Mustafa Barzani, began to withdraw from its close alliance with the Communists. In the first year after the revolution, the two parties had maintained close cooperation against the forces of pan-Arab nationalism. After the events of Kirkuk, however, Barzani—despite his ties with the Soviet Union— began to reduce the extent of cooperation with the Communists.

When the Kurdish revolt broke out in 1961, the Communist Party found itself in an embarrassing position. Despite its support in principle of autonomy for the Kurds, while maintaining Iraqi unity, the party condemned the revolt.[77] The Communist Party censured both Kurdish nationalism and Arab nationalism and demanded the cessation of hostilities; nonetheless, notwithstanding its criticism of Qasim, it did not withdraw its support of his regime. The embarrassing predicament of the Communist Party and its behavior concerning the Kurdish revolt reflected the weakness of its leadership and the no-win situation in which it found itself, having to support Qasim despite its disapproval of him.

The change in Qasim's attitude toward the Communist Party and its weakened status gave rise to criticism by the Soviet Union and to a cooling of the relationship between the two states. Admittedly, the USSR acted in the international arena according to its interests as a Great Power and not as an ideological force, continuing to extend support to regimes that had suppressed Communist parties. Nonetheless, the new anti-Communist trend in Iraq was a disappointment to the Soviet Union, especially in light of the hopes it had held for Qasim's regime in its first year. Despite the embarrassment to the USSR caused by the Kurdish revolt, and notwithstanding Qasim's refusal to accede to Soviet demands to grant autonomy to the Kurds within the framework of the Iraqi state, the USSR continued to support and assist Qasim's regime. Still, the thaw in the relations between the USSR and Nasir, starting in 1960 and especially following the disbandment of the UAR in 1961, restored Egypt to its status as the Soviet Union's principal ally in the Arab world.

Despite its weakness and isolation, the Communist Party maintained a certain degree of influence over the intelligentsia, the workers, and the poorer strata. Still, its effectiveness as a significant political force and a mainstay of the Qasim regime gradually faded away. Qasim had succeeded in neutralizing the Communist Party, which nonetheless continued to support him but could no longer function as an effective part of his regime.

The weakening of the Communist Party in Iraq and neutralization of the trade unions and civilian organizations operated or influenced by Communist activists had long-range historical consequences. Paradoxically, it was precisely the Communist Party—which in most parts of the world was a revolutionary force in opposition to the civil bourgeoisie—that supported the growth of institutions and organizations which in Iraq would constitute a basis for the rise of a civil society. The weakening of the Communist Party had an adverse effect on one of the principal unifying forces in the country, whereby members of various ethnic groups (notwithstanding the contradictions reflected in the events of Kirkuk) cooperated on the basis of an integrative Iraqi national identity.

The Association Law and the Resignation of the National Democratic Party, 1960

January 1960 marked the publication of the Association Law (otherwise known as the Associations Law, or Qanun al-Jami'at). The law was intended to enable the existence of political party life as an expression of the democratic nature of the revolutionary regime. Qasim was interested in the renewal of party activity; however, he was not prepared to waive his control of the political arena, which he exerted by maneuvering among the existing political forces. According to the law, the Ministry of the Interior, which was in charge of its application, was given the power to supervise the various parties, including extensive powers even deciding which parties were entitled to receive legal licenses.[78]

As mentioned above, the Communist Party—the largest and best-organized of all political parties in Iraq—was not granted such a license. Two Islamic parties, the Iraqi Islamic Party and the Liberation Party (Hizb al-Tahrir), did not receive licenses. Those that received licenses, in addition to the "imitation" Communist party, were the National Democratic Party; the faction which had seceded from it, the National Progressive Party (Hizb al-Watani al-Taqaddumi); and the KDP.[79]

The phrasing and application of the Association Law and the absence of any additional measures toward democratization prevented the growth of any political party life capable of reinforcing the legitimacy of the regime or enabling it to grow in strength and recruit political and public support.

In the spring of 1960, the National Democratic Party withdrew its support of Qasim, and its ministers resigned from his government.[80] The attitude of this party toward the Qasim regime had been complicated from the start. The economic, modernization, and social change policies of the Qasim regime were in line with the platform of the National Democratic Party. The ministers who were members of the party (the minister of finance, Muhammad Hadid, and the minister of agriculture, Hudeib al-Haj Hamud) played central roles in the design and implementation of Iraq's economic and social policies. Qasim nationalist views were close to those of the party: they both emphasized integrative, territorial Iraqi nationalism, while placing Arabism in a secondary position, and displayed reservations toward the pan-Arab nationalist supporters of Arab unity.

However, a contradiction existed between the liberal democratic approach of the party, which wanted Qasim's regime to be similar to those of Western democratic regimes, and the actual military-authoritarian nature of the Qasim regime. Veteran party leader Kamil al-Jadirji supported the overthrow of the Hashemite monarchy and believed in social and economic reform, but maintained a suspicious, reserved attitude toward Qasim himself.[81] During the crisis between Qasim and the nationalists in February 1959, when the ministers of al-Istiqlal and the Ba'th Party resigned, the ministers of the National Democratic Party also submitted their resignations. However, under pressure by Qasim, they withdrew their resignations. Kamil al-Jadirji supported resignation from the government.[82] Muhammad Hadid, on the other hand, believed that the party should continue its support of Qasim. Al-Jadirji's weakness (due to illness) and the hopes that many party members still held for Qasim's regime favored Hadid and those of his entourage who believed in continued participation in the government.

Al-Jadirji succeeded in causing the National Democratic Party's withdrawal from the government. His success, along with the change in the balance of power and prevailing sentiments within the National Democratic Party, reflected the middle class's and bourgeoisie's disappointment with the regime. Muhammad Hadid, who demanded that the party continue to support Qasim, was forced to resign from the party. Qasim—acting through the Minister of the Interior, Muhammad Yihya, in charge of supervising the parties—attempted to intervene in the internal elections for party leadership, which were won by al-Jadirji and his supporters, with a view to disqualifying them. However, al-Jadirji approached the Court of Appeals, which confirmed the validity of the elections. (The attitude adopted by the Court of Appeals, which was in opposition to that of Qasim himself, may have reflected the weakening of his status or his basically indecisive nature.)

In June 1960, Hadid and his supporters were expelled from the party. Hadid founded a party of his own, the National Progressive Party.[83] The rift in the National Democratic Party severely affected its power, and the party began to decline. Nor did Hadid's National Progressive Party succeed in coalescing into a significant political force.

The relations between the National Democratic Party and the Communists were complex. While they made common cause for the purpose of modernization, development, industrialization, and agrarian reform, there were fundamental differences between the liberal, Western-based social democratic views of the National Democratic Party, which relied on the support of the middle stratum and the bourgeoisie, and Communist ideology. National Democratic Party activists occasionally cooperated with the Communists; in many cases, however, the two parties were in active competition for control and influence over the trade unions and other social organizations. Within the National Democratic Party, in addition to its liberal social democratic groupings, were also leftist-Socialist factions who tended to cooperate with the Communists.

The decline of the National Democratic Party marked the weakening of a liberal-secular social democratic force characterized by Iraqi-territorialist nationalism. Such a force could have been an important factor in the development of a central democratic political system and a civil society favoring modernization and supra-ethnic, supra-tribal Iraqi nationalism. The decline of the party meant that, from that point onward, the only effective forces in the Iraqi political arena were the radical nationalist parties, the underground Ba'th Party, the Kurdish Democratic Party, and the Communist Party (which was also on the decline), with no moderate liberal democratic or Socialist force remaining.

For Qasim, the rift with the National Democratic Party removed yet another mainstay supporting his regime.

The Kurdish Revolt against Qasim

In its initial stages, the revolutionary regime was extensively supported by the Kurds. Although the agrarian reform harmed or threatened to harm the major landowners among the Kurds, who were resentful of the regime, the KDP and most of the Kurdish population enthusiastically welcomed the revolution. Between 1958 and 1960, they helped Qasim to overcome the pan-Arab nationalists and the Communists. (The KDP had been established as early as 1946.)

In principle, the regime recognized—or at least declared its recognition of—the national rights of the Kurds. (The Provisional Constitution, published on July 27, 1958, stated that the national rights of the Kurds were recognized and that the Arabs and the Kurds were partners in the Iraqi homeland.)[84] By recognizing the Kurdish nationality as a partner to Arab nationality within the Iraqi state, Qasim sought to formulate an integrative Iraqi national identity. However, he rejected a demand by Ibrahim Ahmad, secretary-general of the KDP, that the Constitution include recognition of the Kurds' right to autonomy within the framework of the Iraqi state. Although the Kurds' demand enjoyed the support of the Communists and Kamil al-Jadirji, the leader of the National Democratic Party, Qasim—possibly under pressure by 'Arif and the pan-Arab nationalists—avoided granting official recognition of the Kurds' right to autonomy.

In October 1958, after twenty-one years in exile in the USSR, Mulla Mustafa Barzani returned to Iraq. His return was a demonstration of the Iraqi government's goodwill and a gesture toward the Kurds, for many of whom Barzani—who had headed the Kurdish revolt in 1943–45—symbolized the national struggle. Qasim personally brought about the return of Barzani to create a counterweight against Ibrahim Ahmad.[85] Under the revolutionary regime, the Kurds enjoyed cultural freedom. Books and newspapers in the Kurdish language were published. The annual congress of Kurdish teachers in 1959 and 1960 turned into important events and articulated the demands for Kurdish culture and language use. In September 1959, the Division for Kurdish Education was established in the Ministry of Education. However, integration of the Kurdish language as a language used in administration and bureaucracy in the Kurdish areas was implemented at a snail's pace.

The change in attitude toward the Kurds on the declaratory level, which came about following the establishment of the revolutionary regime and Qasim's victory over the pan-Arab nationalists, did not wipe out the tensions, evident within Iraq since its inception, between the Sunnite Arabs and pan-Arab nationalists on the one hand and the Kurds on the other. The latter, though willing in practice to content themselves with autonomy within the framework of the Iraqi state, still dreamed of Greater Kurdistan.

The relationship between Barzani (who was elected president of the KDP) and Ibrahim Ahmad was characterized by mistrust and rivalry. This tension reflected the differences in their social origins, political and ideological views, and political experiences. Ibrahim Ahmad and most KDP leaders were urban, educated, leftist members of the middle class, who primarily enjoyed the support of the Kurds in Baghdad and the large cities. In contrast, Barzani was a traditional, charismatic tribal leader with great influence over the tribal population of Kurdistan. Barzani also maintained connections with both the landowning Kurdish tribal notables and the poorer strata in the cities. However, Barzani's traditional status was the source of one of his weaknesses—and, in fact, of the principal weakness of the Kurdish national movement. The Kurds were divided into many tribes and clans, and the relations between those tribes were traditionally hostile. Kurds from tribes hostile to the Barzani tribe and its allies distrusted Mulla Mustafa Barzani; they viewed him as a rival tribal notable rather than a national Kurdish leader. At times, traditional tribal rivalry and modern social and ideological rivalry empowered each other—as in the case of Jalal Talabani (a protégé of Ibrahim Ahmad), one of the heads of the KDP. The Talabanis came from the Koysanjaq area of southern Kurdistan, east of Irbil and Kirkuk; the Barzanis came from the village of Barazan, in the high mountains of northern Kurdistan. The Talabani clan was connected with the Qadiri Sufi order, while the ascendancy of the Barzani tribe had been connected with the Nakshbandi Sufi order, beginning in the nineteenth century. The Talabani clan, which was a traditional rival of the Barzani tribe, and Jalal Talabani, in contrast to Barzani, maintained a leftist worldview. Still, despite the tension and rivalry in 1958–59, Barzani and the heads of the KDP maintained a certain degree of cooperation.

Between July 1958 and July 1959, the KDP and the Iraqi Communist Party were close allies. The cooperation and affinity between the Kurds and the Communists in Iraq resulted from the following factors:

1. The objections, on the part of both the Kurds and the Communists, to pan-Arab nationalism. This was a case of political partnership in the face of a common enemy.
2. The Communist Party's support of the Kurdish claims to equality and autonomy within the framework of the Iraqi state.
3. The influence exerted by the Communist Party over many of the Kurdish intelligentsia. Educated Kurds (not unlike a certain group of educated Jews), who could not gain acceptance into the pan-Arab radical movements and were alienated by pan-Arab ideology, found in Communist ideology and the Communist Party a response to their distress and a way of achieving a feeling of partnership with the Arab majority. Most of the supporters of the Kurdistan Democratic Party were not Communists; nonetheless, among its educated members, many were affected by leftist radical views.

Up to and including the events of Kirkuk in July 1959, cooperation between the Communist Party and the KDP continued, especially in their shared objection to the pan-Arab nationalists' demand for Arab unity. Following the events of Kirkuk, however, Barzani began to exert pressure on the KDP to distance itself from the Communists. At the Fourth Conference of the KDP in 1959, Barzani and Ibrahim Ahmad joined forces to weaken the leftist, pro-Communist wing of the party and brought about the expulsion of the leader of that wing, Hamza 'Abdallah, and his supporters.[86]

Although the support of the Kurds made it easier for Qasim to take action against the Communists, his unwillingness to accede to Kurdish demands for autonomy created tension and suspicion in the relations between them. Qasim, like most of the rulers of Iraq, feared that granting Kurdish autonomy would constitute a precedent for demands by the Shi'ites and other minorities,[87] which would undermine the structure of the Iraqi state. Qasim also wanted to avoid arousing the fears of Sunnite Arabs, which would be stirred up by capitulating to the Kurds; such fears could be exploited by his pan-Arab nationalist rivals.

From the beginning of 1959, disquiet increased in Kurdistan. The steps taken to implement agrarian reform among tribal Kurds raised the opposition of the tribal leaders who owned property and those under their influence. The leaders of the KDP, urban and with leftist leanings, supported the agrarian reform and were backed by the urban Kurds and Kurds in those areas where traditional Kurdish notable influence had been weakened. However, in large areas of Kurdistan, the conservative, traditional notables retained their considerable influence. During the first half of 1959, 20,000 Kurds, among them the traditional tribal notables, left Iraq and requested asylum in Iran and Turkey.

In order to neutralize Barzani, Qasim began to nurture Barzani's tribal rivals, while exploiting the tribal fragmentation of the Kurds. (This sort of "divide and conquer" tactic had been used by all of the rulers and regimes of Iraq since its inception, and it was especially favored by Saddam Husayn.) As early as the summer of 1959, the Iraqi Army began arming the Zibari tribe, a traditional rival of the Barzanis.[88]

In the summer of 1960, members of the Zibari, Baradost, and Lulan tribes—all rivals of the Barzanis—began a series of raids on Barzani villages. The Barzani tribe countered by launching an offensive against the rival tribes and showing its strength throughout Kurdistan.

In 1961 and 1962, members of the KDP with links to Barzani sent a series of memoranda to the government of Iraq, in which they set forth the Kurds' demands: cultural autonomy, administrative autonomy within an administrative area which would include all of Iraqi Kurdistan, recognition of the Kurdish language as an official language and that it be taught in schools in Kurdistan, and diversion of a considerable proportion of the income from the oilfields around Kirkuk and Mosul to meeting the needs of the Kurdish population.

In November 1960, Barzani visited the USSR, hoping to get the Soviet Union to exert pressure on Qasim to accede to the Kurds' demands. During his stay in the USSR, which continued until January 1961, clashes between the Zibari and Baradost tribes (supported by the authorities) and his own tribe continued. The Barzani tribesmen claimed that Qasim was trying to exploit their leader's absence in order to undermine his status.[89] Barzani's mission failed.

In February 1961, Qasim officially prohibited the annual convention of Kurdish teachers, in order to prevent the presentation of Kurdish claims for cultural autonomy.[90] This move followed the adoption, at a previous convention, of vigorous resolutions to that effect. In March, the authorities closed *Khabat,* the official journal of the KDP, after it published a strongly phrased nationalist article written by Talabani.[91] As an additional step in the escalating conflict, Qasim began to emphasize that the Kurds and the Arabs of Iraq were a single nation.[92] The Kurds viewed this as manifestly an attempt to eradicate their national identity. However, despite the increasing clashes between Barzani's supporters and his rivals, Qasim and Barzani avoided overt conflict, and the Iraqi Army did not openly intervene in those clashes.

In July 1961, Barzani and the leaders of the KDP presented their demands for total autonomy of Kurdistan:

1. Recognition of the Kurdish language as the official language in the Kurdish Autonomous Region.
2. The local authorities in the Kurdish Autonomous Region would be responsible for the police, transportation, education, and all other municipal services.
3. Iraqi Army and police units stationed in Kurdistan would be composed primarily of Kurds, and all orders would be issued in the Kurdish language.
4. Income from the oil fields located in the Kurdish Autonomous Region would go primarily to developing the Kurdish region.
5. Although foreign and economic policy and defense would remain in the hands of the central government in Baghdad, Kurds would be appointed to such positions as deputy prime minister, deputy minister of defense, deputy chief of staff, and deputies in most government ministries.
6. A Kurdish college would be established that would develop into a Kurdish university. A school of Kurdish language and literature would be established in Baghdad University.

The Iraqi government, which saw these demands as a threat to Iraq's national integrity, rejected them.

In the summer of 1961, clashes took place between the Iraqi Army and rebels from the Aku tribe led by 'Abbas Mamand, a tribal leader and landowner who had been hurt by the agrarian reform. He was an ally of Barzani but was apparently acting independently.[93] In September, 'Abbas Mamand's forces defeated an Iraqi military force. The military action may have been an act of Iraqi provocation, in order to justify the bombing of Kurdish villages, including Barzani's own village. At the same time, the Zibari tribe launched an offensive against Barzani's supporters. The final deterioration into overt conflict resulted from an attempt by Barzani's people, in early September, to take over a strategic road between the towns of Duhuq, Zahu, and 'Amadiyya.[94] This constituted part of Barzani's continued efforts (which he had begun in the spring of 1960) to establish control over all of Kurdistan by subduing the rival tribes.[95] Barzani was joined by other Kurdish tribes, some of which were led by traditional leaders/major landowners who had been adversely affected by the agrarian reform. Starting in September 1961, the intertribal clashes developed into a large-scale Kurdish revolt.

Whether Qasim really wanted to provoke a Kurdish revolt against his regime is doubtful. Nonetheless, his attempts to undermine Barzani's status and his efforts to weaken the KDP, on the one hand, and his efforts to ensure his dominance over Kurdistan, on the other, led to the outbreak of armed national struggle. The alliance between the Kurds and Qasim's revolutionary regime, and Qasim's attempts to integrate the Kurds into the Iraqi nation, were now viewed by the Kurds as an attempt to wipe out their identity as a nation and to subordinate them to an Iraqi-Arab national identity. Qasim's integrative nationalist concept was perceived by the Kurds as a continuation of Arab dominance and Kurdish deprivation. The outbreak of the Kurdish revolt led Qasim to exploit the tribal structure of Kurdish society in order to subdue the Kurds, in accordance with the nationalist concept and governing interests of his regime.[96]

The intertribal clashes in Kurdistan, throughout 1960 and up to September 1961, caused embarrassment in the ranks of the KDP, the power of which was basically concentrated in the large cities. In the summer of 1961, a debate broke out within the party concerning the developing conflict between the Kurds and Qasim. Although Barzani still held the official title of president of the KDP, his already limited influence had decreased even further since March 1961, when he left Baghdad and returned to his village of Barazan. Barzani, Ibrahim Ahmad, and Jalal Talabani cooperated in the struggle against the leftist, pro-Communist wing of the party, but their relations were tainted by rivalry. In the debate within the party in the summer of 1961, following the exacerbation of the clashes in Kurdistan, the majority, led by Ibrahim Ahmad, expressed its disapproval of the tribal revolts and of Barzani's allies. The majority of the party leadership objected to the "reactionary," "conservative," and "antirevolutionary" characteristics of the clashes between the tribes and the army, as well as to the influence exerted by the landowners, who were motivated by their objections to the agrarian reform. Ahmad sought to defer, as far as possible, any military conflict with Qasim. In contrast, Jalal Talabani believed that the party should join forces with Barzani and launch a national revolt, in order to prevent domination by the landowning tribal leaders and to give the Kurdish national struggle a leftist-revolutionary character.[97]

Following the attack by the Iraqi Army on Barzan in September 1961, the party abandoned the debate and called upon its members to join the revolt, going so far as to establish its own paramilitary units. With the government's approval, mass demonstrations took place opposite the offices of the KDP in Baghdad, condemning the Kurdish demands. An attempt by the demonstrators to enter the offices led the building's security guards to open fire on the crowd. This gave Qasim the excuse to outlaw the Kurdistan Democratic Party, which he did on September 24. The party countered by organizing its own forces, the Peshmerga. In the spring of 1962, it launched an offensive against the Iraqi Army in the areas of Sulaymaniyya and Kirkuk.[98] Barzani's prestige and status gave him an advantage among the tribes; the KDP demonstrated a capacity for organization and rapidly enlisted some 15,000 troops in its service, many of them deserters from the Iraqi Army.[99] At the same time, its influence over the traditional tribal population of the Kurdistan Mountains was limited. On the other hand, the party and its forces enjoyed the support of the urban Kurdish population and of the Kurds in areas where agrarian reform had eliminated or weakened the traditional leaders and attenuated intertribal rivalry. By joining the revolt, which had initially shown the character of a tribal struggle, the party reinforced the nationalist nature of the revolt and enlisted the support of the intelligentsia and the workers.

In 1962, the rebels succeeded in taking over extensive sections of Iraqi Kurdistan, from the Iranian border to the Turkish border. The rebels controlled the areas around the cities of Sulaymaniyya, Khanaqin, Kirkuk, and Irbil. Most of this area was controlled by Barzani, while a small part of it was held by the party forces. The Iraqi Army, many of whose Kurdish officers and enlisted men had deserted in order to join the rebels, found it difficult to fight effectively against the irregular units and guerrillas in the mountainous areas. At the same time, many Kurdish soldiers and officers remained loyal to the government of Iraq. The Iraqi authorities established an auxiliary force, composed of Kurds who opposed Barzani; this force, which numbered about 10,000 troops, was called in against the rebels.

The struggle with the Kurds and the inability of the Iraqi Army to subdue them placed an ever-growing burden on the Qasim regime in 1962–63. The Kurdish rebels held several talks with groups of officers and activists who opposed Qasim and began to organize a number of conspiracies to overthrow him. Early in 1962, talks took place between supporters of Ibrahim

Ahmad and a retired colonel named Taher Yihya, regarding cooperation between the army and the Kurds against Qasim. During the course of 1962, various Kurdish representatives—primarily members of the KDP—maintained contacts with various opposition forces. The Kurds demanded explicit assurances that the regime which would come to power following Qasim's overthrow would stop the fighting against them and grant them extensive autonomy. According to Kurdish claims, in talks which took place in the autumn of 1962 and the winter of 1963 with representatives of 'Ali Salah Sa'di, secretary-general of the Ba'th Party, the Ba'th agreed to grant the Kurds self-rule (*hukm dhati*), within the framework of decentralizing the Iraqi state.[100] However, the atmosphere of mutual suspicion, and apparently also the basic unwillingness of the Ba'th to commit in writing to grant Kurdish autonomy, prevented the signing of any formal agreement.

Eventually, the coup launched by the army and the Ba'th Party in February 1963, which led to the overthrow of the Qasim regime, was carried out without any coordination with or assistance from the Kurds. Nonetheless, the transformation of the Kurds from an important mainstay of the regime to an enemy force and the failure of the Iraqi Army to suppress the Kurdish revolt played an important role in the weakening and collapse of the Qasim regime.

The Decline of the Qasim Regime in Historical Perspective

The revolutionary regime, which had initially enjoyed the extensive support of the Iraqi society and political system, began to sink into isolation and stagnation as early as 1959–60.

In the first year of his rule, Qasim was supported by a coalition consisting of the army, the Communists, the Kurds, and the National Democratic Party and enjoyed the support of the middle stratum, the bourgeoisie, the poorer popular strata within the cities, and the fellahin. By relying on the support of the army, the Communists, and the Kurds, Qasim succeeded in overcoming the pan-Arab nationalists. However, between 1959 and 1962, he gradually lost the support of all those forces. Qasim accepted the assistance of the Communist Party, but avoided granting it any representation in his government; starting in 1959, he went so far as to neutralize. Despite his policy of integrating the Kurds on an egalitarian basis and recognizing their national identity within the Iraqi state, Qasim became embroiled in conflict with them. In 1960, based on differences of opinion concerning the nature of the regime and the demand for democratization, the National Democratic Party also resigned from his government. Ministers who were identified with the parties that resigned from the government, or who became entangled in confrontations with Qasim himself, were replaced by technocrats and retired officers from among Qasim's associates and personal friends.

The Association Law was phrased and implemented in such a way that, while indeed ensuring Qasim's control of the political system, prevented the development of democratic political life. By virtue of such democratization, the regime could have reinforced its position, enlisted public support, and substantiated its legitimacy.

As Qasim's isolation increased, so did his efforts to sustain a cult of personality, attempting to obtain mass support on a personal basis. Notwithstanding this cult of personality, which was intended to reinforce Qasim's status and which reflected his populist policy, Qasim's personal life was characterized by monastic asceticism and the total absence of any ostentation or aggrandizement. Throughout the entire period of his rule, Qasim maintained strict personal integrity and avoided any charge of corruption. He lived in his modest study in the Ministry of Defense building and slept next to his desk.

In contrast to most of the radical revolutionary rulers and regimes that arose after World War II in the various Arab states, Qasim did not establish a party of his own as a means of enlisting social and political support and substantiating the legitimacy of his regime. Instead, he attempted to combine a populist approach based on direct contact between the leader and the masses without an intermediary role for the party mechanism or the political system, with maneuvers among the various forces, while at the same time limiting their power. At the end of the day, however, Qasim remained without the support of any political forces whatsoever, nor did he have any organizational system that could have translated the support of the masses (which he retained until the end of his regime) into an effective political force.

In the inter-Arab arena, Iraq became isolated as the result of the suspicions which the conservative monarchies entertained toward its revolutionary radical regime and toward the UAR and its radical forces under Gamal 'Abd al-Nasir. For his part, Nasir consistently strove to overthrow Qasim. Following the Syrian withdrawal from the UAR, which was a severe blow to Nasir's prestige, some degree of Iraqi-Syrian rapprochement took place, temporarily improving Iraq's situation. In March 1962, Qasim met with Nazim al-Qudsi, who had been the president of Syria since Syria had withdrawn from the UAR in September 1961. This was an attempt by the heads of Iraq and Syria to reinforce their relationship in the face of the common threat to their regimes posed by Egypt and Nasir (with the backing of his admirers). However, the weak regime in Syria, prone to attacks and attempted coups by groups of officers and radical forces, and Qasim's sinking regime did not manage to revive their respective positions. They were incapable of formulating a message attractive to the public, nor did they have the strength to neutralize the officers. Iraq's ties with the flaccid, "separatist" Syrian regime could not give Qasim any kind of solid footing against the nationalist, pro-Nasirist enemies of his regime.

On June 25, 1961, only five days after Kuwait received its independence from Britain, Qasim declared at a press conference that Kuwait was an integral part of Iraq.[101] This Iraqi contention was based on the allegation that Kuwait had been ripped away from the Ottoman *vilayet* of Basra in 1899 by Britain, and that the agreement between Britain and the Kuwaiti rulers, the al-Sabah shaykhs, had been dictated by the colonial Great Power to the declining Ottoman Empire. (The demand for Iraqi control of Kuwait had been raised by King Ghazi in 1938; twenty years later, Nuri al-Sa'id had held talks with Britain concerning the addition of Kuwait to the Arab union between Iraq and Jordan.) Qasim's move to annex Kuwait aroused the profound objections of Britain and the Arab states. This mutual objection gave rise to cooperation between the rival forces of revolutionary radical Egypt, conservative Saudi Arabia, and Great Britain. Iraq's isolation increased, and Qasim's personal status and prestige suffered an additional blow. Despite Qasim's efforts to exploit the Kuwait crisis in order to reinforce his nationalist status in Iraq, the crisis was effectively exploited to Qasim's detriment by Egypt and the pro-Nasirist forces.[102]

The regime's economic and social policies were unsuccessful in accomplishing any breakthrough in the sphere of industrialization, nor did the regime narrow the gap between Iraq and the affluent industrialized countries. Despite the relatively large financial resources at the disposal of the government of Iraq—specifically, its oil revenues and the credit granted by the USSR—and despite encouraging investment in industry by the bourgeoisie and private capital, the results in practice were quite limited. In 1963, the Iraqi economy remained dependent on oil and agriculture. Industry accounted for only 12.7 percent of the Iraqi GNP. The great expectations of 1958, that the revolutionary regime would launch dramatic breakthroughs in the standard of living and would drastically increase Iraq's national power, declined within a few short years into empty promises.

In the field of agrarian reform, more significant achievements were accomplished. While Iraq's progress toward modernizing agriculture was extremely slow and implementation of the reforms proved difficult, some 31,000 fellahin became landowners (in addition to the temporary leasing of plots to some 250,000 fellahin families). In addition, a significant change took place in agrarian relations, and the major landowners as a social stratum were effectively eliminated. At the same time, agricultural output per unit of land decreased, due to the difficulties experienced by the fellahin in adapting to the new production conditions and, ironically, the inefficient functioning of the state bureaucratic systems, which had been established to help the fellahin.

The success in the area of secondary and higher education, along with the failure in the area of industrialization, had a tremendous impact on the situation of the modern middle class. Despite its accelerated expansion, it had remained dependent upon the state as its almost exclusive employer. The expansion of Iraq's educational system and state bureaucracy led to the growth of the middle class, most of whose members were salaried rather than self-employed. The proportion of those in the population with a modern education and holding modern occupations rose from 28 percent in 1958 to 34 percent in 1968. The number of civil servants, most of whom belonged to the middle class, increased from 85,000 in 1958 to 318,000 in 1971. However, the numeric growth of this stratum and the fact that it was less affected—both during the monarchy and under Qasim—by conflicts between Sunnites and Shi'ites and by tribal identities and loyalties did not lead to its transformation into a social force with defined interests. Nor did it become the foundation for political forces capable of constructing a modern democratic society and a supra-ethnic, nontribal, integrated national identity.

The agrarian reform and the continued migration of the fellahin and tribesmen to the large cities led to social change among the poorer strata. Despite some improvements in their living conditions, they remained in abject poverty. The transformations achieved by the Qasim regime were not accompanied by any structural changes in the Iraqi economy, due to the absence of any breakthrough in industry, the continued dependency on oil and agriculture, and the absence of political democratization.

Despite the expansion of light industry, which produced for the local market, the bourgeoisie did not grow into a defined economic and political force with clear interests and the ability to influence the public agenda. The weakening of the Communists effectively halted the initial moves toward organization of the working class, which had enjoyed the cooperation of parts of the middle class and especially that of the intelligentsia, into a political force. The decline of the National Democratic Party and (paradoxically) that of the Communists, along with the disintegration of the trade unions and other civil organizations established after the revolution, impeded the growth of a civil society and prevented the formation of conditions that would have enabled political democracy.

Although Qasim's regime was authoritarian and dictatorial, it was not a murderous one. With the exception of the first days of the revolution and a few death sentences passed against those who had headed the security services during the monarchical era and a few rebels, Qasim did not kill off his enemies. Instead, his rivals and the enemies of his regime were imprisoned;

most of them, however, were eventually released. Qasim attempted to convince his rivals of the rightness of his actions. (This relative liberalism was especially exploited by 'Abd al-Salam 'Arif in his organization of a coup against the regime.)

Despite the aggressiveness that characterized Iraqi politics in general, the years of Qasim's revolutionary regime were more affected by ideological disputes and ideological forces than any other period in the history of Iraq. Tribalism and religious sectoethnicity did not disappear from the Iraqi domestic political arena; nonetheless, under Qasim's rule, they were suppressed—at least among the urban Arabic-speaking Sunnite and Shi'ite population—in favor of ideological disputes and class cleavages. This was not the case, however, among the Kurds. Under Qasim, the tensions between Kurds and Arabs escalated to violent conflicts between the Kurds and the government. In a number of cases, political-ideological struggles and class-related tensions became interwoven with conflicts between tribes and between ethnic communities. This was what happened in the case of the Shawwaf revolt in March 1959, as well as in the Kirkuk revolt in July 1959. Even among the Shi'ites, trends began to appear during Qasim's rule which contributed to exacerbating the Shi'ite-Sunnite tensions in Iraq in later years. Still, the aggravation of this tension remained marginal under the Qasim regime.

The situation by which the state drew most of the oil revenues and remained the only factor capable of coping with the centrifugal ethnic trends of its population gave a special strength to the Iraqi state and its apparatus. This strength on the part of the Iraqi state gave those groups which were capable of controlling it a vast amount of power, making them stronger than all of the fragmented social forces put together and enabling them to prevent any development toward democratization. (Nonetheless, it took several years to find the force—in the name of the Ba'th Party by a determined, strong, brutal, and sophisticated leader named Saddam Husayn—that could seize the reins of power and make it absolute, with no other entity able to stand in its way.)

The Qasim regime attained significant achievements in promoting education and health services, reducing inequality in the distribution of wealth, improving the standard of living among the poorer strata (especially with regard to housing), and changing agrarian relations and the system of land-ownership. These successes and improvements in the situation of the poorer strata, combined with nurturing Iraqi nationalism and bolstering Qasim's own status as the leader of the populace, helped him to retain the support of those strata until his regime was overthrown. This support, however, lacked both organization and effective leadership. The militia, established after the revolution and dominated by the Communists, was disarmed following the events of Kirkuk. In practice, the militia was deprived of any further effectiveness in the streets of Iraq—precisely at a time when the Ba'th Party was secretly organizing its supporters and laying the foundations for its own militias in the poorer neighborhoods of the cities.

The Communist Party, despite restrictions on its activities, closure of its newspapers, and persecution and threats against the lives of many of its leaders (by both the Iraqi authorities and the nationalist enemies of the regime), continued to support Qasim—basically because it had no choice but to do so—but ceased to be an effective force that could provide any actual assistance. Despite the Communists' fears that, following the collapse of the Qasim regime, the nationalists would take decisive action toward their elimination, the weak, hesitant Communist leadership did not succeed in organizing party members and supporters in any effective way.

On February 8, 1963, when the Iraqi Army officers and the Ba'th Party launched the coup against Qasim, there remained no organized force to defend his regime. With the outbreak of the coup, spontaneous demonstrations of support took place in the poorer neighborhoods of Baghdad. Although he was repeatedly asked to do so, Qasim refused to distribute arms to the masses. This refusal on his part is difficult to understand. He may have hoped to succeed in establishing a dialogue with the rebels; he may have relied on his own capacity for political maneuvering. But with no organization and no arms, the masses demonstrating in the streets were powerless to stop the army or to withstand the small but well organized, armed, and determined forces of the Ba'th Party, which brought the Qasim regime to its end.

The Seizure of Power by the Ba'th
and Its Overthrow in 1963

The Growth of the Ba'th Party in Syria

The Ba'th Party was established by young, educated Syrians of the middle stratum during the 1940s. Three educated Syrians played pivotal roles in establishing the party: Michel 'Aflaq, Salah al-Din al-Bitar, and Zaki Arsuzi. Although Arsuzi was not a party member, his ideas affected its ideology, and several of his supporters joined the party and held various positions within its ranks. In 1947, the Founding Conference of the party took place. The small party was significantly boosted by its unification with the Arab Socialist Party (Hizb al-'Arabi al-Ishtiraki) headed by Akram Hourani in 1953.[1] Party founders Michel 'Aflaq and Salah al-Din al-Bitar composed a long series of articles that were published in the periodical *al-Ba'th* and compiled into several anthologies constituting a comprehensive and complex ideological system characterized by historiosophic depth.[2] Also contributing to the comprehensive and fascinating ideology of the Ba'th Party were intellectuals Munif al-Razzaz, 'Abdallah Rimawi, and, in the 1960s, Yasin al-Hafiz, Jamal al-Atasi, and others.[3] The ideological basis of the Ba'th was founded on three principles: Arab unity, liberty, and socialism. The concept of nationalism and goal of Arab unity constituted a central and dominant component in the Ba'th ideology. According to Michel 'Aflaq, nationalism is an eternal, meta-historical, universal human phenomenon, and Arab nationalism carries a universal message to all of human civilization. Michel 'Aflaq and Salah al-Din al-Bitar were influenced in their nationalist outlook by German nationalist concepts; they adopted an approach of historiosophic idealism and rejected Marxism and historical materialism. The central axis of human history, according to the Ba'th, is nationalism, rather than social forces or conditions of production. According to the founders of the Ba'th, who supported the secularism of the state, Islam was one form of expression of the Arab nation and one chapter in the eternal history of that nation. The realization of Arab unity is the only way in which Arab individuals and the Arab society can achieve their potential and attain power and equality with the West. In order to achieve Arab unity, the Arabs must free themselves of the dominant Western powers and shake off the control of the reactionary conservative elites subservient to those powers. The socialism of the Ba'th ideology was nationalist Arab in nature, intended to serve the Arab nation. It meant only the reduction of poverty and inequality, the provision of equal opportunity to all Arabs, agrarian reform, and the development of national power by the state—all without class struggle or harm to individual property. While the founders of the party and its ideology rejected Marxist philosophy and dialectical and historical materialism, other Ba'th intellectuals, such as Yasin al-Hafiz, selectively adopted Marxist ideas and combined them with their nationalist ideology. At the same time, this was a minority position within the party.

The Ba'th Party as a historical phenomenon was an expression of the historical, social, and political conditions unique to Syria. However, its growth and expansion reflected the similarities in sociohistorical conditions between the urban centers of the various Arab states. In all of those centers, a modern middle stratum had arisen and was now drawn to the radical nationalist messages of the Ba'th, as a way to alleviate its personal and collective frustration, given the dominance of the conservative ruling elites and the supremacy of the West. Those who were most attracted to the Ba'th included high school and college students and educated young men. The combination of radical nationalism and the vision of national power, as a response to the feelings of indignity and weakness generated by Western domination, coupled with the message of Socialist change and revolution against the conservative elite establishment, was attractive to educated young adults. In accordance with the Ba'th concept of the pan-Arab world, branches of the party were established outside Syria—in Jordan, Lebanon, and Iraq and among the Palestinian Arabs; all of these were subordinate to the Ba'th national leadership in Syria.[4]

Although the Ba'th was a civilian party, young army officers began to join its ranks in the 1950s. Many of these belonged to the 'Alawi, Druze, and Isma'ili minorities, and they perceived the secular pan-Arab nationalist messages of the Ba'th as a response to their social and identity-related distresses. In view of the weakness, existential laxity, and political instability of Syria during the 1940s and 1950s, the Ba'th Party, with its well-formed radical nationalist revolutionary message, achieved considerable influence over the political and ideological climate in Syrian society and in politics. The influence exerted by the Ba'th on Syria's politics during the second half of the 1950s played a role in creating conditions that led to the establishment of the United Arab Republic (UAR), the union between Syria and Egypt in 1958. In the autumn of 1957, the Ba'th and various groups in Syria and army officers were the forces that vigorously supported the establishment of that union.[5] In addition to their longing for Arab unity, the Syrian Ba'th members and army officers were motivated by their suspicions of Iraq and Turkey. These countries—with the assistance of Britain, the United States, and even Israel—were viewed as threatening the sovereignty and territorial integrity of Syria. They also feared the rise of Communism, the traditionally fierce opponent of the Ba'th and pan-Arab nationalism.

Only a few months after the establishment of the UAR, tensions arose between the Ba'th and Gamal 'Abd al-Nasir. Ba'th leaders viewed themselves as the bearers of the pan-Arab vision. In exchange for agreeing to disband, they sought to become the central ideological force and the principal recruiters of public support within the framework of the UAR. Accordingly, they wished to expand their activities in Egypt. Nasir, in accordance with his authoritarian approach, was not prepared to accept the kind of activities proposed by the Ba'th leaders and did not desire the establishment of a power center that was not under his complete control. Nasir's political interests and the political culture of Egypt opposed those of the Syrian Ba'th. In December 1959, the Ba'th ministers resigned from the government of the UAR; in 1960, the party leaders transferred their activities to Lebanon.

Despite the blow to the prestige of the Ba'th given the disappointing failure to realize the vision of Arab unity in the format of the UAR, the party continued to be attractive to young, educated persons and army officers from Syria. Between 1960 and 1962, a sociological and ideological transformation began to take place within the Ba'th. More and more educated people and army officers joined its ranks, including many members of minority groups from the lower middle stratum or even the poorer strata, as well as residents of provincial areas. Their views were more leftist-radical than those of the Old Guard.[6]

Between 1964 and 1966, a struggle took place within the Syrian Ba'th between its left wing and its National Command, headed by 'Aflaq and al-Bitar. The left wing became dominant within the Regional Command (the second most important party institution), and its leaders included Hamud al-Shufi, Jamal al-Atasi, 'Abd al-Karim Zuhur, and Yasin al-Hafiz.[7] The left wing manifested the rise of new social forces, in which minority groups, members of the lower and lower middle strata, and residents of small towns and provincial areas were especially noticeable. These forces also reflected a generational change and the transformations that were taking place within the modern middle stratum, engendered by the expansion of education and modernization into rural areas, small towns, and the poorer strata as well as by the integration of young men from those groups and regions into the military and the political system. The senior national leadership, thanks to cooperation with a group of Ba'th officers, succeeded in maintaining its status until 1966. Between 1963 and 1966, the Syrian state was headed by Amin al-Hafiz, a Ba'th officer who had the support of the National Command.

In February 1966, army officers from the left wing, headed by Salah Jadid, launched a coup that deposed Amin al-Hafiz. The founders of the party were forced to go into exile. The left wing took control of the Ba'th Party and of Syria in general.[8] Under Salah Jadid, the regime maintained a socioeconomic policy characterized by Socialist leanings and reinforced ties with the USSR. Sociopolitical revolution and Arab socialism were more central to the concept of the leftist Ba'th ("neo-Ba'th") than ambitions for Arab unity. In 1970, Hafiz al-Asad, minister of defense and commander in chief of the Syrian Air Force, staged an additional coup against his partners in government and ousted Jadid and his cronies. The seizure of power by Asad marked the beginning of a long period of etatist, authoritarian rule that was nonetheless pragmatic and tended toward controlled economic and social liberalization. While the party remained faithful to the ideological principles of pan-Arabism, the meaning of those principles in practice was reduced to cooperation among the Arab states, rather than their actual unification and abolition. Thus, dialectically, a party which had grown up with a slogan calling for unification of the Arab states became the central force in the cohesion and substantiation of the nation-state in Syria, contributing to the stabilization of the Arab states and the reinforced legitimacy of their separate existence.

Preparing for the Coup against Qasim

The ideas of the Ba'th Party were first disseminated in Baghdad in 1948–49 by Syrian college students. During the initial organizational stages of the party in Iraq, several of its secretaries were Syrian.[9] At the time of the intifada, in November 1952, activists of the tiny party played a small and specific role among the high school and college students, inciting them to become active. Estimates by various researchers regarding the number of Ba'th Party members in Iraq in 1952 run between 50 and 170.[10] From 1952 until 1960, the position of party secretary was held by Fuad al-Rikabi, a Shi'ite from Nasiriyya, a city in southern Iraq. The Ba'th and its ideology were attractive to educated young people whose nationalist views and pan-Arab orientation were increasingly imbued with the awareness of the need for profound social and economic change. These young members of the effendiyya were unable to find their place within the older nationalist party, al-Istiqlal. The socially conservative leadership of al-Istiqlal maintained close ties to the Hashemite regime and its elite; they were unsuccessful in combining radical pan-Arab nationalism with messages of social change in a way that could attract the younger generation in the years following World War II. The outmoded, inactive spirit that prevailed among al-Istiqlal and its elderly, gray leadership failed to attract dynamic young people, who were looking for violent radical revolutionary activity. Embittered young people, especially students, were attracted to radical messages and slogans that combined pan-Arab nationalist ideas and militant Socialist statements. The young age of the Ba'th leaders and the fact that they were not part of the establishment (which was perceived as petrified, corrupt, and reactionary), as well as the mystery surrounding the party, gave it a romantic charm in the eyes of these young people.

Until 1963, the Shi'ites constituted a majority within the party leadership.[11] Many Shi'ites were repelled by the pan-Arab ideas that had been traditionally considered by Iraq as identified with Sunnite Arab dominance. Nonetheless, because the message of the Ba'th was nationalist, secular, and supraethnic, and opposed any distinction between Sunnites and Shi'ites or between Muslims and Christians, other educated young Shi'ites were attracted to the party and its pan-Arab messages as an intermediary between themselves and the Sunnite majority and a response to the identity-related distresses of the educated non-Sunnite Arabs. Between 1953 and 1958, although it was still illegal, the Ba'th maintained contacts and participated in organizations affiliated with legal and illegal opposition parties. Although several army officers had joined the party as early as the 1950s, none were affiliated with the leaders of the Free Officers who had launched the revolution in 1958. In actual fact, the Ba'th played no role at all in toppling the monarchy.

The government that had been established by Qasim in July 1958 included the party secretary-general, Fuad al-Rikabi, as minister of development. During the struggle between Qasim and 'Arif in August and September 1958, Ba'th activists played a role in organizing demonstrations in support of 'Arif, under the slogan "Unity Now." In February 1959, Rikabi resigned from the government due to the rift between Qasim and the nationalists. Following Rikabi's resignation, the Ba'th began to militantly oppose the Qasim regime.[12] The heads of the Ba'th began to form ties with nationalist army officers, with a view to launching a coup against Qasim. It is unclear to what extent plans had been made to topple the Qasim regime in 1959; however, it is known that the Ba'th undertook to assassinate the leader as a first step toward overthrowing the regime. On October 7, a squad of six Ba'th members attempted to kill Qasim. They failed, and those who managed to escape arrest were forced to flee Iraq (one was Saddam Husayn).

The failure of the assassination led to the expulsion of Fuad al-Rikabi from the ranks of the party; he had served as secretary-general of the Ba'th since 1952.[13] The organizational infrastructure of the party was seriously undermined. Early in 1960, the national leadership of the Ba'th, which was pursuing its operations from Beirut at the time due to the rift between the party and Nasir, established the Office for Iraqi Affairs (Maktab al-'Iraq).[14] The rehabilitation of the party in Iraq was assigned to Hazim Jawad, a Shi'ite Ba'th activist from Nasiriyya, and 'Ali Salih al-Sa'di, a Sunnite Ba'th activist from the neighborhoods of Baghdad. Jawad and al-Sa'di displayed an impressive organizational ability in reconstructing the party infrastructure while forced to operate underground.[15] It appears that 1961 and 1962 were good years for al-Sa'di, who began to function as acting party secretary during periods when Jawad was not present. Starting in 1960, the party expanded its activities among the military and the students. To pursue its activities with students, Ba'th activists established the Patriotic Students' Union (al-Ittihad al-Watani l'il-Tulaba al-'Iraq), which was intended to compete with the Communists. The party made contact with active and retired military officers, some of whom held senior ranks. The confrontation between Qasim and 'Arif, the suppression of the Shawwaf revolt, and the identification of Qasim with forces the image of which was antinationalist aroused the discontent of many officers, most of whom were Sunnite Arabs and tended toward Arab nationalism and the vision of pan-Arab unity. The Ba'th was the most cohesive opposition force, and its pan-Arab nationalist, radical, anti-Communist views were attractive to those officers. Among the officers who joined the Ba'th between 1960 and 1962 were Brigadier General (ret.) Ahmad Hasan al-Bakr, who had been a member of the Free Officers in the 1950s, Colonel (ret.) 'Abd al-Karim Mustafa Nasrat, and Colonel (ret.) Tahir Yihya.[16]

In February 1962, the National Command of the Ba'th in Iraq decided to make practical preparations to overthrow the Qasim regime. The National Conference in April was dedicated to accelerating these activities as well as to the initial formation of the Revolutionary Council, with the participation of nationalist, Nasirite army officers. Steps were taken toward establishing an armed party militia. Secret cells were set up for the purpose of providing weapons training to party members and candidates, under the supervision of active and retired officers who were themselves members of the Ba'th.[17] (This proto-militia was later—following the revolution of February 8—given the name of the National Guard, or al-Haras al-Qawmi.)[18]

Starting in February 1962, contacts began between the conspirators and the heads of the Kurdish revolt. Tahir Yihya held talks with Ibrahim Ahmad and Jalal Talabani. The contact person was a Kurdish officer from the Iraqi Army, Karim al-Qarani, a resident of Sulaymaniyya who was trusted by both the Ba'th members and the Kurds.[19] One of the party leaders, Hani al-Fkaiki, states in his memoirs that the contacts with the Kurds through Tahir Yihya took place in October 1962.[20] Al-Sa'di also maintained contacts with the Kurds, so there were actually several channels for dialogue open at the same time. While these talks did not result in any agreement, the Kurds promised to assist in the overthrow of the Qasim regime by calling a truce.

The practical preparations for the revolution were the responsibility of the Ba'th Military Office, which also worked at increasing the party's influence among the military. According to al-Fkaiki, the Office was established as early as 1960; the people involved in it included Salih Mahdi 'Amash, Mundhir al-Wandawi, Hazim Jawad, and 'Ali Salih al-Sa'di.[21] The Office was originally headed by Jawad and subsequently by al-Sa'di. The composition of the Office appears to have fluctuated before stabilizing in 1962. By contrast to the development of the Syrian Ba'th, in which the army officers became the strongest force in the party, in Iraq the civilian leadership maintained dominance of the Ba'th and control of the Military Office. During the period of preparations for the coup in 1962, the Office personnel included civilians Sa'di, Hazim Jawad, and Talib Shabib and quite a number of officers: Ahmad Hasan al-Bakr, Salih Mahdi 'Amash, 'Abd al-Sattar 'Abd al-Latif, Khalid Maki al-Hashimi, Hardan 'Abd al-Ghaffar al-Tikriti, Mundhir al-Wandawi, and Mustafa Nasrat.[22] Tahir Yihya was apparently also involved in the Office. (The composition of the Office changed following the revolution; its additional members included Colonel Tahir Yihya and leading Ba'th figures—all civilians—closely associated with al-Sa'di.)

The Ba'th Coup of February 8, 1963

On February 8, 1963 (the fourteenth day of the Muslim month of Ramadan), the coalition of the Ba'th Party and the nationalist Nasirite army officers led by 'Abd al-Salam 'Arif launched a coup that put an end to the Qasim regime. The Ba'th itself was still a small party, with about 830 members and 15,000 candidates, and accordingly it required the cooperation of nationalist officers who were not Ba'th members.[23] Despite its limited membership, the Ba'th enjoyed a relatively powerful position, thanks to its well organized nature, its influence among the officers, and the laxity of the regime. The weakness and degeneration of the other organizations and parties, and especially the indecision among the leadership of the Communist Party, gave the Ba'th, as the best-organized nationalist force in Iraq, a relatively great degree of power.

'Abd al-Salam 'Arif, who enjoyed all the glory of a nationalist leader, was linked to the Ba'th, although he was not a member of the party. The Ba'th leaders, mostly in their thirties, wanted the coup and the revolutionary regime to be headed by a well-known and influential personage. Their intention was for ʿArif to serve as a symbolic leader and thus ensure the support of the army, while keeping control in the hands of the Baʿth. (It may have been al-Saʿdi who played the pivotal role in forming the coalition between the Baʿth and ʿArif.)[24]

Although the Baʿth officers and the nationalist officers involved in the preparations for the coup formed only a small minority of Iraqi Army officers, some of them, who served in the armored corps and the air force, held positions vital for implementing the coup. In 1962, the Baʿth officers tried to acquire control of the military units that were essential to the coup, especially units of the armored corps and the air force around Baghdad.[25] The conspirators included Colonel Maki al-Hashimi, commander of the Fourth Armored Brigade at the Abu Ghrayb Base near Baghdad, Colonel ʿArif ʿAbd al-Razzaq, commander of the air force base in Habbaniyya, and Colonel Hardan ʿAbd al-Ghaffar al-Tikriti, commander of the air force base in Kirkuk. Qasim received warnings regarding the conspiracy against him. (Even Israel sent a warning, through one of Qasim's personal aides. To Israel, the existence of a regime hostile to that of Nasir, which was viewed by the Israelis as a dangerous threat, was an asset worth preserving.) The army purges, in which officers suspected of activity against the regime or sympathy with ʿArif were summarily discharged, made things more difficult for the conspirators but did not foil the conspiracy. Communist officers conveyed warnings to Qasim concerning the impending coup, but the leadership of the Communist Party made no actual preparations. Moreover, despite these warnings, Qasim himself did not take any decisive steps that could have prevented the coup from taking place.

Early in 1963, Lieutenant Colonel Salih Mahdi ʿAmash, one of the chief conspirators, was arrested. His arrest worried the conspirators, who feared an impending wave of arrests; accordingly, the date set for the coup was advanced to February 8. On that morning, army units from the Abu Ghrayb Base took over the local radio station and the Rashid and Washwash army bases. An armored unit from the Fourth Brigade set out from Abu Ghrayb and turned toward the Ministry of Defense compound in Baghdad, which was defended by a brigade loyal to Qasim.[26] Early in the morning, Jalal al-Awqati, commander in chief of the air force and loyal to Qasim, was murdered near his home. Aircraft taking off from the Habbaniyya AFB, which was commanded by one of the conspirators, Colonel ʿArif ʿAbd al-Razzaq, bombed the Ministry of Defense compound. The conspirators took advantage of the situation whereby most of the Iraqi Army units were far from Baghdad, involved in suppressing the Kurdish revolt. This meant that control of the armored corps base nearest to Baghdad and the air force bases in

Habbaniyya and Kirkuk by officers involved in the plot was enough to tip the balance in their favor. In the streets of Baghdad and its poorer neighborhoods, masses of civilians led by Communist activists attempted to block the advancing columns of troops; attempts were even made to retake the broadcasting station which had fallen into the hands of the Ba'th. With no organization and no arms, however, they could not stand against the army and the well-organized and well-armed Ba'th militia.[27] After a grim battle, during the course of which the Ministry of Defense compound was shelled by tanks and bombed from the air, Qasim and his few remaining supporters surrendered. A brief trial was held, following which Qasim and a number of his associates were executed.

The streets of Baghdad were now seized by the National Guard (the Ba'th militia), the organizational skeleton of which had been established underground by resolutions adopted by the Ba'th leadership early in 1962. The militia was established to serve as the party's proto-military arm against its rivals and as counterweight against the army, the Ba'thist and nationalist officers of which were trusted to only a limited degree by the party leaders. The militia was now issued weapons, and the centers—some of which were set up following the coup, whereas others had been prepared in advance—applied themselves to the task of hunting down Communists and supporters of the Qasim regime. The Communists, as well as people suspected of being pro-Communist or having been active in the Qasim regime, were arrested, and many of them were murdered in the streets or in prison. The terror and confusion were also exploited for personal vendettas and "settling of accounts." The first to be eliminated or arrested, however, were Communist Party activists, intellectuals, labor leaders, and political and community activists. Taking advantage of the terror imposed by the National Guard, the Ba'th wiped out the power of the Communist Party, which had been its most cohesive ideological and political rival in society and in the political arena. The Communist Party leaders—including the party secretary, Husayn al-Radi—were arrested and executed. Between February and October 1963, some 10,000 Communists, Communist sympathizers, and suspected sympathizers were murdered. From the standpoint of Iraqi society, the terror and slaughter wrought by the National Guard did severe damage to all of the socially and politically active elements that could have fostered the development of a democratic civilian society.

With the takeover of the radio station and the Ministry of Defense compound, control was effectively placed in the hands of the National Council of Revolutionary Command (NCRC). The Council, established by the national leadership of the Ba'th as early as 1962, included seventeen party members and 'Abd al-Salam Arif (who was not a party member, but was considered the most senior of the nationalist Nasirite officers). The nine other officers serving on the Council were all party members, although some had only joined the party in 1961–62, and their loyalty to it was limited. The goal of the Ba'th leadership (the Regional Command) was to retain control of the state and supervise the NCRC, which was intended to constitute the supreme official entity of the state. The government, which would include other nationalist elements besides the Ba'th, would comprise only the executive branch.

The NCRC chose 'Abd al-Salam Arif as president of the Republic and assigned the job of forming a government to Ahmad Hasan al-Bakr. The government established by al-Bakr included twenty ministers, twelve of whom were Ba'th members holding the key portfolios. 'Ali Salih al-Sa'di, secretary of the party, was appointed deputy prime minister and interior minister. Salih Mahdi 'Amash, an officer who had joined the Ba'th in 1952, became minister of defense. Talib Shabib became foreign minister, and Hazim Jawad was named minister of state for presidential affairs. Five of the ministers were Shi'ites: Talib Shabib, Hazim Jawad, Salih Kubba (minister of finance), Hammad Khalkhal (minister of social affairs), and Naji Talib (minister of industry). Two of the ministers were Kurds: Baba 'Ali, minister of agriculture, and Fuad 'Arif, minister of state.[28] Colonel Tahir Yihya was promoted and appointed chief of staff; Lieutenant Colonel Hardan 'Abd al-Ghaffar al-Tikriti became commander in chief of the air force.

The Ba'th coup and the suppression of the Communist Party were received with satisfaction by the United States, which had considered Qasim a threat because of his close relations with the Soviet Union and his reliance on the Communists. Certain contacts had apparently been made between the conspirators and the CIA, which favored the elimination of Qasim. The conspirators established contacts with the CIA as early as 1960. The common enemy, the Communists, represented the common denominator for cooperation between the United States and the Ba'th.[29] The USSR viewed the coup with suspicion and reservations. Once the execution of the heads of the Communist Party and the slaughter of the Communists in the streets of Baghdad had become known, the Soviet press began to attack the new regime in Iraq.[30] Further deterioration in the relations between the USSR and Iraq took place when, following the outbreak of riots at the Rashid Base, the Ba'th leaders blamed the Communists, accused them of attempting to launch a coup, and heightened their persecution of Communist Party members. At this point, officials on behalf of the USSR accused the Iraqi regime and the Ba'th Party of fascism, terrorism, and ties with the CIA. Following the renewed outbreak of the Kurdish revolt in June, the Soviet Union stepped up its attacks on the

Ba'th regime and openly expressed its support of the Kurds.[31] (Israel regarded the coup with concern because Nasir was its most dangerous enemy; the Qasim regime, which had been hostile to Nasir, was an asset to Israel.)

The Ba'th Regime and Talks Aimed at a Tripartite Alliance with Egypt and Syria

On March 8, 1963, a coup in Damascus brought the Ba'th Party to power in Syria.[32] The party, which followed the banner of Arab unity in the sense of union between Arab states, now controlled the two largest Arab states in the Fertile Crescent. In this situation, which constituted the practical test of the party's central ideological principle, the tension and internal conflicts between the ideological commitment to achieve Arab unity and the separate interests of the two states and those of the various factions and leaders who struggled for control within them rose to the surface.

Two days after the coup in Damascus, a delegation of the Iraqi Ba'th Party headed by 'Ali Salih al-Sa'di came to Syria. Given the weakness of both Ba'th regimes, they had a vital interest in supporting each other. The collapse of either could have had fatal consequences for the survival of the other. Both Ba'th Parties depended on the Nasirite army officers, who saw Nasir as their inspiration. These officers demanded immediate rapprochement with Egypt and the unification of all three states as soon as possible, in the name of pan-Arabism. Moreover, the civilian component of the national leadership of the Iraqi Ba'th, as well as the senior leaders within the pan-Arab nationalist Ba'th leadership in Damascus, did not trust either the non-Ba'thist officers or the officers who had only recently joined the party. (In Syria, the struggle between the leftist radical wing of the party and the senior leadership, headed by Michel 'Aflaq and Salah al-Din al-Bitar, had already begun.)

On March 14, a series of talks initiated by Syria took place in Egypt between Syrian and Iraqi delegations and Nasir regarding a tripartite union. The ideological commitment of the Ba'th leaders to act toward realization of Arab unity was reinforced by a practical political motive: the desire to neutralize the power of the Nasirite officers and to take the wind out of their sails, by negotiating with Nasir. The addition of Iraq as a third partner in the talks and in the planned unity was intended to reinforce the status of Syria within the talks and, once the union was implemented in practice, to offset the imbalance between the size, power, and stability of Egypt and the weaknesses, small dimensions, and instability of Syria.

The idea of Arab unity was a central component in the ideology and legitimization of the Ba'th and its central argument (and that of the Nasirite officers) against Qasim, who was decried by the party as a separatist and a traitor to Arab unity. The interest in preserving the Ba'th regime in Syria constituted an additional motive for that country to join the talks in Cairo. Just before the departure of the Iraqi delegation for the talks in Egypt, the NCRC held a debate on the issue, which was characterized by two different approaches. Although they supported Arab unity and the establishment of a common political framework, 'Arif, Ahmad Hasan al-Bakr, Salih Mahdi 'Amash, and 'Ali Salih al-Sa'di adopted a cautious stance and stressed the need, within the framework of the proposed unity, to preserve Iraq's special interests regarding the Kurds, petroleum, and relations with its neighbors, especially Iran. By contrast, Hazim Jawad, Talib Shabib, and Hani al-Fkaiki were more enthusiastic about the establishment of a tripartite union, emphasizing that the union was an urgent and vital interest that would help the Arabs stand firm against Israel while assisting Iraq to cope with its socioeconomic and political problems.[33] This dispute does not seem to have given rise to fixed camps within the party. When the struggle within the Iraqi Ba'th broke out several weeks later, the members of the party leadership were divided along different lines.

The talks in Cairo focused on relations between Egypt in Syria and the conflict between Nasir and the heads of the Syrian Ba'th, Michel 'Aflaq and Salah al-Din al-Bitar.[34] Nasir did not trust the Syrian and Ba'th leaders, and he resented them for having deserted the UAR, contributing to its demise in 1962, after having been active in promoting its establishment in 1958. Nasir was now prepared for union only on his terms and suspected the other participants in the talks of intending only to gain time. Their motives for doing so, in his opinion, were to strengthen the positions of their parties relative to the Nasirites and their own positions relative to their rivals within the parties. Despite Nasir's haughty and humiliating attitude, the Syrian and Iraqi delegations agreed to the establishment of a union on the terms dictated by Nasir. The Iraqi delegation, composed of 'Ali Salih al-Sa'di and Talib Shabib, who played a minor role in the talks, generally supported the positions held by the Syrian delegation and made efforts to mediate between the Syrians and Nasir.

On April 17, the tripartite agreement was signed establishing the union of Egypt, Syria, and Iraq. Even on the date of its signing, the signatories themselves believed that the chances of putting the agreement into practice were slim. The agreement immediately became a tool of domestic Syrian and inter-Arab struggles. Tension between Syria and Egypt increased with the exacerbation of the struggle between the Ba'th and the nationalist Nasirite officers in Syria. Following an attempted nationalist Nasirite coup in Syria on July 18, relations between Egypt and Syria deteriorated into an exchange of accusations, and the agreement ceased to be relevant.[35] Regarding the cold war that developed between Egypt and the Syrian Baʿth regime, the Iraqi Baʿth adopted a pro-Syrian line. The Baʿth in Iraq, which was becoming more and more embroiled in severe domestic struggles of its own, once more played only a minor role in the conflict between Nasir and the Baʿth.

Given the rift between the Baʿth and Nasir, Syria and Iraq began a series of talks regarding union between the two states. On September 30, an agreement for economic union was signed, followed by an agreement for military union on October 8.[36] The Iraqi minister of defense, Salih Mahdi ʿAmash, was appointed supreme commander of the armies of Iraq and Syria; the combined headquarters of those armies was established in Damascus. According to the agreement, a Syrian division entered Iraq and joined the fighting against the Kurdish rebels. In practice, however, these agreements constituted no more than a declaration of intent and became irrelevant after the fall of the Baʿth regime in Iraq.

The Attempt to Achieve an Agreement between the Kurds and the Baʿth Regime and the Renewal of the Kurdish Revolt

Following the overthrow of the Qasim regime, the Kurds declared a cease-fire and stated their willingness to negotiate with the new regime.[37] The heads of the KDP, Jalal Talabani and Ibrahim Ahmad, both of whom were educated urban leftists, held out hopes for achieving a dialogue with the leftist radical members of the Baʿth; on the other hand, the more conservative Barzani regarded the Baʿth regime with suspicion and skepticism. He repeatedly warned that, if the Kurds' demands were not met, the fighting would be resumed.[38] In view of the need to negotiate with the government, Barzani and the heads of the KDP reached an understanding, following which Talabani set out for Baghdad on February 19, in order to discuss the Kurdish demands.[39]

Talabani was welcomed in Baghdad with declarations of sympathy and support by the regime, but the actual negotiations were delayed. The members of the new regime gave higher priority to the need to consolidate their rule and gain legitimacy in the international arena and in the Arab world than to the talks with the Kurds. Soon after his arrival in Baghdad, Talabani was asked to participate in a large Iraqi delegation that was being dispatched to Egypt in order to congratulate Nasir on the fifth anniversary of the establishment of the UAR (the union between Egypt and Syria that existed between 1958 and 1961). Talabani's trip to Egypt and his appearance as the spokesman for the Kurds infuriated Barzani, who was not interested in any improvement in the status of the KDP leaders, given the mistrust and rivalry that characterized his relations with them.[40] Talabani, seeking to prevent a rift between the party and Barzani, began to encourage direct contacts between the latter and the government of Iraq. The heads of the regime also considered Barzani to be the leader with whom an agreement should be reached. On March 5, a delegation sent by the Iraqi government and headed by Tahir Yihya, with the participation of two Kurdish ministers, Fuad 'Arif and Baba 'Ali, met with Barzani. Tahir Yihya urgently desired to reach an understanding with the Kurds, but his status was apparently not strong enough to be able to conclude an agreement. Accordingly, several days later, Barzani met with another delegation headed by Defense Minister Salih Mahdi 'Amash, and that meeting resulted in the formulation of guidelines for an agreement.[41]

On March 15, the NCRC published a plan for the administrative decentralization of the state. According to that plan, Iraq was to be divided into six administrative districts that would enjoy a certain degree of autonomous rule.[42] The central government, however, reserved the principal powers for itself, including the appointment of governors and holders of key positions within the districts.

On March 18–22, Barzani organized a Kurdish conference with a large number of participants in Koysanjak.[43] Participating in the conference were representatives of various Kurdish groups and sectors. Among the participants were tribal leaders and notables who had not taken part in the revolt during the Qasim regime and had even maintained a reserved or outright hostile attitude toward it. The conference was intended to reinforce the front presented by the Kurds against the Ba'th regime; however, it also provided Barzani with an opportunity to reinforce his own status vis-à-vis the heads of the KDP. At the conference itself, tensions were obvious between the tribal leaders, who sought to preserve their traditional status, and the members of the KDP, whose urban, modern, educated, leftist leadership was perceived as a threat to the existing order of Kurdish society. It appears that Barzani did not succeed in weakening the party leaders during the course of the conference. Notwithstanding the differences in outlook, social interests, and mentality between the conference participants, the conference succeeded in putting together a plan for extensive Kurdish autonomy, which was presented as part of the Kurdish national demands.

The Kurdish demands, presented in various versions by Barzani early in March in KDP publications and by the Kurdish delegation to the talks with the government in April and May, were as follows:[44]

a. Extensive self-rule, autonomy in practice for all areas populated with Kurds.
b. National equality for the Kurds within the framework of the Iraqi state.

c. Inclusion of the city of Kirkuk and the surrounding oil fields, the area around the city of Khanakin, and the oil fields northwest of Mosul within the Kurdish zone.

d. Allocation of income from petroleum for the needs of the Kurdish zone in proportion to its share of Iraq's population.

e. Equalization of the status of the Kurdish and Arabic languages.

f. Appointment of a Kurd as vice president of Iraq.

g. Appointment of a Kurd as deputy chief of staff of the Iraqi Army.

h. Appointment of Kurds to government positions, in proportion to the Kurds' share of Iraq's population.

i. Establishment of Kurdish units commanded by Kurds within the framework of the Iraqi Army, and the posting of those units within Kurdistan.

On April 24, the Kurdish demands were presented to the government of Iraq. The dispute between the Kurds and the government focused on two types of problems: (a) territorial problems—the Kurdish demands for the inclusion of Kirkuk (which, although its population was basically non-Kurdish, was surrounded by a Kurdish majority), Khanakin and the oil fields around Mosul within the autonomous Kurdish zone; (b) the degree of autonomy to be granted to the Kurdish zone and the powers to be retained by the government. The gap between the positions of the two sides was quite wide. Admittedly, 'Ali Salih al-Sa'di and Tahir Yihya expressed the Ba'th regime's willingness to grant extensive self-rule to the Kurds. In practice, however, the government leaders feared the Kurdish autonomist and even separatist currents. Like any other Iraqi regime, they feared that granting the Kurdish demands could have an adverse effect on the cohesive nature of Iraq, by provoking the Shi'ites to raise demands of their own and thus threatening Iraq's continued existence. The pan-Arab nationalist world outlook of the Ba'th leaders and the Nasirite officers opposed any compromise on issues that could give rise to consequences affecting national sovereignty. The Kurds held a relatively good bargaining position given the weakness and insecurity of the new regime in Baghdad. Moreover, they enjoyed the support of the Soviet Union, which viewed the Ba'th regime that had overthrown its ally, Qasim, and persecuted the Communists with hostility. Furthermore, the Ba'th leaders—especially the civilians among them—sought to prevent a resumption of fighting, fearing that this would strengthen the position of the army officers.

The tripartite alliance talks between Egypt, Syria, and Iraq, which were conducted in Cairo in March and April of that year, aroused the profound concern of the Kurdish leaders. They feared that, if the union were to take place, their relative importance would decline within the framework of the large Arab state and its predictably pan-Arab nationalist character. On April 8, Talabani sent an official message to the Iraqi delegation at the talks in Cairo, with a demand for Kurdish representation at the conference. In addition, the Kurds demanded the assurance of extensive autonomy for Iraqi Kurdistan within the framework of the united Arab state.[45] In view of the lack of progress of the talks and the delaying tactics on the part of the Iraqi government, Talabani set out for Egypt once again, where he met with Nasir on May 25.[46] Talabani then continued to Algeria and met with President Ahmad Ben Bella, with the aim of bringing the radical revolutionary leaders of the Arab world to exert pressure on the government of Iraq.

In Iraq, the Kurds exploited the lull in the fighting to reinforce the Peshmerga and increase its control of various areas within Kurdistan. At the same time, local clashes continued between the Kurds and units of the National Guard. Early in June, tensions between the Kurds in the government increased. On June 6, the government imposed a quarantine and curfew on the city of Sulaymaniyya, which had, in practice, been taken over by the Kurdish rebels. According to the Iraqis, this action was taken in response to an attack which had been launched by the Kurds on an Iraqi military convoy. In Baghdad, arrests of KDP activists began. Among those arrested were members of the Kurdish delegation for negotiations with the government. On June 10, the Iraqi Army launched an all-out offensive against the Kurds.[47] The army officers apparently believed that it would be possible to put down the Kurdish revolt by military means.

In the first stages of the offensive, during the summer and autumn of 1963, the Iraqi Army attained impressive achievements, driving the Kurds out of the cities and their environs and into the high mountains. The Kurds, who were impressively skilled at guerrilla warfare in the mountains, could not withstand a regular army, equipped with armor and backed by an air force, on the low hills and plains. The Iraqi Army offensive was joined by a Syrian brigade, while Syrian aircraft made sorties against Kurdish targets. At the same time, while destroying Kurdish villages and expelling their populations, the Iraqi authorities renewed their efforts to organize the tribal rivals of the Barzani.[48] By autumn, the situation had returned to the status quo under Qasim. In practice, the Kurds had control of the high mountains and the areas of limited accessibility. The Iraqi Army was deeply embroiled in exhausting battles with the Kurdish guerrillas and, unable to suppress the revolt, increased the bombings on the Kurdish civilian population.

The resumption of fighting in Kurdistan reinforced the status of the army and its nationalist Nasirite and Ba'thist officers in the power struggles within the framework of the regime and the party.

Internal Struggles within the Baʿth and Its Overthrows

The Baʿth had established control throughout Iraq and primarily in the large cities by means of the National Guard. The number of National Guardsmen increased from fewer than 5,000 in February to 21,000 in May and 40,000 in August.[49] The National Guard terrorized the streets of Iraq's cities. Anyone who was identified with the Qasim regime or was thought to sympathize or to maintain any contact with the Communist Party was persecuted and arrested. Communist activists were murdered in the streets. The National Guard took over municipalities, expelled the mayors, and appointed Baʿth leaders to head the cities. It paralyzed the courts and freed prisoners (including criminals). In several cases, National Guardsmen attacked foreign diplomats.[50] Colonel ʿAbd al-Karim Mustafa Nasrat, who had founded the underground predecessor of the National Guard, lost control of his men and resigned. He was replaced by Mundhir al-Wandawi, an air force officer and follower of ʿAli Salih al-Saʿdi.[51] Al-Saʿdi and his cronies sought to strengthen the National Guard, as a force capable of preventing any organization of the Communist Party and as a counterweight to the military. Muhsin al-Shaykh Radi, a party activist and leading member of al-Saʿdi's faction, even proposed training the National Guardsmen in the use of heavy arms and equipping them with tanks.[52]

Following the seizure of power, the coalition between the Nasirite army officers and the Baʿth began to fall apart. Some of the Baʿth officers felt closer to the nationalist officers than to the civilian party members.[53] Within the framework of the regime and the party, a struggle between the various factions broke out. The two largest factions, which were most decisive in the fate of the party as a whole, were led by ʿAli Salih al-Saʿdi and by Hazim Jawad and Talib Shabib. In addition to those two factions, there was some degree of factional organization around the prime minister, Ahmad Hasan al-Bakr, who maintained a neutral position regarding the struggle between the two large factions during the summer, and around the minister of defense, Salih Mahdi ʿAmash, and the minister of communications, ʿAbd al-Sattar ʿAbd al-Latif. (The latter was a veteran member of the Free Officers in the 1950s; in 1963, he was a member of the Baʿth leadership and the Revolutionary Council.)[54] President ʿArif, meanwhile, was supported by the nationalist officers who remained personally loyal to him, and by the Nasirites who were not Baʿth members.

Al-Saʿdi was supported by leftist radical activists, such as Hani al-Fkaiki, Hamdi ʿAbd al-Majid, and Muhsin al-Shaykh Radi.[55] The al-Saʿdi faction was considered the "left," and the Jawad and Shabib faction was deemed the "right." Al-Saʿdi himself made use of leftist terminology and attitudes, though not with any degree of consistency, and accused his rivals of being "rightist."[56] With the development of the internal struggle within the Syrian Baʿth, it was both easy and convenient for al-Saʿdi to join forces with the leftist groups in Syria, under the leadership of Hamud al-Shufi, ʿAbd al-Karim Zuhur, Jamal al-Atasi, and Yasin al-Hafiz, who challenged the senior national leadership under Michel ʿAflaq.

Scholars on Iraq differ in their opinions regarding the nature of the struggle that took place within the Baʿth and throughout Iraq in 1963—specifically the importance of the ideological differences, or whether this was primarily a personal power struggle, in which the supposed ideological differences were imaginary and meaningless. Majid Khadduri, who is sympathetic to the Baʿth, emphasizes the importance of the ideological dispute between left and right.[57] Peter and Marion Sluglett, whose approach to the Baʿth is more critical, ascribe very little importance to the ideological dispute and stress the violent, power-hungry nature of the struggle. Hanna Batatu points out the ideological dispute between the factions, but stresses the motives of personal power involved.[58]

Hani al-Fkaiki, one of the heads of the "leftist" faction (al-Saʿdi's faction), emphasizes in his memoirs the importance of the ideological differences, but does not ignore the personal power struggle between al-Saʿdi and Jawad.[59] A report compiled by the national leadership of the Baʿth and published at the inspiration of Michel ʿAflaq, in order to examine the events that eventually led to the loss of power by the Iraqi Baʿth Party—in effect, a sort of "soul-searching" of the party—emphasizes that the struggle in Iraq was basically personal and motivated by power and did not involve an ideological dispute regarding objectives and the way to attain them.[60]

Indeed, the historical picture is a complex one. There can be no doubt that al-Saʿdi's struggle was power-motivated and focused on control of the party and of Iraq, and that it adopted leftist Socialist slogans for that purpose. Moreover, al-Fkaiki, Muhsin al-Shaykh Radi, and others held views that were more leftist radical than those of Shabib and Jawad or those of al-Bakr and ʿArif. Al-Fkaiki and his colleagues maintained contact with the left wing of the Syrian Baʿth even before the 1963 revolution and possibly even before joining forces with al-Saʿdi. They were influenced by the leftist intellectuals within the Syrian Baʿth, Yasin al-Hafiz and Jamal al-Atasi,[61] although they did not fully adopt the Marxist outlook shared by them and by Elias Murkus. During the months of Baʿth rule in 1963, neither the left nor the right succeeded in putting together any kind of well ordered plan or program for social, economic, and political action that could have expressed the ideologies and significance of the differences between their orientations. A number of specific decisions, however, reflected differences in values and outlook within the Ba'th leadership and the NCRC. Thus, for example, the month of March was marked by a debate on the Personal Status Law, which had been passed under the Qasim regime (Law no. 188), granting men and women equal status in matters of inheritance.[62] President 'Arif and Prime Minister Ahmad Hasan al-Bakr acted to repeal the law, which they saw as irreconcilable with Islamic law. 'Arif, however, was not a member of the Ba'th, and Ahmad Hasan al-Bakr did not belong to the faction of Jawad and Shabib, although he cooperated with them against al-Sa'di and his "leftist" faction, a majority of whose members supported repeal of the law. An additional ideological struggle involved the issue of whether to nationalize all the private factories and other private institutions. In summary, the struggle of 1963, while it was motivated by power, was also affected by ideological differences and by the ideological slogans that were used as political weapons.

The relations between al-Sa'di and the Nasirite officers were fraught with tension and suspicion. Al-Sa'di and his faction, which sought to establish a one-party (Ba'thist) regime in Iraq, considered 'Arif as a temporary ally who would eventually have to be disposed of.[63] The expansion and activity of the National Guard and the reinforced status of al-Sa'di—who, through his protégé, Mundhir al-Wandawi, controlled the Guard and enjoyed support in the ranks of the party—aroused the concern of 'Arif and the Nasirite officers. Moreover, many of the Ba'thist officers were just as concerned. Their common desire to hamper al-Sa'di led to cooperation between the Ba'th army officers, Tahir Yihya, Ahmad Hasan al-Bakr, and Salih Mahdi 'Amash, and 'Arif and the Jawad-Shabib faction. Starting in February, two power centers began to coalesce—one in the government, which enjoyed the support of the army and the Jawad-Shabib faction, and the other in the party and the National Guard, which were controlled by al-Sa'di and his "leftist" faction.[64]

In May, the Nasirite and Ba'thist officers, together with the Jawad-Shabib faction, began to exert pressure to expel al-Sa'di from the government. Prime Minister al-Bakr threatened to resign, warning that, if al-Sa'di did not resign, the officers would make sure that he was ousted. Al-Fkaiki, seeking to avoid a rift between the Ba'th and the army, also pressured al-Sa'di to resign.[65] It appears that both al-Sa'di and al-Fkaiki feared confrontation with the army. Al-Sa'di's resignation, however, did not stop his continued empowerment, based on the increasing strength of the National Guard, which controlled the streets, and thanks to the support given to him by the party. Although the struggles within the Ba'th became continually more vehement, it appears that, in May and June, the two factions attempted to avoid an out-and-out rift, fearing that the Ba'th would lose control of the country.[66]

At the Fifth Regional Congress of the Iraqi Ba'th Party, held September 13–25, al-Sa'di and his faction reinforced their control of the party.[67] The

Iraqi delegation to the Sixth National Conference of the Syrian Ba'th, held in Damascus in October, was primarily composed of members of the al-Sa'di faction. At the conference, members of that faction supported the coalition between the left wing of the Syrian Ba'th and the Syrian army officers who were party members and helped them defeat the old leadership headed by Michel 'Aflaq.[68]

Following an attempted Nasirite coup against the Ba'th regime in Syria on July 18, relations between the Ba'th and Nasir deteriorated; strong accusations were exchanged and tensions between Syria and Egypt mounted. Unlike Syria, in Iraq it was actually Shabib and Jawad (who were closer to 'Aflaq) who were targeted by most of Nasir's accusations, whereas the officers supporting Ahmad Hasan al-Bakr and 'Amash tended to cooperate with the Nasirites. The possible victory of the al-Sa'di faction, which sought to establish a one-party Ba'thist regime,[69] in which the NCRC and the government would be under the supervision of the party leadership, would dictate the removal of 'Arif and al-Sa'di's rivals from the party. The continued strengthening of the National Guard, the declarations by its commanders of their intention to provide its members with advanced military training,[70] and the inability of the government and the NCRC to control the guard, increased the concerns of 'Arif and the officers, Nasirite and Ba'thist alike. (Saddam Husayn, a civilian who aligned himself with Ba'th officers and became a protégé of al-Bakr, proposed murdering 'Ali Salih al-Sa'di and Talib Shabib.)[71] On November 1, 'Arif announced the transfer of Mundhir al-Wandawi from his post as commander in chief of the National Guard. (Al-Wandawi was appointed to head the air force, which had been placed under joint Iraqi-Syrian command with headquarters in Syria.) Al-Wandawi, however, felt sufficiently secure of his position to ignore these orders.

On November 11, Jawad and Shabib succeeded in convening the Extraordinary Regional Congress of the Ba'th. 'Arif demanded that the Congress disperse the National Guard; Jawad and Shabib, however, were incapable of having such a resolution passed.[72] The National Guard had become stronger than the party and constituted a threat to any and all rivals of the al-Sa'di faction. In the situation that ensued, 'Arif and the army officers made a dramatic move. A group of officers burst into the hall where the Congress was meeting, during the elections for the party's Regional Command. Under threat of arms, the chairman of the Congress, Hani al-Fkaiki, was removed from the podium, and the management of the Congress was transferred to the Ba'th officers, under Tahir Yihya. The officers dictated the results of the elections, thus ensuring a majority for the colleagues of Ahmad Hasan al-Bakr, Tahir Yihya, and Salih Mahdi 'Amash and the Jawad-Shabib faction.[73] Al-Sa'di and four members of his faction—Hamid 'Abd al-Majid (the party

Secretary), Hani al-Fkaiki, Muhsin al-Shaykh Radi, and Abu Talib al-Hash-imi—were arrested; the next day, November 12, they were placed aboard an aircraft that took them to exile in Spain.[74]

In response, the National Guard incited a series of riots that led to its control of most of the streets of Baghdad, with the exception of the government compound, which was still controlled by the army. Its commander in chief, al-Wandawi, an air force officer and a pilot, took control of a MiG aircraft, bombed the Habbaniyya Air Force Base, and fired a missile at the Presidential Palace.[75] ʿArif and the nationalist Nasirite officers, while they felt the need to take immediate, decisive action against the National Guard, wished to avoid a rift with the Baʿth and to secure the support of those officers who were party members. Given the struggle and the collapse of the government in Baghdad, the heads of the Syrian Baʿth—Michel ʿAflaq, Amin al-Hafiz (who held power in Syria at the time), and Salah Jadid (a leader of the military left wing of the party)—hastened to Iraq. Their intention was to rescue the Baʿth regime in Iraq, lest its collapse lead to the crumbling of the equally weak Syrian Baʿth regime. Under pressure by the heads of the Syrian national leadership (and especially ʿAflaq) and threatened by the National Guard, Talib Shabib and Hazim Jawad, al-Saʿdi's rivals, were forced to leave Iraq and flee to Beirut.[76] The talks conducted by the heads of the Syrian Baʿth failed, due to their inability to impose their will on the National Guard and their weakness in the face of the army officers. Seeing that the National Guard continued rioting and refused to be disarmed, ʿArif sent in the army on November 18. The army bombed the National Guard centers from the air and effectively quelled its resistance. The National Guard was forcibly disarmed and dispersed.

ʿArif assigned the task of forming a new government to Chief of Staff Tahir Yihya, officially a Baʿth member. The new government included a majority of nationalist, non-Baʿthist ministers.[77] While Tahir Yihya was admittedly a party member, his true loyalty was to ʿArif, and he felt no obligation to the party. The position of minister of defense was assigned to another Baʿth officer, Hardan ʿAbd al-Ghaffar al-Tikriti; still, in practice ʿArif and his nationalist Nasirite officers controlled the army. Although Ahmad Hasan al-Bakr was appointed as vice president, this was a meaningless and powerless position, which was abolished early in 1964. (Al-Bakr became a retired officer, with no official position and no political backing.)

The Rule of the 'Arif Brothers, 1963–1968

From Pan-Arab Nationalism and Socialist Etatism to Ideological Confusion and the Weakness of Political Forces

Pan-Arabism and the Socialist Etatist Orientation in the Government Headed by Tahir Yihya, November 1963 to August 1965

'Abd al-Salam 'Arif's regime was supported by army officers who maintained personal loyalty to him. Several of these officers were his relatives from the Al-Jumayla tribe. Among his other supporters were members of the Ba'th Party, some of whom had left the party. 'Arif was also supported by the Nasirists, some of whom were affiliated with the Qawmiyyun al-'Arab movement.[1] Moreover, he still enjoyed the fame and glory that he had earned among the nationalists back in the days when he had been the leader and symbol of the nationalist supporters of Arab unity in their struggle against Qasim and his Iraqi territorialist trends. Between December 1963 and April 1964, 'Arif expelled the Ba'th officers who had helped him to prevail over the civilian factions of the Ba'th. Ahmad Hasan al-Bakr, who had been appointed vice president in November 1963, lost his position when it was abolished early in 1964. While continuing to serve in office, Prime Minister Tahir Yihya only managed to do so by virtue of his personal loyalty to 'Arif and his distance from the Ba'th.

'Arif's approach combined pan-Arab nationalism with a religious Islamic inclination. His relative conservatism in social matters and the combination of Islamic concepts superimposed on a pan-Arab nationalist outlook manifested themselves in differences of opinion between him and the left wing of the Ba'th as early as 1963. At that time an amendment was proposed to the law giving full equality to men and women including matters of inheritance that had been passed in Qasim's time. In contrast to the left wing of the party, both 'Arif and al-Bakr supported the amendment, which would be in line with Islamic traditions and Islamic law (Shari'a).[2] (The Islamic conservative tendencies of 'Arif helped him to maintain good relations with Shi'ite religious leaders. Under his rule the radical Shi'ite organization al-Da'wa expanded its activity. The anti-Communist and anti-Ba'th positions of al-Da'wa were convenient for the regime). 'Arif supported Arab unity; however, following his struggle against Qasim in the name of "Unity Now," he began to adopt an increasingly practical and pragmatic viewpoint regarding the actual meaning of unity in practice. Between 1963 and 1966, 'Arif drifted closer and closer to a pragmatic view of Arab unity in the sense of rapprochement, increased cooperation, political, economic, and military coordination, and even a loose kind of federation, but without abolishing the separate existence of the Arab states within the framework of a union. 'Arif's aim, between 1963 and 1964, to establish a federation with Egypt by adapting Iraq's military and political systems to those of Egypt, while in line with his own world outlook, was also intended to preserve his own status as a pan-Arab nationalist leader and to take the wind out of the sails of the Nasirists. The latter based their own status on the demand for immediate establishment of a union with Egypt. Both Nasir and 'Arif understood Arab unity in terms of coordination between their states, their regimes, and their economic and social practices, but not as a merger involving abolition of the individual states. According to this orientation, Iraq supported Egypt's positions at the Arab summit conferences that took place in Cairo in January 1964, in Alexandria in September 1964, and in Casablanca in September 1965.[3]

A series of political and economic measures that were adopted by Tahir Yihya's government were intended to prepare for the establishment of the union with Egypt. On May 3, 1964, Iraq promulgated a new constitution, which was drawn up so as to be compatible with the Egyptian constitution. On May 26, during his visit to Egypt, on the occasion of the dedication of the Aswan Dam on the Nile, 'Arif and Nasir signed an agreement for union between their states. They agreed on the establishment of a joint Presidential Council, headed by the two presidents, with an equal number of minister-members from each of the two states. In July 1964, following the Egyptian pattern, 'Arif began to establish the ruling party, the Arab Socialist Union. On July 14, the government of Iraq published the Socialist Decrees, which nationalized the banks and the major industrial plants producing textiles, tobacco, vegetable oil, and concrete, as well as wholesale trading and import companies. Small and medium-sized plants were left in private hands. In accordance with the trend of centralizing management and planning of the economy, government institutions were established for economic planning, management, and supervision. The motivating force behind the formulation of the decrees and the adoption of the centralist Socialist orientation was the governor of the Central Bank, Khayr al-Din al-Hasib.[4] An economist with radical pan-Arab nationalist views, al-Hasib was impressed by the adoption of Socialist (in the centralist etatist sense) development methods by the

Nasirist regime in Egypt. Although 'Arif himself tended toward moderation and conservatism in economic and social areas and sought to encourage the private sector and to reassure the bourgeoisie, al-Hasib succeeded in convincing him that adoption of Socialist economic policy was vital for the rapid industrialization and development of Iraq and the adjustment of its economy to that of Egypt.

The socioeconomic orientation in Iraq under Tahir Yihya's government was affected by the Nasirist Egyptian model and was presented as a move toward establishing the federation between Iraq and Egypt. However, it was also the local Iraqi expression of the trend that predominated in the 1960s in many postcolonial states in Asia and Africa. The regimes and the ruling elites in many of these states tended to adopt Socialist etatist methods in the development and management of their states, in the absence or weakness of the local bourgeoisie as an entrepreneurial, developing, and industrializing force. The prevailing global political and economic conditions, too, imposed difficulties on rapid development and modernization in Asia and Africa. The economic backwardness, the grinding poverty, the weakness of national cohesive forces all constituted difficult and complex challenges for the regimes, the elites, and the politicians in the Asian and African countries. In the prevailing ideological climate and the dominant political discourse of the 1960s and 1970s among the new radical elites that had sprung up from among the officers and the middle strata in the Arab states and many other states in Asia and Africa, the state was given the central role in development, modernization, industrialization, and management. Regimes that sought to accomplish rapid modernization and development and to eliminate poverty, while building up their states and the nations within them, selectively adopted etatist centralist patterns of development and management, utilizing the example set by the Soviet Union. The infiltration of Asian and African states, and specifically Arab states, by the Soviet Union from the mid-1950s on encouraged the strengthening of the Socialist etatist authoritarian trends in those states. The nature of the assistance rendered by the Soviet Union, which was primarily directed toward establishing major infrastructure projects and heavy industrial plants, in addition to supplying armaments, provided a response to the ambitions of the elites, the leaders, and the educated strata of the developing countries in Asia and Africa. All such leaders and modern educated people in developing countries sought to promote development and industrialization so as to build up national cohesion and power as quickly as possible. The adoption of the Socialist etatist authoritarian models, inspired by the USSR, was in line with the authoritarian trends that had developed in those states. Lack of national cohesion and severe poverty, difficulties stymieing development, and the complex tasks involved in building up nations and

states and achieving development by small elites—who had their own special interests—under difficult internal socioeconomic circumstances and
international conditions, combined to create fertile ground for the adoption of the authoritarian etatist trends. The authoritarian centralist etatist
economic orientations, which were founded in the ideological concepts
known as "Arab socialism," "African socialism," and so forth, sought to
base the regime on a single ruling party that was intended to serve as a
means for enlisting social and political support and legitimizing the government. Under Qasim and 'Arif, Iraq was at the height of this stage of development.

The Attempt to Reach an Agreement with the Kurds
and the Rift between Barzani and the KDP

'Arif aimed to reach an agreement with the Kurds. According to 'Ali Salah
Sa'di, 'Arif secretly approached Barzani as early as October 1963 and asked
him to stop the fighting, so that he would be able to utilize the army for
coping with the Ba'th.[5] After seizing power, 'Arif sought to reach an agreement with Barzani in order to be able to free Iraq of the burden imposed by
the war in the North and (in the short range) to reorganize the Iraqi armed
forces. In February 1964, a cease-fire agreement was reached between the
Kurds and the government of Iraq.[6] The parties reached the understanding
that the rights of the Kurds would be recognized within the framework of the
new Iraqi Constitution and that negotiations would take place concerning
the remaining Kurdish demands.

The cease-fire agreement was acceptable to Barzani but not to the heads
of the KDP, Jalal Talabani and Ibrahim Ahmad. This fact contributed to the
escalation of the tensions between Talabani and Ahmad, on one hand, and
Barzani, on the other, into an open rift. Barzani tried to overpower his
rivals, whose influence had increased since 1963 and had now begun to
threaten his own position. In March 1964, Talabani and Ahmad convened
a conference of the party, which censured Barzani for having concluded the
agreement with 'Arif. Nonetheless, the supporters of Barzani, who held the
title of president of the party, boycotted the conference and succeeded in
maneuvering Talabani and Ahmad into a situation where they constituted
no more than a faction within the party.[7] Barzani exploited his control of
most of the Kurdish fighters and his influence over the tribal notables and
large segments of the tribal population in order to eject the officers and
activists who were loyal to his rivals from their posts in the revolutionary
movement. In June and July 1964, Barzani's forces took over most of the
areas under Kurdish control. In early August, Barzani convened the Sixth

Conference of the KDP, which gave him its full support. Talabani and Ibrahim Ahmad were forced to flee to Iran, along with about 4,000 of their supporters.

After having overcome his rivals, Barzani continued negotiating with the regime in Baghdad. However, the gaps between their positions concerning the Kurdish demands to include the oilfields of Kirkuk and Khanaqin and the city of Kirkuk itself within the areas of autonomy, as well as the failure to reach agreement regarding the nature of the Kurdish economy and disarmament of the Kurdish Peshmerga militia, led the talks into an impasse and eventual breakdown. Barzani refused to accede to the demands by the government of Iraq to disarm the Peshmerga; instead, he demanded the integration of those forces into the Iraqi Army as organic units under Kurdish command and their posting within Kurdistan. In October, with no progress in the negotiations, the Kurds began to establish institutions of autonomy.[8] These included the Legislative Council, the Kurdish Parliament, and the Executive Office—the latter being equivalent to an autonomous Kurdish government. Among the members of the Executive Office was Jalal Talabani, who had meanwhile become reconciled with Barzani and returned to Iraq. However, Barzani succeeded in guaranteeing himself control of all government agencies. In October, the clashes between the army and the Kurds resumed, with each side attempting to seize strategic areas before snowfall. Notwithstanding these clashes, both sides continued pursuing contacts and exchanging letters; still, there was no definitive breakthrough.[9] Given the impasse, the army officers and the government increasingly adopted a rigid, "hawkish" policy designed to suppress the Kurdish revolt by force, objecting to compromise with Barzani. In February 1965, the Iraqi minister of the interior sent a forceful letter, phrased as an ultimatum, to Barzani. The letter rejected the Kurdish demands concerning autonomy and the dissolution of the Peshmerga; in fact, it demanded disarmament of the Kurds. On April 3, the Iraqi Army began an all-out offensive against the Kurdish areas.

The Political Arena under 'Abd al-Salam 'Arif

The Iraqi political arena under the 'Arif brothers gave a central role to rival groups of officers. The dominance of army officers within the framework of the regime, the weakening of the civilian political parties and organizations, as well as the frustration and disappointment of the general public with the politicians and the resultant indifference, pushed the officers into a central role in politics. Although the Ba'th Party and the Communist Party continued to operate, their effectiveness was hampered by disorganization and ideological confusion. The Nasirist officers were the most prominent in the political arena. Their leaders included ʿArif ʿAbd al-Razzaq, commander of the Iraqi Air Force, Rashid Muhsin, head of the Public Security Agency, and Hadi Hamas, head of Military Intelligence. Following the weakening of the Communist Party, the Nasirists held control of the workers' organizations, which constituted a relatively well organized civilian force.[10] Nonetheless, the Nasirists—whose views were attractive to both officers and civilians—did not succeed in presenting a cohesive political force.

The rivals of the Nasirists included more conservative groups of officers who emphasized the unique conditions of Iraq and sought to block the hasty union that would give superiority to Egypt. The Arab nationalism of those groups was Iraqi territorialist in its orientation. A prominent leader of one of those groups was ʿAbd al-ʿAziz al-ʿUqaili. Another group of officers was led by Colonel ʿAbd al-Ghani al-Rawi, known for his religious Islamic outlook. ʿArif, who was principally supported by officers who maintained personal loyalty to him—some of whom belonged to his own tribe, the al-Jumayla—maneuvered among the various groups of officers, who continued to exert severe pressure on him. In the government headed by Tahir Yihya, the Nasirist members included the minister of the interior, the minister of economic affairs, the minister of justice, the minister of industry, the minister of national guidance, and the minister of rural affairs. Khayr al-Din al-Hasib, an economist with Nasirist views, headed the Central Bank of Iraq and the "Economic Organization," which had been established in order to supervise nationalization and apply the Socialist Decrees.[11]

However, whereas ʿArif himself had abandoned his initial fervor for immediate realization of the vision of Arab unity and had adopted—possibly inspired by Nasir himself—a pragmatic and realistic viewpoint concerning the question of unity in general and union with Egypt in particular, the Nasirists continued to demand accelerated progress toward union. This was based on a combination of ideological dogmatism, faith in the vision of Arab unity, political naivete, and the use of the call for unity as a means of building up their political status within Iraq. Admittedly, in 1964 and 1965, several agreements were signed that were intended to lay the foundations for union with Egypt, and several domestic political and economic measures were taken that were explained as preparations for the union. Still, progress toward its implementation was slow. At the same time, the Socialist Decrees and their partial implementation created economic difficulties and confusion, which gave rise to criticism against the government. The slowness of progress toward union and the economic problems increased the pressure by the Nasirists, who demanded the resignation of the prime minister. In July 1965, the Nasirist ministers resigned and launched an offensive against Tahir Yihya. President ʿArif, who now sought to avoid conflict with the Nasirists, engineered the resignation of Tahir Yihya and assigned the formation of the new government to 'Arif 'Abd al-Razzaq. The government, which was established on September 6, included—in addition to the Nasirist officers—civilian ministers and officers with a personal allegiance to 'Abd al-Salam 'Arif. 'Abd al-Razzaq served as both prime minister and minister of defense, while retaining his post as commander of the Iraqi Air Force. 'Abd al-Rahman al-Bazzaz, a Sunnite politician known for his liberal reformist and moderate nationalist views, was appointed as foreign minister and deputy prime minister.

On September 12, President 'Arif, accompanied by al-Bazzaz, set out for the Arab summit conference in Casablanca, Morocco. 'Abd al-Razzaq attempted to exploit 'Arif's absence in order to overthrow him.[12] Paradoxically, the prime minister and his Nasirist supporters attempted to use slogans calling for union with Egypt under Nasir in order to overthrow President 'Arif, who was Nasir's closest ally in the inter-Arab arena. Pan-Arab ideology and slogans calling for Arab unity fulfilled complex functions in the society, the political arena, and the ideological climate of Iraq, as they did in many of the Arab states. Pan-Arab nationalism and slogans calling for union with Nasirist Egypt were attractive. They provided a response to the identity distress of individuals and of society in general, an alternative to the conservative political and social order, and a hope of extrication from a position of weakness toward the West. At the same time, the slogans that called for Arab unity, and especially for union with Egypt, served as a means of enlisting public support and building status within the political arena. The attempt made by 'Abd al-Razzaq and the Nasirists to overthrow 'Abd al-Salam 'Arif was frustrated by the latter's loyal supporters—chief among them his own brother, 'Abd al-Rahman 'Arif, the chief of staff, and Sa'id Salibi, commander of the Republican Guard. 'Abd al-Salam 'Arif, who returned to Iraq at once, appointed 'Abd al-Rahman al-Bazzaz as prime minister. The appointment of al-Bazzaz reflected the rift between 'Arif and the Nasirists and indicated a shift from Socialist etatism and pan-Arab radicalism to economic liberalization and a policy that, notwithstanding its pro-union rhetoric, favored Iraqi territorialism.

The Al-Bazzaz Government's Efforts toward Economic Liberalization, Civilian Government, and an Arrangement with the Kurds, 1965–1966

'Abd al-Rahman al-Bazzaz, former dean of the Faculty of Law at the University of Baghdad, was the first civilian prime minister since the 1958 revolution. Al-Bazzaz, a Sunnite intellectual, had been active in the circles that opposed the Hashemite regime. In his youth, in the 1930s, he had taken part in the activities of the nationalist club al-Muthanna and had been a supporter of the Rashid ʿAli movement in 1941. His views, as reflected in his lectures, articles, and books, combined pan-Arab nationalism (with an Islamic accent) with moderate Socialist reformism and political liberalism.[13] Al-Bazzaz emphasized the role of Islam in the growth of the Arab nation. According to his outlook, Islam was the national religion of the Arabs, and there was no contradiction in terms between national definitions and Islam. The brand of Socialism supported by al-Bazzaz was quite moderate, with Arab nationalist characteristics. His nationalist and Socialist concept ruled out class struggle and eliminated Marxism (while simultaneously expressing admiration for the Soviet Union, due to his practical perception of realpolitik). Notwithstanding his status as an important ideologue and thinker of the Arab national movement, al-Bazzaz was actually a pragmatic person. Although he sought to intensify cooperation with Egypt, he rejected Nasirism as an ideology and a political force. In executive positions, such as that of prime minister, he displayed a great deal of practical political wisdom. He knew how to separate (or, when necessary, to combine) political vision and political action. In his approach, which combined Arab nationalism with Islamic reformism, moderate Socialist reformism and political liberalism, al-Bazzaz resembled ʿArif himself, who also combined pan-Arab nationalist radicalism with Islamic religious views.

The al-Bazzaz government, which was established on September 21, 1965, included more civilians than army officers. Al-Bazzaz sought to reduce the army's involvement in the ongoing management of state affairs and to transform the government into a civilian organization. He espoused the expansion of representative democracy; accordingly, he supported the renewal of parliamentary activity, the holding of elections, and the establishment of a representative government.[14]

Did ʿArif, in his appointment of al-Bazzaz, actually intend to make the regime more civilian and more democratic, or was he merely seeking to suppress the power of the Nasirist officers? We have no unequivocal answer to this question. He may have been motivated by a combination of both factors. He may have made the appointment in order to reinforce his own status and his personal rule, based on the expansion of public civilian support and legitimization, while suppressing other groups of officers, primarily the Nasirists. In practice, while the government enjoyed a certain freedom of maneuvering, it continued to be dependent upon the goodwill of President ʿArif and his officers. Sovereignty and government rested with ʿArif and the National Defense Council, which was controlled by army officers.

Al-Bazzaz brought about a profound change in Iraq's economic policies.[15] As early as September 1965, he announced that he did not intend to continue the policy of nationalization. In contrast to Tahir Yihya, whose policies had emphasized nationalization and centralist management of resources, al-Bazzaz sought to encourage the private sector, which he viewed as an important element in development and industrialization. The five-year economic plan published on November 5, 1965, although setting forth the importance of centralized planning, nonetheless emphasized the need for decentralization in actual practice. The plan reflected the shift from a policy of Socialist etatist nationalization to one of economic liberalization, which nonetheless retained centralized economic control of planning and infrastructure. The plan stated that encouragement should be given to private investment in the establishment of industrial plants and to the role of the private business sector in the economy and development of Iraq. The government adopted a certain liberalization in the areas of commerce and import. Al-Bazzaz adopted certain Socialist principles, such as striving for social justice, elimination of poverty, and reduction of inequality, all of which were in line with his Islamic-Arab nationalist views. His moderate liberal Socialist outlook emphasized the necessity of adapting Arab socialism to the conditions prevailing within Iraq. The practical interpretation of this attitude included economic liberalization, reduction of etatism, encouragement of private enterprise in the economy while retaining overall state control, and a vague commitment to social justice. The status held by the governor of the National Bank, Khayr al-Din al-Hasib, the architect of the Socialist Decrees and the economic policy under Tahir Yihya, was weakened, whereas that of Minister of Finance Shukri Salah Zaki was strengthened. The Socialist Decrees themselves were severely criticized, and the need for their extensive amendment was recognized. This created conflict between two economic and ideological orientations regarding the development and management of Iraq's economy. With the shift in economic policy, al-Hasib resigned his position.

In his foreign policy, al-Bazzaz took action toward reinforcing Iraq's independent status, while attempting to maintain a close relationship with both the Soviet Union and the Western states. In the inter-Arab arena, al-Bazzaz attempted to combine relations of cordiality and cooperation with Egypt under Nasir and improvement of Iraq's relations with Saudi Arabia, Egypt's bitter rival and the ideological enemy of the Nasirist regime. His policy reflected the changes that had taken place in 'Arif's attitude toward the meaning of Arab unity. Al-Bazzaz, with his pan-Arab nationalist outlook, saw Arab unity as a vision; in practical fact, however, he related to it in a pragmatic manner. He took action to increase inter-Arab cooperation while emphasizing the unique conditions affecting Iraq, without committing to immediate union, as the Nasirists demanded. Al-Bazzaz was the first Iraqi prime minister to visit Turkey and Iran since the 1958 revolution. His visits to

Teheran and Ankara and his moves toward improving Iraq's relations with its pro-Western northern neighbors constituted an expression of his desire to reinforce the regional and international status of Iraq. The attempt to achieve a thaw in Iraqi relations with Iran, the imperial regime of which viewed the radical revolutionary Arab nationalist regime in Iraq with suspicion, was important, especially in light of the increasing rivalry between the two states (and Saudi Arabia) in the Persian Gulf and the assistance that passed through Iran to the Kurdish rebels in Iraq.

Al-Bazzaz succeeded in improving Iraq's relations with the Soviet Union. Despite their suspicion of 'Arif's religious Islamic leanings and al-Bazzaz's economic policies, the Soviets considered both Iraqis worthy allies. In the second half of July 1966, al-Bazzaz made a visit to the USSR, where he was cordially received. The leadership of the Soviet Union preferred to support real national interests, notwithstanding the criticism directed against al-Bazzaz and his economic policy by the Iraqi Communist Party.[16]

The renewal of the Kurdish revolt (and of the attempts to suppress it by force) in northern Iraq, starting in the spring of 1965, increased the power of the army officers and made it difficult for al-Bazzaz to reduce their influence over the management of state affairs. The minister of defense, General 'Abd al-'Aziz al-'Uqaili, known for his "hawkish" views regarding the Kurds, convinced 'Arif to increase military efforts to suppress the Kurdish revolt. When the snow melted in the mountains of Kurdistan in the spring of 1965, the Iraqi Army continued its Kurdish offensive.

In April 1966, 'Abd al-Salam 'Arif was killed when his helicopter crashed during a sandstorm in the course of a visit to southern Iraq. In order to choose a new president, an electoral body convened, composed of members of the National Defense Council and government ministers.[17] The National Defense Council, which had been established under 'Abd al-Salam 'Arif to replace the Revolutionary Command Council, included powerful senior officers and civilians. Although there were only three officers in the government (the ministers of defense, the interior, and finance), these ministers, along with the officers from the National Defense Council, totaled fifteen. (The members of the National Defense Council included twelve army officers and eight cabinet ministers. Since three of the ministers were also officers, the Council was composed of fifteen officers and five civilians. Although, according to the Iraqi Constitution, civilians and army officers were considered equals within the electoral body, in reality the officers held the real power.) Three candidates competed for the office of president: the chief of staff, 'Abd al-Rahman 'Arif (the late president's brother); the minister of defense, 'Abd al-'Aziz al-'Uqaili; and the civilian prime minister, "Abd al-Rahman al-Bazzaz.

In the first round of voting, al-Bazzaz won by a single vote. However, in order to be elected, he required a two-thirds majority. Al-Bazzaz withdrew his candidacy, probably realizing that he had no chance of gaining a sufficient number of votes and that he, as a civilian, would not succeed in controlling the officers; he also hoped that he could continue as prime minister under an officer president. In the second round, 'Abd al-Rahman 'Arif—the weaker of the candidates—was elected. Al-'Uqaili, who enjoyed great prestige among the officers, later claimed that the electors had been subjected to heavy pressure by Egypt and the Nasirists to prevent his election, due to his reserved attitude toward union with Egypt and his insistence on preserving Iraq's interests and independence[18]—that is, due to his Iraqi territorialist leanings. 'Abd al-Rahman 'Arif was supported by the allies of his late brother 'Abd al-Salam, some of whom were members of the al-Jumayla tribe, and the Nasirist officers. Although al-Bazzaz played a central role in the smooth transfer of government, his status was diminished by the weakness of the new president.

'Abd al-Rahman 'Arif charged al-Bazzaz with the task of establishing a new government. This did not include al-'Uqaili, whose militant approach interfered with any initiatives toward dialogue and compromise with the Kurds. Al-Bazzaz believed that continued belligerency against the Kurds was an obstacle to democratizing the government and the political system and making them more civilian in nature. Instead, the government's dependency on the military was preserved. The burden imposed by the fighting on the economy of Iraq had an adverse effect on the country's development.[19] Moreover, al-Bazzaz feared deterioration of Iraq's strategic position in view of the increased involvement and assistance it gave to the revolt.[20] On June 15, 1966, al-Bazzaz declared that the government of Iraq was willing to recognize the national rights of the Kurds and desired to immediately open negotiations with them. During the course of intensive, secret negotiations, the parties reached an agreement that was published on June 29. The secret and intensive nature of the negotiations resulted from a fear shared by al-Bazzaz and Barzani, to the effect that the agreement would encounter the opposition of the senior Iraqi army officers, who had not been party to it. The agreement announced by al-Bazzaz in a speech made on Iraqi Radio included fifteen clauses, three of which were secret.[21] It stated that the Kurds would enjoy self-rule in their areas in education, health, and municipal affairs. The Kurdish language was recognized as an official language, parallel to Arabic. The Kurds were assured representation in government, Parliament, and the civil service, proportionate to their share in the overall population of Iraq. It was agreed that oil revenues would be directed toward areas populated by Kurds—again, proportionally to their share in the population. The secret clauses stated that an additional Kurdish district would be established, to include the oil-rich areas of Kirkuk and Kanaqin. The agreement did not relate to the central Kurdish demands, which had been raised in the past, regarding extensive powers for the Kurdish autonomic region. Apparently, Barzani was willing to sign this agreement in light of the extreme military pressure on the Kurds and the Kurds' difficulty in switching from guerrilla warfare to regular warfare in order to protect their territories from the Iraqi army. Also, he personally believed that al-Bazzaz seriously intended to resolve the Kurdish problem. The status of the al-Bazzaz government, however, was becoming progressively weaker. As early as June 30, the day after the publication of the agreement with the Kurds, an attempted coup took place, under the leadership of 'Arif 'Abd al-Razzaq, who had been allowed to return from exile in Egypt thanks to the personal intervention of Nasir himself. The coup was launched by Nasirist officers who objected to the political line adopted by 'Arif and al-Bazzaz and rejected the agreement with the Kurds. The conspirators succeeded in obtaining partial control of several air force bases and even bombed the Presidential Palace; within several hours, however, they were defeated by forces loyal to 'Arif.[22]

The plot launched by 'Arif 'Abd al-Razzaq failed, but al-Bazzaz's status was weakened even further. His policies aroused the opposition of various groups. Due to his policy regarding union with Egypt and his withdrawal from the economic policies adopted by Tahir Yihya, both the Nasirists and the Ba'th wanted him out of office. The Communists viewed him as a reactionary, because of his conservative socioeconomic orientation and his departure from Socialist policy. Most of the officers, Nasirists and Ba'th members along with more conservative and Iraqi territorialist groups, objected to the compromises with the Kurds. They also feared that al-Bazzaz's attempts to make the government more civilian would damage their status and rights.[23] Although the fragmentation of the various groups of officers prevented them from unifying around a single candidate, their pressure on 'Arif achieved its aim. In the second half of August 1966, while al-Bazzaz was on a visit to the Soviet Union, the parties involved reached an agreement to replace him. Upon his return, al-Bazzaz was dismissed from office by 'Arif. This ended the attempt to transform the government and the political system into civilian institutions, to promote democracy, and to reduce military intervention in the affairs of the state.

The Recovery of the Ba'th Party

Following the blow that it had absorbed in the autumn of 1963, the Ba'th Party underwent a profound crisis and its activity was curtailed. Due to its loss of control of the government and its effective political and organizational collapse, the national leadership in Damascus under Michel 'Aflaq intervened, and a new Regional Command was established for the party. Appointed as party secretary in Iraq was 'Abd al-Karim al-Shaykhali, a Sunnite party activist from Baghdad. Five members were appointed to the party leadership in Iraq: four Sunnite Arabs and one Shi'ite. They included Ahmad Hasan al-Bakr and Saddam Husayn,[24] both from the Al-Bu Nasir tribe from the city of Tikrit. They constituted a sort of faction, which—thanks to the great influence exerted by Saddam on the remnants of the party apparatus—enjoyed considerable power and prestige.

Saddam Husayn stepped up his efforts to take over control of the Ba'th Party, and he played an active role in its organizational rehabilitation. He skillfully utilized the security and intelligence apparatus of the party (al-jihaz al-hass or al-jihaz al-hunayn) to expel his rivals (although he apparently did not officially head the security organization).[25]

In the summer of 1964, the Ba'th again attempted to organize a coup against 'Arif. The plot was exposed in September, resulting in the arrest of seventy central party activists, with others placed under house arrest. This was an additional blow to the Ba'th in Iraq.

Notwithstanding the Ba'th's intrigues against him, 'Arif displayed a forgiving attitude toward the members of the party. Its leaders enjoyed special privileges during their time of imprisonment.[26] Saddam Husayn, while still detained, was allowed to continue studying at the Faculty of Law of the University of Baghdad, and was even given leave from prison in order to take the examinations. Several months later, the authorities began to release the detainees. Saddam, who had been given a longer sentence, escaped in 1966, and the authorities did not make any special effort to return him to prison. The merciful attitude adopted by 'Abd al-Salam 'Arif resulted from a combination of self-confidence in his status as a national leader and his control of the army, along with contempt for the ability of the Ba'th to endanger him in any way. The attitude shown by the authorities toward the Ba'th members was confused and fraught with contradictions. On one hand, the Ba'th members were persecuted and arrested; on the other hand, the attitude toward their leaders was charitable, and 'Abd al-Rahman 'Arif, who succeeded his brother, made efforts to enlist their support of his regime. It is possible that the forgiving attitude displayed toward Ahmad Hasan al-Bakr and Saddam Husayn resulted, at least partially, from the fact that their native city of Tikrit was also that of Tahir Yihya, who had retained considerable influence over the regime even long after his resignation as prime minister.

The events of 1963 constituted a turning point in the history of the Ba'th Party. The expulsion and exile of the leaders of both wings of the party—the left wing, headed by Sa'di, and the right wing, under his rivals Hazim Jawad and Talib Shabib—gave an advantage to those who were not identified with either of those factions, but maneuvered between them. Prominent among the group whose status was reinforced by the expulsion of the rival factions were a number of officers, some retired, others still on active duty: Ahmad Hasan al-Bakr, Hardan 'Abd al-Ghaffar al-Tikriti, Salah Mahdi 'Amash, and others, as well as civilian activists who were close to them, including Saddam Husayn. Within the leadership of the Ba'th and among its principal activists were a number of officers and civilian activists from the Sunnite towns to the north of Baghdad, especially Tikrit and Samarra. Prominent among the group of party leaders from the town of Tikrit were al-Bakr, Hardan, and Saddam Husayn. Their central positions in the Ba'th paved the way for additional officers and activists from that city to advance within the party. At the same time, the advancement and status of any activist were primarily determined by his personal loyalty to one of the "strong men" of the party or by a combination of tribal and familial loyalties. In this manner, Saddam Husayn, Ahmad Hasan al-Bakr, and Khayr Allah Talfah, Saddam's uncle, succeeded in promoting members of their tribe, the Al-Bu Nasir, but also managed to favor their other supporters, thus avoiding any diminution in the foundations of their support.

The events within the party in 1963 affected the ethnic composition of the party leadership and its activists. Starting in 1963, the Sunnites became a dominant majority in the party leadership and among its activists. The expulsion of Jawad and Shabib (both Shi'ites), as well as that of al-Sa'di (who, although himself a Sunnite, counted among his supporters many Shi'ites from the middle and lower strata of Baghdad), and the increasing importance of the army officers (the great majority of whom were Sunnite) reduced both the number and the power of the Shi'ites in the party as a whole and among its leadership.[27] The Ba'th ideology rejected tribalism and the Sunnite/Shi'ite rift, both of which it viewed as phenomena that ran counter to the unity and power of the Arab nation. Generally speaking, the political ideological climate and the *effendiyya,* the intellectuals in the political arenas of the Arab states in the 1940s, 1950s, and 1960s, as expressed in the hegemonic discourse among them, perceived the Sunnite/Shi'ite rift as a reactionary anachronism harmful to modern life, the Arab nation, and the Arab states.

The sociological transformation in the leadership of the Ba'th parties and the regimes of Iraq and Syria, starting in the 1960s, led to the rise of activists and army officers from among the lower strata, residents of peripheral towns, whose familial and tribal connections and regional origins played a practical role in their identity consciousness and in their political advancement. The moves that forced the Shi'ites out of the Ba'th leadership were not directed against the Shi'ites per se; in practice, however, the party, like most of the political forces in Iraq since the establishment of the state, became a force preserving Sunnite Arab dominance, despite the ideological rejection of ethnicity.

Starting in 1966, the separation of the Iraqi Ba'th Party from that of Syria became more pronounced. On February 23, 1966, a military coup took place in Damascus, as a result of which the Syrian government and the Ba'th in that country were taken over by the left wing of the party, which controlled the leadership of the Syrian Regional Command, headed by Salah Jadid. Michel 'Aflaq, leader of the National Command (pan-Arab), which had been allied with the faction led by Ahmad Hasan al-Bakr and Saddam Husayn in Iraq, was expelled from Syria. The Iraqi Ba'th chose a new Regional Command independently, without coordination with the new Ba'th leadership in Damascus. The allies of al-Bakr and Saddam Husayn forced those activists who had maintained connections with the Syrian Ba'th, and primarily with Jadid's faction, out of any position of influence in the Iraqi Ba'th. At the same time, several influential activists remained in contact and continued to cooperate with the Syrian Ba'th. For example, 'Abd al-Karim al-Shaykhali maintained close connections with Hafiz al-Asad and his faction.[28]

At the conference of the Iraqi Ba'th that took place in the autumn of 1966 in the home of one of its activists in Abu Ghrayb, the majority of the party supported Michel 'Aflaq and the senior national leadership that had been ousted in Damascus.[29] In a dialectical manner, the support given by the Ahmad Hasan al-Bakr/Saddam Husayn faction to the right-wing pan-Arab nationalist leadership actually led, during the 1970s, to the long-term strengthening of the pan-Arab Iraqocentric trend and of Iraqi territorialism. This orientation increasingly emphasized the legitimacy and the special national interests of Iraq while adopting an instrumental approach to the pan-Arab vision of Arab unity. This was the beginning of the rift between the two Ba'th parties: Although they possessed separate national identities (Syrian-Arab and Iraqi-Arab), they maintained their pan-Arab commitment and used pan-Arab rhetoric as a basis for their own legitimization, as an expression of identity awareness, and as a political tool. The rift between the Iraqi Ba'th and the Syrian Ba'th became a struggle for legitimacy—that is, a struggle to determine which was the "real" Ba'th Party. Maintaining legitimacy was essential for the ruling group within each of the parties and each of the regimes (this had been true in Iraq since the establishment of the Ba'th regime in 1968) vis-à-vis their rivals within the party and the regime alike.

The independent line adopted by the Iraqi Ba'th, which detached itself from the Syrian Ba'th and adopted a critical attitude toward Nasir and his regime, gave it an advantage over the Nasirists, whose status had declined and whose radical pan-Arab nationalist message had become less attractive.

The Ba'th, which combined pan-Arab ideology (with an Iraqocentric slant) and Iraqi territorialism, in practice reflected the trends that had become more popular with the decline of Nasirism throughout the Arab world: the reinforcement of the separate Arab states, the strengthening of Arab territorial identities within the framework of the existing Arab states, and the increased legitimacy of their separate existence.

The Ba'th was not a mass movement during the presidency of 'Abd al-Rahman 'Arif. However, all the other political forces were weak, the regime itself was impotent, and the ideologically confused Nasirism had lost some of its attraction. Accordingly, the relatively well organized Ba'th, with its attractive ideological message and a leadership that had succeeded in forging strong ties with the power-hungry army officers, became the most effective force in the political arena.

The Weakness and Ideological Confusion of the Regime and the Political Forces under 'Abd al-Rahman 'Arif, April 1966–July 1968

The regime headed by 'Abd al-Rahman 'Arif was devoid of any clear political preference and subject to the contradictory pressures of various groups of officers, whose personal rivalry was exacerbated by differences in their political orientation. The chances for realization of Arab unity through a rapid union with Egypt declined; nonetheless, in the political discourse and rhetoric used by politicians, the pan-Arab, Nasirist "pro-union" slogans and concepts continued to play a role. The political atmosphere and the status of the regime were affected by the decline of Nasirism as a pan-Arab national vision and an alternative to both the conservative regimes and social order or the unrest and lack of cohesion of the revolutionary nationalist radical forces and regimes at the time. Many of the officers, political activists, and educated young men of the period still perceived Nasir as a much-admired national leader, and Nasirism remained the hope for solution of collective and personal distresses. Nonetheless, in practice, there was a growing emphasis on the special conditions and interests of Iraq. In the ideological climate and the political arena, confusion increased regarding national objectives, and the last remnants of the hope and fervor that had accompanied the outbreak of the 1958 revolution faded.

The Iraqi economy benefited from an increase in oil revenues, which amounted to $476 million in 1968.[30] The GNP grew from 760.1 million dinars in 1967 to 832.9 million dinars in 1968, for a total growth of 9.6 percent. This growth was not accompanied by an increase in the cost of living.[31] Thanks to the constant influx of oil revenues, the government had considerable resources at its disposal for development and operating expenses. At the same time, despite this income and a certain amount of progress in the fields of light industry and agrarian reform, the momentum of economic development slowed down. Hopes for a rapid breakthrough that would extricate Iraq from poverty and economic backwardness and transform it into a modern, industrialized state declined. The development programs were implemented slowly and sometimes imperfectly. Only 40 percent of the economic program for 1965–69 was actually implemented.[32] Despite considerable investment in the construction of housing projects and the allocation of lands for do-it-yourself construction in the neighborhoods of Baghdad, the housing crisis continued, due to the influx of large populations from villages to the cities, primarily to Baghdad and Basra.

The parties and forces in politics were characterized by weakness and ideological confusion, and the Iraqi public became progressively more indifferent to politics. The Socialist Arab Union, established in 1964 based on the Egyptian model, with a view to becoming the ruling party, did not manage to become a solid and effective social and ideological mainstay for the regime.

The National Democratic Party, which had declined even under Qasim, now utterly lost its influence and became a group of intellectuals with no extensive public support. The head of the party, Kamil al-Jadirji, died early in 1968, and its other leaders did not attain any significant public influence or status.

The Communist Party, the strongest and most cohesive rival of the Ba'th, suffered a severe setback when the Ba'th National Guard massacred its members in 1963. In spite of the rehabilitation of the Communist Party under Baha al-Din Nuri and 'Amer 'Abdallah, its strength and influence severely declined. The party also suffered from factionalism as a result of the rift between the Soviet Union and Communist China. In September 1967, following the defeat of the Arab states in the war against Israel and the damage to the prestige of the USSR, a group of activists headed by 'Aziz al-Haj resigned from the Iraqi Communist Party and founded an independent Communist organization known as al-Qiyada al-Markaziyya (central headquarters), which adopted positions more leftist radical extremist than those of the Iraqi Communist Party under 'Aziz Muhammad.[33] ('Aziz Muhammad, a Kurd loyal to the line of the USSR Communist Party, had returned to Iraq from exile in 1966 and had been elected as secretary-general of the Iraqi Communist Party.) 'Aziz al-Haj and his faction, which adopted Maoist positions,[34] criticized the pro-compromise attitude of the Communist Party leadership toward the 'Arif regime. Criticism was also voiced concerning the policy of friendship extended by the USSR toward 'Arif and his regime and the USSR's policy on the Arab-Israeli conflict. The members of the faction led by 'Aziz al-Haj also rejected the 1947 partition plan for Palestine, which had been supported by the Soviet Union, and the June 1967 cease-fire; in accordance with Maoist doctrine, they demanded the waging of a "popular revolutionary" war against Israel. Radical young activists provoked local revolts by *fellahin* in southern Iraq, aiming to bring about a Communist revolution, as dictated by Maoist doctrine—that is, a revolution supported by the peasantry. The ʿAziz al-Haj faction established contacts with the Chinese Communist Party and with New Left groups in Europe.

In addition to the factionalism that beset the Communist Party, it also had difficulty in maintaining its attractiveness, in the face of the combination of nationalist radicalism and the leftist slogans and messages of the Baʿth and the Nasirists. The friendly relations maintained by the USSR with the Iraqi regime made it even more difficult for the Iraqi Communist Party to rehabilitate its status as an opposition force. In the elections to the Iraqi Bar Association held in February 1968 and January 1970, Communists and pro-Communists played an important role. The General Federation of Iraqi Students, an organization established under Communist leadership, was the steadfast rival of the Baʿth student organization, the National Federation of Iraqi Students. Only in the 1970 elections did the Baʿth student organization, which enjoyed the support of the authorities, manage to prevail over the Communist organization. All these, however, were only the last vestiges of influence of the thoroughly beaten Communist Party, most of whose principal activists had been murdered or had fled Iraq.[35]

The Nasirists were a large force, but an amorphous one, with no internal organization or cohesion. The Nasirists, who represented the strongest movement among the *wahdawiyun*—that is, the supporters of practical realization of Arab unity—were actually a collection of groups of army officers and nationalist civilian activists. Many of them did believe in the real possibility of implementing Arab unity by rapid union with Egypt under Nasir; at the same time, many others, although they believed in Arab unity and admired Nasir, viewed the slogans and rhetoric that favored union with Egypt as a means of establishing political status and an attractive nationalist image. The Nasirists, while achieving considerable influence among the army officers and the public, never coalesced into an organized political movement. The identification of ʿAbd al-Salam ʿArif as a pan-Arab nationalist leader who supported unity, as well as his close personal contacts with Nasir, made it difficult for any independent Nasirist organization to arise in Iraq. Due to the blow suffered by Nasirism as a result of the 1967 war against Israel and the decline in its attraction throughout the Arab world, the Baʿth now enjoyed a certain advantage. The combination of pan-Arab nationalism with the independent line adopted by the party in Iraq with regard to both the

Ba'th regime in Syria and the Nasirist regime in Egypt gave it an advantage over its nationalist competitors, which became confused and disoriented.

The election of 'Abd al-Rahman 'Arif was enabled by the weakness of the remaining political forces and the fragmentation and impotence of the various groups of officers. Under these circumstances, both al-Bazzaz, who sought to continue with his own reforms, and the officers, who desired to maintain their own status, preferred to ensure the stability and continuity of the regime by electing the brother of the dead president. Nonetheless, 'Abd al-Rahman 'Arif's weakness and the criticism expressed against the al-Bazzaz government by both the Nasirists and their rivals, the nationalist officers, who objected to any agreement with the Kurds, led to the dissolution of the government.[36]

'Arif assigned the establishment of the new government to Naji Talib, a retired army officer. Naji Talib, a Shi'ite and a veteran of the Free Officers, had served as minister of social affairs in Qasim's first government in 1958 and had resigned in the winter of 1959 during the course of the rift between Qasim and the nationalists. With his moderate nationalist views and accommodating personal character that enabled him to maintain ties with the various groups of officers, Naji Talib was a compromise solution. His government lacked any clear-cut political line and did not obtain the support of either the officers or the public, which had become indifferent to politics as a whole. The weakness and passivity of the government drew the criticism of both the Nasirists and the Ba'th, which accused it of not promoting the cause of Arab unity and not adopting a militant stance against Israel.

'Arif himself took over as prime minister in May 1967. At the same time, he appointed four deputies: Tahir Yihya, a pan-Arab nationalist popular with the Nasirists; 'Abd al-Ghani al-Rawi, a conservative with religious Islamic trends; Fuad 'Arif, a Kurd; and Isma'il Mustafa, a Shi'ite with an Iraqi territorialist orientation and a link to the group of officers headed by 'Abd al-'Aziz al-'Uqaili.

During the course of 'Arif's term in office as president and prime minister, in May and June 1967, he was forced to cope with the crisis between the Arab states and Israel, as well as with the consequences of the Arab defeat in the war against Israel in June of that year. The defeat adversely affected the prestige and legitimacy of the radical regimes and hastened the decline of pan-Arab nationalist radicalism throughout the Arab world and in Iraq. The shock of the defeat and the reduced attraction of pan-Arabism and Nasirism in general gave rise to conditions that accelerated the reinforcement of local nationalist currents (*iqlimiyya, wataniyya*) throughout the Arab world. These currents, while retaining a pan-Arab orientation and at times continuing to make use of pan-Arab rhetoric, in practice gave priority to the interests and legitimacy of the existing state frameworks. Nonetheless, in the initial stage, following the 1967 War, the Ba'th and the Nasirists hastened to exploit the feelings of rage and frustration in order to attack the government for the idleness shown by Iraq and its failure to provide sufficient support to the struggle against "the Zionist enemy." In a mass demonstration directed against the government, which took place in Baghdad on June 20, the heads of the Ba'th, who had played a central role in organizing the demonstration, were roundly applauded.[37] Additional demonstrations, inspired by the Ba'th and the Nasirists, which took place during the autumn of that year, called for the renewal of the war against Israel.

In June 1967, two conservative, non-Nasirist groups of officers, headed by 'Abd al-'Aziz al-'Uqaili and Deputy Prime Minister 'Abd al-Ghani al-Rawi, submitted demands for the replacement of the government and the holding of free elections.[38] In December of that year, a petition signed by twenty-two politicians and public personages, including 'Abd al-Rahman al-Bazzaz, Faiq al-Samarai (a leader of the defunct al-Istiqlal), Jamil Husayn of the Democratic Party, and others, was submitted to 'Arif. The petition—the result of a soul-searching process that took place following the crisis in pan-Arab nationalism after the defeat of the Arab armies against Israel—called upon the regime to be more democratic in its practices, in order to reinforce the connection between it and the public. Among the clauses of the petition was a demand for the establishment of a parliamentary regime.[39]

In July 1967, President 'Arif handed over the post of prime minister to his deputy, Tahir Yihya. Admittedly, this action restored the government to the leadership of a man who, during his previous term as prime minister (1963–65), had taken measures intended to promote the union with Egypt and had adopted a relatively radical and etatist socioeconomic policy. Nonetheless, against the background of the changes that had taken place in the conditions affecting the Arab world and the shock that had overcome it following the 1967 war, the government had difficulty in setting forth national objectives in a clear and convincing manner, and even more so, in adopting an unequivocal operative procedure to attain those objectives. The relatively poor record of the governments headed by Naji Talib and Tahir Yihya reflected the internal decay of the 'Arif regime and the ideological confusion that prevailed in Iraq and the Arab world regarding national objectives and socioeconomic trends. The Nasirists and Arab unity had ceased to be the compass that guided the regime in determining its goals and the ways of achieving them. The groups of officers, who had difficulty formulating clear and attractive ideological messages and proposing unequivocal socioeconomic orientations, were unsuccessful in winning a base of public support for themselves, and were perceived as power groups struggling for ascendancy. As the ideo-logical confusion increased and the attraction of the political and ideological messages declined, the political struggles became obvious power struggles. After almost an entire decade (starting in 1958) of disappointed hopes and traumas induced by violence, the Iraqi public was no longer involved in the recurrent power struggles between the officers.

The one area in which significant progress was made was that of oil. The Iraqi government headed by Tahir Yihya reduced Iraq's dependence on the IPC, expanded the influence exerted by the government on the IPC, and increased its oil revenues.[40] Due to the protracted disputes and tension be-tween the Iraqi government and the IPC, the Tahir Yihya government passed a law (no. 97) according to which the Iraqi National Oil Company (INOC) was granted the exclusive right to drill for oil and to produce oil throughout the entire territory of Iraq, with the exception of the oilfields already oper-ated by the IPC. The rigid position adopted by the Iraqi government in the dispute with the IPC resulted directly from the atmosphere prevailing throughout the Arab world following the 1967 war.[41] In order to free Iraq from its exclusive dependence on the IPC, the INOC—and, in practice, the government of Iraq—granted a franchise for oil drilling and production to the French oil company ERAP (Entreprise de Recherches et d'Activités Pét-rolières).[42] In December 1967, an additional agreement was signed between the INOC and the government of the USSR, according to which the USSR undertook to assist Iraq in developing its oil industry.[43] These agreements, resulting from political and economic considerations (80 percent of the in-come earned by the government of Iraq came from oil), helped to increase Iraq's control of its principal natural resource.

Hopes raised for accelerated development and industrialization in the first period of 'Abd al-Salam 'Arif's rule, and especially under the government headed by Tahir Yihya, were not realized. While the government enjoyed extensive oil revenues, the plans for development and industrialization were not implemented in practice. The contribution made by industry to the GNP remained at about 10 percent, and the economy of Iraq remained dependent on revenues from oil, which, in 1968, accounted for 93 percent of exports and the majority of the state income.

In 1967 and 1968, 'Arif attempted to expand the base of support for his government through dialogue with the Ba'th and the nationalist groups of officers and activists—both the Nasirists and their more conservative Iraqi territorialist rivals. This was an attempt to enlist the support of the national-ist forces without adopting the multiparty political system, which both 'Arif and Tahir Yihya considered inappropriate, given the conditions prevailing within Iraq.

While 'Arif was attempting to achieve a dialogue with some of the opposition forces, contacts took place among the various opposition forces to formulate a united front and bring about his ouster. The Ba'th even attempted to confer with its sworn enemies, the Communists. The most significant move, however, was a series of meetings between the Ba'th leaders and nationalist opposition politicians in March and April 1968.[44] Among the participants in these meetings, some of which took place in Ahmad Hasan al-Bakr's own home, were Naji Talib, 'Abd al-'Aziz al-'Uqaili (who had been minister of defense in the al-Bazzaz government), Hardan 'Abd al-Ghaffar al-Tikriti (an army officer and member of the Ba'th), and other nationalist and Nasirist politicians. Notwithstanding the differences of opinion among the participants, the meetings succeeded in formulating a series of demands that were submitted to 'Arif on April 16: the dismissal of the Tahir Yihya government, the establishment of a Legislative Council, the holding of elections, the establishment of a coalition government, and the adoption of a forceful policy against Israel. 'Arif, who objected to a multiparty regime and to holding elections, did not accede to these requests. Tahir Yihya, fearful for his own status, objected to the contacts and talks with the opposition. 'Arif's contacts with the Ba'th and the various groups of officers continued until the fall of the regime on July 18. 'Arif did not succeed in reconciling his desire to stay in power as the sole leader of Iraq with the need to expand the base of support for his regime.

The Ba'th leaders al-Bakr and Hardan played a key role in the talks and meetings between 'Arif and the opposition; at the same time, together with Saddam Husayn, they prepared the conspiracy that led to the downfall of the 'Arif regime. Their participation in the talks was intended to reinforce their status among the opposition forces, while distracting the attention of the authorities from the preparations for the coup.

Under the 'Arif brothers, and especially under 'Abd al-Rahman 'Arif, the state continued to grow in strength and (thanks to its oil revenues) maintained control of considerable resources, while, at the same time, the regime, the political system, and the political forces suffered from weakness, decay, and confusion. The impotence of the political system, the paralysis of the political arena, the personal weakness of 'Abd al-Rahman 'Arif, and the weakness of all of the political forces combined to create the situation that was exploited by the Ba'th in its seizure of power.

11

The Rise of Saddam Husayn's Regime

The Establishment of the Baʿth Regime and the Rise of Saddam Husayn

While ʿArif was unsuccessfully attempting to expand the base of support for his regime, a conspiracy to overthrow it was being formed between the Baʿth and the army officers who held key positions within the regime itself. These officers included ʿAbd al-Razzaq Naif, head of Military Intelligence, ʿAbd al-Rahman Dawud, commander of the Republican Guard, and Saʿdun Ghaydan, commander of the Armored Brigade of the Guard. (The Republican Guard, which had been established by ʿAbd al-Salam ʿArif as the force in charge of defending the regime, became, under his weak brother, the force that overthrew it.) The officers were joined by the commander of the Baghdad garrison, Hammad Shihab al-Tikriti. All of these officers were very close to ʿArif and enjoyed his complete trust. ʿAbd al-Razzaq Naif was even a member of ʿArif's tribe, the al-Jumayla.

On July 17, 1968, the conspirators launched a bloodless coup, deposed ʿArif, and exiled him from Iraq. Ahmad Hasan al-Bakr was appointed president, ʿAbd al-Razzaq Naif prime minister, and ʿAbd al-Rahman Dawud minister of defense. Two officers who were members of the Baʿth were also given key positions: Hardan ʿAbd al-Ghaffar al-Tikriti was appointed deputy prime minister, deputy commander in chief of the armed forces, and commander of the air force, while Salah Mahdi ʿAmash was appointed minister of the interior. The government, which included twenty-six ministers, was a coalition between the Baʿth and a group of nationalist officers with pro-Western tendencies and a relatively reserved attitude toward leftist radicalism.

Thirteen days later, on July 30, the Baʿth seized the opportunity of Defense Minister Dawud's departure for Jordan, on a visit to the Iraqi forces who had been posted there since the 1967 war, and launched a second coup, in which they ousted the non-Baʿth officers, Naif and Dawud.

The Iraqi public reacted with indifference to the coups of July 17 and 30 and the takeover of the state by the Baʿth. After the intense political involve-

ment of the public between 1958 and 1963, and following the disappointment of the great hopes, especially the still-fresh memories of the domestic
terror and bloodshed in 1963, the middle stratum and the working class were
exhausted and reluctant to become involved in politics. Politics had become
the domain of army officers and small groups of power-hungry activists. The
weary middle class did not support political movements, especially given the
fact that the prohibition against political party activity had remained in force
under the ʿArif brothers. Nasirism had lost its attraction as a nationalist-
radical political trend, and its radical pan-Arab message was on the decline
and no longer a basis for any political force that could successfully take on
the Baʿth. The decline of Nasirism, the weakness of Communism, and the
decay of the remaining political forces created conditions that made it easier
for the Baʿth—which continued to excel in the use of radical pan-Arab nationalist messages and frequently and effectively used terror as a means of
eliminating its opponents—to take over the state and impose its hegemony
over Iraq. The Baʿth regime enjoyed the support of Michel ʿAflaq, the historical leader of the Baʿth. ʿAflaq had found himself in exile following the rise of
the Regional Command (the left wing, supported by the army) to power in
Syria. The support of ʿAflaq and the pan-Arab Baʿth, the National Command, reinforced the legitimacy of Baʿth rule in Iraq. Within the leadership of
the Baʿth and the regime that it established were large numbers of representatives of the lower middle and lower strata from Sunnite provincial towns,
in which tribal identities and contexts remained preserved.[1]

The Baʿth leadership, which had learned from the bitter experience of
being ousted by the army officers in November 1963, turned its efforts to
taking over the army immediately after seizing power in 1968. In the framework of this "Baʿthization," many officers, including most of the division
and brigade commanders who were not Baʿth members, were dismissed from
service and replaced by rapidly promoted officers who were members or
affiliates of the party. Some 2,000 Baʿth members and sympathizers were
recruited and rapidly trained, and many of them became officers. The relatively rapid takeover of the army was enabled by the existence of a core of
officers who were members or sympathizers of the Baʿth, as well as by the
fact that the Nasirist nationalist officers were divided among themselves,
disorganized, and politically inept.

Between 1968 and 1970, the faction led by Saddam Husayn and Ahmad
Hasan al-Bakr arrested thousands of politicians, activists, army and police
officers, and members of the security services. From time to time, the authorities published reports of attempted conspiracies to overthrow the government. Some of these reports concerned real attempts, organized by the oppo-

sition; others were published by the regime as justification for the arrests and the elimination of any potential focus of power not controlled by the Ba'th.

In December 1968, thirty people were arrested in Basra and charged with conspiring with the CIA and spying for Israel. In January 1969, following a public trial, fourteen of them—including nine Jews—were sentenced to death. Early in 1970, the authorities disclosed a conspiracy led by Colonel 'Abd al-Ghani al-Rawi, an officer with a rightist-Islamic orientation who enjoyed the support of Iran. In May 1973, an attempted coup was launched by Nadhim Kazzar, Saddam Husayn's right-hand man, who took advantage of Ahmad Hasan al-Bakr's visit to Eastern Europe to attempt to depose him. The plot failed, and all the conspirators were executed. Kazzar, a Shi'ite, may have been attempting to stop the takeover of the state by the al-Bakr/Saddam Husayn/Tikriti faction. (The rapid liquidation of all the conspirators raises the question of whether this was not, in fact, an attempt by Saddam himself to get rid of al-Bakr, and whether the execution of all the participants was intended by Saddam to avoid suspicion against himself.)

The Shi'ite ferment and tensions between the Shi'ites and the authorities increased as a result of the moves made by the Ba'th regime to take over the Shi'ite independent educational system. This ferment and tension increased following the demand by the Ba'th for the Shi'ite religious establishment and its leaders to publicly identify with the regime and denounce Iran. Iran's relations with Iraq had deteriorated since the spring of 1969, and it was viewed as a strategic threat to Iraq and the Ba'th regime.

Due to the increasing unrest among the Shi'ites and the openly opposition-ist attitudes of their religious leaders, the regime took harsh measures to suppress Shi'ite resistance. The sons of the revered Shi'ite religious leader Muhammad Muhsin al-Hakim were arrested. Severe measures were taken against the al-Da'wa al-Islamiyya Party. In 1970, Muhammad Baqir al-Sadr, a rather young and charismatic Shi'ite political leader, was arrested for some time. The tensions between the regime and the Shi'ites were directly and reciprocally related to the exacerbation of the tensions between Iraq and Iran. Starting in 1969, the Iraqi authorities deported thousands of Shi'ites of Iranian origin, some of whom had been living in the holy cities of Najaf and Karbala for generations.

The measures adopted by the Ba'th in coping with the various threats to the regime were accompanied by a constant struggle within the party and the regime. Saddam Husayn exploited his influence over the security services to arrest and physically eliminate anyone suspected of being connected with the Syrian Ba'th.

The faction led by Ahmad Hasan al-Bakr and Saddam Husayn was challenged by various groups and factions within the Ba'th. The most dangerous rivals, from the standpoint of al-Bakr and Saddam, were the factions led by Ba'thist army officers Hardan 'Abd al-Ghaffar al-Tikriti and Salah Mahdi 'Amash. Hardan tried to use his status as minister of defense and deputy commander in chief of the armed forces in order to strengthen his position in the army and among the officers. Salah Mahdi 'Amash used his position as minister of the interior to reinforce the security apparatus that was subordinate to his ministry. However, the faction led by al-Bakr and Saddam was the best organized, and Saddam, who was both crueler and more politically adept than his rivals, maintained actual control of both the constantly expanding security services and the party apparatus.

Early in 1969, a new national leadership for the Iraqi Ba'th was elected. It was promised a majority in the faction led by al-Bakr and Saddam. In November 1969, the faction led by al-Bakr and Saddam succeeded in increasing the number of members of the Revolutionary Council from five to fifteen. The new members were civilian members of the Ba'th national leadership, including Saddam Husayn. As a result of this move, the civilian Ba'th activists obtained an absolute majority on the Council, and the influence of the army officers declined. The failure of the officers to restrain the faction led by al-Bakr and Saddam is a historical question that requires further study.

In the autumn of 1969, the RCC abolished the functions of deputy prime minister, which had been held by 'Amash and Hardan, in addition to their positions as ministers of interior and defense. In January 1970, Saddam was elected deputy commander of the Revolutionary Command Council (RCC); several months later, he became vice president of Iraq. (At the same time, Saddam held the position of deputy secretary-general of the Regional Command of the Iraqi Ba'th Party.) Saddam, who was thirty-two years old at the time, thus became the no. 2 person in the regime—and, in practice, the "strong man" of Iraq.[2]

In April 1970, Saddam and al-Bakr were able to exploit the extreme rivalry prevailing between Hardan and 'Amash in order to remove them from their positions of power as minister of defense and minister of the interior. Hardan and 'Amash were appointed vice presidents—positions which, despite their lofty titles, were devoid of any real power. In October 1970, Hardan was expelled from the RCC and subsequently exiled to Kuwait, where he was murdered a year later. 'Amash was expelled from the RCC in 1971 and appointed Iraqi ambassador to the USSR.

The struggle between the various factions and personages was not based on ideology but rather was a struggle for personal power. Nonetheless, the rise of Saddam Husayn and his takeover of the party and the state had far-ranging historical consequences. Saddam and al-Bakr led a civilian, mostly Sunnite Arab group. Its leaders were members of the Al-Bu Nasir tribe, especially of the Begat subtribal unit. Starting in 1963, Saddam and al-Bakr promoted their relatives from the Al-Bu Nasir tribe in general and the Begat wing in particular to key positions in the party and, from 1968, in the government as well. At the same time, they succeeded in preserving the loyalty of other activists who did not come from their tribe or from their town of Tikrit. Although Saddam's allies also included several Shi'ite activists and one Christian, the relative importance of the Shi'ites in the top ranks of the Ba'th and in key positions within the regime declined sharply. This was not the result of any deliberate anti-Shi'ite policy but rather a consequence of the Sunnite, Tikriti, and tribal nature of Saddam's faction.

Foreign Policy and Domestic Threats: From the Declaration of March 1970 and the Treaty with the USSR in 1972 to the Algiers Agreement of 1975

In the early years of the Ba'th regime, as it struggled to consolidate its position, it was faced with a combination of foreign and domestic threats: tensions and rivalry with Iran, the renewal and intensification of the Kurdish revolt, unrest among the Shi'ites, the rift and the rivalry with the Syrian Ba'th, and the danger of isolation in the international arena. Iraq adopted a rigid, radical, militant pan-Arab rhetoric. Saddam's radical-revolutionary orientation, his warmongering rhetoric, and his unrelenting policy toward Iran and Kuwait aroused suspicion and resistance, both among the conservative, pro-Western regimes of Iran, Kuwait, and Saudi Arabia and among the radical regimes of Egypt and Syria. The Ba'th regime adopted an extremist militant line with regard to Israel, demanding incessant struggle against it, and opposing any cease-fire or armistice agreement between any Arab state and Israel. Egypt's attitude toward the Ba'th regime in Iraq, in the early years, was reserved and cautious—both because of the overthrow of 'Arif, who had been its ally, and because of the contacts between the Iraqi Ba'th and the National Command of the Ba'th under Michel 'Aflaq, whom Nasir despised and hated. The criticism expressed by Iraq of Egypt's agreement to the political initiatives that were intended to bring the War of Attrition with Israel to an end contributed to the tensions between Iraq and Egypt. Iraq's relations with Egypt reached a low point in 1971, when Iraq gave its support and assistance to a Communist attempt to overthrow the Numeyri regime in Sudan. (Sudan constituted Egypt's major national interest in the international arena and was of supreme importance from the standpoint of Egypt's national security.)

The most dangerous threat, from the standpoint of Iraq and its Ba'th regime, was the combination of deteriorating relations with Iran, which threatened Iraq's one outlet to the sea on the Shatt al-'Arab River; with the Shi'ite unrest in the south and the Kurdish revolt in the north.

In the autumn of 1968, Iraq and Iran made efforts to settle the differences between them. The Iraqi minister of defense, Hardan 'Abd al-Ghaffar al-Tikriti, and the Iraqi foreign minister, 'Abd al-Karim al-Shaykhali, visited Iran in December 1968 and held talks aimed at reducing tensions between the two states. However, as early as the spring of 1969, tensions recurred and increased. The conservative monarchical regime of Iran viewed the radical, revolutionary, pan-Arab regime of Iraq with suspicion and mistrust. The radical pan-Arab nationalist militancy of the Iraqi regime was viewed by Iran as a threat to its own regime and its own national interests.

In 1968, Britain announced its intention of pulling its military forces out of the Persian Gulf. This British move created a change in the strategic balance in the Gulf area. The distrust and hostility prevailing between the regimes of Iraq and Iran were now exacerbated by rivalry over dominance of the Gulf. The rivalry and tension between Iraq and Iran encompassed ideological contrasts between the radical revolutionary regime of Iraq and the conservative monarchy of Iran, national rivalry between the Arabs and the Iranians, interstate rivalry for dominance of the region, and a mutual threat to each other's vital national interests, especially oil exports. (Iran threatened the Shatt al-'Arab, Iraq's only outlet to the sea and the route of its oil exports; Iraq threatened the important Iranian port of Abadan and the oil fields in southern Iran.) Iran's attempts to achieve the status of the dominant regional power in the Persian Gulf was perceived by the Iraqi regime as a severe strategic threat.

In April 1969, Iran unilaterally abrogated the agreement with Iraq that had governed shipping on the Shatt al-'Arab since 1937. (As early as 1966, Iran had announced its intention of abrogating the agreement; however, during the rule of the 'Arif brothers and the early Ba'th regime, the two states had managed to prevent the dispute from developing into a crisis.) Tensions escalated. Between 1969 and 1971, a number of border incidents took place along the Shatt al-'Arab. Iraq expelled thousands of Iranian Shi'ites and persons suspected of maintaining ties with Iran. At the same time, Iraq began activities intended to provoke the Arabic-speaking tribes in the Khuzistan (or 'Arabistan) area of southwestern Iran. The existence of this Arabic population was occasionally exploited by Iraq, as well as by Egypt, in times of tension between Iraq and Iran or between Iran and Egypt.

On November 30, 1971, Iran took over three small but strategically important islands at the mouth of the Persian Gulf. (The control of the islands was disputed by Iran, the Arab Emirates, and Britain.) Following this Iranian move, made so as to give it control of the entrance to the Gulf, tensions increased even further.

The threat posed by Iran, on one hand, and the threat created by the Kurds and Shiʿites, on the other, were important causes for the changed priorities of the Baʿth regime. Between 1970 and 1971, due to the direct threat posed by Iran and by the Kurds and Shiʿites, the regime began to change the emphasis that it placed on its regional policy. Whereas it had originally considered the struggle against Israel to be the central issue in Iraqi and Arab foreign policy, it now viewed the struggle against Iran as critical to Iraq and the Arab nation. Of course, the Baʿth regime continued to maintain an extremist militant position against Israel and vehemently opposed the peace agreements between Egypt and Israel in 1977–79. Iraq maintained its implacable position as the symbol of Arab intransigence in the struggle against Israel, for the sake of Iraq's position in the inter-Arab arena. In practice, however, a transformation occurred in its policies, characterized by a shift toward national Iraqi interests and toward pan-Arab Iraqocentrism. This amounted to the subordination of pan-Arab considerations to pragmatic nationalist Iraqi interests.

In the autumn of 1968, the Kurdish revolt resumed and the Iraqi Army had difficulty dealing with it. Efforts to suppress the revolt and isolate Barazani did not succeed. Due to the Kurdish-Iranian threat against Iraq, and in light of the wish of the ruling civilian faction of the Baʿth to free itself from its dependence on the army, the heads of the Iraqi government decided on a course of negotiation with the Kurds. On March 11, 1970, President Ahmad Hasan al-Bakr published a declaration regarding a far-ranging agreement with the Kurds.[3] The Baʿth regime adopted a position of compromise, including Iraqi concessions, in response to the Kurdish demands. A vital role in preparing the agreement was played by Vice President Saddam Husayn. The agreement, which terminated the Kurdish revolt, made it possible for Iraq to cope with the threat posed by Iran, whose ambition to become a regional power in the Gulf area was supported by the United States.

Notwithstanding the agreement with the Kurds, the Iraqi government continued to feel threatened. International isolation and the severe threat posed by Iran were apparently among Saddam Husayn's motives in his decision to begin encouraging the development of nuclear weapons by Iraq in 1971. (It should be noted, however, that the large-scale diversion of resources to the development of nuclear and nonconventional weapons did not begin until after Saddam Husayn rose to power in 1979. This sphere began to receive special emphasis during the war with Iran, principally after 1981.) Because the agreement with the Kurds was only a tactical move on the part of Saddam Husayn and al-Bakr, the regime began, within a relatively short time, to take measures intended to weaken Barzani's position and sap the strength of the Kurds. These measures, including attempts on Barazani's life, led to the resumption of the revolt in 1974. Saddam Husayn made a move that was intended to drive a wedge between the Kurds and Iran and to cut off Iranian assistance. Early in 1975, Iraq and Iran reached an agreement concerning the border between the two states and shipping rights on the Shatt al-ʿArab— areas which had been a major bone of contention between Iraq and Iran. Iraq made a significant concession to Iran by retreating from its traditional position, which called for sovereign control of the entire width of the river (except for short sections opposite the Iranian ports of Abadan and Khoramshar, where Iraq recognized Iranian sovereignty as far as the middle of the river) and accepted the Iranian demand that the border run down the middle of the river, along the Thawleg line. The agreement between Iraq and Iran was signed in 1975 in Algiers; it was inspired by U.S. Secretary of State Henry Kissinger, who sought, in this way, to prevent the USSR from exploiting the tensions between Iraq and Iran in order to promote its own status in the Middle East. The agreement led to the cessation of Iranian support to the Kurds, and thus brought about the collapse of the revolt. However, the concession made by Iraq was no more than a tactical move on Saddam Husayn's part. When Saddam came to believe, following the Islamic revolution led by Khomeini, that Iran's position in the region had weakened, Iraq decided to take back what it had conceded in the Algiers Agreement. Saddam's desire to restore control of the Shatt al-ʿArab to Iraq was one of his motives for declaring war against Iran in 1980. (The additional motives stemmed from Saddam Husayn's fear of Iranian influence, following Khomeini's Islamic revolution, on the Shiʿites of Iraq and from the possibility of a renewal of the Kurdish revolt, with Iranian assistance.) The complicated maneuver between the Kurds and Iran was intended to strengthen the Baʿth regime in Iraq and to reinforce Saddam's own status as its leader.

Saddam viewed the Baʿth regime in Syria as a dangerous rival. The establishment of the Baʿth regime in Iraq and the rise to power of the left wing of the Syrian party, the Regional Command, transformed the rift between the two Baʿth parties into a conflict between the two states. The rift reflected an exacerbation of the contradictions between the pan-Arab ideological outlook of the Baʿth and the development of each of the parties under the unique conditions affecting its own country, which strengthened each state's separate territorial and political identity. As long as the status of both Baʿth regimes was relatively weak and the factions and leaders heading each regime were forced to cope with their rivals within the party, the rival regime provided support for the opposition within each respective party and a means of undermining the legitimacy of the rulers. Accordingly, Saddam and his associates persecuted anyone suspected of maintaining contacts with the Syrian

Baʿth. The alliance between the Iraqi Baʿth and the pan-Arab faction of the Syrian Baʿth under Michel ʿAflaq reinforced the legitimacy of the Baʿth in Iraq, but also encouraged the rivalry with the Syrian Baʿth.[4]

Following the consolidation and stabilization of the two regimes in 1972–73, the rivalry between them continued, while shifting its emphasis to competition for regional dominance. At the same time, the threat to the legitimacy of the regimes and the leadership of their respective parties continued to play a role in the relations between Syria and Iraq. The mutual feelings of suspicion and hostility that prevailed on a personal level between Saddam Husayn and Hafiz al-Asad also contributed to the tensions between the two states.

Upon its rise to power, the Baʿth regime found itself in an uncomfortable position in its relations with the Great Powers. The USSR showed reservations vis-à-vis the Baʿth, which had overthrown the Qasim regime and slaughtered the Communists in 1963; moreover, it suspected the Baʿth of maintaining contacts with the Americans. While it was true that the Baʿth had cooperated with the CIA in preparing for the coup of 1963 and had renewed its contacts with the CIA in 1968, its revolutionary-radical position aroused suspicion and resistance on the part of both the United States and Great Britain. The United States viewed Iran and its imperial regime as an important buffer to keep the Soviet Union from penetrating into the Gulf area; accordingly, it supported Iran's ambitions of becoming the dominant entity in the area.

Notwithstanding their objection to communism as an ideology and the Communist Party as a political rival, both Saddam Husayn and al-Bakr believed that the USSR was Iraq's bastion of support regarding Iran and the United States (despite the Soviet attempts to act as an intermediary between Iraq and Iran). The centralist-etatist development patterns of the USSR and its authoritarian regime were in line with the concepts held by Saddam, al-Bakr, and the heads of the Iraqi Baʿth concerning the need to fortify their rule, build a strong state, control society, and accelerate development and modernization within the state. The Baʿth leaders—like other radical leaders in the Arab states in particular and in Asia and Africa in general—rejected communism as an ideology and a system of human values and disagreed with the Marxist worldview. In addition, they fought against the Communist Party domestically, which was their chief rival for the support of educated young people in Iraq. At the same time, however, they considered the Soviet Union as a partner in the prevailing historic trend, by contrast to the determinist weakening of the Western powers. However, the supreme consideration guiding Saddam Husayn above all other principles was his ambition for personal power and the consolidation of his role in Iraq.

An additional reason for Iraq's belief in the need to improve its relations with the USSR was a deep concern for the relations between Iraq and the Iraqi Petroleum Company (IPC). While the USSR did not encourage Iraq to nationalize its oil resources, it supported Iraq's positions. The heads of government in Iraq knew that, if Iraq were to nationalize its oil, the USSR would be obligated to provide assistance. Ever since Qasim's time, the Soviet Union had been Iraq's principal arms supplier. Improving relations with the USSR was vital.

The Iraqi government accelerated a series of moves, begun under 'Abd al-Rahman 'Arif, to integrate the USSR into the Iraqi oil industry and to grant concessions to the Soviet petroleum company. In order to show goodwill toward the USSR, starting in 1971, the Ba'th regime changed its attitude toward the Communists, with a view to involving them in the regime without giving them any real influence.

In 1972, the Communist Party entered the government; in July 1973, it joined the Patriotic National Front, which had been established by the Ba'th. The Ba'th and the faction led by al-Bakr and Saddam Husayn were interested in showing that they enjoyed broad-based support. The integration of the Communists was also intended to neutralize the remnants of the Communist Party as an independent force. In 1970 and again in 1972, Saddam Husayn visited the Soviet Union. Early in April 1972, Soviet Prime Minister Alexei Kosygin visited Iraq to mark the commencement of oil production from the Rumeila oil fields. On April 9, Iraq and the Soviet Union signed a treaty of friendship and cooperation.

An additional objective of the treaty with the USSR and the integration of the Communists into the Iraqi regime was to achieve the isolation of the Kurds. Tensions increased between the Kurds and the Iraqi government, following the official moves that had been made to erode the Kurds' strength and in light of the government's obvious intention of interpreting the Declaration of March 1970 as it saw fit.

The treaty of friendship with the USSR improved Iraq's regional and international status, ensured the supply of Soviet arms to the Iraqi Army, and reinforced the status of Saddam Husayn and al-Bakr in the domestic arena. However, it did not abolish either the Iranian threat or the danger of resumption of the Kurdish revolt. Following the fundamentalist Islamic revolution led by Khomeini in Iran in 1979, which brought about a dramatic change in that country's policy (which became anti-American), the rapprochement between the United States and Iraq gained momentum. Iraq's objection to the invasion of Afghanistan by the USSR in December 1979, along with the anti-Communist and anti-Soviet declarations made by Saddam, further contributed to the improvement of relations between Iraq and the United States.

During the Iraq-Iran war (1980–88), the United States provided indirect and direct assistance to Iraq. The formulators of the U.S. foreign policy and the heads of the CIA viewed Saddam Husayn and his regime as an important barrier that could prevent the strengthening of Iran and the spread of Islamic fundamentalism, and they estimated that Saddam was well aware of the risk posed by the Soviet Union.

The Shi'ite Challenge

From its earliest inception, the Ba'th regime was forced to deal with increasing unrest among the Shi'ites. Sunnite/Shi'ite relations in general, the Shi'ite feelings of discrimination and alienation from the Iraqi state (which they viewed as being controlled by the Sunnites), and the Sunnite fears of a Shi'ite takeover in Iraq and of pro-Iranian Shi'ite subversion were the basic causes of the political conditions prevailing in Iraq. Although the tension between Sunnites and Shi'ites was an inherent component of political conditions in Iraq, its importance and severity constantly changed, in direct proportion to other social and political forces and tensions and as a result of the ideological climate and international status of Iraq.

Starting in the 1930s, the basic weakness of the Iraqi state, the weakness of the national identity among its heterogeneous population, and of the threat posed by the Kurds and the Shi'ites within Iraq, as well as by Turkey and Iran on its borders, constituted a catalyst for Iraq's growing dependence on its armed forces. The threat to Sunnite dominance posed by the Shi'ites and the separatist trends of the Kurds led the Sunnites to rely on the state and the army as the pillars of the status quo in Iraq.

While the Sunnite-Shi'ite tensions continued during the 1940s and 1950s, with occasional outbursts of unrest among the Shi'ites exploited for domestic political purposes, the severity of other tensions and social divisions was no less problematic. In view of the sociopolitical tension between the upper socioeconomic class and the conservative ruling political elite, on one hand, and the new social forces on the other, and the dominance of secular pan-Arab radicalism in the political climate of the Arab world, the Sunnite-Shi'ite rift was perceived as an anachronism inimical to the progress and interests of the Arab nation. The strengthening of the state and its military force, ever since the 1930s, rendered Shi'ite tribal revolts absolutely hopeless. Also, the policy of the Hashemite regime, which combined nurturing of Arab identity and pan-Arab ideology among the modern middle stratum with the creation of common interests between the Shi'ite tribal landowners and the ruling elite, were useful in dealing with the Shi'ite threat. Although Iraq's educational system was incapable of eliminating the Sunnite-Shi'ite division or eradicating Shi'ite feelings of discrimination or Sunnite anxiety, it succeeded in fostering a layer of Iraqi-Arab identity and a certain degree of acceptance of the Iraqi state among the Shi'ite middle stratum. The integration of Shi'ite politicians into Iraq's political system and the weakening of the Shi'ite religious leaders, along with the decline of the traditional Shi'ite centers of religious learning and holy cities, were also valuable in helping the regime to cope with the Shi'ite threat during the 1950s. (At the same time, the Sunnite-Shi'ite tensions were occasionally exacerbated in connection with other social tensions or the inclusion of Shi'ites in key positions in certain governments—a factor that gave rise to Shi'ite hopes for the improvement of their status and increased the Sunnite fears of a Shi'ite takeover.)

Nevertheless, in the late 1950s, when the Shi'ite centers of religious learning had reached an unprecedented low, a period of intellectual unrest began among the younger Shi'ite religious leaders. The catalysts for this development were the challenges posed by the activities of the Communists and the impact of pan-Arab nationalist-radical messages on young, educated Shi'ites. In 1957, the Shi'ite religious leaders—including a prominent young leader with impressive intellectual capacities, Muhammad Baqir al-Sadr, established a Shi'ite political organization that was later called Hizb al-Da'wa al-Islamiyya, or "The Islamic Call."[5]

The influence exerted by the Communists and the trends toward secular legislation under the Qasim regime aroused the resistance of the Shi'ite religious leaders and encouraged the growth of a new generation of young, activist, radical Shi'ite religious leaders. The secular-nationalist nature of Qasim's regime, as well as the pan-Arab radical messages of the Ba'th, increased the opposition of the Shi'ite religious leaders to the Iraqi state. Many Shi'ites perceived these regimes as the embodiment of Sunnite domination in the guise of Iraqi nationalism or pan-Arab radicalism. Another factor contributing to the increased influence of the religious leaders and the heightened feelings of discrimination among the Shi'ites was the rising socioeconomic distress. The migration of Shi'ite fellahin and poor tribesmen to the large cities and the weakening of the traditional social frameworks, while admittedly contributing to increasing cooperation between Sunnites and Shi'ites similarly afflicted by poverty and distress, also strengthened the Shi'ites' awareness of their status as a large majority of the poorer strata, whereas the state and the ruling elite were dominated by Sunnites. The Qasim regime, and to a great extent those which followed it, invested efforts in improving the living conditions of the poorer strata; thanks to the expansion of Iraq's educational system, and especially higher education, the middle stratum (including both Shi'ites and Sunnites) grew rapidly in Iraq. At the same time, the proportion of Shi'ites among the poorer strata remained high, and the members of the Shi'ite middle stratum blamed their difficulties on the Sunnites and the (real or alleged) discrimination practiced by Sunnites against Shi'ites. Shi'ite political activism gained momentum during the rule of the 'Arif brothers because of their tolerant attitude toward the activity of the Shi'ite radical organization al-Da'wa.

Ever since 1963, the Sunnites had been the dominant component in the Ba'th leadership. Despite the fact that Saddam Husayn's own associates included several Shi'ite activists, the number and influence of the Shi'ites in high places within the Ba'th Party and the regime established by it in 1968 decreased sharply. While it is true that Saddam and his regime did not enact any deliberate anti-Shi'ite policy, both the state and the regime in Iraq were, in practice, dominated by Sunnite Arabs.

In 1969, with the exacerbation of tensions between Iraq and Iran, and in light of the fear of increased Shi'ite influence in Iraq, the Ba'th regime began to deport Shi'ites of Iranian origin. Many of them were residents of the Shi'ite holy cities, where their families had lived for generations. During the 1970s, about 150,000 Shi'ites—defined by the authorities as "Iranian"—were deported. Starting in June 1969, the authorities arrested a large number of Shi'ite religious leaders, who were suspected of opposing the regime and sympathy for the opposition al-Da'wa movement. Scores of these leaders were executed. At the same time, in order to gain sympathy among the Shi'ites, economic benefits were granted to certain Shi'ite sectors. Campaigns of terror and attempts on the lives of Iraqi officials by members of al-Da'wa gave rise to drastic reactions by the regime, especially after the outbreak of violence in 1977 and early in 1980. The first large-scale outburst among the people took place in 1969, the second in February 1970, and the third, which broke out under the influence of the Khomeini revolution in Iran, continued from March 1979 until the spring of 1980. The poor harvests in 1975 and 1976 amplified the dissatisfaction and ferment that led to the outbreak of violent Shi'ite demonstrations among the populace in the region of Najaf and Karbala. Students in Shi'ite religious institutions and Shi'ite religious leaders were arrested and expelled from Iraq by the authorities.[6] (In April 1980, the Iraqi authorities arrested and executed the Shi'ite leader and religious authority Muhammad Baqir al-Sadr and his sister Bint al-Huda.) The rise of the fundamentalist-Islamic regime under Khomeini in Iran in February 1979 led Saddam and his government to fear cooperation between Iran and the Shi'ites in Iraq. It was this fear, along with a desire to prevent any cooperation between Iran and the Kurds in Iraq, a wish to exploit what appeared to be Iranian military weakness and to ensure control of the Shatt al-'Arab waterway, that led to cancellation of the concessions Iraq had made in the Algiers Agreement of 1975 and impelled Saddam Husayn to declare war against Iran in September 1980.

Along with the cruel and ruthless suppression of opposition to his regime, Saddam launched a series of measures intended to enlist the support of the Shi'ites. These included giving those Shi'ites who were willing to support the regime opportunities to advance within the bureaucratic system and even to attain senior political appointments. These incentives were coupled with nationalist indoctrination and the forging of an ideology that emphasized the historical uniqueness of Iraq and Iraqi-Arab unity, in which Sunnites and Shi'ites were proclaimed as equal partners. During the Iraq-Iran war, the Iraqi regime made efforts to exploit the differences between the Arabic-speaking Shi'ites of Iraq and Persian Shi'ism as a part of Persian nationalism alien to the Arab nation.

Saddam's policy regarding the tribes was also apparently based on an attempt to prevent the risk of Shi'ite cohesion and possible uprising. During the great Shi'ite revolt that broke out in the winter of 1991, following the war in Kuwait, Saddam exploited tribal dissension in order to weaken the rebels and suppress the revolt.

The Growth of Saddam's Power during the 1970s

Upon assuming power in 1968, the Ba'th regime began the merciless suppression of all of its opponents and launched a program of dynamic activity intended to take over all of Iraq's social and political institutions and organizations. During the 1970s and 1980s, the Ba'th Party increased tremendously in scope, transforming itself from a tiny organization to a mass party with nearly 1.5 million members and candidates. The party, as well as a ramified network of political and social organizations established under its auspices by its activists, expanded and intensified the purview of the security services and strengthened Saddam Husayn's control of the population of Iraq.

The nationalization of Iraqi oil in 1972 was an important move in ensuring state control of Iraq's principal natural resource and the primary source of the Iraqi government's income. The vast amounts of oil revenues—totaling $5.7 billion in 1974—provided the Iraqi regime with considerable financial capacity for developing its military power, its economic infrastructure, its security apparatus, and its educational system. Iraq was the only major Arab oil producer that did not join the oil boycott in 1973 and 1974. This financial and economic capacity was combined with the fostering of a national identity and a broad and complex ideological system in order to enlist support for the regime and to reinforce its status and power.

In its initial years, the regime adopted a radical policy, accelerating agrarian reform, encouraging the collectivization of agriculture, developing industry, and especially establishing irrigation systems and constructing dams. Emphasis was placed on the development of Iraq's educational system, especially that of its institutions of higher education. The expansion of the educational system led to the rapid growth of the middle stratum. The rapid expansion of the state bureaucratic apparatus and the educational and public health systems under state control, contrasted with the limited development of the private sector, meant that the middle stratum continued to depend upon the state and the regime for its livelihood. The number of people employed in civil service and the state bureaucracy exceeded 620,000 in 1978, exclusive of those employed by the army and security services. The oil revenues enabled the government of Iraq to maintain a populist policy that improved the living conditions of various strata and sectors within the population of Iraq and helped the regime to enlist the support of the common people through the distribution of economic and other benefits. The combined effect of the economic dependency on the state bureaucracy and civil service, intensive indoctrination intended to generate a sense of identification with the regime, and terror campaigns conducted by the security services against any and all opposition to the regime was to keep the middle class politically subdued and passive.

Starting in 1970, a gradual change took place in the approach adopted by the Ba'th in Iraq—from pan-Arab radicalism, which focused on Arab national identity and aimed toward unity of the Arab states as equals, to Iraqocentric pan-Arabism, which focused on the unique identity of the residents of Iraq and the leading role of Iraq among the Arab states. The center of attention of the regime shifted from the universal Arab struggle against Israel to the specific, direct Iraqi struggle against Iran. The gradual transformation in emphasis toward Iraqi territorialism and Iraqocentric pan-Arabism had begun to manifest itself as early as the Eighth Conference of the Ba'th in 1974. This change manifested itself in Ba'th documents starting in 1978, which began to include explicit expressions of the Iraqocentric and "Mesopotamian" approach. Saddam increasingly emphasized Iraq's historical and present privacy in the Arab world. As he put it, "What is good for Iraq is good for the Arabs."[7] This change in attitude resulted from the pragmatic needs of the regime and was intended to subject pan-Arabism to Iraqi national interests as perceived by the Ba'th and by Saddam Husayn. Saddam's speeches, the Iraqi educational system, and the cultural policy of the regime increasingly emphasized ancient Mesopotamian elements unique to Iraq. The Ba'ath regime under Saddam devoted efforts to constructing and fostering pre-Islamic myths—Sumerian, Akkadian, Babylonian, and the like. Various ancient leaders—Sargon, Hammurabi, Nebuchadnezzar, and Sennacherib—were presented as the forefathers of the modern Iraqi nation. (Gradually, and especially in the 1980s, allusions were made to the similarity between these heroic leaders—and even the ancient gods—and Saddam Husayn.)

The fostering of an Iraqi-Mesopotamian-territorialist national identity, the roots of which predated Islam, was not intended to replace the Iraqi-Arab-Islamic identity. Instead, this bizarre combination of divergent concepts of identity was intended to build up the unique facet of Iraqi Arab nationalism without neglecting either pan-Arab radicalism or Islam. It is a fusion between Iraqi-Mesopotamian identity and Iraqi-centered pan-Arabism. All were intended to build a national identity that would confer power and stability upon the regime and its ruler. In the 1970s and 1980s, when the attractiveness and influence of pan-Arab radicalism declined in the other Arab states, in favor of a pragmatism which—while centered on territorial nationalism—preserved a certain degree of inter-Arab identity and cooperation, this process in Iraq assumed a character in line with the pragmatic considerations and the grandiose visions of Saddam Husayn.

Starting in 1968, the radical trends of the regime began to give way to a more pragmatic approach. The Eighth Conference of the Ba'th Party, early in 1974, continued to stress the party's ideological commitment to Arab unity and to socialism. At the same time, however, it emphasized Iraqi patriotism (*wataniyya*). The fostering of an Iraqi-territorial identity, which resulted from the pragmatic needs of the regime, was not intended to replace pan-Arabism but rather was presented as its principal and practical means of expression. In this way, while preserving its commitment to pan-Arab radicalism, the party also gave legitimacy and even precedence to Iraqi identity and interests. More than any other leader in the Arab world in the last half of the twentieth century, Saddam was responsible for fostering a complex and comprehensive ideological system. He did not withdraw from his pan-Arab radical positions. Instead, he nurtured an Iraqi national identity with a framework of Iraqo-centric Arab nationalism. In both the Iraqi and the Syrian Ba'th parties, the reinforcement of the territorialist-nationalist (Iraqi-Arab and Syrian-Arab) positions took place in connection with an internal sociological change: the rise of new forces and activists from among the poorer popular strata, residents of provincial towns, members of the 'Alawite minority in Syria, and Sunnites (principally from Tikrit) with allegiance to their tribal origins in Iraq.

On the practical level, the emphasis was shifted from collectivization and agrarian reform in agriculture based on Socialist principles to greater pragmatism and flexibility in encouraging private enterprise and the private sectors in service-based industries and the economy. At the same time, there was no backing away whatsoever from the strategic decision to retain state control of the economy and of all areas of life, and to exploit them to strengthen the regime and build national power. Both the expressions of dogmatic ideological doctrine and the tendency toward flexibility and quasi-liberalization were intended to serve the supreme goal: the consolidation and reinforcement of Saddam's rule and the building of national power, leading to the transformation of Iraq into a regional Great Power under the complete and absolute control of Saddam Husayn and to the strengthening of Saddam's own status as the leader of all Arabs. By contrast to the ideology of the Ba'th, which considered tribalism an anachronism and a reactionary phenomenon opposed to the unity of the Arab nation, Saddam began to encourage tribalism and to emphasize the identities of the tribes, presenting them as an essential component of Arab and Iraqi-Arab national identity. This policy, which began in the 1970s and reached its height in the 1980s and 1990s, was intended to ensure the support of the tribes for the regime and to avoid the consolidation of the Shi'ites as a united force through the creation of tribal identities and loyalties. Saddam's tribal policy strengthened the legitimacy and the dominance of Al-Bu Nasir, the tribal relatives of Saddam. From the sociological standpoint, tribal connections became a useful means for the survival of many Iraqis, since the state ceased to provide personal security, and tribal connections became advantageous for economic and social survival, even within the state bureaucracy.[8]

Although Saddam Husayn had been the "strong man" of the Iraqi government since 1972–73, he preferred to settle for the roles of deputy secretary of the party, vice president of Iraq—prima facie #2. Ahmad Hasan al-Bakr continued to hold the positions of president of Iraq and secretary of the Ba'th Party, but his status gradually diminished while that of Saddam increased.

On July 16, 1979, al-Bakr announced his resignation for personal reasons and the transfer of power to Saddam Husayn. Saddam immediately launched an extensive purge of the Ba'th Party, the security services, and the armed forces. At a convocation of party leadership called immediately after al-Bakr's retirement, the discovery of a plot led by Syria, aimed at toppling the regime in Baghdad, was announced.

The brief "honeymoon" period between the two states came to an end. The thaw between Iraq and Syria had resulted from an Israeli-Egyptian peace initiative launched by President Anwar al-Sadat of Egypt in 1977. The shared opposition to separate peace agreements between Egypt and Israel, the desire to exploit the isolation of Egypt in the Arab world in order to seize Arab leadership, and the desire of Syrian President Hafiz al-Asad to form an Arab front against Egypt had brought about a rapprochement between Syria and

Iraq. In October 1978, al-Asad visited Baghdad and met with the Iraqi president with a view to establishing a union between the two states. From the
viewpoint of Ahmad Hasan al-Bakr and his supporters, this also represented
the last attempt to halt the rise of Saddam Husayn. Had Iraq and Syria entered into a federation, that federation would have been headed by the two
presidents and Ba'th Party leaders, Ahmad Hasan al-Bakr and Hafiz al-Asad.
Such a situation would have weakened the status of Saddam Husayn, who
would have been forced back to third place, along with the vice president of
Syria. This threat to Saddam's status was apparently what impelled him to
take the measures that led to al-Bakr's resignation, the frustration of the
federation, and the transfer of power into his own hands. To help him carry
out his moves within Iraq, Saddam enlisted the support of other Arab
states—specifically Jordan and Saudi Arabia, which feared the possible
union of the two Ba'th-led states and the consequent renewal and strengthening of a radical force, which in turn would threaten their own conservative
regimes.

The alleged discovery of a plot led by Syria was a convenient pretext for a
wave of arrests and executions among those leaders of the party and the state
who were not loyal to Saddam or who could have opposed or criticized him.[9]
Ever since the failure of the Ba'th in 1963, Saddam and al-Bakr had tried to
enlist the support of residents of their town, Tikrit, and members of their
tribe, the Al-Bu Nasir, in rehabilitating the party and strengthening the candidates from within it. The importance of the Tikrit residents, and that of
Sunnite Arab tribesmen from the Tikrit area in particular, increased as a
result of the takeover of the party and the regime by the al-Bakr-Saddam
faction. Residents of Tikrit from the Al-Bu Nasir tribe and other Sunnite
Arab tribes were enlisted into the various security services and to Saddam's
personal guard. Tribal loyalty became the mainstay of the regime's security
and a means of reinforcing Saddam's rule and authority.[10]

As mentioned above, during the 1980s and 1990s, Saddam encouraged
tribalism and fostered tribal identities as an essential component of the identity of the Iraqi Arab nation. This approach was in conflict with the basic
concept of the Ba'th, according to which the tribes and tribal identities are an
anachronism and the expression of a reaction that opposes the unity of the
Arab nation. Saddam's tribal policy was intended to give legitimacy to the
major role played by members of his tribe and other tribes in reinforcing the
regime. The fostering of tribalism was also of benefit to the regime relative to
the Shi'ites, as it impeded the formation of any large-scale Shi'ite ethnic resistance, since for rural Shi'tes, their tribal identity was paramount.

Saddam Husayn's ambition was to fortify his absolute rule and to neutralize any other focus of power in the Iraqi state and society, while at the same

time acquiring the status of a regional power and an important element in the global arena for Iraq. Saddam's estimate of the threats posed to Iraq by Iran and Turkey, along with his fears of the ethnic Shiʿite and Kurdish forces within Iraq, led him to strive constantly to win special power for his country. Based on Iraq's vast oil reserves, good agricultural conditions, relatively educated population, and ancient history, Saddam believed it was worthy of a leadership role in the Middle East, the Arab world, and even among the states of Asia and Africa. Saddam nurtured his personality cult, placing himself on an equal footing with such renowned Islamic and Arab leaders as Salah al-Din and ʿAbd al-Nasir and even with the heads of pre-Islamic cultures and empires, Hammurabi, Sargon, and Nebuchadnezzar.

In the fortification of his own regime and rule, Saddam adopted a sophisticated combination of measures:

1. Elimination of all foci of power and potential resistance, by means of a network of security services and the mechanisms of the Baʿth Party.
2. Unprecedented support for Saddam's personality cult.
3. Fostering tribalism as a means of neutralizing the possibility of Shiʿite or Kurdish coalescence and legitimizing the special status of Saddam Husayn's supporters, his family, and the members of his tribe.
4. Nurturing an ideological system intended to shape the worldview of the residents of Iraq, in accordance with Saddam's interests and beliefs.

The methods adopted by Saddam led to the fragmentation of Iraqi society and the weakening of the modern middle class. He suppressed all social frameworks not under the absolute control of the regime, exploited economic sanctions, revitalized and nurtured tribalism, and made use of domestic terror. In so doing, he pulverized the modern middle class—a central element of most of the modern regimes and states across the globe.

As long as he and Iraq had the resources to do so, Saddam fostered the national system of higher education. He understood that education and scientific and technological achievements are prerequisites for attaining power by any state in the modern era. The nurturing of Iraqi-Mesopotamian-Arab identity and the argument that tribal identities are an expression of authentic Arabism were intended to build up the Iraqi nation headed by Saddam. But the patterns of cruelty and brutality that characterized his regime and his ambition to seize and hold all power in his own hands and control the Iraqi state led to the destruction of the social foundation of Iraq and exacerbated the interethnic tension manifested by the Shiʿite and Kurdish revolts.

By contrast to all the rulers of Iraq throughout the twentieth century, and by contrast to all his rivals, Saddam Husayn made use of physical elimination—the execution not only of those who took up arms or conspired against the regime but also of his rivals and potential rivals within the regime, the party, and his own ruling group. By means of this method, which was unprecedented throughout the Arab world, Saddam got rid of anyone suspected of less than total loyalty. This method, which he used against friends and rivals alike, had implications regarding the way anyone was handled within Iraqi society who was thought to entertain critical or oppositionist views. The tactics of brutal terror adopted by Saddam Husayn exceeded anything ever before seen among the politicians and rulers of Iraq and the Middle East, and recalled the methods and operational means used by Stalin in the Soviet Union (1925–53) against his associates in the Communist Party, the holders of key positions in the regime, and any powerful person in society. In fact, Saddam Husayn greatly admired Stalin.

The Hashemite monarchical regime, although neither liberal nor democratic, refrained from executing its rivals, with only two exceptions: officers of the Golden Square who were tried and executed, and the heads of the Communist Party in 1948–49. Qasim also avoided putting his friends to death—even those who revolted against his regime and tried to overthrow it. It is true that during the first days of the revolution, members of the royal family were executed, and in the Mahdawi trials, several heads of the monarchical security services were sentenced to death as well as rivals of the regime who had attempted to overthrow it by force. In general, however, Qasim's regime limited itself to arrest and imprisonment. Notwithstanding the authoritarian-dictatorial nature of the Qasim regime, it was not a murderous regime. Qasim did imprison his great rival, 'Abd al-Salam 'Arif, but 'Arif enjoyed relatively good conditions and eventually Qasim released him.

Under the Ba'th regime in 1963, members of the Ba'th militia murdered thousands of Communists and sympathizers, whom they considered to be dangerous rivals. Nonetheless, despite the bitter struggles within the party, its members generally did not kill each other. 'Abd al-Salam 'Arif and his brother 'Abd al-Rahman also desisted from executing even the conspirators against their regime (except for the murder of Qasim himself, in the course of the revolution against him).

The pattern of physical elimination of friends and rivals in the party and the regime adopted by Saddam Husayn was not characteristic of other regimes in the Middle East either. Neither 'Abd al-Nasir in Egypt nor Hafiz al-Asad in Syria executed their rivals within the regime, although both were authoritarian and dictatorial by nature.

The Three Gulf Wars and the Fall of Saddam Husayn

In his ambition to fortify his rule of Iraq and earn it the status of a regional power, coupled with his failure to comprehend the international political scene, Saddam led Iraq into three wars that caused immeasurable suffering for its population, utterly destroyed its economy, and grievously damaged its society. In two of those wars—the one against Iran between 1980 and 1988 and the war against Kuwait in 1990 and its continuation against the Western-Arab coalition led by the United States—Iraq was the initiator and the aggressor. The third war, initiated by the United States and Britain in 2003, marked the zenith of a protracted crisis in Iraq's relations with the United States and the UN.

From the early 1970s, a change had taken place in the priorities of Iraq's regional foreign policy, from the Fertile Crescent and the Arab world to the Persian Gulf and its relations with Iran. Iraq had not abandoned its pretensions to status and leadership of the Arab world, and Saddam, who viewed himself as a great Iraqi and Arab leader, continually strove to raise Iraq to a position of supremacy among the Arab states. Saddam especially invested political efforts in ensuring the support of the Arab states for Iraq during the war against Iran. Despite the extremist anti-Egyptian position that Iraq had adopted in the wake of the separate peace between Egypt and Israel, the war years marked a certain rapprochement between Iraq and Egypt. Iraq's pragmatic need to obtain the assistance of both Arab and Western states during the war against Iran led Saddam to adopt a policy that helped Egypt to find a way out of the isolation imposed upon it by the Arab world without abrogating the peace treaties with Israel. Nonetheless, Saddam continued to view Iran as the most dangerous threat to Iraq and its rival for dominance in the Gulf and the entire area. Iran's control of the Shatt al-'Arab outlet to the sea, its influence on the Shi'ites of Iraq, and the likelihood of renewed Iranian assistance to the Kurds in Iraq (the latter two factors especially probable since Khomeini's Islamic revolution of 1979) made it the most serious threat to Iraq and its regime. The issue of an outlet to the sea for Iraq and securing its oil exports were crucial to Saddam's efforts to win the status of a regional power for Iraq and to bolster his absolute rule. Accordingly, although Saddam did not abandon his ambitions and his activities in the inter-Arab arena, the focus of Iraq's foreign policy shifted to its relations with Iran and the struggle for dominance of the Gulf.

The fear of Iranian superiority and the desire to achieve the status of a regional power for Iraq were apparently what motivated Saddam to develop, or to acquire, unconventional weapons of mass destruction.

The crises and wars inflicted by Saddam on Iraq were among the factors that directed inter-Arab activity to concentrate on the Gulf area. Until the 1980s, the conflict with Israel and the struggle in Lebanon had been the principal foci of inter-Arab activity. In accordance and combination with the social, cultural, and political developments in Egypt, Syria, and Lebanon, those foci had dictated the lines of development of the Arab world. The increasing importance of the oil-producing countries in the Gulf and the increasing significance of oil income under the economic, political, and cultural conditions prevailing in the Middle East since the 1970s and 1980s, together with the crises and wars between Iraq and Iran, between Iraq and Kuwait, and between Iraq and the United States and United Nations, had helped to raise the importance of the Gulf area in global and inter-Arab terms as well as within each of the Arab states involved.

The Islamic revolution under Khomeini in Iran in February 1997 increased Saddam's fears of radical Islamic influence on the Shi'ites in Iraq. At the same time, Saddam believed that Iran had been weakened by the chaos that had followed the Islamic revolution and the dismissal and arrest of the Iranian Army and Air Force officers who had been trained in the United States while the shah was in power. Saddam viewed Iran's weakness as a historic opportunity for Iraq to gain the upper hand, once and for all, in the territorial dispute over the control of the Shatt al-'Arab outlet and thus to ensure that Iraq would always have an outlet to the sea.

Saddam sought to remove himself from the 1975 Algiers Agreement, in which Iraq had made far-ranging concessions to Iran in exchange for the cessation of Iranian support for the Kurdish rebellion. In August 1980, Iraq launched a war against Iran. Saddam's war aims were to dispel the threat posed by the influence of radical Islamic ideology on the Shi'ites in Iraq, to prevent a renewal of Iranian support for the Kurds in Iraq, and to weaken Iraq's power as a competitor for the leading role in the Gulf. All these were intended to lay the groundwork for transforming Iraq into the strongest power in that part of the Middle East.

However, against all Iraqi expectations, what should have been a short campaign turned into a bloody war that lasted eight years. During that time, Iraq was forced to cope with a rival three times its size in terms of population and more cohesive nationally, with a more determined leadership whose message was attractive to significant segments of the Iraqi population.

During the course of that war, Iraq gained the support of most of the Arab governments, the United States, and many European states as the force holding back the threat of Islamic fundamentalism.

Saddam's regime succeeded in surviving the war, and Iraq managed to force Iran into a cease-fire in September 1988. The price, however, was catastrophic: between 150,000 and 350,000 Iraqi dead, and some $160 billion worth of damage to Iraq's economy. Still, although he had embroiled Iraq in a war that had brought it death and destruction—which, at times, threatened the regime in Baghdad—Saddam managed to hold onto power and even to exploit the difficulties of the war in order to fortify his position and intensify his control of Iraq.[11]

In 1990, following a protracted crisis over territorial questions and the issue of oil prices, Iraq invaded and conquered Kuwait. Saddam sought to secure for Iraq a broad outlet to the sea that was free of the Iranian threat and to give Iraq control of Kuwait's oil resources. Iraq traditionally had claimed that the British had arbitrarily removed Kuwait from the vilayet of Basra at the end of the nineteenth century, when the Ottoman Empire was too weak to prevent it. The takeover of Kuwait's oil resources was also intended to extricate the Iraqi economy, which had been drained by the eight years of war with Iran. Had Iraq managed to gain control of Kuwaiti oil, it would have become the second largest oil exporter in the world (after Saudi Arabia) and would thereby have obtained a special international status.

Saddam, who failed to understand the international and global reality following the end of the cold war and the fall of the Soviet Union, and who did not expect the harsh reaction of the Arab world, led Iraq into another crisis and another war. The war with the coalition of Western and Arab states, under U.S. leadership, nearly brought about the fall of Saddam's regime. Complex considerations by the United States and Saudi Arabia, including their unwillingness to support a Shi'ite revolt that could very likely have toppled Saddam, helped him to remain in power. The regime in Baghdad lost control of northern Iraq, in which the main Kurdish factions—the Kurdistan Democratic Party (KDP) under Mas'ud Barzani and the Patriotic Union of Kurdistan (PUK) under Jalal Talabani—established autonomous Kurdish areas. Yet even though Iraq had lost control of Iraqi Kurdistan, the Kurds were unable to exploit the situation and establish an independent Kurdish state. Their inability stemmed both from internal struggles and from the intense opposition by Turkey, Iran, and the Arab states. (The United States, Russia, and the European states also objected to the establishment of a Kurdish state and favored the preservation of Iraqi unity.)

Although the sanctions imposed on Iraq as a result of its invasion of Kuwait caused great suffering to the Iraqi population, they did not undermine Saddam's regime. Saddam managed to use the results of the war and the sanctions on Iraq in order to strengthen his absolute control over Iraqi society. The steps he took to do so included constructing security organizations that practiced domestic terror in order to subdue Iraqi society, strengthening his own personality cult, indoctrination, nurturing his ideological system, control of all of Iraq's economic resources (which could thus be exploited for the benefit of the regime), fostering tribalism, and disbanding all social structures not under his absolute control. Both Saddam's policies leading to the constant sieges and wars and the international sanctions imposed on Iraq led to the destruction of the middle class. All these, given the conditions created by the war and the economic sanctions, served to secure Saddam's absolute totalitarian rule over Iraq.

Starting in 1991, Iraq struggled to throw off the economic sanctions and rid itself of the UN teams inspecting for unconventional warfare. The plight of the Iraqi people was displayed by Iraq in order to gain international support for removing the sanctions and the supervision. Yet, although the population of Iraq underwent incredible suffering as a result of the sanctions, the heads of the regime and their supporters enjoyed vast wealth and exploited the fact of the sanctions in order to fortify the regime and increase their own affluence. Iraq's income, within the framework of the sanctions, would have enabled the regime to supply the basic needs of the population and even to improve its conditions. Nonetheless, Saddam preferred to invest the income placed at his disposal when the sanctions were relaxed, and the additional funds obtained by breaching the sanctions, to gain the loyalty of the sectors vital to the regime, expand the mechanisms of control and domestic security, and to develop the military strength of the state.

Saddam did not give up his aim of canceling the sanctions and the UN supervision of Iraq, restoring his full control of Kurdistan, obtaining a leadership role in the Arab world for Iraq, and proving himself as a historic Iraqi leader possessed of international significance and influence.

The growing tension in Iraq's relations with the United States became a profound crisis after the 2000 election of George W. Bush and the establishment of a Republican administration. In the atmosphere that prevailed after the attack on the World Trade Center on September 11, 2001, and after the war in Afghanistan, Iraq under Saddam and the United States under Bush were set on a collision course. The neoconservative worldview and ideology propounded by Bush and shared by the majority of his administration led to the adoption of rigid positions regarding Saddam's regime.

Saddam's aggressive policy toward Iraq's neighbors, along with the suspicions that he was trying to obtain unconventional weapons, placed his regime in acute conflict with the U.S. government and with those states which sought to prevent proliferation of this type of armament. During 2002, the U.S. administration came to the conclusion that Saddam's regime represented a threat to the stability of the Middle East, world peace, and American interests and that, accordingly, the United States—even without the support of the United Nations—must bring about his downfall.

Iraq's efforts to develop nuclear weapons encountered difficulties in 1990–91 and has stagnated since, with no evidence of progress. Despite indications that Iraq tried to develop chemical and biological weapons in the 1990s, it is unclear how closely it approached the stage of possessing effective weapons of these types. To demonstrate Iraq's might, Saddam created the impression that Iraq possessed unconventional weapons; evidently, though, Iraq did not have any effective unconventional weapons. To what extent Saddam's concern with unconventional weapons was a motivating factor for American decision makers, or whether it was only a pretext used by them to go to war with Iraq in 2003, exceeds the bounds of the present book. The issue of the development of unconventional weapons and its role, among other factors, in fueling the crisis that led to the destruction of Saddam's regime, demands further research in Iraqi and American history.

Further research and historical discussion of Saddam Husayn's regime and the crisis and war that brought it to an end would transcend the scope of this book. That is the job of future historians.

Saddam Husayn's regime and the wars that he inflicted on Iraq were disastrous for its population and destructive to its economy. They shattered Iraqi society, obliterated the middle class, destroyed the educational system, and exacerbated interethnic tension. Following the fall of the Saddam regime, chaos and a political vacuum arose in Iraq. Given the economic and social ruin, the political and ideological vacuum, the psychological burden, and the interethnic tensions and suspicion, the rehabilitation process in Iraq can be expected to be long and complicated, with international implications.

Writing the history of the period in which the relationship between Iraq and the United States created a crisis, leading to the war that brought about the conquest of Iraq by the United States and the fall of Saddam's regime, will require examination of two main aspects. Developments in Iraq and the political conflicts within the politico-social forces in Iraq, as well as the political developments and the ideological currents in the United States since the end of the twentieth century and the election of George W. Bush as president, must be analyzed in depth. In fact, this war has now become not only a milestone in Iraq's history but a significant landmark in the history of the United States as well.

Conclusion

The Conditions of Iraq and the Rise of Saddam Husayn's Regime

Study of the historical perspective is vital to understanding the political and social conditions that facilitated the rise of the Ba'th Party and Saddam Husayn to power and consolidation of their rule. The weakness of the modern middle stratum, the capitalist entrepreneurial bourgeoisie, and the working class and their dependence on the state, as well as the impotence of civilian society and the political forces against the might and resources of the state, were exploited by the Ba'th and Saddam Husayn to take over the state. Once they had established the totalitarian regime, the prevailing conditions actually helped it to survive and to exploit the crises and wars into which Saddam led Iraq over the years.

During the 1940s and 1950s, an imbalance arose in Iraq between the relative strength and considerable financial resources of the state and the weakness of civilian society and political forces. This imbalance, which resulted from the special importance of the state apparatus and the army, due to the perpetual threat posed by ethnic centrifugal forces (the Shi'ites and Kurds) within Iraq and the strategic threat posed by its neighbors, was exacerbated following the dramatic increase in oil revenues which gave the state even greater financial capacities than it had previously enjoyed. The conservative nature of the regime and the ruling elite, due to their dependence on the large landowners, the concentration of capital in the hands of the state, and the world economic conditions which hampered the development of industrialization and the industrial bourgeoisie, all contributed, under the Hashemite monarchy, to the weak bourgeoisie's and the modern middle stratum's dependence on the state and its conservative regime. The inflexible domestic policy resulting from the conservatism of the ruling elite and the upper socioeconomic class prevented the development of political parties in the 1940s and 1950s. Such parties could have represented the interests of both the modern middle stratum and the bourgeoisie in promoting entrepreneurship, industrialization, and reform as well as representing the interests of the working class and the poorer strata.

Several factors led the regime and the ruling elite into a no-win situation culminating in the collapse of the regime and the revolution launched in 1958 by the radical army officers. The conservative interests of the ruling political elite and the upper socioeconomic class prevented them from responding to the needs of the new social forces. In addition, the conservative nature of the regime and the political system—which did not allow a means of political expression for the new social forces or a response to the challenge of pan-Arab nationalist radicalism—was incompatible with the dynamically changing social structure of Iraq. These officers, under the leadership of Qasim and 'Arif, reflected the nationalist-radical trends of the new social forces, the modern middle stratum and the poorer strata. In 1958, conditions existed which enabled the rise of organizations that could constitute a basis for a civilian society. These conditions gave rise to the growth of strong political forces that could provide a counterweight to the power of the state in the political arena. However, the major political forces that characterized Qasim's time—the pan-Arab radical nationalists ("Nasirists"), the Iraqi-territorialist radical nationalists, and the Communists—weakened each other, while failing to develop into cohesive, well-organized forces with strong public backing. Qasim's populist, antiparty approach prevented the establishment of a ruling party, such as those which had been established in the authoritarian radical-nationalist regimes of Egypt and other countries in Asia and Africa. At the same time, the parties which had existed in Iraq for some years, al-Istiqlal and the National Democratic Party, were unsuccessful in adapting to the new conditions; they lost their attraction and crumbled. The decline of the workers' organizations and other civilian organizations that had been established under the inspiration of the Communists following the revolution of 1958, the collapse of the National Democratic Party (which had represented the liberal social-democratic alternative), and the blow struck against the Communist Party by the Ba'th early in 1963, together truncated the development of the strong political forces and the growth of the civilian society in Iraq. The Ba'th, which thus became the only strong force to survive in Iraq's political arena, was ousted in the autumn of 1963 by a group of army officers headed by 'Abd al-Salam 'Arif, who exiled the heads of the rival factions within the party. But even 'Arif and his officers did not succeed in building a strong political force capable of enlisting broad-based public support of their regime. The attempt by Prime Minister 'Abd al-Rahman al-Bazzaz to renew political party life and refresh the political arena, which could have constituted a counterweight against the power of the officers and the state, never came to fruition.

Under the 'Arif brothers, and primarily under 'Abd al-Rahman 'Arif, the weakening of the political forces continued and the ideological crisis and confusion worsened. The nationalist supporters of Arab-Nasirist unity were unsuccessful in coalescing into a political force. The message of Nasirist pan-Arab radicalism began to lose its attraction as the Nasirists declined in Egypt, especially after the 1967 war with Israel. The older political parties fell apart and disappeared. The Communists never recovered and could not resume their earlier position as a central force. The intervention of the army officers prevented the resumption of political party life under al-Bazzaz, but the officers were divided among themselves. Their prestige and that of 'Arif and his regime had suffered a blow as a consequence of the poor performance shown by the Iraqi Army in the 1967 war, and they were unable to establish a political force that could stabilize the regime and enlist the support of the Iraqi public.

The political vacuum was accompanied by the weakness and confusion of the social forces in Iraq. The new middle class, the working class, and the bourgeoisie became exhausted by the violent struggles that had continued since 1958, and they did not achieve a civilian society or establish strong and effective political forces. The regimes led by Qasim and the 'Arif brothers did not establish bureaucratic political parties that could enlist extensive social support.

The success of the Ba'th, Saddam Husayn, and Ahmad Hasan al-Bakr in exploiting the weakness of the regime, the impotence of the political forces and the army officers, and the ideological confusion in order to seize power was based on social phenomena. The rise of the Ba'th regime and the transformation of Saddam Husayn and his supporters into the dominant force within the regime and the party was an expression of the rise of a group from among the lower-middle and lower classes of a provincial town, Tikrit, and the tribe of Al-Bu Nasir. Among the lower-middle and lower strata of the provincial towns, there was more of a tendency toward tribal and familial affinity than existed among the "older" modern middle stratum in Baghdad, which had formed during the 1930s, 1940s, and 1950s and had given rise to the now-weakened political forces. Tribal and familial affinities and loyalties were more significant and more relevant to Saddam Husayn and his faction and could therefore be transformed into more effective political means. Against the background of this sociological change in the modern middle stratum, accompanied by the lessened attraction of the message of secular pan-Arab radicalism, and especially following the failure of attempts to bring about Arab unity, the Ba'th quickly gained in strength and succeeded in consolidating its regime, eventually leading to totalitarianism under Saddam Husayn.

The decay of the social forces and the ideological confusion prevailing in Iraq gave rise to conditions that enabled the Ba'th Party, despite its initially small size, to be an effective force. The Iraqi Ba'th, which had detached from the Syrian Ba'th and was embroiled in rivalry with both the "Nasirist" nationalists and the Communists, was not as severely harmed by the crisis and the ideological confusion that followed 1967. The Ba'th had the advantage of its pan-Arab radicalism, which preserved radical pan-Arab rhetoric and expressed the concept of Arab identity. Nevertheless, the main factor in the success of the Ba'th lay in its leadership, the members of which—primarily Saddam Husayn—succeeded in forming ties with power-hungry army officers and in overthrowing the 'Arif regime. Given the fragmentation prevailing among the officers and the decline of all remaining political forces, the Ba'th—more and more prominently represented by a group of activists and army officers, most of the members of the Al-Bu Nasir tribe, and/or residents of Tikrit—constituted a relatively cohesive force. The success of the Ba'th, and mainly of the group headed by Ahmad Hasan al-Bakr and Saddam Husayn, resulted from the political skills, determination, and ruthless cruelty of Saddam Husayn to a great degree. More than any of his rivals, Saddam succeeded in exploiting the unique conditions prevailing in Iraq.

The ethnic splits and the fragmentation of Iraqi society made it difficult for civilian society in Iraq to develop a strong national identity and constituted a threat to the legitimacy and stability of the various regimes and rulers in Iraq. The weaknesses of Iraqi society and the external and internal threats against the state and all of its regimes, on one hand, and, on the other, the financial resources and income from oil which were at the disposal of the state and its rulers, created conditions that favored the establishment of tyranny.

The imbalance between the strength and resources at the disposal of the Iraqi state and the weakness of Iraq's political forces and civil society made it easy for anyone who could take over the state apparatus and use it with skill, cruelty, and sophistication to attain complete control, eliminate any resistance, generate loyalty among large sections of society, and consolidate his rule in the long term. Merciless domestic terror, development of mechanisms for the control of society and the state, the fostering of an ideological system that favored identification with the regime, and a well-developed personality cult were the means used by Saddam in the construction of his totalitarian regime in Iraq. He succeeded in exploiting the power and resources of the state, the conditions of Iraqi society, the errors of his rivals, and the disastrous series of crises and wars caused by his policies during the 1990s, in order to survive and reinforce his rule. The weakness of Iraq and the threats against it became motives which fueled Saddam's aim to achieve and maintain national power and the status of a regional power.

Notes

Chapter 1. Historical Perspective of Iraq before 1941

1. Longrigg, *Four Centuries of Modern Iraq*, Nieuewenhuis, *Politics and Society in Early Modern Iraq: Mamluk Pashas, Tribal Shaykhs, and Local Rule between 1802 and 1831*.

For a different critical view of the Mamluks, see Toledano, "The Emergence of Ottoman–Local Elites (1700–1800)," and Toledano, "The Ottoman Middle East and North Africa from Hegemonic Rule to Dynastic Order." Toledano argues that the households were a local–Ottoman framework.

On the local forces and society in Mosul, see Khoury, *State and Provincial Society in Ottoman Empire: Mosul, 1540–1834*. On the Mamluk local–Ottoman rule, see 'Ali al-Wardi, *Lamhat ijtima'iyya min taarikh al-'Iraq al-hadith*, 1:170–296.

2. Longrigg, *Four Centuries of Modern Iraq*, 298–311; Jwaidah, "Midhat Pasha and the Land System in Lower Iraq."

3. Farouk-Sluglett and Sluglett, "The Transformation of Land Tenure and Rural Social Structure in Central and Southern Iraq, 1870–1958"; Jwaidah, "Aspects of Land Tenure and Social Change in Lower Iraq during the Late Ottoman Period."

4. Nakash, *The Shi'is of Iraq*; Litvak, *Shi'i Scholars of Nineteenth-Century Iraq*.

5. The activity of the Western powers in the vilayets of Baghdad and Basra has been extensively researched. At the same time, many issues are eminently deserving of further study, in view of the focus of historic research on the foreign policy and the colonial policy of the Western powers and economic entities. See Cohen, *British Policy in Mesopotamia, 1903–1914*; Hasan, "The Role of Foreign Trade in Economic Development of Iraq, 1864–1964."

6. Mejchner, *Imperial Quest for Oil: Iraq, 1910–1928*; Kent, *Oil and Empire: British Policy and Mesopotamian Oil, 1900–1920*.

7. Atiyyah, *Iraq, 1908–1921*, 51–70.

8. Wilson, *Loyalities: Mesopotamia, 1914–1917*; Barker, *The Neglected War: Mesopotamia, 1914–1918*; Millar, *Death of an Army: The Siege of Kut, 1915–1916*; Townshend, *My Campaign in Mesopotamia*.

9. Constitution of Iraq, 21 March 1925, in Khalil, ed., *Arab States and the Arab League*, 1:10–27. On the effect of the tribal regulations on the inferior status of women and their contribution to impeding women's liberation in Iraq, see Efrati, "Women, Elites, and Discourse in Pre-Revolutionary Iraq, 1932–1958."

10. Haldane, *The Insurrection in Mesopotamia, 1920*; al-Far'un, *Al-Haqaiq al-Nasia fi al-Iraqiya Sanat 1920 wa-Nataijaha*; 'Atiyyah, *Iraq, 1908–1921*, 307–54;

Nakash, *Shi'is of Iraq*, 66–74; Wilson, *Mesopotamia, 1917–1920: A Clash of Loyalities;* al-Hasani, *Al-Thawra al-Iraqiyya al-Kubra.*

11. Vinogradov, "The 1920 Revolt in Iraq Reconsidered: The Role of Tribes in National Politics."

12. Bell, *The Letters of Gertrude Bell;* Klieman, *Foundation of British Policy in the Arab World: The Cairo Conference of 1921;* Atiyyah, *Iraq, 1908–1921,* 355–80.

13. Olson, "Battle for Kurdistan: The Churchill–Cox Correspondence Regarding the Creation of the State of Iraq"; McDowall, *A Modern History of the Kurds,* 151–83.

14. On state-building in Iraq in the 1920s, see Ireland, *Iraq: A Study in Political Development;* Main, *Iraq from Mandate to Independence;* Foster, *The Making of Modern Iraq;* Longrigg, *Iraq, 1900–1950;* Kelidar, ed., *The Integration of Modern Iraq.*

15. Hemphill, "The Formation of the Iraqi Army, 1921–1933."

16. Sluglett, *Britain in Iraq, 1914–1932;* Shikarah, *Iraqi Politics, 1921–41: The Interaction between Domestic Politics and Foreign Policy,* 30–106.

17. Batatu, *The Old Social Classes and the Revolutionary Movements of Iraq,* 1–366.

18. Eppel, "The Elite, the Effendiyya, and the Growth of Nationalism and Pan-Arabism in Hashemite Iraq, 1921–1958."

19. Simon, *Iraq between the Two World Wars,* 75–114; Simon, "The Teaching of History in Iraq before the Rashid 'Ali Coup of 1941"; Marr, "The Development of a Nationalist Ideology in Iraq, 1920–1941."

20. Zubaida, *Islam, the People, and the State.*

21. Batatu, *Old Social Classes;* Tejirian, "Iraq, 1932–1956: Politics in Plural Society."

22. Pool, "From Elite to Class: The Transformation of Iraqi Leadership, 1920–1939"; al-Qazzaz, "Power Elite in Iraq, 1920–1958." For a very useful and enlightening analysis of the class structure of Iraqi society, see Batatu, "Class Analysis and Iraqi Society."

23. Masalha, "Faisal's Pan-Arabism"; Shikarah, *Iraqi Politics, 1921–41,* 1–30, 130–64.

24. Michael Eppel, *The Palestine Conflict in the History of Modern Iraq: The Dynamics of Involvement, 1928–1948,* 17–79; Simon, "The Hashemite 'Conspiracy': Hashemite Unity Attempts."

25. Shikarah, *Iraqi Politics, 1921–41,* 107–29; Khadduri, *Independent Iraq,* 36–70. On the conduct of Iraqi government, see al-Hasani, *Taarikh al-Wizarat al-'Iraqiyya.*

26. Khadduri, *Independent Iraq,* 56–62; MacDonald, "The Political Developments in Iraq Leading Up to the Rising in the Spring of 1935"; Marr, "Yasin al-Hashimi: The Rise and Fall of a Nationalist, 1920–1936," 279–300; Nakash, *Shi'is of Iraq,* 120–24.

27. Marr, "Yasin al-Hashimi," 299, 368.

28. Tarbush, *The Role of the Military in Politics: A Case Study of Iraq to 1941;*

Eliezer Beeri, *Army Officers in Arab Politics and Society,* 17–25; Simon, *Iraq between the Two World Wars,* 116–44; Khadduri, *Independent Iraq,* 71–181.

29. Tarbush, *Role of the Military,* 123–49; Beeri, *Army Officers,* 17–22; Eppel, "The Hikmat Suleyman–Bakr Sidqi Government in Iraq, 1936–37, and the Palestine Question"; Eppel, *Palestine Conflict,* 50–66.

30. Silverfarb, "The British Government and the Question of Umm Qasr, 1938–1945."

31. Eppel, *Palestine Conflict,* 104–15; Sabbagh, *Fursan al-'Uruba Fi al-Iraq,* 139.

32. Eppel, *Palestine Conflict,* 93–100.

33. Khadduri, "General Nuri's Flirtation with the Axis Powers."

34. Tarbush, *Role of the Military,* 156–82; al-Hasani, *Asrar al-Khafiyya Fi al-Hawadith al-Sana, 1941*; al-Durra, *Al-Harb al-'Iraqiyya al-Britaniyya, 1941*; al-Sabbagh, *Fursan al-'Uruba Fi al-Iraq*; Haddad, *Harakat Rashid 'Ali al-Kaylani*; Simon, *Iraq between the Two World Wars,* 145–66; Khadduri, *Independent Iraq,* 153–222.

Chapter 2. Iraq during World War II

1 . Minister resident in Iraq (Sir Arnold Wilson) to Secretary of State, 20 January 1942, *Foreign Relations of the United States,* 4:636.

2. G. H. Thompson (chargé d'affaires in the British embassy, Baghdad) to Foreign Office (hereafter referred to as FO), no. 841, 7 September 1943, PRO/FO/371/34998/E/5377 (PRO stands for Public Records Office, Kew Gardens, Britain).

3. Shwadran, *The Middle East, Oil, and the Great Powers,* 252.

4. Iraq Ministry of Economics, *Laborers' Cost of Living Index.*

5. Middle East Financial Conference, *Notes and Statistics Relating to Inflation in the Middle East* (Cairo, 1944), PRO/FO/921/235.

6. On the economic and political situation in Iraq during World War II, see Silverfarb, *The Twilight of British Ascendancy in the Middle East,* 9–54.

7. Ghareeb, *Al-Haraka al-Qawmiyya al-Kurdiyya,* 35–37.

8. Cornwallis (Baghdad) to Eden, 8 February 1944, PRO/FO/371/40041/E/1143.

9. Silverfarb, *Twilight,* 45.

10. On Iraqi activity in the inter-Arab arena during World War II, see Porath, *In the Search of Arab Unity, 1930–1945,* 39–57, 257–89; Gomaa, *The Foundation of the League of Arab States.*

11. Khadduri, *Independent Iraq,* 208–14; Constitution of Iraq, 21 March 1925, with amendments to 1943, in Khalil, ed., *Arab States and the Arab League,* 1:10–27: see Article 26, 13–14.

12. Al-Hashimi, *Mudhakkirat Taha al-Hashimi,* 2:278, 282; Sir Alec Kirkbride (British resident in Transjordan), Amman, to the high commissioner of Palestine, no. 429, 28 December 1944, PRO/FO/624/38/503; Eppel, "Iraqi Politics and Regional Policies, 1945–1949," 112.

13. Hurewitz, *Diplomacy in the Near and Middle East,* 236–37.

14. From British embassy in Cairo to British embassy in Baghdad, 7 October 1944, PRO/FO/624/37/368/65.

Chapter 3. Iraq after World War II: Domestic Economic Crisis and Sociopolitical Tensions and the Struggle for Seniority in the Inter-Arab Arena

1. Stonehewer Bird (British ambassador to Iraq, 1945–47) to FO, no. 377, 25 March 1947, PRO/FO/371/61588; al-Hashimi, *Mudhakkirat Taha al-Hashimi,* 2:105.

2. "Parliamentary and Press Campaign for Revision of the Anglo-Iraqi Treaty of Alliance, 1930," 5 February 1945, in Stonehewer Bird to FO, no. 241, 8 July 1945, PRO/FO/371/68448.

3. Stonehewer Bird to FO, no. 400, 27 May 1945, PRO/FO/371/45302; Eppel, *Palestine Conflict,* 135–36.

4. Iraq Ministry of Economics, *Laborers' Cost of Living Index.*

5. Sir Henry Mack, British ambassador to Iraq, to FO, 10 November 1948, PRO/FO/371/68467; Silverfarb, *Twilight,* 190–91.

6. Silverfarb, *Twilight,* 190–91.

7. Al-Hashimi, *Mudhakkirat Taha al-Hashimi,* 2:160; British embassy, Baghdad, to FO, "Political Review of Iraq for the Year 1947," PRO/FO/371/684443; G. C. Pelham, commercial counselor, British embassy, Baghdad, to FO, 25 November 1947, PRO/FO/371/61660; Franck and Franck, "Economic Review: The Middle East Economy in 1948," 202.

8. Penrose and Penrose, *Iraq: International Relations and National Development,* 151; Silverfarb, *Twilight,* 111–23.

9. Batatu, *Old Social Classes,* 532–33; Farouk-Sluglett and Sluglett, "Labor and National Liberation: The Trade Union Movement in Iraq, 1920–1958," 152.

10. Owen, "British and Decolonization: The Labour Governments and the Middle East"; Eppel, "The Decline of British Influence and the Ruling Elite in Iraq," 188–89; Louis, *The British Empire in the Middle East, 1947–1951,* 315–17; Stonehewer Bird (Baghdad) to Bevin, 10 March 1947, PRO/FO/371/52365.

11. Khadduri, *Independent Iraq,* 265; Elliot, *"Independent Iraq": The Monarchy and British Influence, 1941–1958,* 54.

12. Khadduri, *Independent Iraq,* 254.

13. Busk (British chargé d'affaires in Iraq) to FO, no. 761, 23 September 1946, PRO/FO/371/52402.

14. Al-Hasani, *Taarikh al-Wizarat,* 7:24–48; Batatu, *Old Social Classes,* 531.

15. Batatu, *Old Social Classes,* 531.

16. Al-Jamali, *Mawaqif wa-ʿibar fi siyasatina al-duwaliyya: safhat min taarikhuna al-muasir,* 264–65; Al-Hasani, *Taarikh al-Wizarat,* 7:87–90; Al-Hashimi, *Mudhakkirat Taha al-Hashimi,* 2:129; Eppel, "Iraqi Politics," 113.

17. Bruce Maddy-Weitzman, *The Crystallization of the Arab State System, 1945–1954,* 25–37.

18. Al-Hashimi, *Mudhakkirat Taha al-Hashimi,* 2:96, 122; Cornwallis (Baghdad) to FO, no. 93, 14 March 1945, PRO/FO/371/45332; Eppel, "Iraqi-Syrian Relations," 1:37–39.

19. Eppel, "Iraqi Politics."

20. Eppel, *Palestine Conflict,* 17–100.

21. Ibid., 183.

Chapter 4. The Earthquake of the Iraqi Regime: The Wathba Crisis and Iraq's Role in the 1948 War in Palestine

1. This chapter is based on my previous research on Iraq's involvement in the Palestine question, published in Eppel, *Palestine Conflict.*

2. Busk (Baghdad) to Bevin, 19 September 1946, PRO/FO/371/52402/E 9584; Busk (Baghdad) to Bevin, no. 761, 23 September 1946, PRO/FO/371/52402/E 9584.

3. Silverfarb, *Twilight,* 147–49; Franck and Franck, "Economic Review," 202; Pelham (Baghdad) to FO, "Political Review of Iraq for the Year 1947," PRO/FO/371/68443/E/834; John Troutbeck (British Middle Eastern Office, BMEO, Cairo) to M. R. Wright, FO, 31 December 1947, PRO/FO/371/68387; Batatu, *Old Social Classes,* 471–73.

4. Al-Barazi, *Al-Mudhakkirat Muhsin al-Barazi, 1947–1948,* 15–18.

5. Eppel, *Palestine Conflict,* 158–76.

6. Louis, *British Empire,* 322–36; Silverfarb, *Twilight,* 125–56.

7. Eppel, *Palestine Conflict,* 173–75; Silverfarb, *Twilight,* 141–55; Batatu, *Old Social Classes,* 545–66; Kubba, *Mudhakkirati Fi Samim al-Ahdath, 1918–1958,* 226–31.

8. Edward J. Crocker, U.S. ambassador to Iraq, to Secretary of State, 18 May 1949, National Archives 890G.515/5–1849.

9. See chapter 8.

10. "Political Situation," in Mack to Bevin, no. 104, 29 March 1948, PRO/FO/371/68448/E14291; *al-Ahram,* 18 February 1948; Jamil al-Urfali, *Lamhat Min Dhikriyyat Wazir al-'Iraqi Sabiq,* 210.

11. Busk (Baghdad) to Wright, Secret, 30 January 1948, PRO/FO/371/68446/E/2554G.

12. Mack (Baghdad) to FO, no. 326, 24 March 1948, PRO/FO/371/68447/1E3986.

13. Mack to FO, no. 408, Secret, 15 April 1948, PRO/FO/371/68448/E/4661.

14. Eppel, *Palestine Conflict,* 158–59.

15. Fadil al-Jamali (Baghdad) to FO, 3 March 1948, PRO/FO/624/126.

16. Eppel, *Palestine Conflict,* 184.

17. Ibid., 190–92; Silverfarb, *Twilight,* 159–72; al-Jaburi, *Mihnat Filastin.* Salih Saib al-Jaburi was chief of staff of the Iraqi Army in 1948.

18. *Taqrir Lajnat al-Tahqiq al-Niyabiyya fi Qadiyyat Filastin.*

19. Elliot, *"Independent Iraq,"* 70–72; al-Hasani, *Taarikh al-Wizarat,* 8:8–52.

Chapter 5. The Economic Development of Iraq and the Social Processes of the 1950s

1. Penrose and Penrose, *Iraq,* 170.

2. Shwadran, *Middle East, Oil, and the Great Powers,* 262.

3. Jalal, *The Role of Government in the Industrialization of Iraq, 1950–1965,* 11.

4. Longrigg, *Oil in the Middle East,* 191.

5. Shwadran, *Middle East, Oil, and the Great Powers,* 260–61; Longrigg, *Oil in the Middle East,* 189–94; Stocking, *Middle East Oil,* 200–214.

6. International Bank for Reconstruction and Development, *The Economic Development of Iraq,* 272; United Nations, Department of Economic Affairs, *Review of the Economic Conditions in the Middle East, 1951–1952,* 43.

7. International Bank, *Economic Development,* 149; United Nations, *Review of the Economic Conditions of the Middle East, 1951–1952,* 43; Sassoon, "Industrial Development in Iraq, 1958–1968," 24.

8. Sassoon, "Industrial Development," 25.

9. Haseeb, *The National Income of Iraq, 1953–1961,* 23.

10. Al-Uzri, *Taarikh fi Dhikrayat al-ʿIraq, 1930–1958,* 314; Jalal, *Role of Government,* 14–29; Grewin Gerke, "The Iraqi Development Board and the British Policy, 1945–1950," *Middle Eastern Studies* 27 (1991): 231–54.

11. Jalal, *Role of Government,* 15; al-Uzri, *Taarikh,* 331.

12. Jalal, *Role of Government,* 32–38.

13. Salter, *The Development of Iraq: A Plan of Action.*

14. Jalal, *Role of Government,* 33.

15. Ibid., 36.

16. Ibid., 63; Penrose and Penrose, *Iraq,* 170.

17. Doreen Warriner, *Land Reform and Development in the Middle East,* 175.

18. Penrose and Penrose, *Iraq,* 166–70.

19. The cost of living index, which increased by some 500 percent between 1939 and 1948, decreased to 369 percent over the next five years (or 469 points where 1939 = 100). According to other data, the cost of living in 1953 was 440 points, for a 340 percent increase relative to 1939. See Statistical Summary for August 1952, PRO/FO/371/104683.

The convenient agricultural conditions in Iraq generally enabled the supply of basic foods, which prevented protracted famine and fellahin revolts (provided that there was no disastrous combination of natural disasters, drought, and locusts). In mountainous Kurdistan, where living and agricultural conditions were more severe than in the Euphrates and Tigris plains, severe famine prevailed during World War II. In the 1950s, the resources available to the government enabled it to ensure a reasonable food supply.

20. Haseeb, *National Income,* 15.

21. Penrose and Penrose, *Iraq,* 165.

22. International Bank, *Economic Development,* 469; Qubain, *The Reconstruction of Iraq, 1950–1957,* 230; Jalal, *Role of Government,* 8.

23. Adams, "Current Population Trends in Iraq," 152; Qubain, *Reconstruction,* 212–25.

24. Batatu, *Old Social Classes,* 57, 58–62, 837. According to Rony Gabbay, about 3,418 landowners, each of whom owned more than 1,000 dunams, held a total of 15.8 million dunams, or 68 percent of cultivated land in Iraq, while 86 percent of the fellahin held only about 11 percent of lands. Gabbay, *Communism and Agrarian Reform in Iraq,* 37.

25. Farouk-Sluglett and Sluglett, *Iraq since 1958,* 34; Philips, "Rural to Urban Migration in Iraq," 409.

26. See, for example, the report by the British ethnographer Wilfred Thesiger, "The Mass Movement of Tribesmen from Amara Liwa to Baghdad and Basra," in the dispatch from the British embassy in Baghdad to Levant Department, 5 August 1955.

Chapter 6. The Political Conflict in Iraq between 1950 and 1954: Failed Attempts at Reform within the Regime

1. Khadduri, *Independent Iraq.*

2. On the establishment of the Constitutional Union Party, see *Al-'Ahd* (Baghdad), 22 November 1949; *Al-Zaman* (Baghdad), 26 November 1949; Mack (Baghdad) to Clement Attlee, no. 229, 30 November 1949, PRO/FO/371/75128/E/14883; Mack to Attlee, no. 211, 21 September 1950, PRO/FO/371/82408/EQ/1016/26; Mack to Bevin, no. 71, 23 March 1950, PRO/FO/371/82407/EQ/1016/6; 'Abd al-Razzaq Muhammad al-Aswad, ed., *Mawsuwat al-'Iraq al-Siyasiyya,* 6:259–78. For a document on the parties in Iraq, see also Troutbeck (Baghdad) to Churchill, no. 108, 22 June 1953, PRO/FO/371/104665/EQ/1016/32.

3. Mack to Attlee, no. 211, 21 September 1950, PRO/FO/371/82408/EQ/1016/26; "Iraq: Annual Review for 1950," in Mack to Bevin, no. 4, 5 January 1951, PRO/FO/371/91629/EQ/1011/1. About al-Suwaydi's government, see Tawfiq al-Suwaydi, *Mudhakkirati: Nisf al-Qurn Min Taarikh al-'Iraq Wa-al-Qadiyya al-'Arabiyya,* 491–512.

4. Al-Uzri, *Taarikh,* 370–77; Mack (Baghdad) to Bevin, no. 71, 23 March 1950, PRO/FO/371/82407/EQ/1016/6; Mack to FO, no. 130, 9 March 1950, PRO/FO/371/82407/EQ/1016/4. On tension in the government between Shi'ites and Sunnites, see Kedourie, "Anti-Shi'ism in Iraq under the Monarchy."

5. For Nuri's criticism of al-Suwaydi's policy with a view to improving Iraqi-Egyptian relations, see Mack to FO, 19 April 1950, PRO/FO/371/8407/EQ/1016/7.

6. Al-Aswad, *Mawsuwat,* 6:269–82; Harold Beeley, British chargé d'affaires in Iraq, to Furlonge, FO, 25 July 1951, PRO/FO/371/91634/EQ/1019/6.

7. Troutbeck (Baghdad) to Eden, no. 79, 5 June 1952, PRO/FO/371/98734/EQ/1016/15.

8. Troutbeck to Churchill, no. 108, ibid., notes.

9. On al-Istiqlal, see al-Aswad, *Mawsuwat,* 6:152–80; Kubba, *Mudhakkirati Fi Samim al-Ahdath;* Mack (Baghdad) to Bevin, no. 245, 15 October 1950, PRO/FO/371/82408/EQ/1016/35.

10. Fadhil Musayn, *Taarikh al-Hizb al-Watani al-Dimuqrati, 1942–1958;* al-Jadirji, *Mudhakkirat Kamil al-Jadirji, Wa-Taarikh al-Hizb al-Watani al-Dimuqrati.*

11. Troutbeck (Baghdad) to Churchill, no. 108, 22 June 1953, PRO/FO/105665/EQ/1016/32.

12. Batatu, *Old Social Classes,* 567–71.

13. Ibid., 604–27.

14. "Ratification of the Iraqi Petroleum Agreement: Proceedings in the Iraqi Parliament and Effect on Political Situation," in Troutbeck (Baghdad) to Eden, no. 30, 21

February 1952, PRO/FO/371/98764/EQ/1531/34; Troutbeck (Baghdad) to Eden, no. 40, 6 March 1952, PRO/FO/371/98734/EQ/1016/4.

15. Beeley (Baghdad) to Churchill, no. 118, 21 August 1952, PRO/FO/371/98737/EQ/1017/15; Burton Berry, U.S. ambassador to Iraq, to Department of State (Washington), no. 232, 23 September 1952, National Archives 783A.00.

16. Beeley to Churchill, no. 118, 21 August 1952, PRO/FO/371/98737/EQ/1017/15.

On the way in which the opposition parties in reformist circles of the elite were encouraged by the events in Lebanon regarding the possibility of making changes in the Iraqi regime without endangering its existence and stability, see Troutbeck to Eden, no. 137, 9 October 1952, PRO/FO/371/98734/EQ/1016/35.

17. Law no. 74 of 1952 Amending the Electoral Law no. 76 of 1946; *Official Gazette,* no. 3129, 12 July 1952; Troutbeck (Baghdad) to Eden, no. 79, 5 June 1952, PRO/FO/371/98734/EQ/1016/15; Beeley (Baghdad) to Eden, no. 87, 3 July 1952, PRO/FO/371/98734/EQ/1016/21.

18. Salih Jabr in conversation with Harold Beeley, in Beeley (Baghdad) to Eden, no. 106, 24 July 1952, PRO/FO/98734/EQ/1016/28.

19. Troutbeck (Baghdad) to Eden, no. 79, 5 June 1952, PRO/FO/371/98734/EQ/1016/15.

20. Memorandums of the Political Parties, in Troutbeck (Baghdad) to Eden, no. 145, 5 November 1952, PRO/FO/371/98735/EQ/1016/39.

21. Troutbeck (Baghdad) to Eden, no. 146, 8 November 1952, PRO/FO/371/98735/EQ/1016/42; Kubba, *Mudhakkirati Fi Samim al-Ahdath,* 341–44; al-Hasani, *Taarikh al-Wizarat,* 8:315–18.

22. Disturbances in Baghdad, Events of 22–24 November 1952, in Troutbeck (Baghdad) to Eden, no. 156, 28 November 1952, PRO/FO/371/98736/EQ/1016/78; Batatu, *Old Social Classes,* 666–70; Kubba, *Mudhakkirati Fi Samim al-Ahdath,* 345–48; al-Hasani, *Taarikh al-Wizarat,* 8:310–23.

23. Troutbeck (Baghdad) to Eden, no. 16, 24 January 1953, PRO/FO/371/104665/EQ/1916/10.

24. Al-Hasani, *Taarikh al-Wizarat,* 9:6–52.

25. Ibid., 9:52–108; Eppel, "The Fadhil al-Jamali Government in Iraq, 1953–1954"; Elliot, *"Independent Iraq,"* 105–11.

26. 'Abd al-Karim al-Uzri, *Taarikh,* 417–20; Troutbeck (Baghdad) to Eden, no. 195, 10 October 1953, PRO/FO/371/104666/EQ/1016/65.

27. Al-Jamali, "Iraq under General Nuri," 19.

28. Hooper (chargé d'affaires in the British embassy in Iraq) to Eden, no. 86, 24 April 1954, PRO/FO/371/110988/VQ/1015/21.

29. On the 1954 elections in particular, and the process of elections to Parliament in Iraq during the 1950s in general, see Grassmuck, "The Electoral Process in Iraq, 1952–1958"; al-Hasani, *Taarikh al-Wizarat,* 9:121–22.

30. On Nuri's talks with senior British Foreign Office officials in London, see FO to Hooper (Baghdad), no. 130, 20 July 1954, PRO/FO/371/110990/VQ/1015/16.

31. On British pressure on 'Abd al-Ilah to achieve a compromise with Nuri, see al-

Hasani, *Taarikh al-Wizarat,* 9:133–34; FO to Hooper (Baghdad), no. 130, 20 July 1954, PRO/FO/371/110990/VQ/1015/46.

32. Troutbeck (Baghdad) to Eden, no. 194, 10 September 1954, PRO/FO/371/110991/VQ/1015/70.

33. Troutbeck (Baghdad) to Eden, no. 190, 3 September 1954, PRO/FO/371/110991/VQ/1015/66; al-Hasani, *Taarikh al-Wizarat,* 9:147–50, 153–55.

34. Gallman, *Iraq under General Nuri,* 6–7.

Chapter 7. The Monarchy in Iraq versus the Radical Revolutionary Forces in the Arab World, 1954–1958

1. Iraq: Annual Review for 1950, Mack (Baghdad) to Bevin, no. 4, 5 January 1951, PRO/FO/371/91629/EQ/1011/1.

2. Mack (Baghdad) to Bevin, no. 13, 24 January 1951, PRO/FO/371/91636/EQ/1023/1.

3. On the political atmosphere in Iraq in 1950–52 and the attitudes toward the cold war and neutralism, see Batatu, *Old Social Classes,* 681–83; *Al-ʿAlam al-ʿArabi* (Baghdad), 20 January 1951, *Sada al-Ahali* (Baghdad), 11 January 1951.

4. Beeley (Baghdad) to Eden, no. 198, 3 December 1951, PRO/FO/371/91634/EQ/1019/10.

5. For the text of this treaty, see *Middle East Journal* 6 (1952): 238–40.

6. Jamiʿat al-Duwal al-ʿArabiyya, *Madabit Jalsat Dawr al-Ijtimaʾi al-ʿAadi al-Hadi ʿAshar Limajlis al-Jamiʿat* (Proceedings of the Eleventh Gathering of the League of Arab States), 17 October 1949, 60; American embassy in Cairo to Secretary of State, no. 986, 23 October 1949, National Archives 890/B.00.

7. Elie Podeh, *The Quest for Hegemony in the Arab World,* 50–53.

8. Ibid., 53–63.

9. Troutbeck (Baghdad) to FO, no. 177, 23 March 1954, PRO/FO/371/110787/E/1073/21; *Al-Ahram* (Cairo), 22 March 1954.

10. Podeh, *Quest for Hegemony,* 80.

11. On Nuri's conversation with Selvin Lloyd, see FO to Hooper (Baghdad), no. 130, 20 July 1954, PRO/FO/371/110990/VQ/1015/46.

12. Podeh, *Quest for Hegemony,* 82–87; Mahmud Riad, *Mudhakkirat Mahmud Riad,* 2:57–58.

13. Seale, *The Struggle for Syria,* 206–8; Podeh, *Quest for Hegemony,* 87–90.

14. British embassy in Cairo to FO, no. 234, 28 December 1954, PRO/FO/371/115483/V/1072/1; Podeh, *Quest for Hegemony,* 96–97.

15. Podeh, *Quest for Hegemony,* 100–103; Seale, *Struggle for Syria,* 208–12.

16. On Nasir's intention to receive economic and military aid from the West and especially from the United States, but to avoid Egyptian and Arab commitment to a military pact with the Western powers, see Stephens, *Nasir: A Political Biography,* 148.

17. Gardener (British ambassador in Syria) to FO, no. 17, 15 January 1955, PRO/FO/371/115484/V/1073/91.

18. Gardener (Damascus) to Rose (Levant Department, FO), 26 February 1955,

PRO/FO/371/115945/ VY/1015/12. According to the British ambassador in Lebanon, Sir Chapman Andrews, Sabri al-'Asli believed that the only way to save Syria was through Iraqi military intervention.

19. Eppel, "Iraqi-Syrian Relations, 1945–1958," 2:284–94.

20. On a conversation between Syrians and Tawfiq al-Suwaydi, who visited Damascus in May 1955, see Moose (Damascus) to Department of State, no. 695, 25 May 1955, 686.

On the proposals of Syrian defense minister Rashad Barmada, see testimony of Burhan al-Din Bash 'Aayan at his trial before the Special Revolutionary Court in 1958: Iraq, Wizarat Dif'ai, al-Mahakamat al-'Askariyya al-'Ulia al-Hassa (cited hereafter as Mahakamat al-Sha'b), 4:101; Gardener to FO, no. 483, 17 November 1955, PRO/FO/371/115954/VY/1039/18; Gardener (Damascus) to FO, no. 495, 25 November 1955, PRO/FO/371/115950/VY/1022/61.

21. Batatu, Old Social Classes, 752–57.

22. Al-Hayat (Beirut), 14 November 1956; British Broadcasting Corporation, Summary of World Broadcasting: The Middle East and Africa (cited hereafter as BBC, SWB), no. 98, 15 November 1956.

23. Podeh, Quest for Hegemony, 214–15.

24. Wright (Baghdad) to FO, no. 1238, 1 November 1956, PRO/FO/371/121489/ VJ/10393/176; Wright to FO, no. 1268, 3 November 1956, PRO/FO/371/121787/ VR/1091/557.

25. BBC, SWB, no. 107, 26 November 1956, no. 113, 3 December 1956; Al-Ba'th (Damascus), 27 November 1956; Al-Sha'b (Baghdad), 3 December 1956; Mideast Mirror (Beirut), 1 December 1956, 8 December 1956; Seale, Struggle for Syria, 272–82.

26. BBC, SWB, no. 112, 1 December 1956, no. 114, 4 December 1956, no. 147, 16 January 1957, no. 199, 7 January 1957; Al-Jumhuriyya (Cairo), 5 January 1957.

27. From FO to embassy in Baghdad, no. 2255, 11 September 1957, PRO/FO/ 371/128227/VY/1015/186.

28. Wright (Baghdad) to FO, no. 1292, 24 October 1957, PRO/FO/371/128243/ VY/10344/63.

29. Mahakamat al-Sha'b, 6:294–95.

30. Al-Suwaydi, Mudhakkirati, 571–74; Podeh, Quest for Hegemony, 230–34.

31. On the 'Ali Jawdat government, see Beaumont (Baghdad) to Selvin Lloyd, no. 251, 1 October 1957, PRO/FO/371/128041/VQ/1015/42; Beaumont (Baghdad) to Lloyd, no. 982, 13 August 1957, PRO/FO/371/128249/VY/10393/5. On 'Ali Jawdat's efforts to improve Iraqi relations with Syria and Nasir's Egypt, see Ahmad Mukhtar Baban, Mudhakkirat Ahmad Mukhtar Baban, Aahir Rais al-Wuzara Fi al-'Ahd al-Malaki Fi al-'Iraq, 233–38; 'Ali Jawdat al-Ayubi, Dhikriyyat, 1900–1958 (Beirut, 1967), 306–8; al-Hasani, Taarikh al-Wizarat, 10:175–78.

32. Al-Zaman (Baghdad), 15 September 1957, Mahakamat al-Sha'b, 4:330.

33. On the Government of the Arab Federation: Podeh, Quest for Hegemony, 239; al-Uzri, Taarikh, 544–621; al-Suwaydi, Mudhakkirati, 575–82.

34. Baban, Mudhakkirat, 194–211.

35. Wright (Baghdad) to FO, no. 162, 5 February 1958, PRO/FO/371/134386/

VY/10316/37; Wright to FO, no. 163, 5 February 1958, PRO/FO/371/133813/V/ 1072/1; Wright to FO, no. 343, 1 March 1958, PRO/FO/371/1338813/V/1072/39; BBC, SWB, no. 477, 15 February 1958; al-Suwaydi, *Mudhakkirati,* 583–85; Khadduri, "Nuri al-Sa'id's Disenchantment with Britain in His Last Years," 93; al-Uzri, *Taarikh,* 615–17, 621–29.

36. Khadduri, "Nuri al-Sa'id's Disenchantment."

37. Baban, *Mudhakkirat,* 202–3; al-Hasani, *Taarikh al- Wizarat,* 10:262.

Chapter 8. The 1958 Revolution and the Qasim Regime

1. Dann, *Iraq under Qassem,* 28–32; Khadduri, *Republican Iraq,* 40–43; Batatu, *Old Social Classes,* 800–807.

2. Dann, *Iraq under Qassem,* 30.

3. Khadduri, *Republican Iraq,* 44–46.

4. Ibid., 55–56; Lord Birdwood, *Nuri al-Sa'id: A Study in Arab Leadership,* 270.

5. See, for example, Thesiger's report on the developments in the relations between the tribal landowners and the tribesmen who became fellahin: "The Mass Movement of Tribesman."

6. Dann, *Iraq under Qassem,* 19–25; Batatu, *Old Social Classes,* 764–807.

7. Dann, *Iraq under Qassem,* 26.

8. *Al-Ahram,* 19 July 1958.

9. Dann, *Iraq under Qassem,* 13.

10. BBC, SWB, pt. 4, no. 612, 28 July 1958; Provisional Constitution of the Republic of Iraq, 27 July 1958, in Khalil, ed., *Arab States and the Arab League,* 1:30. See also Dann, *Iraq under Qassem,* 36–37.

11. Dann, *Iraq under Qassem,* 38–42.

12. *Mahakamat al-Sha'b.*

13. Batatu, *Old Social Classes,* 802.

14. Smolansky, *The Soviet Union and the Arab East under Khrushchev,* 104; *Pravda* (Moscow), 17 August 1958, full text.

15. Smolansky, *Soviet Union and the Arab East,* 109.

16. Ibid.; Khadduri, *Republican Iraq,* 158; Dann, *Iraq under Qassem,* 186–87.

17. Rashid Khalidi, "The Impact of the Iraqi Revolution on the Arab World."

18. *Al-Hayat,* 20 July 1958.

19. Dann, *Iraq under Qassem,* 74–75.

20. Ibid., 54–61; Farouk-Sluglett and Sluglett, *Iraq since 1958,* 76–78.

21. *Iraq Times,* 23 July 1958; Dann, *Iraq under Qassem,* 54.

22. Batatu, *Old Social Classes,* 841; Penrose and Penrose, *Iraq,* 248–49.

23. Sluglett, *Iraq since 1958,* 218–19.

24. United Nations, Department of International Economy and Social Affairs, *National Experience in Formulations and Implementation of Population Policy, 1958–1979,* 11.

25. Penrose and Penrose, *Iraq,* 248–49.

26. *Middle East Record, 1960,* 231.

27. One Iraqi dunam (or meshara) = 0.618 acre = 0.251 hectare = 2509 m^2.

28. Batatu, *Old Social Classes,* 57, 58–62, 837, 1115.

29. Iraq High Committee for Celebrations of the 14 July, *The Iraqi Revolution in Its Second Year,* 256.

30. *Iraq Times,* 1 October 1958; *Al-Zaman,* 3 October 1958.

31. Gabbay, *Communism and Agrarian Reform,* 116; Penrose and Penrose, *Iraq,* 250; Batatu, *Old Social Classes,* 837.

According to Iraqi data, by March 1961 about 4,381,500 dunams had been expropriated from 700 large landowners. These, along with state lands, accounted for a total of 5,396,000 dunams made available for distribution to the fellahin. Most of the plots were leased on a temporary basis. A total of 308,000 fellahin benefited from these lands. It should be noted that there is some degree of incompatibility in the official data published in Iraq. Iraq High Committee for Celebrations of the 14 July, *The Iraqi Revolution in Its Third Year.*

32. Haseeb, *National Income,* 42–43; Penrose and Penrose, *Iraq,* 243–45.

33. Jalal, *Role of Government,* 71.

34. Penrose and Penrose, *Iraq,* 253–55.

35. Batatu, *Old Social Classes,* 838–40.

36. Penrose and Penrose, *Iraq,* 254.

37. Batatu, *Old Social Classes,* 840, Haseeb, *National Income,* 17.

38. Dann, *Iraq under Qassem,* 54; statement by the prime minister concerning petroleum policy, 23 July 1958, in Khalil, ed., *Arab States and the Arab League,* 1:29–30.

39. *Iraq Times,* 9 April 1959.

40. Sluglett, *Iraq since 1958,* 78.

41. *Middle East Economic Digest* (Nicosia, Cyprus), 29 July 1960; *Middle East Record, 1960,* 269; Stocking, *Middle East Oil,* 218–19.

42. *Iraq Times,* 11 April 1961; Stocking, *Middle East Oil,* 213–39; *Middle East Record, 1961,* 291.

43. Longrigg, *Oil in the Middle East,* 355–56.

44. Ibid., 356.

45. Ibid., 351; Stocking, *Middle East Oil,* 352–53.

46. Dann, *Iraq under Qassem,* 73; Sluglett, *Iraq since 1958,* 58.

47. Khadduri, *Republican Iraq,* 87–88.

48. Ibid., 87.

49. Dann, *Iraq under Qassem,* 79.

50. Khadduri, *Republican Iraq,* 94; Dann, *Iraq under Qassem,* 81–84.

51. Dann, *Iraq under Qassem,* 127–35; Khadduri, *Republican Iraq,* 100–104.

52. Dann, *Iraq under Qassem,* 130.

53. Ibid., 151–53.

54. Ibid., 164–77; Batatu, *Old Social Classes,* 867–89.

55. Batatu, *Old Social Classes,* 866.

56. Khadduri, *Republican Iraq,* 110–11.

57. *Al-Ahram,* 27 January 1959.

58. Dann, *Iraq under Qassem,* 176.

59. Ibid., 193; Podeh, *The Decline of Arab Unity,* 85–88; Heikal, *The Sphinx and the Commissar,* 106–9.

60. Dann, *Iraq under Qassem*, 253–64.

61. Ibid., 263; *Al-Zaman*, 7 January 1960.

62. *Al-Ahram* (Cairo), 6 April 1959.

63. *Middle East Record, 1960*, 133.

64. *Middle East Record, 1960*, 132–38.

65. Batatu, *Old Social Classes*, 642.

66. See detailed tables in Batatu, *Old Social Classes*, 1175–76.

67. See chapter 1 for the 1941 suppression of the Rashid 'Ali revolt.

68. Dann, *Iraq under Qassem*, 177–218.

69. Ibid., 104–6.

70. Batatu, *Old Social Classes*, 894–97.

71. Dann, *Iraq under Qassem*, 207.

72. Ibid., 223–34; Batatu, *Old Social Classes*, 912–21.

73. *Middle East Record, 1960*, 243–44.

74. Dann, *Iraq under Qassem*, 144–45; Baram, "Two Roads to Revolutionary Shi'ite Fundamentalism in Iraq," 536–39. On the fatwa published by Muhsin al-Hakim, see *Die Welt des Islams* 6 (1959–60): 263–64; T. M. Aziz, "The Role of Muhammad Baqir al-Sadr in Shi'i Political Activism in Iraq from 1958 to 1980," 209.

75. Batatu, *Old Social Classes*, 945.

76. Ibid., 936–41; Dann, "Licensed Parties in Qasim's Iraq: An Experiment in Constitutionalism."

77. Saadi Ali, "The Events in Iraqi Kurdistan," *World Marxist Review*, March 1962.

78. Dann, "Licensed Parties"; Dann, *Iraq under Qassem*, 265–69; Khadduri, *Republican Iraq*, 139–43.

79. Dann, *Iraq under Qassem*, 269–310.

80. *Middle East Record, 1960*, 234.

81. Dann, *Iraq under Qassem*, 42, 143.

82. Ibid., 151–56.

83. *Middle East Record, 1960*, 246; Khadduri, *Republican Iraq*, 143.

84. See also Jawad, *Iraq and the Kurdish Question, 1958–1970*, 37–38.

85. McDowall, *Kurds*, 303.

86. Schmidt, *Journey among Brave Men*, 123.

87. Ghareeb, *The Kurdish Question in Iraq*, 39.

88. Schmidt, *Journey among Brave Men*, 75.

89. Dann, *Iraq under Qassem*, 334.

90. McDowall, *Kurds*, 308; Schmidt, *Journey among Brave Men*, 73.

91. McDowall, *Kurds*, 308; Edgar O'Ballance, *The Kurdish Revolt, 1961–1970*, 72.

92. *Al-Zaman*, 22 February 1961; Dann, *Iraq under Qassem*, 331; Jawad, *Iraq and the Kurdish Question*, 73.

93. McDowall, *Kurds*, 309; Jawad, *Iraq and the Kurdish Question*, 78–79; Edgar O'Ballance, *Kurdish Revolt*, 75.

94. Schmidt, *Journey among Brave Men*, 78.

95. *Middle East Record, 1961,* 285, based on *Al-Jihad* (Amman), 11 October 1961; *MENA,* 17 September 1961.

96. *Middle East Record, 1961,* 283–84.

97. McDowall, *Kurds,* 310–11; Jawad, *Iraq and the Kurdish Question,* 80–81; O'Ballance, *Kurdish Revolt,* 78, Schmidt, *Journey among Brave Men,* 77.

98. Jawad, *Iraq and the Kurdish Question,* 82.

99. O'Ballance, *Kurdish Revolt,* 87–88; Schmidt, *Journey among Brave Men,* 80–81.

100. O'Ballance, *Kurdish Revolt,* 97; Jawad, *Iraq and the Kurdish Question,* 108–10.

101. *Middle East Record, 1961,* 117–38.

102. Miriam Joyce, "Preserving the Sheikhdom"; Abadi, "Iraq's Threat to Kuwait during the Qasim Era"; Podeh, "'Suez in Reverse': The Arab Response to the Iraqi Bid for Kuwait, 1961–1963"; Shwadran, "The Kuwait Incident"; Finnie, *Shifting Lines in the Sand: Kuwait's Elusive Frontier with Iraq.*

Chapter 9. The Seizure of Power by the Ba'th and Its Overthrow in 1963.

1. Devlin, *The Ba'th Party: A History from Its Origins to 1966,* 7–23, 47–63; Kamel Abu Jaber, *The Arab Ba'th Socialist Party.*

2. 'Aflaq, *Fi Sabil al-Ba'th al-'Arabi;* 'Aflaq, *Ma'rakat al-Masir al-Wahid.*

3. Al-Razzaz, *Ma'lim al-Hayaa al-'Arabiya al-Jadida;* al-Hafiz, *Hawla B'ad Qadaya al-Thawra al-'Arabiyya;* al-Hafiz, ed., *Fi Fikr al-Siyasi.*

4. Devlin, *Ba'th Party,* 99–114.

5. Seale, *Struggle for Syria,* 307–25; Devlin, *Ba'th Party,* 79–97; Malcolm Kerr, *The Arab Cold War: Gamal 'Abd al-Nasir and His Rivals, 1958–1970,* 11–39.

6. Avraham Ben-Tsur, "The Neo-Ba'th Party of Syria"; Itamar Rabinovich, *Syria under the Ba'th: The Army Party Symbiosis,* 36–43; Devlin, *Ba'th Party,* 195–204.

7. Rabinovich, *Syria under the Ba'th,* 75–179.

8. Ibid., 180–208.

9. Abu Jaber, *Arab Ba'th Socialist Party,* 52; Batatu, *Old Social Classes,* 741.

10. According to Batatu, in 1952 the Ba'th Party in Iraq had only 50 members: *Old Social Classes,* 742. According to the detailed research performed by Ronel Zeidel, there were 170 Ba'th members in 1952: Zeidel, "The Iraqi Ba'th Party, 1948–1995: Personal and Organizational Aspects," 33.

11. Zeidel, "Iraqi Ba'th Party," 69–70. See membership lists for the regional leadership of the Ba'th in Iraq in Batatu, *Old Social Classes,* 748.

12. At the end of the twentieth century, the leaders of the two rival groups, Hani al-Fkaiki and Talib Shabib, published their memoirs, which give us two perspectives of the participants in the struggle in Iraq in 1963. Talib Shabib's memoirs were published as a continuous interview by 'Ali Karim Sa'id. On the relations between the Ba'th and Qasim, see Hani al-Fkaiki, *Awkar al-Hazima,* 81–135; 'Ali Karim Sa'id, ed., *Iraq 7 Shbat 1963 Min Hiwar al-Mafahim Ila Hiwar al-Dam Muraja't fi Dhakirati Talib Shabib,* 23–28 (hereinafter: Sa'id, *Talib Shabib*).

13. Sa'id, *Talib Shabib,* 26–35; al-Fkaiki, *Awkar al-Hazima,* 99–100. On the at-

tempted assassination and its consequences, see also Fuad al-Rikabi's own testimony: al-Rikabi, *Al-Hall al-Awhad*, 45–90.

14. Batatu, *Old Social Classes*, 966.

15. Al-Fkaiki, *Awkar al-Hazima*, 108.

16. Ibid., 217–19; Zeidel, "Iraqi Ba'th Party," 107–8.

17. Al-Fkaiki, *Awkar al-Hazima*, 216–19.

18. Sa'id, *Talib Shabib*, 165.

19. Dana Adams Schmidt, *Journey among Brave Men*, 248.

20. Al-Fkaiki, *Awkar al-Hazima*, 294.

21. Ibid., 217.

22. Sa'id, *Talib Shabib*, 47.

23. Batatu, *Old Social Classes*, 1010.

24. Khadduri, *Socialist Iraq: A Study in Iraqi Politics since 1968*, 15.

25. Al-Fkaiki, *Awkar al-Hazima*, 217–20.

26. For testimony by the leaders and participants of the 8 February revolution, see Sa'id, *Talib Shabib*, 61–128; Al-Fkaiki, *Awkar al-Hazima*, 229–54; 'Ali Khayun, *Dababat Ramadan, Qissat Thawra 14 Ramadan Fi al-'Iraq*. See also Batatu, *Old Social Classes*, 974–76; Khadduri, *Republican Iraq*, 189–96.

27. Batatu, *Old Social Classes*, 976–95; Sluglett, *Iraq since 1958*, 83–84; al-Fkaiki, *Awkar al-Hazima*, 254–56.

28. Aburish, *Saddam Hussein: The Politics of Revenge*, 54–60; Bulloch and Morris, *Saddam's War: The Origins of the Kuwait Conflict and the International Response*, 54.

29. Khadduri, *Republican Iraq*, 196–200.

30. Smolansky, *Soviet Union and the Arab East*, 224–39.

31. Ibid., 235–37.

32. Rabinovich, *Syria under the Ba'th*, 48–51.

33. Al-Fkaiki, *Awkar al-Hazima*, 289.

34. On the tripartite alliance talks in Cairo, see the transcript published by the Egyptians: *Mahadir Muhadathat al-Wahda*; Kerr, *Arab Cold War*, 44–77. On the Cairo talks from the Syrian perspective, see Rabinovich, *Syria under the Ba'th*, 59–66. For the Iraqi perspective, see the testimony by members of the Iraqi delegation: Sa'id, *Talib Shabib*, 205–27; al-Fkaiki, *Awkar al-Hazima* 286–91.

35. Rabinovich, *Syria under the Ba'th*, 66–84.

36. Kerr, *Arab Cold War*, 92–94.

37. O'Ballance, *Kurdish Revolt*, 99–100; Schmidt, *Journey among Brave Men*, 252–53.

38. Al-Durra, *Al-Qadiyya al-Kurdiyya*, 308; Jawad, *Iraq and the Kurdish Question*, 145.

39. Schmidt, *Journey among Brave Men*, 252.

40. Ibid., 254.

41. Ghareeb, *Kurdish Question*, 59–60.

42. Ibid., 64.

43. Schmidt, *Journey among Brave Men*, 259–60; Ghareeb, *Kurdish Question*, 60.

44. Khadduri, *Republican Iraq*, 270–71; Adamson, *The Kurdish War*, 208–15; Durra, *Al-Qadiyya al-Kurdiyya*, 308–9; Schmidt, *Journey among Brave Men*, 259–60; Jawad, *Iraq and the Kurdish Question*, 134–35.

45. Durra, *Al-Qadiyya al-Kurdiyya*, 315–17.

46. Schmidt, *Journey among Brave Men*, 264.

47. Ghareeb, *Kurdish Question*, 65–68.

48. Durra, *Al-Qadiyya al-Kurdiyya*, 344.

49. Al-Fkaiki, *Awkar al-Hazima*, 326.

50. Saʿid, *Talib Shabib*, 165–69.

51. Ibid., 172.

52. Ibid., 166.

53. Al-Fkaiki, *Awkar al-Hazima*, 282.

54. Ibid.

55. Ibid., 267–70; Saʿid, *Talib Shabib*, 149–240.

56. Batatu, *Old Social Classes*, 1020.

57. Khadduri, *Republican Iraq*, 211.

58. Sluglett, *Iraq since 1958*, 92–93; Batatu, *Old Social Classes*, 1016–18.

59. On the personal roots of the rivalry between Jawad and al-Saʿdi, see al-Fkaiki, *Awkar al-Hazima*, 173.

60. Bengio, ed., *The Reasons for the Collapse of the Baʿthi Regime in Iraq, 1963*, 48–49. The Baʿth document was presented to the Eighth National Congress of the Baʿth in April 1965.

61. Al-Fkaiki, *Awkar al-Hazima*, 205.

62. Batatu, *Old Social Classes*, 1018; al-Fkaiki, *Awkar al-Hazima*, 274.

63. Batatu, *Old Social Classes*, 1018.

64. Ibid., 1012.

65. Saʿid, *Talib Shabib*, 170.

66. Al-Fkaiki, *Awkar al-Hazima*, 312–15.

67. Devlin, *Baʿth Party*, 264.

68. Rabinovich, *Syria under the Baʿth*, 79–83.

69. Saʿid, *Talib Shabib*, 129–34.

70. Devlin, *Baʿth Party*, 262.

71. Al-Fkaiki, *Awkar al-Hazima*, 328; Aburish, *Saddam Hussein*, 62.

72. Saʿid, *Talib Shabib*, 174.

73. The detailed dramatic events of the party Congress were described twenty-five to thirty years thereafter by the leaders of the rival factions: Saʿid, *Talib Shabib*, 327–51; al-Fkaiki, *Awkar al-Hazima*, 348–51.

74. Devlin, *Baʿth Party*, 270; al-Fkaiki, *Awkar al-Hazima*, 356–58; Said, *Talib Shabib*, 328–30.

75. Batatu, *Old Social Classes*, 1023–24.

76. Said, *Talib Shabib*, 333.

77. Khadduri, *Republican Iraq*, 218.

Chapter 10. The Rule of the 'Arif Brothers, 1963–1968

1. On the influence of the Harakat Qawmiyyun al-'Arab (Arab Nationalist Movement) in Iraq, see Batatu, *Old Social Classes,* 1029–30.

The Harakat Qawmiyyun al-'Arab was established in Lebanon in 1949 by faculty and students at the University of Beirut. The ideology of the movement was pan-Arab nationalist. In its initial years, Qawmiyyun al-'Arab had a nationalist-rightist orientation; however, during the 1950s, with the strengthening of radical and leftist trends in the Arab world and the drift toward the left among pan-Arab nationalists, Qawmiyyun al-'Arab also adopted leftist trends. Some of its members were influenced by Marxist ideology and combined pan-Arab nationalism with leftist revolutionarism. In the late 1950s, the movement assumed a Nasirist nature, and its people began to view Nasir as the great leader of the Arab nation. Qawmiyyun al-'Arab did not become a mass movement in any Arab state, but its members filled key positions in regimes and political movements throughout the Arab world in the 1960s, 1970s, and 1980s.

2. On the Qasim regime, see chapter 8 above.

3. Sela, *Unity within Conflict in the Inter-Arab System,* 26–62.

4. Marr, *The Modern History of Iraq,* 192–95; Penrose and Penrose, *Iraq,* 324–25; Khadduri, *Republican Iraq,* 228–34.

5. Jawad, *Iraq and the Kurdish Question,* 155.

6. Ibid., 156–58.

7. O'Ballance, *Kurdish Revolt,* 119–22; Jawad, *Iraq and the Kurdish Question,* 159–73.

8. O'Ballance, *Kurdish Revolt,* 123; Gantner, 90; *New York Times,* 6 November 1964.

9. Jawad, *Iraq and the Kurdish Question,* 177–79.

10. Batatu, *Old Social Classes,* 1028.

11. Khadduri, *Republican Iraq,* 218–21.

12. Batatu, *Old Social Classes,* 1033–34; Khadduri, *Republican Iraq,* 244–46.

13. Al-Bazzaz, *Min Wuhi al-Uruba;* al-Bazzaz, *Buhuth fi al-Qawmiyya al-'Arabiyya;* al-Bazzaz, *Al-Dawla al-Muwahidda wa-al-Dawla al-Ittihadiya;* al-Bazzaz, *On Arab Nationalism.*

14. Khadduri, *Republican Iraq,* 252–54; Penrose and Penrose, *Iraq,* 333–51.

15. Marr, *Modern History,* 195–98; Sluglett, *Iraq since 1958,* 97–99; Khadduri, *Republican Iraq,* 256.

16. On al-Bazzaz's visit to the Soviet Union and his cordial welcome, see Haim Shemesh, *Soviet-Iraqi Relations, 1968–1988,* 11. On al-Bazzaz's attitude toward the Soviet Union and the Communist Party of Iraq, see al-Bazzaz, *Safhat Min Ams al-Qarib,* 9, 13, 35, 124–25.

17. Marr, *Modern History,* 197; Khadduri, *Republican Iraq,* 264–66.

18. Khadduri, *Republican Iraq,* 265.

19. Ibid., 273; Batatu, *Old Social Classes,* 1064.

20. Jawad, *Iraq and the Kurdish Question,* 198–99.

21. Ibid., 194–202; *Al-Jumhuriya* (Baghdad), 30 June 1966; Khadduri, *Republican Iraq*, 275–77.

22. Khadduri, *Republican Iraq*, 278–81.

23. Batatu, *Old Social Classes*, 1064.

24. Zeidel, "Iraqi Ba'th Party," 141; Amir Iskandar, *Saddam Husayn, Mundilan, Mufakiran Wa-Insanan*, 80.

25. Iskandar, *Saddam*, 101.

26. Ibid., 88.

27. Batatu, *Old Social Classes*, 1078–79.

28. Eberhard Kienle, *Ba'th v. Ba'th: The Conflict between Syria and Iraq, 1968–1989*, 37.

29. Iskandar, *Saddam*, 98–102.

30. Shwadran, *Middle East, Oil, and the Great Powers*, 270.

31. *Middle East Record, 1968*, 530–33.

32. Penrose and Penrose, *Iraq*, 466–67.

33. *Middle East Record, 1968*, 514; Batatu, *Old Social Classes*, 1069–70; Khadduri, *Socialist Iraq*, 80–81.

34. Maoism was a pro-Chinese trend in the Communist movement, named for Mao Tse-tung, longtime chairman of the Chinese Communist Party and of Communist China. This trend was more radical and "leftist" than Soviet Communism. Maoism emphasized the Socialist Revolution in Third World countries—developing countries in Asia, Africa, and Latin America—and viewed the peasantry as a force whose enlistment in the cause of the revolution would bring about the change that would lead to the establishment of a Communist regime.

35. Dann, "The Communist Movement in Iraq since 1963," 388–89.

36. Khadduri, *Republican Iraq*, 281–85; Penrose and Penrose, *Iraq*, 343–45.

37. *Middle East Record, 1967*, 350.

38. Khadduri, *Socialist Iraq*, 18.

39. Batatu, *Old Social Classes*, 1078–79.

40. Ibid., 1066; Sluglett, *Iraq since 1958*, 100.

41. Stocking, *Middle East Oil*, 304.

42. *Middle East Economic Survey* (London), 12 January 1968; Stocking, *Middle East Oil*, 306–8.

43. Stocking, *Middle East Oil*, 314–15.

44. *Middle East Record, 1968*, 514–15.

Chapter 11. The Rise of Saddam Husayn's Regime

1. Baram, "The Ruling Political Elite in Ba'thi Iraq, 1968–1986."

2. Farouk-Sluglett and Sluglett, *Iraq since 1958*, 112–23.

3. Bengio, *The Kurdish Revolution in Iraq*; Farouk-Sluglett and Sluglett, *Iraq since 1958*, 140–42.

4. Eppel, "Syrian-Iraqi Relations," 210–27; Eppel, "Syria: Iraq's Radical Nemesis"; Baram, "Ideology and Power Politics in Syrian-Iraqi Relations, 1968–1984."

5. Aziz, "The Role of Muhammad Baqir al-Sadr in Shi'i Political Activism in Iraq."

6. Baram, "Two Roads to Revolutionary Shi'ite Fundamentalism in Iraq"; Aburish, *Saddam Hussein,* 184–89.

7. Baram, "Re-inventing Nationalism in Ba'thi Iraq, 1968–1994." On comprehensive research about the discourse and ideology in Saddam's Iraq, see Bengio, *Saddam's Word: Political Discourse in Iraq.*

8. Jaber, "Shaykhs and Ideologues."

9. Baram, "Neo-Tribalism in Iraq: Saddam Hussein's Tribal Policies, 1991–1996."

10. Cordesman, *Iran and Iraq: The Threat from the Northern Gulf;* Cordesman, *The Iran-Iraq War;* Dilip, *The Longest War;* al-Azhary, *The Iran-Iraq War: A Historical, Economic, and Political Analysis;* Karsh, *The Iran-Iraq War;* Ismael, *Iraq and Iran: Roots of Conflict.*

11. Cordesman and Wagner, *The Gulf War.*

Bibliography

Abadi, Jacob. "Iraq's Threat to Kuwait during the Qasim Era." *Journal of South Asian and Middle Eastern Studies* 22 (1998): 1–22.

Abu Jaber, Kamel. *The Arab Ba'th Socialist Party: History, Ideology, and Organization.* Syracuse, N.Y.: Syracuse University Press, 1966.

Aburish, Saïd K. *Saddam Hussein: The Politics of Revenge.* New York: Bloomsbury, 2000.

Adams, Doris G. "Current Population Trends in Iraq." *Middle East Journal* 10 (1956): 151–64.

Adamson, David. *The Kurdish War.* London: G. Allen and Unwin, 1964.

Aflaq, Michel. *Ma'rakat al-Masir al-Wahid* (The battle of the one destiny). Beirut, 1958.

———. *Fi Sabil al-Ba'th al-'Arabi* (On the road of renaissance). Beirut, 1959, 1963.

al-'Alawi, Hasan. *Al-Shi'a wa-al-Dawla al-Qawmiyya fi al-'Iraq, 1914–1990.* N.p., 1990.

Anderson, J. N. D. "A Law of Personal Status for Iraq." *International and Comparative Law Quarterly* 9 (1960): 542–63.

———. "Changes in the Law of Personal Status in Iraq." *International and Comparative Law Quarterly* 12 (1963): 1026–31.

Aswad, 'Abd al-Razzaq Muhammad, ed. *Mawsuwat al-'Iraq al-Siyasiyya.* 6 vols. Beirut: al-Dar al-'Arabiyya al-Mawsumat, 1986.

Atiyah, Ghassan R. *Iraq, 1908–1921: A Socio-Political Study.* Beirut: Arab Institute for Research and Publications, 1973.

al-Ayubi, 'Ali Jawdat. *Dhikriyyat, 1900–1958.* Beirut, 1967.

al-Azhary, M. S. *The Iran-Iraq War: A Historical, Economic, and Political Analysis.* New York: St. Martin's Press, 1984.

Aziz, T. M. "The Role of Muhammad Baqir al-Sadr in Shi'i Political Activism in Iraq from 1958 to 1980." *International Journal of Middle Eastern Studies* 25 (1993): 207–22.

Baban, Ahmad Mukhtar. *Mudhakkirat Ahmad Mukhtar Baban, Aahir Rais al-Wuzara fi al-'Ahd al-Malaki fi al-'Iraq.* Beirut: al-Muasasat al-'Arabiyya Lildirasat Wa-al-Nashr, 1999.

Baram, Amatzia. "Culture in the Service of Wataniyya: The Treatment of Mesopotamian-Inspired Art in Ba'thi Iraq." *AAS* 17 (1983): 265–313.

———. "Mesopotamian Identity in Ba'thi Iraq." *Middle Eastern Studies* 19 (1983): 426–55.

———. "Ideology and Power Politics in Syrian-Iraqi Relations, 1968–1984." In *Syria under Assad,* ed. Moshe Ma'oz and Avner Yaniv. London: Croom Helm, 1986.

———. "The Ruling Political Elite in Ba'thi Iraq, 1968–1986: The Changing Features of Collective Profile." *International Journal of Middle Eastern Studies* 21 (1989): 447–93.

———. *Culture, History, and Ideology in the Formation of Ba'th Iraq, 1968–1989.* London: Macmillan, 1991.

———. "A Case of Imported Identity: The Modernizing Secular Elites of Iraq and the Concept of Mesopotamian-Inspired Territorial Nationalism, 1922–1992." *Poetics Today* 15 (summer 1994): 279–319.

———. "Two Roads to Revolutionary Shi'ite Fundamentalism in Iraq." In *Accounting for Fundamentalisms: The Dynamic Character of Movements,* ed. Martin E. Marty and R. Scott Appleby, 531–90. Chicago: University of Chicago Press, 1994.

———. "Re-Inventing Nationalism in Ba'thi Iraq, 1968–1994." *Princeton Papers,* no. 5 (1996).

———. "Neo-Tribalism in Iraq: Saddam Hussein's Tribal Policies, 1991–1996." *International Journal of Middle Eastern Studies* 29 (1997).

Baram, Amatzia, and Barry Rubin, eds. *Iraq's Road to War.* New York: St. Martin's Press, 1993.

al-Barazi, Muhsin. *Al-Mudhakkirat Muhsin al-Barazi, 1947–1948.* Edited by Khayriyya Qasmiyya. Beirut, 1994.

Barker, A. J. *The Neglected War: Mesopotamia, 1914–1918.* London: Faber, 1967.

Batatu, Hanna. *The Old Social Classes and the Revolutionary Movements of Iraq.* Princeton, N.J.: Princeton University Press, 1978.

———. "Class Analysis and Iraqi Society." In *Arab Society: Social Science Perspectives,* ed. Saad Eddin Ibrahmin and Nicholas S. Hopkins, 379–92. Cairo: American University in Cairo Press, 1985.

al-Bazzaz, 'Abd al-Rahman. *Al-Dawla al-Muwahidda wa-al-Dawla al-Ittihadiya* (The United States and the federated state). Baghdad, 1958.

———. *Min Wuhi al-'Uruba* (Inspiration of Arabism). Cairo: Dar al-Qalima, n.d.

———. *Safhat Min Ams al-Qarib* (Pages from the recent past). Beirut: Dar Lilmalain, 1960.

———. *Buhuth fi al-Qawmiyya al-'Arabiyya* (Studies in Arab nationalism). Cairo: Jami'at al-Duwal al-'Arabiyya, 1962.

———. *On Arab Nationalism.* London, 1965.

Beeri, Eliezer. *Army Officers in Arab Politics and Society.* New York: Praeger, 1970.

Bell, Lady Florence. *The Letters of Gertrude Bell.* London: Boni and Liveright, 1927.

Bengio, Ofra. "Saddam Husayn's Quest for Power and Survival." *AAS* 15 (1981): 323–42.

———. "Shi'is and Politics in Ba'thi Iraq." *Middle Eastern Studies* 21 (1985): 1–15.

———. *The Kurdish Revolution in Iraq.* Tel Aviv, 1989 (Hebrew).

———. "Iraq: Shi'a and Kurdish Communities from Resentment to Revolt." In *Iraq's Road to War,* ed. Amatzia Baram and Barry Rubin, 51–97. New York: St. Martin's Press, 1993.

———. "Nation-Building in Multiethnic Societies. The Case of Iraq." In *Minorities and State in the Arab World*, ed. Ofra Bengio and Gabriel Ben Dor. Boulder, Colo.: Westview, 1997.

———. *Saddam's Word: Political Discourse in Iraq*. New York: Oxford University Press, 1998.

———, ed., *The Reasons for the Collapse of the Ba'thi Regime in Iraq, 1963*. Tel Aviv, 1981 (Hebrew).

Ben-Tsur, Avraham. "The Neo-Ba'th Party of Syria." *Journal of Contemporary History* 3 (1968): 161–81.

Birdwood, Lord. *Nuri al-Sa'id: A Study in Arab Leadership*. London: Cassell, 1959.

Brown, Michael S. "The Nationalization of the Iraqi Petroleum Company." *International Journal of Middle Eastern Studies* 10 (1979): 107–29.

Bruinessen, Martin van. *Agha, Shaikh, and State: The Social and Political Structures of Kurdistan*. London: Zed Books, 1992.

Bulloch, John, and Harvey Morris. *Saddam's War: The Origins of the Kuwait Conflict and the International Response*. London: Faber and Faber, 1991.

Butti, Rafail. *Dhakkirat 'Iraqiyya, 1900–1956*. 2 vols. Edited by Faiq Butti. Damascus: al-Mada, 2000.

Cohen, Stuart. *British Policy in Mesopotamia, 1903–1914*. Oxford: St. Antony's College, 1976.

Cordesman, Anthony H. *The Lessons of Modern War*. Vol. 2: *The Iran-Iraq War*. Boulder, Colo.: Westview Press, 1990.

———. *Iran and Iraq: The Threat from the Northern Gulf*. Boulder, Colo.: Westview Press, 1994.

Cordesman, Anthony H., and Abraham R. Wagner. *The Lessons of Modern War*. Vol. 4: *The Gulf War*. Boulder, Colo.: Westview Press, 1996.

Dann, Uriel. "Licensed Parties in Qasim's Iraq: An Experiment in Constitutionalism." *Asian and African Studies* 3 (1967): 1–33.

———. *Iraq under Qassem: A Political History, 1958–1963*. Jerusalem: Israel Universities Press, 1969.

———. "The Communist Movement in Iraq since 1963." In *The USSR and Middle East*, ed. Michael Confino and Shimon Shamir, 377–94. New York: Wiley; Jerusalem: Israel Universities Press, 1973.

Dawr Al-Jaish Al-'Iraqi fi Harb Al-Tishrin 1973 (The role of the Iraqi Army in the October War, 1973). Beirut: 'Idad Al-Markaz Al-'Arabi Lildirasat Al-Istratijiyya, Al-Muasasat Al-'Arabiyya Lil-Dirasat Wa-Nashr, 1975.

Devlin, John F. *The Ba'th Party: A History from Its Origins to 1966*. Stanford, Calif.: Hoover Institution Press, 1976.

Dilip, Hiro. *The Longest War: The Iran-Iraq Conflict*. London: Grafton Books, 1989.

al-Durra, Mahmud. *Al-Qadiyya al-Kurdiyya* (The Kurdish problem). Beirut, 1966.

———. *Al-Harb al-'Iraqiyya al-Britaniyya, 1941*. Beirut, 1969.

Efrati, Noga. "Women, Elites, and Discourse in Pre-Revolutionary Iraq, 1932–1958." Ph.D. diss., University of Haifa, 2001.

Elliot, Matthew. *"Independent Iraq": The Monarchy and British Influence, 1941–1958*. London: Tauris Academic Studies, 1996.

Eppel, Michael. "The Hikmat Suleyman-Bakr Sidqi Government in Iraq, 1936–37, and the Palestine Question." *Middle Eastern Studies* 24 (1988): 25–41.

———. "Iraqi-Syrian Relations, 1945–1958." Ph.D. diss., Tel Aviv University, 1990 (Hebrew).

———. "The Iraqi Domestic Scene and Its Bearing on the Question of Palestine." *AAS* 24 (1990): 51–73.

———. "Iraqi Politics and Regional Policies, 1945–1949." *Middle Eastern Studies* 28 (1992): 108–19.

———. "Syria: Iraq's Radical Nemesis." In *Iraq's Road to War,* ed. Amatzia Baram and Barry Rubin, 177–90. New York: St. Martin's Press, 1993.

———. *The Palestine Conflict in the History of Modern Iraq: The Dynamics of Involvement, 1928–1948.* London: Frank Cass, 1994.

———. "Nuri al-Sa'id and 'Abd al-Ilah's Ambitions in Syria." In *The Hashemites in the Modern Arab World: Essays in Honour of the Late Professor Uriel Dann,* ed. Asher Susser and Aryeh Shmuelevitz, 152–63. London: Frank Cass, 1995.

———. "The Elite, the Effendiyya, and the Growth of Nationalism and Pan-Arabism in Hashemite Iraq, 1921–1958." *International Journal of Middle Eastern Studies* 30 (1998): 227–50.

———. "The Decline of British Influence and the Ruling Elite in Iraq." In *The Demise of the British Empire in the Middle East,* ed. Michael J. Cohen and Martin Kolinsky, 185–97. London: Frank Cass, 1998.

———. "The Fadhil al-Jamali Government in Iraq, 1953–1954." *Journal of Contemporary History* 34 (1999): 417–42.

———. "Syrian-Iraqi Relations: Iraq as a Factor in Syrian Foreign Policy." In *Modern Syria: From Ottoman Rule to Pivotal Role in the Middle East,* ed. Moshe Ma'oz, Joseph Ginat, and Onn Winckler, 210–27. Brighton: Sussex Academic Press, 1999.

Farouk-Sluglett, Marion, and Peter Sluglett. "The Transformation of Land Tenure and Rural Social Structure in Central and Southern Iraq, 1870–1958." *International Journal of Middle Eastern Studies* 15 (1983): 491–505.

———. *Iraq since 1958: From Revolution to Dictatorship.* London: KPI, 1987.

———. "Labor and National Liberation: The Trade Union Movement in Iraq, 1920–1958." *Arab Studies Quarterly* 5 (1987): 139–54.

al-Far'un, Fariq al-Muzhir. *Al-Haqaiq al-Nasia fi al-Iraqiya Sanat 1920 wa-Nataijaha.* Baghdad, 1952.

Fernea, Elizabeth Warnock. *Guests of the Sheik.* Garden City, N.Y.: Doubleday, 1969.

Fernea, Robert A. *Shaykh and Effendi: Changing Patterns of Authority among the Shabana of Southern Iraq.* Cambridge: Harvard University Press, 1970.

Fernea, Robert, and Wm. Roger Louis, eds. *The Iraqi Revolution of 1958: The Old Social Classes Revisited.* London: I. B. Tauris, 1991.

Finnie, David H. *Shifting Lines in the Sand: Kuwait's Elusive Frontier with Iraq.* Cambridge: Harvard University Press, 1992.

al-Fkaiki, Hani. *Awkar al-Hazima.* London, 1993.

Foster, H. A. *The Making of Modern Iraq*. Norman: University of Oklahoma Press, 1935.

Franck, Dorothea Seelye, and Peter G. Franck. "Economic Review: The Middle East Economy in 1948." *Middle East Journal* 3 (1949): 201–20.

Gabbay, Rony. *Communism and Agrarian Reform in Iraq*. London: Croom Helm, 1978.

Gallman, Waldemar. *Iraq under General Nuri*. Baltimore: Johns Hopkins University Press, 1970.

Gat, Moshe. *Jewish Exodus from Iraq, 1948–1951*. London: Frank Cass, 1997.

Gerke, Grewin. "The Iraqi Development Board and the British Policy, 1945–1950." *Middle Eastern Studies* 27 (1991): 231–54.

Ghareeb, Edmund. *Al-Haraka al-Qawmiyya al-Kurdiyya*. Beirut, 1973.

———. *The Kurdish Question in Iraq*. Syracuse, N.Y.: Syracuse University Press, 1981.

Gomaa, Ahmad. *The Foundation of the League of Arab States*. London, 1977.

Grassmuck, George. "The Electoral Process in Iraq, 1952–1958." *Middle East Journal* 14 (1960): 397–415.

Gunter, M. Michael. *The Kurds of Iraq: Tragedy and Hope*. New York: St. Martin's Press, 1996.

Haddad, Uthman Kamal. *Harakat Rashid 'Ali al-Kaylani*. Sidon, 1959.

al-Hafiz, Yasin. *Hawla B'ad Qadaya al-Thawra al-'Arabiyya* (About some problems of the Arab revolution). Beirut, 1965.

———, ed. *Fi Fikr al-Siyasi* (On political thought). Damascus, 1963.

Haj, Samira. "The Problems of Tribalism: The Case of Nineteenth-Century Iraq." *Social History* 16 (1991): 45–58.

———. *The Making of Iraq, 1900–1963: Capital, Power, and Ideology*. Ithaca, N.Y.: State University of New York Press, 1997.

Haldane, A. L., Sir. *The Insurrection in Mesopotamia, 1920*. Edinburgh, 1922.

Hamdi, Walid M. *Rashid 'Ali al-Gailani and the Nationalist Movement in Iraq, 1939–1941*. London: Darf, 1987.

Hasan, M. S. "The Role of Foreign Trade in Economic Development of Iraq, 1864–1964: A Study of Development of a Dependent Economy." In *Studies in Economic History of the Middle East*, ed. M. A. Cook. London, 1970.

Haseeb, K. *The National Income of Iraq, 1953–1961*. New York: Oxford University Press, 1964.

al-Hasani, 'Abd al-Razzaq. *Al-Thawra al-Iraqiyya al-Kubra*. Sidon, 1952.

———. *Asrar al-Khafiyya fi al-Hawadith al-Sana, 1941*. Sidon, 1958.

———. *Taarikh al-Wizarat al-'Iraqiyya* (The history of governments of Iraq). 8 vols. Sidon, 1958–61.

———. *Al-Usul al-Rasmiyya Li-Taarikh al-Wizarat al-Ìraqiyya fi 'Ahd al-Malki al-Zail*. Sidon: al-'Urfan, 1964.

al-Hashimi, Taha. *Mudhakkirat Taha al-Hashimi*. 2 vols. Beirut, 1978.

Hassanpour, Amir. *Nationalism and Language in Kurdistan, 1918–1925*. San Francisco: Mellen Research University Press, 1992.

Heikal, Muhammad Hassanein. *The Sphinx and the Commissar.* London: Collins, 1978.

Hemphill, Paul. "The Formation of the Iraqi Army, 1921–1933." In *The Integration of Modern Iraq,* ed. Abbas Kelidar. London: Croom Helm, 1979.

Hirszowicz, Lukasz. *The Third Reich and the Arab East* (Toronto: Toronto University Press, 1966).

Hurewitz, J. L. *Diplomacy in the Near and Middle East,* vol. 2, 1914–1956. Princeton: Princeton University Press, 1956.

Husayn, Jamil. *Al-'Iraq, Shahada Siasiya, 1929–1950.* London, 1987.

International Bank for Reconstruction and Development. *The Economic Development of Iraq.* Baltimore: Johns Hopkins University Press, 1952.

Iraq High Committee for Celebrations of the 14 July. *The Iraqi Revolution in Its Second Year.* Baghdad, 1960.

———. *The Iraqi Revolution in Its Third Year.* Baghdad, 1961.

Iraq Ministry of Economics. *Laborers' Cost of Living Index.* Baghdad, 1946.

———. *Report of the Industrial Census of Iraq.* Baghdad, 1956.

Iraq, Wizarat Dif'ai (Defense Ministry of Iraq). *al-Mahakamat al-'Askariyya al-'Ulia al-Hassa* (Mahakamat al-Sha'b) (Proceedings of the Special Revolutionary Court). 23 vols. Baghdad, 1959–62.

Ireland, Philip. *Iraq: A Study in Political Development.* London: J. Cape, 1937.

Iskandar, Amir. *Saddam Husayn, Munadilan, Mufakiran wa-Insanan* (Saddam Husayn, the fighter, the thinker, the man). Paris: Hachette, 1980.

Ismael, Tariq. *Iraq and Iran: Roots of Conflict.* Syracuse: Syracuse University Press, 1982.

Jaber, A. Faleh. "Shaykhs and Ideologues, Detribalization and Retribalization in Iraq, 1968–1998." *Middle East Report* 125 (summer 2000): 28–31.

al-Jaburi, Salih Saib. *Mihnat Filastin* (The experience of Palestine). Beirut, 1970.

al-Jadirji, Kamil. *Mudhakkirat Kamil al-Jadirji, Wa-Taarikh al-Hizb al-Watani al-Dimuqrati.* Beirut: Dar al-Tali'a, 1970.

Jalal, Ferhang. *The Role of Government in the Industrialization of Iraq, 1950–1965.* London: Frank Cass, 1972.

al-Jamali, Muhammad Fadhil. *Al-'Iraq Bayn Ams Wa-al-Yawm.* Baghdad, 1954.

———. "Iraq under General Nuri." *Middle East Forum* 40 (1964): 12–25.

———. *Mawaqif wa-'ibar fi siyasatina al-duwaliyya: safhat min taarikhuna al-muasir* (Situations and lessons in our international politics: Pages from our modern history). Tunis: al-Sharika al-Tunisiyya Liltawzi'i, 1991.

Jami'at al-Duwal al-'Arabiyya. *Madabit Jalsat Dawr al-Ijtima'i al-'Aadi al-Hadi 'Ashar Limajlis al-Jami'at* (Proceedings of the Eleventh Gathering of the League of Arab States). 17 October 1949.

Jawad, Saad. *Iraq and the Kurdish Question, 1958–1970.* London: Ithaca Press, 1981.

Joyce, Miriam. "Preserving the Shiekhdom: London, Washington, Iraq, and Kuwait, 1958–1961." *Middle Eastern Studies* 31 (1995): 281–92.

Jwaidah, Albertine. "Midhat Pasha and the Land System in Lower Iraq." *St. Antony's Papers: Middle Eastern Affairs* 3 (1963): 106–36.

———. "Aspects of Land Tenure and Social Change in Lower Iraq during the Late Ottoman Period." In *Land Tenure and Social Transformation in the Middle East,* ed. T. Khalidi. Beirut, 1984.

Karsh, Efraim. *The Iran-Iraq War: Impact and Implications.* London and Tel Aviv: Macmillan and Jaffe Center, 1989.

Kedourie, Elie. "Anti-Shiʿism in Iraq under the Monarchy." *Middle Eastern Studies* 24 (1988): 249–53.

———. "The Shiʿite Issue in Iraqi Politics, 1941." *Middle Eastern Studies* 24 (1988): 495–500.

Kelidar, Abbas. *Iraq: The Search for Stability.* London, 1975.

———. "Aziz al-Haj: A Communist Radical." In *The Integration of Modern Iraq,* ed. Abbas Kelidar. London: Croom Helm, 1979.

———, ed. *The Integration of Modern Iraq.* London: Croom Helm, 1979.

Kent, Marian. *Oil and Empire: British Policy and Mesopotamian Oil, 1900–1920.* New York: Barnes and Noble, 1976.

Kerr, Malcolm. *The Arab Cold War: Gamal ʿAbd al-Nasir and His Rivals, 1958–1970.* London: Oxford University Press, 1971.

Khadduri, Majid. *Independent Iraq, 1932–1958: A Study in Iraqi Politics.* London: Oxford University Press, 1960.

———. "General Nuri's Flirtation with the Axis Powers." *Middle East Journal* 16 (1962): 328–36.

———. *Republican Iraq: A Study in Iraqi Politics since the Revolution of 1958.* London: Oxford University Press, 1969.

———. *Socialist Iraq: A Study in Iraqi Politics since 1968.* Washington, D.C.: Middle East Institute, 1978.

———. "Nuri al-Saʿid's Disenchantment with Britain in His Last Years." *Middle East Journal* 34 (1999): 83–96.

Khalidi, Rashid. "The Impact of the Iraqi Revolution on the Arab World." In *The Iraqi Revolution of 1958: The Old Social Classes Revisited,* ed. Robert A. Fernea and Wm. Roger Louis, 106–17. London: I. B. Tauris, 1991.

Khalil, Muhammad, ed. *The Arab States and the Arab League.* 2 vols. Beirut, 1962.

al-Khalil, Samir (Kanan Makiya). *Republic of Fear.* London: Hutchinson Radius, 1989.

———. *The Monument: Art, Vulgarity, and Responsibility in Iraq.* Berkeley: University of California Press, 1991.

al-Khamasi, ʿAbd al-Hadi. *Al-Amir ʿAbd al-Ilah.* Beirut: al-Muasasat al-ʿArabiyya Lildrasay Wa-al-Nashr, 2001.

Khayun, ʿAli. *Dababat Ramadan, Qissat Thawra 14 Ramadan fi al-Iraq* (Tanks of Ramadan: The story of the 14th of Ramadan revolution in Iraq). Baghdad, 1989.

Khoury, Dina Rizk. *State and Provincial Society in Ottoman Empire: Mosul, 1540–1834.* Cambridge: Cambridge University Press, 1998.

Kienle, Eberhard. *Baʿth v. Baʿth: The Conflict between Syria and Iraq, 1968–1989.* London: I. B. Tauris, 1990.

Klieman, Aaron. *Foundations of British Policy in the Arab World: The Cairo Conference of 1921.* Baltimore: Johns Hopkins University Press, 1970.

Kubba, Muhammad Mahdi. *Mudhakkirati fi Samim al-Ahdath, 1918–1958*. (My memoirs from the heart to events). Beirut, 1963.

Langley, Kathleen M. *The Industrialization of Iraq*. Cambridge: Harvard University Press, 1961.

Litvak, Meir. *Shi'i Scholars of Nineteenth-Century Iraq: The 'Ulama of Najaf and Karbala*. New York: Cambridge University Press, 1998.

Longrigg, Stephen Hemsley. *Four Centuries of Modern Iraq*. London, 1925.

———. *Iraq, 1900 to 1950*. New York: Oxford University Press, 1953.

———. *Oil in the Middle East: Its Discovery and Development*. New York: Oxford University Press, 1961.

Louis, Wm. Roger. *The British Empire in the Middle East, 1945–1951*. Oxford: Claredon Press, 1984.

Lukitz, Liora. *Iraq: The Search for National Identity*. London: Frank Cass, 1995.

MacDonald, A. D. "The Political Developments in Iraq Leading Up to the Rising in the Spring of 1935." *Journal of Royal Central Asian Society* 23 (1936): 27–44.

Maddy-Weitzman, Bruce. *The Crystallization of the Arab State System, 1945–1954*. Syracuse, N.Y.: Syracuse University Press, 1993.

Mahadir Muhadathat al-Wahda. Transcript of the Unity Talks. Cairo: Muasasat al-Ahram, 1963.

Main, Ernest. *Iraq from Mandate to Independence*. London: G. Allen and Unwin, 1935.

Makiya, Kanan (Samir al-Khalil). *Cruelty and Silence: War, Tyranny, Uprising, and the Arab World*. New York: W. W. Norton, 1993.

Mardan, Jamal Mustafa. *'Abd al-Karim Qasim: al-Bidaya Wa-al-Sukut*. Baghdad, 1989.

Marr, Phebe. "Yasin al-Hashimi: The Rise and Fall of a Nationalist, 1920–1936." Ph.D. diss., Harvard University, 1966.

———. *The Modern History of Iraq*. Boulder, Colo.: Westview Press; London: Longman, 1985.

———. "The Development of a Nationalist Ideology in Iraq, 1920–1941." *Muslim World* 75 (1986): 86–101.

Masalha, Nur al-Din. "Faisal's Pan-Arabism." *Middle Eastern Studies* 27 (1991): 679–91.

McDowall, David. *A Modern History of the Kurds*. London: I. B. Tauris, 1996.

Mejchner, Helmut. *Imperial Quest for Oil: Iraq, 1910–1928*. London: Ithaca Press, 1976.

Middle East Record, 1960. Ed. Yitzhak Oron. Tel Aviv: Israel Oriental Society and Review, Shiloah Research Center for Middle Eastern and African Studies; and London: Weinfeld and Nicolson, 1962.

Middle East Record, 1961. Ed. Yitzhak Oron. Tel Aviv: Tel Aviv University, Shiloah Research Center for Middle Eastern and African Studies, 1963.

Middle East Record, 1967. Ed. Daniel Dishon. Tel Aviv: Tel Aviv University, Shiloah Center for Middle Eastern and African Studies, Israel Universities Press, 1971.

Middle East Record, 1968. Ed. Daniel Dishon. Tel Aviv: Tel Aviv University, Shiloah Center for Middle Eastern and African Studies, Israel Universities Press, 1973.

Middle East Record, 1969–1970. Ed. Daniel Dishon. Tel Aviv: Israel Universities Press, 1977.

Millar, Ronald William. *Death of an Army: The Siege of Kut, 1915–1916.* Boston: Houghton Mifflin, 1970.

Musayn, Fadhil. *Taarikh al-Hizb al-Watani al-Dimuqrati, 1942–1958.* Baghdad, 1963.

Mushtaq, Talib. *Awrak Ayyami.* Beirut, 1968.

Nakash, Yitzhak. *The Shi'is of Iraq.* Princeton: Princeton University Press, 1994.

Nieuewenhuis, Tom. *Politics and Society in Early Modern Iraq: Mamluk Pashas, Tribal Shaykhs, and Local Rule between 1802 and 1831.* The Hague: Marting Nijhoff, 1982.

O'Ballance, Edgar. *The Kurdish Revolt, 1961–1970.* Hamden, Conn.: Archon Books, 1973.

———. *The Kurdish Struggle, 1920–94.* New York: St. Martin's Press, 1996.

Olson, Robert. "Battle for Kurdistan: The Churchill–Cox Correspondence Regarding the Creation of the State of Iraq." *Kurdish Studies* 5 (1992): 29–44.

Owen, Nicolas. "British and Decolonization: The Labour Governments and the Middle East." In *Demise of the British Empire in the Middle East,* ed. Michael J. Cohen and Martin Kolinsky, 3–22. London: Frank Cass, 1998.

Penrose, Edith, and E. F. Penrose. *Iraq: International Relations and National Development.* Boulder, Colo.: Westview Press, 1978.

Philips, Doris G. "Rural to Urban Migration in Iraq." *Economic Development and Cultural Change* 20 (1959): 405–21.

Podeh, Elie. *The Quest for Hegemony in the Arab World: The Struggle over the Baghdad Pact.* New York: A. E. J. Brill, 1995.

———. *The Decline of Arab Unity: The Rise and Fall of the United Arab Republic.* Brighton: Sussex Academic Press, 1999.

———. "Suez in Reverse: The Arab Response to the Iraqi Bid for Kuwait, 1961–1963." *Diplomacy and Statecraft* 14 (2003): 103–30.

Pool, David. "From Elite to Class: The Transformation of Iraqi Leadership, 1920–1939." *International Journal of Middle Eastern Studies* 12 (1980): 331–49.

Porath, Yehoshua. *In the Search of Arab Unity, 1930–1945.* London: Frank Cass, 1986.

al-Qassab, 'Abd-al-'Aziz. *Min Mudhakkirati.* Beirut, 1962.

al-Qazzaz, Ayad. "Power Elite in Iraq, 1920–1958." *Muslim World* 61 (1971): 267–82.

Qubain, Fahim I. *The Reconstruction of Iraq, 1950–1957.* London: Stevens, 1958.

Rabinovich, Itamar. *Syria under the Ba'th, 1963–66: The Army Party Symbiosis.* Jerusalem: Israel Universities Press, 1972.

al-Rawi, 'Adnan. *Min Al-Qahira Ila Muatkal Qasim.* Beirut, 1963.

al-Razzaz, Munif. *Ma'lim al-Hayaa al-'Arabiya al-Jadida* (Landmarks of the New Arab Life). Cairo, 1953.

Riad, Mahmud. *Mudhakkirat Mahmud Riad.* 2 vols. Cairo, 1986.

al-Rikabi, Fuad. *Al-Hall al-Awhad.* Cairo, 1964.

Sabbagh, Salah al-Din. *Fursan al-ʿUruba fi al-Iraq* (The knights of Arabism in Iraq). Damascus, 1956.

Saʿid, Ali Karim, ed. *Iraq 7 Shbat 1963, Min Hiwar al-Mafahim Ila Hiwar al-Dam, Murajaʿt fi Dhakirati Talib Shabib* (Iraq of February 8, 1963, from the dialogue of conceptions to the dialogue of blood, interviews in Talib Shabib's memory). Adabiyah, 1999.

al-Saʿigh, Najib. *Min Awrak Najib al-Saʿigh fi ʿAhdain al-Malqi Wa-al-Jumhuri, 1947–1963.* Baghdad, 1996.

Salter, Lord. *The Development of Iraq: A Plan of Action.* Baghdad: Iraq Development Board, 1955.

Sassoon, Joseph. "Industrial Development in Iraq, 1958–1968." *Hamizrah Hehadash* 30 (1981): 21–49.

———. *Economic Policy in Iraq, 1932–1950.* London: Frank Cass, 1987.

Schmidt, Dana Adams. *Journey among Brave Men.* Boston: Little, Brown, 1964.

Schofield, Richard, ed. *Kuwait and Iraq: Historical Claims and Territorial Disputes.* London: Royal Institute of International Affairs, 1991.

Seale, Patrick. *The Struggle for Syria: A Study of Post-War Arab Politics, 1945–1958.* New Haven: Yale University Press, 1986.

Sela, Avraham. *Unity within Conflict in the Inter-Arab System.* Jerusalem, 1982. (Hebrew).

———. *The Decline of the Arab-Israel Conflict, Middle East Politics and the Quest for Regional Order.* New York: State University of New York Press, 1998.

Shemesh, Haim. *Soviet-Iraqi Relations, 1968–1988: In the Shadow of the Iraq-Iran Conflict.* Boulder, Colo.: Lynne Rienner, 1992.

Shikarah, Ahmad Abd al-Razzaq. *Iraqi Politics, 1921–41: The Interaction between Domestic Politics and Foreign Policy.* London: LAAM, 1987.

Shwadran, Benjamin. *The Power Struggle in Iraq.* New York: Council for Middle Eastern Affairs Press, 1960.

———. "The Kuwait Incident." *Middle Eastern Affairs* 13 (1962): 2–13, 43–53.

———. *The Middle East, Oil, and the Great Powers.* New York: Wiley, 1974.

Silverfarb, Daniel. "The British Government and the Question of Umm Qasr, 1938–1945." *Asian and African Studies* 16 (1982): 215–38.

———. *The Twilight of British Ascendancy in the Middle East: A Case Study of Iraq, 1941–1950.* New York: St. Martin's Press, 1994.

Simon, Reeva. "The Hashemite 'Conspiracy': Hashemite Unity Attempts." *International Journal of Middle Eastern Studies* 5 (1974): 314–27.

———. *Iraq between the Two World Wars: The Creation and Implementation of a Nationalist Ideology.* New York: Columbia University Press, 1986.

———. "The Teaching of History in Iraq before the Rashid ʿAli Coup of 1941." *Middle Eastern Studies* 22 (1986): 37–49.

Sluglett, Peter. *Britain in Iraq, 1914–1932.* London: Ithaca Press, 1976.

Sluglett, Peter, and Marion Farouk-Sluglett. "Sunnis and Shiʿis Revised: Sectarianism and Ethnicity in Authoritarian Iraq." In *Problems of the Modern Middle East in Historical Perspective: Essays in Honour of Albert Hourani,* ed. John P. Spagnolo, 259–73. Reading: Ithaca Press, 1992.

Smolansky, Oles M. *The Soviet Union and the Arab East under Khrushchev.* Lewisburg, Pa.: Bucknell University Press, 1974.

Smolansky, Oles M., and Bettie M. Smolansky. *The USSR and Iraq: The Soviet Quest for Influence.* Durham, N.C.: Duke University Press, 1991.

Springborg, Robert. "Iraqi Infitah: Agrarian Transformation and the Growth of the Private Sector." *Middle East Journal* 40 (1986): 33–52.

Stephens, Robert. *Nasir: A Political Biography.* New York: Simon and Schuster, 1972.

Stevens, Paul. "Iraqi Oil Policy, 1961–1966." In *Iraq: The Contemporary State,* ed. Tim Niblock. London: Croom Helm, 1982.

Stocking, George W. *Middle East Oil.* Kingsport, Tenn.: Vanderbilt University Press, 1970.

al-Suwaydi, Tawfiq. *Mudhakkirati: Nisf al-Qurn Min Taarikh al-'Iraq Wa-al-Qadiyya al-'Arabiyya* (My memoirs: Half a century of the history of Iraq and the Arab problem). Beirut: Dar al-Kitab al-'Arabi, 1969.

Taqrir Lajnat al-Tahqiq al-Niyabiyya fi Qadiyyat Filastin (Report of the Iraqi Parliamentary Committee for Investigation of the Palestine Problem). Baghdad: Government of Iraq Press, 1949.

Tarbush, Mohammad A. *The Role of the Military in Politics: A Case Study of Iraq to 1941.* London: Kegan Paul, 1982.

Tejirian, Eleanor Harvey. "Iraq, 1932–1956: Politics in Plural Society." Ph.D. diss., Columbia University, 1972.

Thesiger, Wilfred. "The Mass Movement of Tribesmen from Amara Liwa to Baghdad and Basra," in dispatch from British embassy (Baghdad) to Levant Department, 5 August 1955, PRO/FO/371/115748/VQ/1015/11.

———. *The Marsh Arabs.* London: Longman, 1964.

Toledano, Ehud. "The Emergence of Ottoman–Local Elites (1700–1800): A Framework for Research." In *Middle Eastern Politics and Ideas: A History from Within,* ed. Ilan Pappe and Moshe Ma'oz, 141–62. London: Tauris Academic Studies, 1997.

———. "The Ottoman Middle East and North Africa from Hegemonic Rule to Dynastic Order: The Case of Ottoman Iraq in the 17th–19th Centuries" (forthcoming).

Townshend, Charles V. F. *My Campaign in Mesopotamia.* London: T. Butterworth, 1920.

Tripp, Charles. *A History of Iraq.* Cambridge: Cambridge University Press, 2000.

United Nations, Department of Economic Affairs. *Review of Economic Conditions in the Middle East: Supplement to World Economic Report, 1949–1950.* New York: United Nations, 1951.

United Nations, Department of Economic Affairs. *Review of the Economic Conditions in the Middle East, 1951–1952.* New York: United Nations, 1953.

United Nations, Department of International Economy and Social Affairs. *National Experience in Formulations and Implementation of Population Policy, 1958–1979.* New York: United Nations, 1981.

United Nations. *Economic Development in the Middle East, 1961–1963: Supplement to World Economic Survey, 1963*. New York: United Nations, 1969.

United States. *Foreign Relations of the United States (FRUS)*. Diplomatic Papers, the Near East and Africa, 1943. Vol. 4. Washington, D.C.: Government Printing Office, 1964.

al-Urfali, Jamil. *Lamhat Min Dhikriyyat Wazir al-'Iraqi Sabiq*. Beirut, 1970.

al-Uzri, 'Abd al-Karim. *Taarikh fi Dhikrayat al-'Iraq, 1930–1958*. Vol. 1. Beirut, 1982.

Vinogradov, Amal. "The 1920 Revolt in Iraq Reconsidered: The Role of Tribes in National Politics." *International Journal of Middle Eastern Studies* 3 (1972): 123–39.

al-Wakil, Fuad Hussain. *Jami'at al-Ahali fi al-'Iraq*. Baghdad, 1986.

al-Wardi, 'Ali. *Dirasat fi Tabi'at al-Mujtam'at al-'Iraqiyya*. Baghdad, Matba't al-A'ani, 1965.

———. *Lamhat Ijtima'iyya Min Taarikh al-'Iraq al-Hadith*. 6 vols. Baghdad, Matba'at al-Ishad, 1974.

Warriner, Doreen. *Land Reform and Development in the Middle East*. London: Royal Institute of International Affairs, 1957.

Wiley, J. N. *The Islamic Movement of Iraqi Shi'as*. Boulder, Colo.: Lynne Rienner, 1992.

Wilson, Arnold Talbot, Sir. *Loyalities: Mesopotamia, 1914–1917*. London: Oxford University Press, 1930.

———. *Mesopotamia, 1917–1920: A Clash of Loyalities*. Oxford: Oxford University Press, 1931.

Zeidel, Ronen. "The Iraqi Ba'th Party, 1948–1995: Personal and Organizational Aspects." M.A. thesis, University of Haifa, 1997.

Zubaida, Sami. *Islam, the People, and the State: Essays on Political Ideas and Movements in the Middle East*. London: Routledge, 1989.

Index

Michael Eppel is a senior lecturer in the Middle Eastern History Department of the University of Haifa and in the Oranim College of Education. He is the author of *The Palestine Conflict in the History of Modern Iraq, 1928–1948* (1994) and many articles in professional journals.